Philosophy as Metanoetics

Nanzan Studies in Religion and Culture

James W. Heisig, General Editor

Hans Waldenfels, *Absolute Nothingness: Foundations for a Buddhist-Christian Dialogue*. 1980.

Frederick Franck, ed., *The Buddha Eye: An Anthology of the Kyoto School*. 1982.

Keiji Nishitani, *Religion and Nothingness*. 1982.

Yoshinori Takeuchi, *The Heart of Buddhism: In Search of the Timeless Spirit of Primitive Buddhism*. 1983.

Winston King, *Death Was His Kōan: The Samurai Zen of Suzuki Shōsan*. 1986.

Hajime Tanabe, *Philosophy as Metanoetics*. 1986.

Robert Morrell, *Early Kamakura Buddhism: A Minority Report*. 1986.

PHILOSOPHY AS METANOETICS

TANABE Hajime

Translated by
TAKEUCHI Yoshinori

with
Valdo Viglielmo
and
James W. Heisig

UNIVERSITY OF CALIFORNIA PRESS
Berkeley   Los Angeles   London

University of California Press
Berkeley and Los Angeles, California

University of California Press, Ltd.
London, England

Copyright © 1986 by The Regents of the University of California

Library of Congress Cataloging in Publication Data

Tanabe, Hajime, 1885–1962.
  Philosophy as metanoetics.

  Includes index.
  1. Philosophy, Buddhist. 2. Self-realization.
I. Title. II. Title: Metanoetics.
B5244.T34T29165 1986   181'.12   85-20840
ISBN 0-520-05490-3 (alk. paper)

Printed in the United States of America

1 2 3 4 5 6 7 8 9

Contents

Foreword

James W. Heisig

High up in the foothills of Mount Asama in Kita-Karuizawa a block of black marble rests peacefully at the edge of a solitary wood; on it is inscribed the epitaph *My search is for truth, and it alone.* The words sum up a lifetime of total, nearly fanatical devotion to philosophy that raised Tanabe Hajime (1885–1962) to the ranks of the most original and influential thinkers of modern Japan. That they might also mark a milestone on the path from East to West, and back again, is the hope in which this translation is being published.

Despite the numerous delays that this first book-length issue of Tanabe's work in English has suffered, it could hardly come at a more opportune time. For one thing, the impact of the collision of Western "being" with oriental "nothingness" has sent a tremor through received traditions that seems now to be commanding equal concern on both sides. For another, the translation of several books of Nishida Kitarō (1870–1945) over the past two decades and the recent appearance of Nishitani Keiji's (1900–) *Religion and Nothingness*, all of them important responses to this very challenge, help Tanabe's own contribution to emerge in clearer relief to the Western eye than it might have done on its own. In the estimation of Takeuchi Yoshinori, whose own considerable writings distill years of discipleship under all three teachers, there is no better way to survey the state of the question in Japanese philosophy than to triangulate from the standpoints of Nishida, Tanabe, and Nishitani.[1] Nor, I would add, is there any more representative statement of Tanabe's position than *Philosophy as Metanoetics*.

I

The epitaph carved on Tanabe's tombstone was of his own phrasing but was intended for quite another context. It appears in a late essay on the problem of death composed for a festschrift to honor Martin Heidegger on his seventieth birthday. There, no sooner does he express his gratitude to Heidegger as a teacher than he immediately takes his distance in the name of a weightier demand: "Of course, my search is for truth, and it alone." When Tanabe's family and intimates agreed to Tsujimura Kōichi's choice for the epitaph, they were no doubt thinking of the nobility of the ideal it expressed. But more, the words must have reverberated with their memories of a temperament so thoroughly bent to philosophy that it could not bring itself to compromise the raw, cold force of truth for the warmth and comfort of social relationships. Everything I have heard and read about Tanabe portrays him as a man who never hesitated to rise to the demands of a new idea whatever its source— be it books or teachers or students or colleagues—and never let go of what he judged valuable, even when it meant parting company with those whose influence on him had been most decisive.[2] To see his grave, anonymous and undated, one cannot help but think it fitting that the ego he had slowly sacrificed to the rigors of a most uncommon self-discipline should now, in death, have been effaced once and for all.

Even accounts written of Tanabe while he was still alive agree that he was a man of strong and tautly stretched moral fiber, demanding much of others but always more of himself, never letting up, never pampering himself, stern and ascetic, even scrupulous in his life-style, a singularly humorless personality who never smiled in the presence of his students and commanded an almost terrified respect from them inside and outside the classroom. Even in the company of colleagues and peers he was not given to joviality or banter. He always welcomed serious questions, naive though they might be, but would not put up with clever wordplay, caricature, sarcasm, or willful abstraction from real problems. Throughout the thirty years he spent at Kyoto he avoided sightseeing and side trips, "fleeing the world as if it were a virus."[3] Nor did he take up his pen for light or popular composition; his writings, like his life, were the very incarnation of the philosophy he practiced. In the words of a senior colleague, "this severity may be seen as a hard and self-fortifying armor of moral *Sollen* designed to carry Tanabe beyond the sentimentalism to which his inner warmth of affection might have led him."[4]

The last sixteen years of his life were spent in the relative isolation of a small mountain cottage where he wrote and studied almost without interruption. During the summer months he would receive visitors, but for at least half of the year he was virtually cut off, often snowbound, with only the postman to negotiate his contact with the outside world. Still, a glance through late photographs of Tanabe showing him sitting in the fields of Kita-Karuizawa, gesturing amicably, or smiling an almost boyish smile, and a comparison of the tone of his last essays with those written during his time in Kyoto reveals how much his manner had mellowed in his late years—"rounded out and filled up," as Japanese would have it.

As a teacher Tanabe enjoyed extraordinary popularity. The hall in which he lectured was regularly filled to overflowing with both students and teachers from the department of philosophy and other departments. He was engaging but never entertaining. "Like a lion roaming restlessly about in its cage," one of his former students recalls, he would stalk back and forth across the front of the lecture hall speaking freely and without notes, but in a way that showed meticulous preparation and impeccable organization of ideas. So seriously did he take his lectures, normally held twice a week, that he had the custom of refusing all visitors the day before.[5]

One of the most attractive aspects of Tanabe's philosophical teaching and, if I am rightly informed, the one that caused him most pain to the end of his life, was his keen social consciousness. The Japanese army's overrunning of Manchuria in 1931 affected him keenly, but not nearly so much as the alliance with Germany and Italy that led to Japan's involvement in the Second World War. Outraged by the irrational tendencies of the state at the time, he is said often to have compared the plight of intellectuals with the persecution of Galileo by the Roman church. The occasion on which the wife of the minister of finance, a schoolmate of Tanabe's wife, came to pay a visit only to be roundly shouted out of the house is only one illustration of his passionate involvement with political issues. Like Plato, who helplessly beheld the decline of Athens, Tanabe knew the painful dilemma of the "unhappy philosopher," unable either to leave his country or to belong fully to it,[6] a dilemma eloquently spelled out in the Preface with which this book opens.

Of itself, the bare skeleton of Tanabe's philosophical career might well give the impression of an inveterate skeptic who spent his time pulling up stakes and breaking camp with one philosophical position after another and was never able to bring his own thinking to any kind of final synthesis. Such an impression is likely to be confirmed by the present book, which faces tradition from a position of "neither/nor," argues for the ultimate futility of all philosophy, and proposes instead a "philosophy that is not a philosophy." Such impressions work injustice to Tanabe's total effort. The itinerary of Tanabe's ideas is not a tale of *ressentiment* born of difficulties with systematic philosophy but of an alert sensitivity to the failure of ideas to match the actuality of his experience. Indeed, I have the impression that there has been no philosopher in Japan before or since who has been so concerned with constructive and systematic presentation as Tanabe. But with the sources for an adequate assessment of Tanabe's philosophy locked away in fifteen heavy volumes of *Collected Works* published in Japanese (to give an idea of just how heavy, the work translated here takes up one half of one of the volumes), and very little else in Western languages to rely on,[7] it is necessary to give some fuller shape to the story of his thought, if only to disarm the reader of misconceptions to which *Philosophy as Metanoetics* might lead.

II

Draw the lines between the stages of development of Tanabe's philosophy as one will, there is no telling the story without constant reference to his clashes of mind with those whose influence on him was strongest. While he cannot be said always to have represented his adversaries fairly or to have understood them as they wished to be understood, the best measure of the seriousness with which Tanabe faced any philosophical position seems to be the degree of turmoil and counterposition it spurred him to in his own thinking.[8]

Tanabe's philosophical career began in 1913, when he took up the post of lecturer in the Tōhoku Imperial University's Department of Natural Sciences. Within two years he had published a book of reflections on science which marks the first important watershed for the philosophy of science in Japan. This was followed by a series of articles written one after the other in quick succession, and a second book on scientific logic. Given these pioneering efforts, the preoccupation of Japanese philosophers after the First World War with neo-Kantian thought, and the encouragement given by the government for study abroad, it was only natural that Tanabe should have been drawn to the work of Cohen and Natorp (rather than to Rickert, Windelband, and the Heidelberg School) and felt it his special calling to travel to Marburg in order to learn for himself at first hand. Once returned, he might not only make their thought better known but also pursue a critique of his own in the light of the other interests he was cultivating at the time: the recreation of Kantian transcendentalism through phenomenology, the vitalism of Bergson, and the notions of pure experience and absolute free will circulating in Japan through the writings of a brilliant young philosopher in Kyoto named Nishida Kitarō. In 1918 Cohen died, and Tanabe's dream evaporated.

Fortunately, he had already attracted the attention of Nishida, who recognized his talents and helped him secure a post as assistant professor at Kyoto University's Faculty of Arts and Letters. As noted above, Tanabe was already familiar with Nishida's thought, and in fact had been one of the first to recognize the significance of his struggles with the Marburg School and the epistemological limitations of Kant's thought. (Most of this was worked out by Nishida piecemeal between 1913 and 1917 in a self-tortured, drawn-out experiment with neo-Kantianism that nail by nail sealed the coffin on his own interests and those of his successors in neo-Kantianism. The results were later published under the title *Intuition and Reflection in Self-Consciousness.*) "Even were I to go abroad," Tanabe is said to have remarked to one of his colleagues at the time, "I could not find a better teacher than Nishida." [9]

While Tanabe was in Kyoto, his dream of study abroad came to life again through Nishida's encouragement, and in 1922 he left for Europe with a grant from the Japanese Ministry of Education. The first year he spent in Berlin studying under Alois Riehl, who urged him to go next to Heidelberg and cast his lot in with Rickert. Tanabe would have none of it, and moved instead to Freiburg to study with Husserl and pursue his fascination with phenomenology. During this period he was invited to Husserl's home to address a small gathering on Nishida's philosophy. The impression he left, reports of which reached Nishida directly from a German philosopher who had been present, was highly favorable. [10] Husserl seems even to have nurtured the hope that Tanabe might bring phenomenology to the Orient, much as Heidegger was expected to carry on the tradition in Germany. As things turned out, Tanabe had other ideas. Disenchanted with the promise of the movement, he turned instead to the ideas of the young Heidegger, who had been tutoring him privately in German philosophy. Through this contact he came to the grandiose idea of working out a systematic philosophy that would bring together a "philosophy of life" and a "philosophy of the human sciences."

In 1924 he returned to Kyoto, his head buzzing with new ideas but almost no forethought of the new obligations that would await him as a favored young disciple of Nishida who had studied under Husserl. Before he could begin work on his own projects, he found himself thrown back into the grip of Kant. The initial impulse came from what he was later to refer to as "the fateful external circumstances" of the celebration of the two hundredth anniversary of Kant's birth, for which he was asked to deliver a memorial lecture. His preparations drove him deep into an investigation of Kant's teleology and surfaced in an attempt to carry critical philosophy through to its ultimate conclusions: to answer the demand for a metaphysics without falling into either the dogmatism of German idealism or the epistemological muddle of neo-Kantianism. Even though the results of his work on Kant were much acclaimed, and helped him to see how the Kantian teleology leads in the end to a religious standpoint, this seems to have been an academically difficult time for Tanabe, unsettling in the extreme. Luckily, it was not long before he had shaken free and was on his feet again, thanks to his rediscovery of Hegel. At first his aim was simply to right what he saw as a lack of dialectic in his own thought, but soon he found himself faced with major confrontations on three fronts at the same time—with Hegel, with Marx, and with Nishida.

Tanabe began his long engagement with Hegel by way of Fichte and Schelling, on whose thought he lectured for two years, followed by two years on Hegel's *Encyclopedia* and then thirteen years on the *Phenomenology*. These efforts led him not only to appreciate the genius of the Hegelian dialectic but to see how, when carried out absolutely, it led to what he called a standpoint of "absolute mediation." Meanwhile, the social philosophies of such thinkers as Miki Kiyoshi (1897–1945), whose company he had shared in Freiburg, and Tosaka Jun (1900–1945) forced him to recognize the seriousness of the challenge that Marxist thought posed to the intellectual community in Japan. A keen sensitivity to the historicity of the philosophical task and the moral dimension this entails had always been present just under the surface of Tanabe's thought, but now broke out with full force and resulted in what many still consider his most original contribution to philosophy: the "logic of species." Finally, these two complementary ideas—the formal dialectic of absolute mediation and the concrete reality of species—prompted a growing critical posture to two similarly complementary ideas that Nishida was working on: the "logic of locus (topos)" and "active intuition."

The consequences of Tanabe's confrontation with Nishida, which may be dated formally from a 1930 essay fitted out with the reverently ambiguous title "Looking to the Teachings of Nishida" and was to carry on even after Nishida's death in 1945, were unexpectedly divisive. Just two years before, it should be remembered, Nishida had retired from Kyoto University, leaving Tanabe to assume the vacant chair. Tanabe rose to the challenge with great outward intensity and even greater inner turmoil. Students noticed a nervous edge to the usual earnestness of his lectures; the scattered streaks of gray in his hair spread visibly. Patching together scattered and parenthetical remembrances of this period, I conclude that it was far less the prestige of the appointment that weighed heavily on him than the lingering presence of the absent Nishida. What began as no more than a slight crease in Tanabe's esteem for his mentor ended up as a yawning chasm of discord that neither was able to bridge. They grew further and further apart until they could not suffer one another's company and in fact could hardly read one another's writings without misunderstanding.[11] It is no accident, for example, that *Philosophy of Metanoetics* does not once mention the name of Nishida, even though various aspects of Nishida's thought come up for explicit criticism; nor that Nishida's last essay, "The Logic of Locus and a Religious Worldview," completed in the same year, submits Tanabe to criticism in no less anonymous a manner. This is not to say that they did not continue to learn from their differences, and even to sharpen or alter their views, but only that their personal relations had soured to the point that those who counted them both as their teachers were helpless to do more than look sadly on as their sympathies for each other deteriorated further and further.

At the same time, there is no denying that this daring departure from his teacher set Tanabe off in the direction of his most creative philosophical years and opened a way for others to appropriate Nishida's thought more critically. Had there been no such head-on clash with Nishida by someone of his own intellectual stature, it is arguable that there would be no Kyoto School as it is known today, and little if any contact between Nishida's thought and the West, but only a tradition of "Nishida Philosophy" scattered throughout Japan. In this sense, Tanabe may rightly be reckoned the founder of the Kyoto School.[12]

In any event, it was against the backdrop of these confrontations that Tanabe turned his attention to the philosophy of religion in *Philosophy as Metanoetics*, a book that set him squarely on the existentialist standpoint he was to uphold for the rest of his life. The argument of the book moves elliptically around a confrontation with Shinran (1173–1262), founder of the True Pure Land sect of Buddhism, on the one hand, and a series of confrontations with Western thinkers—Eckhart, Kant, Schelling, Hegel, Pascal, Kierkegaard, Nietzsche, and Heidegger—on the other. Tanabe hoped to locate an Archimedean point outside of the world of philosophical tradition from which to dislodge that world and set it spinning in a new orbit. Proclaiming it the standpoint of one "sinful and ignorant" yet trusting in Other-power, he set about a religiously motivated "non-philosophy" that would undermine the claims of the "saints and sages" based on self-power. The inconsistency entailed by the claim to abandon philosophy by means of purely philosophical arguments, all of which are intended for public scrutiny and critique, was not lost on Tanabe's disciples.[13] But neither was the sense that only a convinced sage can make the kind of transition from knowing to unknowing that he was trying to elaborate in the "philosophical religion" of a metanoetics.[14]

To be sure, it is the great and ineluctable paradox of the book that only reason can ultimately persuade reason of its own debilities. At the same time, the sense of finitude that Tanabe was attempting to convey is qualitatively different from what we find in Nishida and Nishitani. Theirs is a position closer to Heidegger in the sense that its primary focus is the existential condition of being human. Tanabe ventured to take the further step of grounding the critique of reason in a recovery of basic sincerity that can come only from shifting the focus to one's own individual experience of existential limits. To miss this shift of focus is to deprive the book of its greatest originality.

After *Philosophy as Metanoetics* Tanabe returned to many of the concerns, if not the language, of his "logic of species" in the attempt to fill out his philosophy of religion. Given the experience of the war itself, and the harsh measures that had been taken during the time immediately following the war against a number of key figures in Kyoto University's Department of Philosophy for their supposed complicity in bolstering the myth of nationalism, Tanabe let his past political philosophy lie where he had left it—at the idea of a social democracy that would preserve the best of communism and democracy—and turned his gaze to wider horizons. Against all the culture-worshiping voices of intellectuals raised to invigorate the national spirit for the restoration of Japan, he insisted that it was necessary that Japan commit itself positively to a sociohistorical praxis based on love—an idea that began in the form of "nothingness-*qua*-love" and evolved to a triunity of God-*qua*-love, love of God, and love of neighbor—and aimed at world peace.[15]

At the same time, he returned to his interest in science, carrying on what Takeuchi has described as his lifelong "guerrilla warfare" against the inflated claims of natural science. The progress gained through an accumulation of knowledge, he saw, was ultimately no more than the working out of the innate methodological fragmentariness of science itself, which impeded a true synthesis of knowledge, and suggested that the contradictions the new physics was uncovering at its own foundations should be read as existential *kōan*.[16] In this way, the "metanoetic" spirit of his later writings is apparent in his attempt to define the goal of philosophy as to insert itself into both science and religion, so that the two might unite and cooperate in promoting love and peaceful collaboration among the peoples of the earth.[17]

In 1951 Tanabe's wife of thirty-five years died after a protracted illness, leading him to what was to be the final great confrontation of his life: the encounter with death itself. In memory of his wife, whose long devotion to him and whose exemplary attitude to her approaching death seemed to embody the philosophy he had been writing about so assiduously for so many years, he composed a short *waka*, or Japanese poem. Rendered literally and without meter it reads: "My wife who gave her life on my behalf and died has been reborn and lives within me." This intensely personal experience of the transformation of life into death and death into life attracted Tanabe's attention to the Christian symbol of the *communio sanctorum*, and wiped away the last vestiges of vitalism from his dialectic of absolute mediation to make room for a new dialectics of death that was central to the writings of his last decade.[18]

III

As with any abridgment of ideas woven tightly together over the course of a lifetime, it is impossible to pull out the main threads without getting tangled up along the way. In the case of Tanabe, the stubbornest snarls are those that gather at his notions of the logic of species and the dialectics of absolute mediation. Because of the importance of these notions for understanding the transformation his thought went through in *Philosophy as Metanoetics*, it is worth trying to clarify our account a bit at these points.

The term "logic" in "logic of species," as also in the case of Nishida's "logic of locus," does not refer in the first place to a formal metalanguage yielding inference and proof or to a generalized theory of semantics, but simply to a cluster of principles or linguistic recommendations for carrying on theoretically. The Japanese word, however, slides back and forth between these two senses rather more easily than Western philosophical terminology, allowing Tanabe to develop a rational theory about the workings of irrationality in history (which is what the logic of species is ultimately all about) with an occasional sideswipe at the strictures of formal logic, particularly its principle of self-contradiction, but not obliging him to a thorough review of the formalities of traditional logic.

In contrast then with traditional logic, which places the category of species below genus and above individual, and seems to deny it anything but an ancillary role in order to account for the varieties of particulars belonging to the same universal class, Tanabe proposed that species be understood as the substratum of human Existenz itself, the ground of the "will to life." His aim was to replace the series of negations he saw worked out in Hegel, in which the individual is made to pass through the specificity of history to a transcendent universal, with a positive affirmation of the permanent role of species. In other words, to account for the basic structure of consciousness, it does not suffice to state that we are born as individuals into the human race, and then turn to a phenomenology of our generic humanity; nor is it enough simply to carry on a phenomenology of the processes operative in the individualizing of transcendental or generalized values in specific historical societies (after the manner, say, of Rickert's *Kulturwissenschaft* or Dilthey's *Geisteswissenschaft*). The concrete specificity of a tribe or people or nation is more than a theoretical filter after the manner of what the young Hegel called a "national imagination." It is the most immediate ground of human being, an immediate, formal disposition not existing itself but forming a concrete substrate in terms of which the individual formally actualizes its genus in history.

Where Hegel and Marx seek to locate rationality in a generic substratum of spirit or matter working itself out in history, Tanabe's species begins from a radical irrationality of pure desire for life at the core of human consciousness, a desire defined by social conditions. Although attracted to Schelling's idea of an irrational, unconscious impulse to will outlined in *Philosophical Inquiries into the Nature of Human Freedom*, Tanabe wanted to define species as a kind of social archetype that is more clearly visible in the uniting symbols of a society, such as the totemic imagery that he found treated in the works of Lévy-Bruhl, than in any purely individual expression.

It is not hard to see how, on this basis, Tanabe should come to see a positive significance in acknowledging the emperor of Japan as a symbol of the sacredness of the nation. But neither is it hard to see how such statements might be misinterpreted, as in fact they were both by nationalist-minded intellectuals before and during the Great War and by critics of nationalism after it. No fair account of Tanabe's logic of species can fail to see, however, that its goal was a "theory of national existence" that would serve as a direct critique of the blind nationalism he saw inspiring Japan's engagements in Asia and fascism in Europe. Taking the distinction between "open" and "closed" societies from Bergson's *Two Sources of Morality and Religion*, he strove to show how a society based on a "closing of species" subjugates a particular race or people to the irrationality of its particularity, cutting it off from affinities with generic humanity or blurring the distinction idealistically (his criticism of Hegel's genus-nation and Kant's "world citizen"), and how only an "opening of species" to genus through the dialectical mediation of rationality has any hope of promoting freedom in history. It is therefore altogether wrongheaded to suppose, as some Japanese historians were to do from post-War bandwagons, that Tanabe had composed his *Philosophy as Metanoetics* in order to dissociate himself from nationalist views he had once espoused. Not only did he never hold such views, but the lectures on which the work were based were delivered during the war.

The second nodal idea, the "dialectics of absolute mediation," represents the formal lining to the material logic of species. For Tanabe, the concrete individual of history, while grounded in the contingent definition of its locus as a being in the world ("species"), is also the subject of freedom and spontaneity. The unity of these two dimensions is worked out as a dialectic of what he calls "determination-*qua*-reverse determination," and it is this dialectic in turn that defines the nature of human rationality. In other words, the fullness of reason demands not only that the individual exert its freedom *from* its contingency but also that it make itself free *for* that contingency, and this can be accomplished only through an absolute negation of reason. In mediating the "will to life" of its specific contingency, the individual exercises the "will to power" of its particular freedom, and vice versa.

What distinguishes this from Hegel seems at first to be no more than a procedural device: Tanabe begins at the moral standpoint that Hegel only arrives at three-quarters of the way through the *Phenomenology*, namely with the conviction that dialectical mediation must never be viewed contemplatively as a static unity between every I and Thou but always and primarily as an ongoing process, full of struggle and confrontation, between species and individual within which the I-Thou dialectic takes its meaning. This shift from a generative account of the emergence of the individual to a concrete, existential account served two additional purposes, however. First, it established the role of the logic of species as a hermeneutic device for reading philosophical texts. Second, it set up a direct, and we can only say in hindsight greatly exaggerated, opposition between his "dialectics of *absolute mediation*" and Nishida's "self-identity of *absolute contradictories*." That Tanabe, wrongly I think, traced the philosophical pedigree of Nishida's position to the emanational logic of Plotinus and the Neoplatonists need not detain us here. More important is the fact that this confrontation further stabilized his commitment to a radically historical I, the subject of rationality, engaged in a permanent mutual mediation with its species, the realm of the irrational in history. Whatever harmony may be achieved between individuals, this fact plants a fundamental irrationality and "egoity" at the core of the I which sooner or later will pull on rationality until it is torn out by the roots. This radical negation was the beginning of the conversion that Tanabe called metanoesis.[19]

The key problem here was to ground the conflict and mutual mediation of specificity and individuality. Tanabe's commitment to rationalism would not allow him to find such a ground in an absolute irrationality, since that would effectively sterilize the position of the individual subject and disallow its freedom. But neither could he find it in the absolute rationality of the free subject, since that would effectively dehistoricize the individual. He therefore came to speak of a principle of self-alienation at the core of *everything* that is. Formally put, this means that the absoluteness of absolute mediation stems from the fact that the mediation between individual and species in human life is itself mediated by the general impossibility of unmediated existence. It is not just that the two dimensions are engaged dialectically with each other as a result of the free choice of the subject, but that neither can be what it is except in terms of an essential internal contradiction: to be what it *is*, it must appropriate to itself the other, which it *is not*. There is no species without individual, no individual without species—in short, nothing unmediated in the human world, and therefore no actual achievable unity of opposites. It is not only the individual but also species that suffers the self-alienation of a desire for unmediated existence frustrated by the concrete demands of mediation.

Apart from the role accorded species, which was pointed out earlier, the logical scheme of what Tanabe is doing again looks like vintage Hegel. And indeed it would be, but for the fact that Tanabe had already shifted the accent of absoluteness from the realm of being and reason—and therefore also from a personalized and anthropomorphic view of the world—to the realm of nothingness. The consequences of this shift of the concrete universal from absolute being to absolute nothingness unfolded gradually in Tanabe's thought until he was able to display the full compass of his dialectic of absolute nothingness in *Philosophy as Metanoetics*. To appreciate that what is taking place here is not just a crude distortion of Hegel's thought to an Eastern eye but an original rereading of its religious dimension, it is necessary to speak briefly to the question of what Tanabe understood by nothingness.

The infrastructure Tanabe has in common with Nishida. Both approached Western philosophy from a basic stance of absolute nothingness. That this happens to be a prejudice of Eastern intellectual history should trouble us no more than the fact that philosophy itself began under the Western prejudice of the supremacy of being. (I assume "prejudice" here to carry the fuller meaning that Gadamer has restored to it.) This absolute nothingness is not some cold and calculating metaphysical negation of everything that is or might be, but first and foremost "an awakening to the drive to know the truth about what it is to be alive; it is the very stuff of human Existenz." In other words, the standpoint of nothingness does not begin from reflection on the world of objects but from reflection of the self upon itself; and it finds its moorings not in the everyday external realities of perception but in the realization that all things functioning in existence are "shadows emptying the self of itself and projecting it back into itself."[20] Where Western philosophies of being begin from an ontological reflection on science and myth, the standpoint of nothingness rests on a primarily psychological realization of the world akin to religious experience.

Just how that "realization" (or self-consciousness) is conceived in practice is no less open to a variety of viewpoints than Western ontologies. In fact, Tanabe's break with Nishida began with a disagreement over the latter's "standpoint of absolute nothingness," which he considered so bound up with the self-consciousness of a realm of universal ideas that he even revolted for a time against using the term at all. In the end, the common bond proved too strong and fundamental to be sacrificed so simply, and Tanabe returned to the notion of absolute nothingness in *Philosophy as Metanoetics*, where it is said to become manifest in the absolute mediation of absolute Other-power to the subject of metanoesis. (This Other-power has the curious logical quality of having been deduced a posteriori from the personal experience of a transcendent force, and at the same time of having been postulated a priori after the manner of the Hegelian Absolute Spirit.) Thus while Nishida took absolute nothingness as the transcendent ground of all reality, toward which the self that has let go of the subject-object dichotomy breaks through to face reality as it is, Tanabe ultimately came to understand it as the ground of a transcendent force that breaks in upon the self from without. For Nishida, the quality of "religious experience" associated with absolute nothingness is reviewed by the self-conscious subject philosophically and at a remove from historical conditions; for Tanabe, this very review itself belongs to history and therefore demands an absolute "disruption" of the conscious subject and an absolute "crisis" in reason.

This two-dimensional understanding of absolute nothingness, namely in its logical and its experiential functions, affected Tanabe's dialectic of absolute mediation in three ways. First, it carried the Hegelian dialectic of the *Phenomenology* to what he saw as its inevitable conclusion (close to what Hegel himself did in the *Encyclopedia*,[21] though Tanabe does not acknowledge this): the outright rejection of an abstract and nonmediated absolute, antecedent to and transcendent to the relative beings that make up history.[22] Second, under the rubrics of the Shin Buddhist notions of *gensō* and *ōsō* it raised absolute mediation to the status of religious experience, not only at the level of the experience of the transcendent but also at the level of the return to care for one's fellow living beings. And third, under the influence of Kierkegaard, it shifted the ideal of the I-Thou relationship from Hegel's unity of the self with the other through self-negation to a "nothingness-*qua*-love" that lets go of self-power altogether, and thus elevated the I-Thou relationship to the same level as the individual-species relationship, if not actually above it. In each case, the dialectics of absolute mediation that was forged to undergird the logic of species ended up transfiguring it.

IV

The logic of species that governs the "will to life" of historicity, and the dialectic of absolute mediation that governs the "will to power" of the individual, are brought to term in what may be called a "logic of envelopment"[23] that characterizes the "will to salvation" at the level of genus. The working out of this final step is the philosophy of religion that

Tanabe began with *Philosophy as Metanoetics* and enhanced during the years of his retreat to Kita-Karuizawa.

At the start of his confrontation with Nishida in 1930, Tanabe accused his teacher of a mystical erasure of the distinction between philosophy and religion by stressing the "self-consciousness of absolute nothingness." Not only did Tanabe later return to use that term himself, as already noted, but he did so in a way that threatened the distinction far more than Nishida had ever done.[24] How this works out in practice will be clear enough from the text of the translation that follows. While this is a trait that, to one degree or another, all the thinkers of the Kyoto School have in common,[25] we need not trouble ourselves with those differences here. It is enough if we can lay a finger on the principal peculiarities of the way Tanabe brought "religion" into his philosophical thought.

To begin with, Tanabe abstained stoically from association with any one religious tradition, Eastern or Western, in order that he might the better address the problem of religion in a more general sense. Some of his commentators judge him closer to Christianity, others to Shin Buddhism, and still others to Zen. The evidence to support any of these conclusions is there in abundance, but only because it was his goal to keep equidistant from all three, thereby to work a general dialectical synthesis of the philosophic core of Zen Buddhism (concern with totality), *Nembutsu* Buddhism (concern with the individual), and Christianity (concern with species).

In the second place and within these perimeters, Tanabe saw no reason to extend his investigation of religion outside of Buddhism and Christianity, the two major world religious traditions that must in any event be drawn into a philosophical encounter between Eastern nothingness and Western being. To all other forms of religion, he simply closed his eyes. My own suspicions, as yet unconfirmed, are that this was in part a device to avoid having to face the fuller religious dimensions of Shinto as part of Japanese historical specificity, in spite of the way it was being used for nationalistic purposes repulsive to his moral sensitivities.

Third, in treating Buddhism and Christianity he did not oblige himself in any strict sense to the same historical and textual standards that he applied to philosophy and science, preferring to countenance these traditions in a direct and for all practical purposes ahistorical manner. Indeed, so little did he bother with theology (aside from a scattering of ideas from Augustine to Bultmann that attracted his philosophical appetite) and denominational distinctions, that he all but reduced the Christian Scriptures to the Gospel accounts. Likewise, his understanding of Shin Buddhism, the crux of his argument in the present book, is based on a highly original but critically suspect reading of the *Kyōgyōshinshō*.[26]

In the fourth place, he lopped off from religion the whole dimension of ritual and symbolic expression, as well as of dogmatic constructs based on faith in special revelation, a strategy he found he could support by a radical appeal to the method of demythologization.[27] Here too, for all the importance he gave the notion of species, not to mention the immediate historic setting of his "metanoesis," the historical-institutional aspect of the religions he studied is brushed to one side.

Fifth, Western reflections on religion are restricted to their philosophic aspects. Poetry, literature, music, the arts, and so on that speak to religion in a nonphilosophic manner are all but neglected, a bias he tried to set straight in some late writing on poets such as Rilke, Mallarmé, and Valéry.

Lastly, he did not harass Western intellectual history for its misrepresentations of Buddhism and oriental religions, of which he would have found more than enough to complain about in Hegel, perhaps in order to avoid attracting like criticism of his own reading of Christianity.

There is no point in faulting a philosopher for not doing what it is not, or what he does not see it as, the business of philosophy to do. But even when we have to do with a thinker so heroically single-minded in his pursuit of philosophy as Tanabe, the complaint that his generalizations simply do not fit the facts of religious consciousness in history is serious. Without the continued nuisance of data, philosophy cannot sustain the moral edge that Tanabe always insisted on. At the same time, fairness requires that students of religion acknowledge how right his philosophic instincts were at times in getting to the heart of problems that other approaches tend to obscure.

To return where we began, the judgment that Tanabe's writings grind away the edges between the religious and philosophical dimensions of the human is no more true than the same conclusion he once drew in regard to Nishida's writings. There is of course no denying a tension in Tanabe's late work. On the one hand, it is clear that "metanoesis" and dependence on Other-power are closer to religious faith than Nishida's "self-consciousness of absolute nothingness." On the other, his notion of absolute critique does not permit him to leave the realm of philosophy to chase after the "absolute freedom from error" that he associated with faith, dogma, and theology.[28] But to conclude, as one commentator has done, that there is no more religion in Tanabe as a person than one finds in his philosophic texts, and that therefore he is an "unchurched religious vagabond" with whom millions of people in Japan and Europe who cannot make a home for themselves in any specific religious tradition can identify,[29] is both naive and indiscreet.

There is far too much in Tanabe's late writings suggestive of what we might call with Jaspers a "philosophical faith" to lump him together with the largely unreflected and untutored religious consciousness of the secularized world. If one limits religion to standing within a particular confessional tradition and practicing its rites in public, it is easy to classify him as irreligious. A broader perspective, such as I believe the last two hundred years of intellectual history oblige us to, surely allows the possibility of characterizing a critique of the religious dimension in self-consciousness as itself a religious act. Though Tanabe himself would not have welcomed the comparison, his religiosity falls squarely in line with a Western tradition that goes back at least as far as Plotinus and the Neoplatonists.

Moreover, there is far too little of Tanabe's private papers (practically nothing compared with the copious correspondence and diaries that Nishida left behind), to permit such a conclusion. Attempts to speak of Tanabe's inner religious life must remain at best hunches from evidence that is inadequate and ambiguous. What we can say, it seems to me, is that Tanabe saw in the abstractions of philosophy a defense behind which to safeguard his private life and feelings from public view, and yet from whose privileged position he could address the modern soul directly. The personal metanoesis he performs for us in *Philosophy as Metanoetics* under the continually repeated leitmotiv "sinful and ignorant as I am" so rarely touches down on the solid ground of particular historical fact that the reader cannot but slide over the words after a while. Since I find it hard to imagine that Tanabe was not aware of this as he was writing, I can only conclude that he had taken what was originally a genuinely personal (though in its details genuinely impersonal) sentiment and turned it into the mask of an Everyman so that his readers might gradually be led to think "sinful and ignorant as *we* are," and be drawn into the same experiment of life-and-resurrection through Other-power that Tanabe was conducting himself. Far from being an asbestos cloak that protected his inward self from catching fire, the outer mask then takes on the glow of a religious conviction burning within.

Confessional writings based on religious experience are nothing new to Western philosophy, but it is hard to know just where to place Tanabe's brand of metanoesis in their ranks. One thinks of Augustine, Pascal, Hamann, Kierkegaard, and Blondel, to mention but a few possibilities for comparison. Yet the peculiar blend of self-criticism without autobiographical detail, appeal to religious experience without firm commitment to a given religious tradition, sharp moral sense without an ethical theory,[30] and overall critique of the rational subject that we find in Tanabe undermines the likenesses from the start. The difficulty of locating his "metanoetics" in intellectual history implies more than the fact that every speculative thinker of rank enjoys some degree of distinctiveness from every other. The context itself has shifted from Western philosophy's objective associations with religious experience to an oriental understanding where the very grounds of distinctiveness rest in the experiencing subject. More particularly, it has shifted to the Japanese philosophy of the Kyoto School, where this context forms the vanguard of a confrontation with Western thought.

V

The translation of this book has had an odyssey all its own, which bears brief telling if only because of the many delays involved in its publication, first announced some fifteen years ago. Around 1965 UNESCO, which had been collaborating with the Japanese Ministry of Education to sponsor and publish English translations of Japanese philosophy in Japan, made it known to Shimomura Toratarō that it was interested in Tanabe's work and would offer a grant for its translation. Shimomura conveyed the offer to the other editors of Tanabe's *Collected Works* at a meeting in Kyoto, and the decision was reached to translate 『懺悔道としての哲学』 (*Philosophy as Metanoetics*). One of the group, Takeuchi Yoshinori, then professor of philosophy at Kyoto University, was entrusted with the task. Takeuchi approached Yamamoto Seisaku, a gifted young philosopher who had just returned from doctoral studies in the United States and who has since distinguished himself as the translator of Whitehead's *Process and Reality* and as one of the foremost process thinkers in Japan. In rather short order, Yamamoto prepared a rough draft of about 80 percent of the book. After checking it himself, Takeuchi sent sections of the English typescript to UNESCO, who in turn contacted its publishers for an opinion. The judgment was favorable but cautioned that stylistic improvements were needed. Anxious to have the polishing done by someone familiar with Japanese philosophy in the Kyoto tradition, Takeuchi invited Valdo Viglielmo (whose translation of Nishida's *A Study of Good* UNESCO had published in 1960) to assist him in the work.

At the time Viglielmo was busy with a translation of Nishida's 『自覚における直観と反省』 (*Intuition and Reflection in Self-Consciousness*) and in need of assistance himself. For several years Takeuchi and Viglielmo spent their summers together in Japan, giving their mornings to Tanabe and their afternoons to Nishida. About half of the untranslated portion was passed on to Jan Van Bragt and Hase Shōtō; the rest they decided to do on their own, the grant having already been exhausted. In the hope of publishing the book in 1968, Takeuchi issued a draft of the Preface in 1967. Once again, in 1971, it being felt that publication was imminent, an earlier draft of part of the fourth chapter that had been polished stylistically by Gerald Cooke of Bucknell University was published.[31]

Soon thereafter it became clear that UNESCO was intending to discontinue its publishing ventures, though no formal statement was made to this effect. Still incomplete, the manuscript book fell into a temporary limbo until 1980, when Takeuchi persuaded the responsible authorities to release the rights for publication to the Nanzan Institute for Religion and Culture in Nagoya. Once again Viglielmo began his summer visits to Japan to work with Takeuchi on the remaining chapters. In fall of 1984, the entire manuscript was handed over to the Institute to prepare for presentation to the University of California Press, which had already expressed interest in it.

Over the twenty years of interrupted labors, the translation had lost its sense of unity and consistency of phrasing and style. For better or worse, it fell to me to take up the task, restoring portions lost in the shuffle of papers from one draft to the next, polishing the rough edges, and tracking down the notes. From the first I was struck by the precision and almost mathematical balance of Tanabe's prose, well suited to the sources and topics he was treating. (I was not at all surprised recently to come across the following comment by one of Japan's former ministers of education, Aihara Shinsaku: "The secret of Tanabe's ability as an author to draw such a large number of readers lies in the highly fascinating way he has of orchestrating complicated theoretical works in the clear and critical tones of rationality."[32]) The deeper I got into the work, the more did my admiration grow for the immense labors that had thus far gone into the translation and the more convinced I became that nothing short of a total review would do justice to the work already invested in it. With the encouragement of both Takeuchi and Viglielmo, I spent the next several months shaping and reshaping the winding sentences and massive paragraphs (one of which runs no less than twelve pages) into what seemed to me more flowing and digestible segments, until the text reached the form in which it is presented here. Rather than yield to the temptation to take the still more arbitrary step of inserting subtitles into the text, it was decided to follow the somewhat dated procedure of including at the head of each chapter the major themes treated there. I am only too aware that my contribution is one that others could have carried out with greater eloquence than I can command and that Tanabe's brilliance was often diminished through my phrasing of his ideas. For this I beg the reader's indulgence and correction.

In the course of preparing these remarks, I have been tempted again and again to make predictions about the reception Tanabe will receive in the West, particularly among those philosophers of religion and theologians whose interests have drawn them to Japanese philosophy and the Kyoto School. On each occasion I have found my mind the same blank slate with no higher inspiration to guide my hand. Part of the problem, no doubt, is the enigma the Kyoto School itself presents to Japanese philosophy as a whole. Neither Nishida nor Tanabe, surely the two "classical" philosophers of modern Japan, have left behind disciples in the strict sense of the term. There are no Nishideans or Tanabeans to be compared with the Kantians, the Hegelians, or the Heideggerians of the West. One Japanese critic has singled out four reasons for this in the case of Tanabe. First, Japanese academics are not yet prepared to compare the level of Japanese philosophy in any form with its Western counterparts. Second, the demand that philosophy be defined, as Tanabe himself had done, as the result of one's own highly subjective quest chills one philosopher's relationship to another's systematic thinking, as if before an antique that should be looked at but not touched. Third, there may be something badly wanting in the academic quality of Tanabe's own thought as such. And finally, a philosophy that concerns itself with absolute nothingness abandons the canons of philosophy for those of religion, turning even the philosophy *of* religion into a philosophy–*qua*–religion.[33]

It is surely an irony of some significance that on each point of this assessment, it is the very opposite view that has been promoting Western interest in contemporary Japanese philosophy. Aside from a growing revisionist strain, one would have to say that the cutting edge in American and European philosophy still rests in the area of a critique of the limits of speculative language and logic, and that it is this concern more than any other that accounts for the recent spate of comparative studies on Buddhist thought and mainline Western philosophies. Tanabe's arrival at a comparable critique, though one worked out in what we might now consider a dated language, has remarkable affinities with the thrust of this concern. At the same time, if one may view the revisionist stance—especially the return to classical metaphysics—as an attempt to reconstruct what has been torn down by largely critical philosophies, there would seem to be great promise in pursuing a standpoint of nothingness that offers a positive alternative precisely by upholding its critique of the rational metaphysics of being. There is no knowing what the fate of oriental philosophy in the countries of the West is to be. For now we can only say that the question has risen up too strong and clear above the voice of the past to be silenced without a suitable reply.

NOTES

1. Takeuchi Yoshinori, 「田辺哲学と絶対無」 ("Tanabe's Philosophy and Absolute Nothingness"), 『絶対無と神』 (*Absolute Nothingness and God*) (Tokyo: Shunjusha, 1981), p. 198.

2. The Japanese reads: 私の希求するところは真実の外にはない. It appears in 「生の存在学か死の弁証法か」 ("An Ontology of Life or a Dialectics of Death?"), in 『田辺元全集』 (*Collected Works of Tanabe Hajime*) (Tokyo: Chikuma Shobō, 1963–1964), 13:529. Tsujimura had edited this essay and translated it into German, with the collaboration of Hartmut Buchner, as a contribution to *Festschrift Martin Heidegger zum 70. Geburtstag* (Pfullingen, 1959), pp. 93–133.

The immediate impetus to commit such a sentiment to print seems to been a Latin proverb Tanabe came across in Carlyle: *Amicus Plato, magis amica veritas* (*Sartor Resartus*, chap. 2), though the saying itself is much older. The original Greek proverb, stemming from a passage in Plato's *Phaedo* (91) and referring to Socrates, was given its form in Ammonius's *Life of Aristotle*. Latin translations and variants are to be found in Erasmus, Luther, and Cervantes.

3. Aihara Shinsaku, 「田辺先生について」 ("Professor Tanabe"), in 『田辺哲学』 (*The Philosophy of Tanabe*) (Tokyo: Kōbundō, 1951), p. 270.

4. See Takahashi Satomi, 「田辺元君の死を悼む」 ("In Memoriam: Tanabe Hajime"), 『思想』 (*Thought*) 9, no. 459 (1962):1258–1259. In his eulogy, Takahashi likens Tanabe's philosophical disposition to a blend of the temperaments of Kant, Schelling, and Schiller. See also the special issue of 『理想』 (*Ideals*), 1963, no. 2, devoted to Tanabe.

5. See Ōshima Yasumasa, 「教師としての田辺先生」 ("Professor Tanabe the Teacher"), in *The Philosophy of Tanabe*, pp. 273–284.

6. Ibid., p. 269. It should be noted that there were certain left-wing students in

Kyoto who tried to use Tanabe's ideas for their own purposes and in the process circulated their share of distortions. Since the essay being cited here was read by Tanabe, however, we have reason to presume he approved of it.

7. References to Tanabe in the West begin about 1959, with Tsujimura's translation referred to above (n. 2); an English translation of his "Memento Mori" in the opening volume of *Philosophical Studies of Japan*, pp. 1–12 (a later German translation appeared in *Gott in Japan*, ed. Yagi Seiichi and Ulrich Luz [Munich, 1973], pp. 113–126); and an extended reference in Takeuchi Yoshinori's English essay, "Buddhism and Existentialism: The Dialogue between Oriental and Occidental Thought," in *Religion and Culture: Essays in Honor of Paul Tillich*, ed. W. Leibrecht (New York, 1959), p. 301. Takeuchi later expanded these remarks in his contribution to the entry on "Japanese Philosophy" for the 1967 *Encyclopaedia Britannica*. A brief resume of Tanabe's thought based on secondary sources was included in Gino Piovesana's *Recent Japanese Philosophical Thought, 1862–1962* (Tokyo: Enderle, 1963), pp. 145–158. In 1967 and 1971 first drafts of the Preface and an extract of chapter 4 of the present book were printed in *Japanese Religions* (5, no. 2, pp. 29–47; 7, no. 2, pp. 50–75). In 1969, *Monumenta Nipponica* published an English version of the opening chapter of *The Logic of Species as Dialectics* (24, no. 3, pp. 273–288); and in 1971 a translation of Tanabe's "Zu Hegels Lehre vom Urteil" was printed in *Hegel-Studien* (6:211–229).

While these translations have stirred a certain amount of interest in the German-speaking world, there has been virtually no major work done on Tanabe elsewhere in Europe or in America. The only book-length treatment of Tanabe to appear in a Western language is Johannes Laube's *Dialektik der absoluten Vermittlung* (Freiburg: Herder, 1984). Although Laube had previously published a number of articles on Tanabe's thought, and includes a good bibliography of source materials, his book falls under some suspicion for its alarming overdependence on a single work that Tanabe had prepared for a more popular audience and published in 1949 under the title *Introduction to Philosophy*. His more recently published critiques of Fritz Buri's treatment of Tanabe in *Der Buddha-Christ als der Herr des wahren Selbst* (Basel: Paul Haupt, 1982), pp. 81–112, however, applies rather more rigorous standards (*Zeitschrift für Missionswissenschaft und Religionswissenschaft* 67 [1983]:154–155; and *Neue Zeitschrift für Systematische Theologie und Religionsphilosophie* 27 [1985], 207–218).

8. I rely chiefly here on the following sources: Tsujimura Kōichi, 「田辺哲学について」 ("Tanabe's Philosophy"), in his edited selection entitled 『田辺元』 (*Tanabe Hajime*) (Tokyo: Chikuma Shobō, 1965), pp. 7–62; Nishitani Keiji, 「田辺哲学について」 ("Tanabe's Philosophy"), in 『田辺元集』 (*Tanabe Hajime: A Collection*), ed. Nakano Hajimu (Tokyo: Chikuma Shobō, 1975), pp. 399–424 (this volume is a completely revised edition of the former, appearing in the series *Library of Japanese Thought*, no. 23); Shimomura Toratarō, 「田辺哲学の発展とその性格」 ("The Development and Character of Tanabe's Philosophy"), in *The Philosophy of Tanabe*, pp. 23–52; Kōsaka Masaaki, 『西田哲学と田辺哲学』 (*The Philosophies of Nishida*

and Tanabe), reprinted in vol. 8 of 『高坂正顕著作集』(*The Works of Kōsaka Masaaki*) (Tokyo: Risōsha, 1965), pp. 235–372; and Kōyama Iwao, 「田辺哲学の史的意識と特色」("The Historical Consciousness and Distinctiveness of Tanabe's Philosophy"), ibid., pp. 3–22.

9. Aihara, "Professor Tanabe," p. 262.

10. Ibid., p. 264.

11. See Abe Nōsei, 「田辺元君と私」("Tanabe Hajime and I"), in *The Philosophy of Tanabe*, p. 256.

12. In saying this I cannot fail to mention the important role that Kōsaka Masaaki played in stabilizing the position of the school. The exemplary lucidity and fairness of his comparative studies of Nishida and Tanabe, and of Nishida and Watsuji Tetsurō, have set the highest of standards for Japanese historians of philosophy. One can only hope that increased interest in the Kyoto School will inspire their translation into Western languages in the near future.

13. Nishitani Keiji, 「西田哲学と田辺哲学」("The Philosophies of Nishida and Tanabe"), in *The Philosophy of Tanabe*, p. 200.

14. "The Historical Consciousness and Distinctiveness of Tanabe's Philosophy," in *The Philosophy of Tanabe*, p. 22.

15. See Mutō Kazuo, 「政治・社会—田辺博士の社会民主主義の哲学—」("Politics and Society: Dr. Tanabe's Philosophy of Social Democracy"), in *The Philosophy of Tanabe*, pp. 138–153.

16. Takeuchi, "Tanabe's Philosophy and Absolute Nothingness," p. 216.

17. On this point, see Ueda Yasuharu's recent article, 「田辺哲学における生物学」("Biology in Tanabe's Thought"), in 『哲学の世界』(*The World of Philosophy*), ed. Takeuchi Yoshinori et al. (Tokyo: Sōbunsha, 1985), pp. 205–227.

18. See Takeuchi, "Tanabe's Philosophy and Absolute Nothingness," pp. 215–217.

19. See Kōsaka, *The Philosophies of Nishida and Tanabe*, p. 322.

20. Nishitani, "The Philosophies of Nishida and Tanabe," pp. 164–165.

21. Consider the following passage which Hegel quotes from the *Vorbegriff* to the third edition of the *Encyclopedia of the Philosophical Sciences*, Sec. 61 ff., in Book I of *The Science of Logic*: "there is nothing, nothing in the heavens or in nature or in the spirit or anywhere, which does not contain both immediacy and mediation."

22. One is tempted here to start drawing comparisons with Whitehead, as indeed Ueda has hinted ("Biology in Tanabe's Philosophy," p. 207), but the clear burden of any such attempt would be to show that beyond the level of logical formalities about the interdependence of God and the world, Whitehead had produced any clear notion of subjectivity capable of facing the questions that are central to Tanabe.

23. The word 摂取 is a Buddhist term, referring to the protection and assimilation of the believer by Amida Buddha.

24. Funayama Shin'ichi reckons that if Tanabe had broken from Nishida earlier, his thought might have developed in a more profitable and less religious

direction than metanoetics and a philosophy of death (*Ideals*, p. 33; see above, n. 4). I could not disagree more.

I would also note that in the earlier stages of this translation, Professor Take-uchi had often inserted the qualification "religious" before the words "self-consciousness" and "consciousness" to stress the point, feeling that it might otherwise have been lost on the reader. I later took the liberty of deleting these additions in the hope that our prefatory remarks would suffice to make the point.

25. Nishida's final essay, "The Logic of Locus and a Religious Worldview," a translation of and commentary on which should be forthcoming soon in the pages of *The Eastern Buddhist*, the opening essays of Nishitani's *Religion and Nothingness*, (Berkeley, Los Angeles, London: University of California Press, 1982) and Takeu-chi's *The Heart of Buddhism* (New York: Crossroad, 1983) all attest to the same tendency.

26. Nakayama Enji takes Tanabe to task here in the second and third chapters of his book 『仏教と西田・田辺哲学』 (*Buddhism and the Philosophies of Nishida and Tanabe*) (Kyoto: Hyakkaen, 1979). The main thrust of his argument centers on two points: that Tanabe had failed to distinguish the coming-to-faith from the actual state of faith achieved in coming-to-the-Pure-Land, and had misrepresented the radical otherness of Other-power. Similar complaints are lodged against Tanabe's reading of Shinran's notion of *zange* (repentance) in his late works.

As the offhand, scissors-and-paste comparison of Tanabe and Nishida in the early chapters of this book makes amply clear, Nakayama is far more out of his depth in the world of philosophy than Tanabe was in Shin Buddhism. The book contributes too little to our understanding of Tanabe to warrant more than the rubric of a footnote.

27. For a résumé and critique of Tanabe's position here, see Mutō Kazuo, 「非神話化—自然神学の問題と関連して—」("The Relation of Demythologizing to the Problem of Natural Theology"), in *Absolute Nothingness and God*, pp. 104–130.

28. Nishitani, "The Philosophies of Tanabe and Nishida," p. 197.

29. Laube, *Dialektik der absoluten Vermittlung*, p. 222.

30. In spite of this, Nishitani takes the notion of *Tat* as the "alpha and omega" of Tanabe's endeavors. See his memorial lecture, devoted largely to *Philosophy as Metanoetics*, "Tanabe's Philosophy."

31. See above, n. 7.

32. "Professor Tanabe," p. 263.

33. Nakano Hajimu, "Commentary," in *Tanabe Hajime*, ed. Nakano, pp. 454–456.

Translator's Introduction

Takeuchi Yashinori

Tanabe Hajime[1] was born in Tokyo on 3 February 1885. Already from his elementary and middle school days his extraordinary intellectual abilities were in evidence. After completing his studies at the First High School, he entered the Tokyo Imperial University to study mathematics, and during the course of his studies he transferred to the Department of Philosophy, graduating in 1908 with a brilliant academic record. Regarding his first published work, an essay entitled "On Thetical Judgment" published in the *Journal of Philosophy* two years later, Takahashi Satomi remarks:

> The piece not only showed the young Tanabe's talent for scholarship but contained hints of sympathy with the intuitionism of Nishida Kitarō (1870–1945), Japan's foremost modern philosopher. At the time I was not even aware of the term "thetical judgment," and was amazed to find someone writing so splendidly on it. I was greatly encouraged by the prospects of having such an able young colleague as my senior.[2]

After graduation Tanabe served for a time as an English teacher at the Fourth Tokyo Municipal Middle School, where he himself had been a student, and later moved to the Kaisei Middle School, where his father was serving as principal. In 1915 he moved again, this time to Sendai, where he took up the post of lecturer in the philosophy of science at Tōhoku University. His next essay, "The Significance of Description in Physical Cognition," dates from this period.

Concerning his transfer from mathematics to philosophy, Tanabe was later to reflect in a public lecture:

> Having graduated from the Faculty of Science in high school, I enrolled in the
> Faculty of Science at Tokyo University with the intention of specializing in
> mathematics. In the course of the first three months at the university, from
> September to November, I realized that I lacked the qualifications to become a
> mathematician and shifted to the Faculty of Letters. Even now I can recall how
> poorly I did in my mathematical exercises. As I listened to the lectures of such
> teachers as Professor Takagi and Professor Sakai, both of whom are present here
> today, I found the material extremely interesting and intelligible. Even the
> reference material cited was clear to me, but somehow, when it came to the
> exercises, everything got muddled. Having completed my studies in mathema-
> tics at High School, I presumed I would continue in the same line at university,
> only to find that I had no ability when it came to actual mathematical problems.
> Convinced that I lacked the talent to become a mathematician, in the following
> year I transferred to arts and letters, in which I had also been interested for a
> long time.[3]

No doubt there is some truth in Tanabe's self-deprecating comments. Still, it should be borne in mind that even after changing his
major field, Tanabe maintained his lively interest in mathematics and
the natural sciences. Among his major works we find such monographs
in his early period as *An Introduction to the Philosophy of Science* and a
massive volume entitled *A Study of the Philosophy of Mathematics*; and
in later years, *Historicism in the Recent Development of Mathematics*,
Methodology in Theoretical Physics, and *The Dialectics of the Theory of
Relativity*. When we see how faithfully Tanabe devoted his energies to
these researches throughout his life, it becomes clear that his own
judgment about his "lack of talent" for mathematics is hardly the whole
story. Had he been a Western scholar, he might not have hesitated to
state more openly his reasons for changing fields: a disenchantment with
the state of mathematical studies in Japan at the time.

My own personal recollections of talks with Tanabe as well as the
many things I have heard from older colleagues lead me to suppose that
what first attracted him to mathematics was the rigor of its approach to
truth, and that what led him into philosophy was his discovery of how
bogged down in technical intricacies the study of mathematics had
become at the university. A comment by one of Tanabe's close friends,
Ueno Naoake, probably reflects his mood at the time accurately:

> Tanabe entered the Department of Mathematics in the Faculty of Science while
> I entered the Faculty of Law. Both of us later became disgusted with the content
> of our courses. . . . We discussed the matter together, aired our disappointment,
> and found ourselves kindred spirits.[4]

Another school friend, Fujiwara Tadashin, aptly describes Tanabe's personality after transferring to the Philosophy Department:

> During his university days Tanabe was serious and aloof and did not readily seek out friends or indulge in idle chatter. Indeed, apart from academic topics he almost never spoke at all. His approach to his studies was the very soul of gravity. After listening to an important lecture he would pore over his notes carefully and then compare his teachers' interpretations with the pertinent passages in the original texts. This was especially true in epistemology: wherever he went, he carried about with him the Reclam edition of Kant's *Critique of Pure Reason,* checking his notes against the text meticulously and making corrections. In this way his critical faculties grew stronger and sharper day by day, until eventually one had to wonder whether he had come to the school to learn or to criticize his teachers' lectures.[5]

Given the high intellectual standards Tanabe had set for himself, it is no surprise that he quickly found himself attracted to the work of Nishida and undertook to study his thought earnestly. Nishida's first book and a major milestone in Japanese philosophy, *Zen no kenkyū* (*A Study of Good*),[6] was published in 1911, the year after Tanabe's first essay, though most of it had already appeared in the *Journal of Philosophy* between 1907 and 1909. In addition, Nishida had given a lecture to the Philosophical Association of Tokyo University in November of 1909 entitled "On Reciprocal Relationships in Pure Experience." Quite by coincidence the text of this lecture appeared in the same journal one month before Tanabe's essay. All of this helps to explain why Tanabe should have attached such importance to Nishida's standpoint of pure experience from the very outset of his academic career and why he should have made it the foundation of his own thought.

At the same time, it is interesting to note that already in Tanabe's first essay, "On Thetical Judgment," we find the core of what was later to become his own original philosophical contribution. Departing from Nishida's standpoint of pure experience, Tanabe there attempts to grasp, by way of thetical judgment, the primordial form in which the subject-object opposition is generated and in which pure experience is transformed into judgment. Later he advanced a unique interpretation of Hegel centered on Hegel's theory of judgment, thereby laying the cornerstone for "Tanabe philosophy." In that sense, this early essay makes a fascinating study in itself.

Tanabe's third essay, "The Limits of Rationalism in Epistemology," was published in 1914 and drew explicit mention by Nishida. It is not clear precisely when Tanabe first turned to Nishida for philosophical guidance. I am told that Tanabe wrote a letter directly to Nishida asking for advice, but have not been able to confirm any further details. Tanabe's name appears for the first time in Nishida's diary only in 1913, after Nishida had moved to Kyoto University. The entry is dated Sunday, 6 April, and reads:

> In the morning I left for Tokyo.... There I accompanied Tokunō to the university, where I gave a lecture on "History and Science." Later, in the evening, there was a dinner party. Among those in attendance were Professors Inoue, ... Suzuki [Daisetsu], Yamazaki, Tokunō, Miyamoto, Tanabe Hajime, Takahashi [Satomi], and Itō [Kichinosuke].[7]

In his lecture Nishida discussed the methodological differences between the natural sciences and the historical sciences. He also introduced ideas of Windelband and Rickert, and even made reference to the hermeneutics of Dilthey. Tanabe's fourth essay, "Natural Science vis-à-vis Intellectual Science and Cultural Science," may be said to have been written directly under the influence of this lecture, though already in Tanabe's second essay we find Nishida's work cited. For his part, Nishida's first published reference to Tanabe's work is to "The Limits of Rationalism in Epistemology."[8] The essay is important because it shows not only at how early a stage Tanabe had assimilated neo-Kantian epistemology and begun a sharp critique of the theories of Rickert and Cohen based on Nishida's notion of pure experience, but also how rapidly his own philosophical position was maturing.

II

Philosophy as Metanoetics was published by Iwanami Shoten in April of 1946, a year and a half after the completed manuscript had been sent. In his Preface, Tanabe describes in very moving terms how he came to write this work. The basic framework for his metanoetics, as he explains, was laid out in a final series of lectures delivered in the Faculty of Letters at Kyoto University during November and December of 1944. In fall of that year, he goes on, "I also offered an outline of my lectures in the form of a public lecture with the same title sponsored by the Kyoto Philosophical Society." It was customary on such occasions for a professor about to retire from the Department of Philosophy to give a farewell address that would bear witness to the deep fund of knowledge he had acquired. In Tanabe's case, however, the lecture coincided with the final days of World War II, at the very time that the fate of Japan was being decided.

The atmosphere was tense as the hall filled to overflowing. The audience sat spellbound, not knowing what to expect.

"The people of Japan watch in alarm as their nation sinks deeper and deeper into hell," Tanabe began, and against this background of grave concern for the future of our country proceeded to set forth his ideas. Those of us who lived through the political situation described in the Preface to this book understood at once that his words of warning could be uttered only by a philosopher willing to risk his life for his convictions. Apart from the footsteps of the indignant few who left the hall in the middle of the lecture, the audience hung on Tanabe's every word with utmost seriousness. Kōsaka Masaaki, who was also present on the occasion, records his impressions in the following way:

> At the time I did not have the leisure to attend Tanabe's lectures at the university, nor was there much chance to visit him at his home. Thus I was glad to be able to hear the public lecture he gave at the Kyoto Philosophical Association. . . . I was deeply moved by the feelings of despair and powerlessness pervading his entire lecture as well as by his exposition of the concepts of *zange* (metanoia) and *tariki* (Other-power), and was surprised at the startling change he had made in his philosophical position.[9]

Earlier, as Amano Teiyū reports,

> not only students attended Tanabe's lectures, but also professors from the Philosophy Department and other departments, as well as graduates from Kyoto and even from the Osaka-Kobe area, so that every Tuesday, which was the day set for his lectures each semester, came to be known as "Philosophy Day."[10]

As the war intensified and more and more young men set off for the battlefields, and as even the teachers and students who remained behind were conscripted into the labor force, the numbers of those able to attend his lectures diminished noticeably. Nonetheless, Tanabe exerted ever greater energy in the preparation of lectures on such topics as "Absolute Knowledge" (October 1942–March 1943), "The Logic of Self-Consciousness" (1943), and "Metanoetics" (1944). In this way, the five-year period between the time that his collected essays on the logic of species were published in the *Philosophical Studies* and the publication of *Philosophy as Metanoetics* in 1946 came to represent a dramatic turning point both for Tanabe's thought and for the fate of the nation as such. And yet, as Kōsaka has shown, even those closest to Tanabe in the Kyoto school of philosophy found it difficult to keep abreast of the changes in his thought. Ōshima Yasumasa, Ueda Yasuharu, and I were among the fortunate few who were able at that time to continue receiving instruction from him, and thus were able to follow the development of his thought closely during that period.

On the day Tanabe and his wife left Kyoto in July of 1945, Ueda and I saw them off at Kyoto Station. I can still recall vividly, as if it were yesterday, the agreement we made in the crowded streetcar on the way home that the one who survived the war should transmit Tanabe's thought to future generations. I knew at the time how much he had weakened in body and spirit, and feared that he might not have much longer to live. But I also felt—as I still feel today—that the ideas Tanabe was thinking through in the composition of the present book were of extraordinary significance. The importance of the mission that might fall into my trust, coupled with a sense of my own powerlessness to carry it out, caused me considerable unrest and tension. When I learned that Tanabe had recovered his energies at his mountain home in Kita-Karuizawa and was seeing his work to completion, I was more than relieved.

The greater part of the thought set forth in *Philosophy as Metanoetics* is therefore directly connected with the tense wartime situation in which we studied and reflected on philosophical problems. For this reason I find it unfortunate that its publication in the immediate postwar period, which was also a time of uncommon intellectual turbulence, should have overshadowed its true origins and caused it to be absorbed into the general atmosphere of mass appeals for national repentance being generated by opportunistic politicians.

III

By way of introduction to Tanabe's philosophy of metanoetics, I should like to quote at length from my personal correspondence with him. On 7 July 1944 he wrote to me as follows:

> ... I found the detailed passages you referred to in Matsumoto's work on the future Buddha Maitreya and his Pure Land, and they have proved most useful. While I wish to express my gratitude to you for having kindly lent me this book for the time being, I would also ask you to see if by any chance that work and its companion volume on Amida's Pure Land[11] can be found in any secondhand bookstore so that I might have them with me permanently. I have been intending to ask you to do this for some time, but other business has delayed my writing. At any rate, I am not in any particular rush, nor are these books absolutely essential, but I should be happy if you could do this favor for me if you happen to be in the area of a secondhand bookstore.
> Recently I have become interested in a somewhat different subject, "analy-

tic dynamics," and I have been reading books in that area in the hope of finding a relationship between dynamics and the Great Compassion. (Perhaps it will turn out to be the path that Leibniz took.) While proctoring examinations I have become engrossed in the poems of Rilke's *The Book of Hours* and am delighted to have been able to understand his religious symbols to some extent. At this time of national crisis I must look like a mere bystander with these pursuits of mine, but I am too old and frail to do anything else. My one hope is that I might assimilate thoroughly within my being the way of transcendence to "death-and-life," and so prepare myself to participate in the task of leading those who will choose to take that path in the future. The national mood is extremely somber, and yet I feel a strange sense of light streaming over me that fills me with indescribable gratitude. It seems to me that there can be no other path toward national rehabilitation than for our people as a whole to engage in repentance. My philosophy of metanoetics may come to have a strange kind of historical objectivity about it. . . .

That year the academic year was shortened and examinations were begun toward the end of June. At the time I was often asked by Tanabe to purchase books on Buddhism for him. I have ten or more postcards from him that year with requests similar to the one cited above. By the beginning of September he began to ask me about commentaries on Shinran's *Kyōgyōshinshō* and *Ganshō-ge* (*Ode to Rebirth in the Pure Land*). At the end of one of those postcards he wrote: "I have been considering the important questions raised by the reflections of the two sages Hōnen and Shinran on the *nembutsu*, but the material is difficult and I am having a hard time finding my way through it." Obviously Tanabe was busy preparing his lectures on "Metanoetics," which were to begin in October. The relationship between Hōnen and Shinran was a question Tanabe dealt with specifically in chapters 6 and 7 of the present work,[12] leading us to suppose that he was already nearing the conclusion of the manuscript. Incidentally, Tanabe's reference to Rilke marks the first time I had heard him mention the great German poet, of whose work he had already acquired a profound understanding. Thereafter, whenever I would hear him talk about Rilke, I could not help recalling the deep religious concern of this letter and the impression it made on me at the time.

A second letter I should like to cite was written a little more than a year later, immediately after the end of the war. As noted above, Tanabe was living in his mountain home in Kita-Karuizawa, where he had fled to escape the bombings. As his students, we were concerned about the austere life he was leading in that remote place and asked him to keep us informed of his situation in detail. This was his response, dated 27 August 1945:

As I have finished my work in life and my frail and sickly state can only make me a burden to others, I wish to continue my retirement in this place. My health will not improve. My arms and legs are weak, and my sight is failing. But despite the severe food shortage—at times one cannot avoid a state of near-starvation—my ability to work has not been seriously impaired. My efficiency has improved markedly since my Kyoto days. On these points, as far as work is concerned, I find this place excellent for me. It is a great help to have few distractions. Thus, if possible, I should like to live here permanently....

I purposely refrain from mentioning the war, which would only be a source of pain. The course Japan takes from now on will be an extraordinarily difficult one; the rebuilding will not be easy. I especially fear an impasse in the financial and economic realms, and we shall have to be prepared for an aggravation of social problems. It is doubtful whether our livelihood can be maintained. Economic reform is essential above all. Even though academic studies are necessary, for a time their decline may be unavoidable. The state of the world is such that academic pursuits are out of the question. I am extremely pessimistic about the postwar period....

May there not possibly come a time when religion will be sought for the sake of people's spiritual peace and enlightenment? If so, it would signal that the period of repentance for the entire Japanese people has begun. I myself have the feeling that my philosophy of metanoetics has opened the way for such action. Be that as it may, my work seems to have responded coincidentally to the temper of the times, and I am rewriting it with the strong desire to have it published. Each day I write as much as I can.

Between the time he wrote this letter and composed the Preface to *Philosophy as Metanoetics*, his assessment of the state of postwar academia and culture in general changed somewhat. I remarked earlier that Tanabe's metanoetics had developed in advance of the postwar situation. Yet once his work was completed and it came time to add a Preface, he showed himself keenly aware of the state of affairs and moved by the timeliness of his own call for repentance a year previously:

Of course, I despise the shamelessness of the leaders primarily responsible for the defeat who are now urging the entire nation to repentance only in order to conceal their own complicity. Metanoesis is not something to be urged on others before one has performed it for oneself. Still, it is clear that we the nation of Japan, having fallen into these tragic and appalling circumstances, should practice metanoesis (*zange*) together as a people. Since I am one of those who believe in the collective responsibility of a nation, I am convinced that all of us should engage in collective metanoesis (*sō-zange*) in the literal sense of the term.[13]

The repentance that Tanabe had hoped for was in fact not carried out by the Japanese people. Even those who felt moved by his deep concern for Japan not only did not heed his call but did not understand it fully.

Instead of the metanoesis that Tanabe saw as necessary for authentic national rehabilitation, Japan took the speedy but superficial road to recovery whose consequences we see about us today, a recovery that we may say without exaggeration was restricted to the material and economic realms. As was the case with postwar Germany, there is no concealing the fact that our restoration took place at the cost of evading, if not directly sacrificing, the most fundamental issues. Creative energy for spiritual recovery declined rapidly in direct proportion to the recovery of material prosperity.

Many spoke of the advent of a nihilistic mentality. Nothing was emerging in postwar Japan to speak to the needs of the new generation in the way that existentialism and dialectical theology, for example, emerged out of the experience and confusion that the devastations of World War I had wrought on philosophy and the philosophy of religion. It seemed that the brutalities and severities of World War II had not allowed people the emotional margin they needed in order to reflect their situation accurately in literature and philosophy. For my own part, I am inclined to think that the basic reason for this phenomenon lies in a neglect of the sort of groundwork for spiritual self-consciousness that Tanabe propounded in his metanoetics. As a result of this neglect a far more serious problem hangs over us than if Tanabe's expectations had been fulfilled. Perhaps, as with all highly significant historical prophecies, Tanabe's very failure demonstrates all the more clearly how close he was to the heart of the matter. But more than that, the problem of metanoetics looms before us as a challenge to the future. In his own words:

> Speaking frankly, I would say that the occupying powers themselves have yet to achieve a harmony between democracy and socialism, and that this will remain a difficult problem for them in the foreseeable future. But so long as that problem is not resolved, it is inevitable that these nations will be beset by a host of difficulties both internal and external. All nations, be they democratic or socialist, have their own need to perform metanoesis.[14]

IV

After completing his study of the philosophy of metanoetics, Tanabe produced a number of major works in rapid succession. From October of 1945 he turned his attention to writing *The Dialectics of the Logic of Species*, which he completed in February of 1946 and published in the August issue of the *Philosophical Quarterly*. Together with its complement, *Philosophy as Metanoetics*, this work represents the mainstay of his thought at the time and the foundation for his final period.

Although there is some difference of opinion as to how to divide Tanabe's lifework into periods, I am largely in agreement with Kōsaka Masaaki[15] in defining a second period in terms of the three works that make up volume 3 of Tanabe's *Collected Works*: *Kant's Theory of Teleology* (1924), *Hegelian Philosophy and Dialectics* (1932), and *A General Theory of Philosophical Method* (1933). Everything prior to these would belong to his first period. A third period may be circumscribed by his *Collected Essays on the "Logic of Species,"* published in *Philosophical Studies* between 1932 and 1941 and making up volumes 6 and 7 of the *Collected Works*. The fourth period would then be centered on his concern with metanoetics. Of this final period we may now speak in greater detail.

Tanabe's encounter with Shinran's *Kyōgyōshinshō* was central to the development of his *Philosophy as Metanoetics*, and while his criticisms of a number of Western philosophers in this connection were rather severe, he never hesitated to proclaim his indebtedness to them. We find the same standpoint dominant in his *Dialectics of the Logic of Species*, where he exerts himself more directly to bring the truth of religious existence into contact with social praxis. In *Existenz, Love, and Praxis* (1947), he pursues this concern with the social praxis of religious love through a criticism of Kierkegaard's existentialism for its excessive emphasis on the importance of becoming an individual and the ethical imperative of religious love. In that work he also took up the problem of superseding Plato's later dialectics by means of the faith of the Gospel. During this period, Jesus' teaching of repentance was becoming central in Tanabe's religious view of society, and was developed concretely in *The Dialectics of Christianity* (1948).

Tanabe's own assessment of these developments was that his philosophy was drawing closer and closer to the core of Christianity. His last essays, however, seem to show a standpoint closer to Zen, his affinities with which are clear from *Hegelian Philosophy and Dialectics* (1931) and other works. But these differences are not of great weight when set in the balance against his overriding concern with the fundamental problems of the philosophy of religion. Here I am in full agreement with Nishitani Keiji when he claims that the cornerstone of Tanabe's thought can as well be Buddhism or Christianity or Shin or Zen, or all of these or none of these, since his is really a philosophy—or more accurately, a philosophy of religion—in the genuine sense of the term.

Tanabe's pilgrimage in the philosophy of religion, which looks in one sense to have been an aimless wandering from Dōgen to Shinran, from Shinran to Jesus, and then back again to Zen, was actually a consistently rigorous and highly disciplined spiritual journey. In seeking to satisfy the existential requirements of philosophy, Tanabe almost seems to have made a "leap" from a philosophical position to a religious one in working out his position of "absolute critique" in which the essential problems of religion are to be treated in terms of genuine religious subjectivity. Indeed, seen from the standpoint of absolute critique, "philosophy as metanoetics" appears to be almost a confession, or a conversion of philosophy itself into religion, so that his thought can unfold as an honest encounter and dramatic confrontation between the two realms. But seen from the standpoint of orthodox religion—that is, from the viewpoint of theology and religious doctrine—Tanabe would appear to be making his judgments from without, or to retreat to philosophy each time he gets to the verge of a genuine religious position. I would rather say that Tanabe struggled to sustain a sort of "philosophical faith" created from philosophy but transcending philosophy. Just as the road from the grove of trees at the base of the volcano Mount Asama, where Tanabe had his cottage, twists and turns until it makes its way to the magnificent panorama at the summit, so too does the philosophical position he spoke of as "nothingness-*qua*-love," "Great Nay–*qua*–Great Compassion," or "death-and-resurrection" always loom large in the heights ahead, no matter how many twists and turns his thought takes along the way.

One further point to be emphasized in this regard is that Tanabe himself repeatedly made clear that even in *Philosophy as Metanoetics* Shinran's influence on his thought was an indirect one. Consider, for example, the following passage:

> I do mean to imply that this was how the Pure Land doctrine set forth by Shinran effected a conversion in my philosophy. It is only that when the critique of reason that takes place in philosophy progresses to the point of an absolute critique and thus reaches the end of its tether, a way to the suprarational "death-and-resurrection" of reason is necessarily thrown open....
>
> In short, it has been the destiny of my life philosophy that it necessarily develop into metanoetics. It is not that I mean to graft Pure Land Shin faith in Other-power onto philosophy, but rather that the confrontation of philosophy with my personal experience of reality has forced me to develop my thought in this direction.[16]

By the same token, he has the following to say regarding his relationship to Zen:

> I was also surprised to find that once I had arrived at belief in Other-power, I found myself feeling still closer to the spirit of Zen, whose emphasis on self-power is generally considered opposed to Pure Land doctrine. Nor was this the last of my surprises. A key to solving a problem in mathematical philosophy, which would at first glance seem to be rather far removed from religious concerns, also emerged at this time. I refer to the puzzle of infinite-set theory, over which I had cudgeled my brains for many years in vain.[17]

These ideas were later carried out in various works published between 1949 and 1955 on the philosophy of mathematics and the philosophy of science. Of course this "new direction" had already begun in sections of *Existenz, Love, and Praxis* dealing with Plato's later doctrine of Ideas and their relation to number, Plato's notion of division, and the Dedekind cut.[18]

Meantime, Tanabe's notion of the mediation between dynamics and the Great Compassion flowed like a steady undercurrent through his later essays, culminating in two important final pieces, "The Ontology of Life or the Dialectics of Death" (1961) and "My View of the *Ch'an-yuan*" (1960).[19]

As Tanabe states in his preface to *Existenz, Love, and Praxis*, his understanding of Christianity was also broadened by his metanoetics, as had been the case with Zen. I can testify personally to the fact that at the time he was working on his metanoetics, Tanabe's interest in the study of early Christianity was every bit as strong as his devotion to the study of Buddhism. Already in January of 1943, for instance, he had read Schweitzer's *The Mysticism of the Apostle Paul*, which played such a prominent role in his later *The Dialectics of Christianity* (1948). I myself once borrowed Tanabe's copy of the book, the margins of which were filled with notes, and remember feeling that I was learning a great deal more from those detailed scribblings than from the actual text itself.[20] From the very outset, then, his study of Christianity had an indirect influence on his philosophy of metanoetics, which in turn served to deepen his understanding of Christianity.

Tanabe's long "third period" that produced the *Collected Essays on the "Logic of Species"* was crystallized in new form with the publication of *Philosophy as Metanoetics* followed by *The Dialectics of the Logic of Species*. These two volumes, which we have referred to as the mainstay of his final period, represent the result of an intellectual and spiritual leap. The fact that he felt he had resolved the problem of the logic of species demonstrates how convinced he was of the truth of his metanoetics. In hindsight, we discover that already in his third period, Tanabe's ideas on metanoetics have begun to take shape, thus showing a continuous line of development from the logic of species to metanoetics. At the same time, *The Dialectics of the Logic of Species* is more than just a completion of the logic of species; it signals a new approach to the same problem, which dates from the composition of *Existenz, Love, and Praxis*. And this confirms the view that the logic of species represents the thought of a lifetime, the central problem of his philosophical career, or perhaps we should rather say a labyrinth of problems that land us in endless complexities.

I once asked Tanabe what sort of changes his concept of species had undergone in being applied to such issues as race, class, and nation. His response was that to think dialectically one must always do philosophy in confrontation with the real world. At the time I did not fully grasp his meaning. But now that I reflect on the matter, it strikes me that just as philosophy as metanoetics can only arise metanoetically, that is, from a standpoint wherein philosophy itself becomes existential and subjective metanoia, so, too, does the dialectics of the logic of species represent a system of thought that demands a perspective on the real world. Herein lies its difficulty and its danger, which can be faced only by way of a metanoetics. The complementary and interrelated nature of the philosophy of metanoetics and the dialectics of the logic of species remains one of the fundamental problems of Tanabe's philosophy to which I should like to return at a later date.

V

While he was composing *Philosophy as Metanoetics, Existenz, Love, and Praxis*, and *The Dialectics of the Logic of Species*, Tanabe's idea of metanoia took on fresh nuance. Without entering into details here, let us conclude by singling out the main features of the idea as expressed in the first two of those works.

Tanabe conceived of *zange* in terms of the Greek terms μετάνοια or μετανόησις, which refer to a sort of "thinking-afterward" or "repentance" that entails the painful recollection of one's past sins, a feeling of remorse accompanied by the strong wish that those sins had not been committed. But this reflective afterthought is not the central issue for Tanabe. Since metanoia is the "action" of self-negation, one cannot simply establish the self and then practice metanoia. What is required, in the first place, is rather a breakthrough of the self through which metanoia clashes head-on with the radical evil that negates our existence at its very core, where one boldly faces the discipline of a death that lets go of the self. Metanoia begins at the point where, in the midst of suffering, one recognizes the evil of the self and abandons its right to exist. Tanabe distinguishes this "voluntary despair" from a "rebellious despair," showing the former to be a profound and self-conscious grasp of a compound negation in which existence and value are intertwined.

From there he proceeds to argue for the dual nature of this negation. The reason that voluntary metanoia can negate and break through the self is that it is a self-negation prompted by an absolute nothingness that transcends the self. Because of its grounding in this transcendent absolute nothingness, the self-negation of metanoia possesses a twofold negative structure in which the self acts while being acted upon. This activity of self-negation, supplemented by transcendence (absolute nothingness), effects a conversion from negation to affirmation, from death to life. This is the second meaning of metanoia: metanoia as conversion or transformation. Tanabe's own mysterious experience of conversion is related in the Preface to the present work, where he reveals how his philosophical torment and his awareness of his personal short-comings came together to provide the platform for a spiritual leap.

The complete death and self-negation wherein one acts while being aided and acted upon by absolute nothingness signal the start of a new life, a life in which one *lives* as one who has been *brought to life*. Here we can no longer speak of either life or death in the strict sense, but of a restoration of existence in which both life and death have been swallowed up. Conversion in this sense consists in the religious practice of a faith and action directed toward the transcendent negation of absolute nothing-ness at work in the self. In other words, it is "absolute nothingness–*qua*–love" or "Great Nay–*qua*–Great Compassion." Since a resurrected existence based on the love and salvation of such absolute transforming power spells the end to the acquisition of self-identity by one's own power (Tanabe uses the Shin Buddhist notion of "self-power" or *jiriki*), it does not entail the absolute extinction of sin. On the contrary, one's self-awareness of sin only grows deeper and keener, and the voluntary despair of the self continues to torment the self with suffering and sorrow. In spite of this—or rather, precisely because of it—the purifica-tion and joy of salvation are bestowed, and sadness is transformed into bliss, in the midst of one's sinful condition. Moreover, since metanoia means an absolute transformation by absolute nothingness, the return to affirmation from negation requires this transformation to be repeated again and again. Through this repetition, the self comes to an awareness of metanoia as a dynamic and unending process of development.

In the third place, in considering the basic structure of *zange*, Tanabe based himself on a distinction he had worked out at the time of his *Hegelian Philosophy and Dialectics* (1931), contrasting the *differential* standpoint of action and faith with the *integral* standpoint of immediate intuition. In this way he could insist that metanoia is achieved in an active faith of religious existence that abandons contemplation of existence as a totality. Thus metanoetics, as a "meta-noetics," surpasses the position of mere contemplation (philosophical speculation). This in turn allows him to argue that his is a "philosophy beyond philosophy." In the terms of the Kegon (Hua-yen) school of Chinese Buddhism, it is at one and the same time a suprarational philosophy where reason (*ri*) is thoroughly destroyed by fact (*ji*) and a philosophy where reason and fact interpenetrate each other (*riji-sōnyū*) without hindrance or obstacle (*riji-muge*).

In the fourth place, Tanabe deals with the question of the transcendence of the speculative position by appealing to a philosophy of absolute criticism. The overcoming of speculative metaphysics in "meta-noetics" is achieved by the path of an absolute critique that results from carrying out the critique of reason to its ultimate consequences. Kant's position grounds philosophy, both theoretical and practical reason, in the autonomy of reason alone, exempting nothing that exists, not even God and the state, from his critique. But he did not allow reason the full rein of its critique inasmuch as the reason that is performing the critique is not turned around to criticize itself. If reason is not made to perform this task, Tanabe argues, it must perforce fall into a state of utter confusion and end up in antinomy. Hegel's philosophy is marked by the attempt to pursue Kant's critique of reason to its limits in both its theoretical and practical dimensions, and on this basis to set philosophy up as a practical dialectics. It is here that we find his profound notion of "reconciliation with destiny through love," which Tanabe sees as exemplary for the philosophy of metanoetics. No less important is Hegel's location of the self-awareness of the sinfulness of human existence and its transformation by means of religion at the heart of his dialectics.

However, inasmuch as Hegel ended up retreating to a rational standpoint concerned with a purely conceptual and speculative structuring of the totality of being, he left his thought open to the critical corrective of

Kierkegaard's attacks. Accordingly, in the fifth place, Tanabe's philosophy makes use of the notion of metanoia to undertake a spirited presentation of Kierkegaard's dialectics of religious existence.

In a sense, Kierkegaard's notion of "repetition" corresponds to the demand for constancy in metanoia, but what it lacks is a self-consciousness of the element of compassionate *return to* care for the world that must underlie the element of *going forth* on the way of one's own salvation, a distinction that Tanabe develops through Shinran's ideas of *gensō* and *ōsō* respectively. This leads to a sixth characteristic of metanoia: its unending "repetition" through which the self incarnates itself in faith and practice. It is in this process, where "the turning (conversion) of the self on its own axis empathizes with and arouses the turning of an infinite number of other axes (one's neighbors)," that we see Tanabe making Kierkegaard's profound but incomplete grasp of the logic of "return" more concrete. God's love must join with our love of God and our love of one another to form a trinity that may be described as a "nothingness-*qua*-love." It is here that Tanabe ultimately comes to turn metanoetics back to social praxis grounded in religious love.

NOTES

1. Although even in academic circles in Japan one will often hear Tanabe's personal name pronounced *Gen*, after its Chinese reading, instead of the Japanese reading, *Hajime*, this is incorrect.

2. Cited from Takahashi Satomi, 「田辺元君の死を悼む」 ("In Memoriam: Tanabe Hajime"), 『思想』 (*Thought*) 9, no. 459 (1962):1253–1259.

3. "The Development of Mathematics Viewed from the History of Ideas," in 『田元辺全集』 (*Collected Works of Tanabe Hajime*), ed. Nishitani Keiji et al. (Tokyo: Chikuma Shobō, 1962–1963), 5:95.

4. 「田元辺追想」 ("In Memory of Tanabe Hajime"), publisher's supplement to vol. 11 of the *Collected Works*.

5. 「田元辺君の学生時代から」 ("From Tanabe's School Days"), publisher's supplement to vol. 3 of the *Collected Works*.

6. English translation by Valdo Viglielmo, *A Study of Good* (Tokyo: Japan Ministry of Education, 1960).

7. 『西田幾多郎全集』 (*Collected Works of Nishida Kitarō*), ed. Watsuji Tetsurō et al. (Tokyo: Iwanami, 1947–1953), 17:313.

8. Ibid., 1:366. See also 17:173, citing a letter of Nishida to Kuwaki Ayao.

9. 『西田哲学と田辺哲学』 (*The Philosophies of Nishida and Tanabe*) (Nagoya: Reimei Shobō, 1949), p. 131.

10. ("Tanabe the Man") in 『田辺哲学』 (*The Philosophy of Tanabe*) (Tokyo: Kōbundō, 1951), pp. 257–261.

11. The two volumes he refers to are Matsumoto Bunsaburō, 『彌勒浄土論』 *A Treatise on the Pure Land of Maitreya* (Tokyo: Heigo, 1904), and 『娯楽浄土論』 *A Treatise on the Pure Land of Enjoyment* (Tokyo: Kinkō, 1911).

12. A preliminary draft of these two chapters, based on lecture notes, was published separately, with Tanabe's permission, by one of his students, a sociologist named Minami Dentarō, in 1944 under the title 『私観教行信証の哲学』 (*A Personal View of the Philosophy of the "Kyōgyōshinshō"*).

13. See Preface, p. lx.

14. See Preface, pp. lxi–lxii.

15. *The Philosophies of Nishida and Tanabe*, pp. 65–76.

16. See Chap. 1, pp. 28–29.

17. See Preface, p. liv.

18. *Collected Works* 9 : 446–457.

19. The *Ch'an-yuan-chu-ch'uan'chi* is a collection of famous Zen sayings dating from the T'ang dynasty in China. Only the preface remains.

20. I recall receiving a postcard from Tanabe dated 17 January (1945) in which he remarked, "I have already finished reading it [the Schweitzer volume], so you may have it at any time." I believe it was also at this time that I borrowed his copy of the English translation of Gustav Deissman's *Light from the Ancient East* (London: Hodder & Stoughton, 1910), the margins of which were similarly filled with notes.

Preface

Last summer, when the fortunes of war had turned against Japan and the nation was under the increasing threat of direct raids and attacks, the government found itself at a loss as to how to handle the situation, and in the stalemate that ensued, it showed itself completely incapable of undertaking the reforms necessary to stem the raging tide of history. Instead, government officials tried to keep the actual course of events secret from the people in order to conceal their own responsibility. Criticism of any kind became impossible. All public opinion, except for propaganda in favor of the government's policy, was suppressed. Freedom of thought was severely restricted, and the only ideas given official recognition were those of the extreme rightists. In the midst of economic distress and tensions, and an ever deepening anxiety, our people were greatly concerned about their nation's future but did not know where to turn or to whom to appeal.

I myself shared in all these sufferings of my fellow Japanese, but as a philosopher I experienced yet another kind of distress. On the one hand, I was haunted by the thought that as a student of philosophy I ought to be bringing the best of my thought to the service of my nation, to be addressing the government frankly with regard to its policies toward academic thought and demanding a reexamination, even if this should incur the displeasure of those currently in power. In such a critical situation, where there was no time for delay, would it not be disloyal to my country to keep silent and fail to express whatever ideas I had on reform? On the other hand, there seemed something traitorous about expressing in time of war ideas that, while perfectly proper in time of peace, might end up causing divisions and conflicts among our people that would only further expose them to their enemies.

Caught between these alternatives, I was unable to make up my mind and was tormented by my own indecision. In the impasse I even wondered whether I should go on teaching philosophy or give it up altogether, since I had no adequate solution to a dilemma that philosophically did not appear all that difficult. My own indecision, it seemed to me, disqualified me as a philosopher and university professor. I spent my days wrestling with questions and doubts like this from within and without, until I had been quite driven to the point of exhaustion and in my despair concluded that I was not fit to engage in the sublime task of philosophy.

At that moment something astonishing happened. In the midst of my distress I let go and surrendered myself humbly to my own inability. I was suddenly brought to new insight! My penitent confession—metanoesis (*zange*)—unexpectedly threw me back on my own interiority and away from things external. There was no longer any question of my teaching and correcting others under the circumstances—I who could not deliver myself to do the correct thing. The only thing for me to do in the situation was to resign myself honestly to my weakness, to examine my own inner self with humility, and to explore the depths of my powerlessness and lack of freedom. Would not this mean a new task to take the place of the philosophical task that had previously engaged me? Little matter whether it be called "philosophy" or not: I had already come to realize my own incompetence as a philosopher. What mattered was that I was being confronted at the moment with an intellectual task and ought to do my best to pursue it.

The decision was reached, as I have said, through metanoia, or the way of *zange*, and led to *a philosophy that is not a philosophy*: philosophy seen as the self-realization of *metanoetic consciousness*. It is no longer I who pursue philosophy, but rather *zange* that thinks through me. In my practice of metanoesis, it is metanoesis itself that is seeking its own realization. Such is the nonphilosophical philosophy that is reborn out of the denial of philosophy as I had previously understood it. I call it a philosophy that is not a philosophy because, on the one hand, it has arisen from the vestiges of a philosophy I had cast away in despair, and on the other, it maintains the purpose of functioning as a reflection on what is ultimate and as a radical self-awareness, which are the goals proper to philosophy.

To be sure, this is not a philosophy to be undertaken on my own power (*jiriki*). That power has already been abandoned in despair. It is rather a philosophy to be practiced by Other-power (*tariki*), which has turned me in a completely new direction through metanoesis, and has induced me to make a fresh start from the realization of my utter helplessness. Metanoesis (*zange*) signifies repentance for the wrongs I had done, with the accompanying torment of knowing that there is no way to expiate my sins. It also signifies shame for the powerlessness and inability that have driven me to despair and self-surrender. Yet insofar as this entails an act of self-denial, it points to a paradox: even though it is my own act, it cannot be my own act. It has been prompted by a Power outside of myself. This Other-power brings about a conversion in me that heads me in a new direction along a path hitherto unknown to me.

Zange thus represents for me an experience of Other-power acting in and through *zange* to urge me to a new advance in philosophy. I entrust my entire being to Other-power (*tariki*), and by practicing *zange* and maintaining faith in this Power I confirm the truth of my own conversion-and-resurrection experience. In this way the practice-faith-witness (*gyō-shin-shō*) of my *zange* becomes the philosophy of my re-generated existence. This is what I am calling "metanoetics," the philosophy of Other-power. I have died to philosophy and been resur-rected by *zange*. It is not a question of simply carrying on the same phi-losophy I had abandoned in my despair, as if resuming a journey after a temporary interruption. It cannot be a mere repetition without negation and change. In the life of the spirit, "repetition" must mean self-transcendence; "resurrection" must mean regeneration to a new life. I no longer live of myself, but live because life has been granted to me from the transcendent realm of the absolute which is neither life nor death. Since this absolute is the negation and transformation—that is, conversion—of everything relative, it may be defined as absolute noth-ingness. I experience this absolute nothingness through which I am reborn to new life as nothingness-*qua*-love. One might also say that it is an experience of the truth of absolute negation: the confirmation of the Great Nay as the Great Compassion. The truth of my conversion and resurrection in dependence on *tariki* (Other-power) is confirmed in the practice and faith (*gyō-shin*) of *zange*.

While I have no doubt that metanoetics is the way to a new philos-ophy of Other-power as the "action-faith-witness" of *zange*, I am but a finite and imperfect being whose *zange* may not be fully pure and true. It may sometimes happen that my *zange* is not accompanied by a resurrec-tion, or that even after a resurrection experience, I may fall away from *zange* into reliance on self-power. I may grow complacent with my accomplishments and in my arrogance imagine myself a wise man. In that case I should inevitably be driven back to my former despair, since anything I achieve apart from true *zange* can only be immediately contradicted by reality itself. Only through continual *zange* can we achieve the faith and witness (*shin-shō*) of continuous resurrection. By acting in and witnessing to the circular process of death-and-resurrection that characterizes *zange* and indeed accords with the unfolding of reality itself, the infinity and eternity of *zange* are revealed to us and the dialectical unity of absolute and relative affirmed. This is in fact the basic principle that shapes history. In terms of its concrete content, metanoetics is a radical historicism in that the continuous repetition of *zange* provides basic principles for the circular development of history.

My experience of conversion—that is, of transformation and resurrection—in metanoesis corresponds to the experience that led Shinran (1173–1262) to establish the doctrine of the Pure Land Shin sect (*Jōdo Shin-shū*). Quite by accident I was led along the same path that Shinran followed in Buddhist discipline, although in my case it occurred in the philosophical realm. Reflection on this parallel led me to an interpretation of Shinran's *Kyōgyōshinshō* from a metanoetical point of view. I had, of course, been interested in Shinran before that time. In particular I found his *Tanni-shō* and one of the hymns from his *Shōzōmatsu Wasan* entitled "Confession and Lamentation" deeply moving for their treatment and tone of metanoesis.

Shinran's doctrine of salvation through the praise and recitation of the name of Amida Buddha, as an expression of faith in Amida Buddha alone, has often been mistaken for a kind of spiritual laxity, especially seen in conjunction with his advocacy of the "easy way" of salvation (*igyōdō*). This is due to the common error of confusing the realm of the transcendent—where we must speak of people being saved "just as they are," without any merit on their part, as a result of the conversion and transformation brought about by absolute compassion—with the realm of the relative—normal, everyday life. Thus his doctrine of the salvation of people "just as they are" led to the error of disregarding morality, and at times even served the evil purpose of providing excuses for wrongdoings.

In contrast with these abuses of his teaching, Shinran's own faith was based on the bitter experience of metanoesis. This had been my firm conviction from the outset in reading Shinran's works. But I had no idea at the time that his *Kyōgyōshinshō* was in its very essence nothing other than metanoetics. The oversight was a natural one in that metanoesis does not appear as one of the central ideas of the work, even though Shinran mentions and explains the "three kinds of metanoesis" developed by the Chinese priest Shan'tao (Jap., *Zendō*, 613–681) in one of his doctrinal discourses, and in his hymns in praise of Amida Buddha we find strong elements of metanoesis at various places. Among contemporary scholar-priests of the Shin sect, Soga Ryōjin (1875–1971) should be mentioned for his appreciation of and deep insight into the basic notion of metanoesis, as well as for his recognition of its significance for understanding Shinran's faith. I have found his interpretation and doctrinal analysis most enlightening, and owe him a great debt of gratitude in this regard.

Understanding the *Kyōgyōshinshō* as the metanoetical development of Buddhism has not received general approval as a correct interpretation. I myself had long been reluctant to accept such a viewpoint. My innate attraction for the idealistic doctrine of self-power made me more sympathetic to the Zen sect than to sects that taught "salvation by Other-power." Although I had never undergone discipline in a Zen monastery, I had long been familiar with the discourses of Chinese and Japanese Zen masters. I was ashamed that I still remained an outsider to Zen and could not enter into the depths of its holy truth, and yet I felt closer to Zen than to Shin doctrine. This was why I had taken little notice of the *Kyōgyōshinshō* up until that time.

One of my students, Takeuchi Yoshinori (1913–), had published a book under the title *The Philosophy of the "Kyōgyōshinshō"* (1941). Drawing on the intellectual acumen he had developed through reading Hegel under me, he was able to produce an outstanding interpretation of the work. While I learned much from reading this study, it was impossible for me at the time to develop a philosophy of my own based on the thought of the *Kyōgyōshinshō*. It was only when I set out to develop a new philosophy, a philosophy of metanoetics based on Other-power, that I returned to reread the *Kyōgyōshinshō* carefully and was able to find a way to understand it. I regard Shinran with gratitude, love, and respect as a great teacher from the past. As I shall demonstrate in chapters 6 and 7, his idea of the three stages of religious transformation and his interpretation of the "Three Minds" (*sanshin*) is unique in the history of the philosophy of religion as an explanation of the structure of salvation. I cannot but feel thankful for the grace of Other-power that led me to metanoetics and to reliance on the guidance of Shinran.

I was also surprised to find that once I had arrived at belief in Other-power, I found myself feeling still closer to the spirit of Zen, whose emphasis on self-power is generally considered opposed to Pure Land doctrine. Nor was this the last of my surprises. A key to solving a problem in mathematical philosophy, which would at first glance seem to be rather far removed from religious concerns, also emerged at this time. I refer to the puzzle of infinite-set theory, over which I had cudgeled my brains for many years in vain. Moreover, it became clear that a philosophy of history could be based on metanoetics, inasmuch as the content of metanoetics itself consists in a "radical historicism." In this way I grew confident of the range of applicability of metanoetics with its broad and ample perspective, although I must admit that at first I had no idea it was capable of such scope.

Some may contend that metanoesis is so extraordinary a phenomenon in one's spiritual life that it is hardly possible to develop a universal philosophy out of it. But I have been convinced from the start that metanoetics involves social solidarity inasmuch as we are always obliged to practice metanoesis so long as we are aware of our collective responsibility for every event that takes place in our society. In my case, metanoesis was aroused because I had been driven to the limits of my philosophical position as I confronted the desperate straits into which my country had fallen. My distress resulted not only from my own personal inability to execute my responsibilities as a philosopher at the time but also from my feeling the responsibility that each of my fellow Japanese had to assume in his or her particular situation. Naturally I was indignant at the militarists and the government authorities for having duped the people and suppressed criticism among them, for having had the audacity to pursue the most irrational of policies in violation of international law, causing our nation to be stripped of its honor before the rest of the world. But in the strict sense we Japanese are all responsible for the failure and disgrace since we were unable to restrain the reckless ways of the government and the militarists. After those who are directly to be blamed for the disasters that befell Japan, the leaders in the world of social and political thought are most responsible. There is no excusing the standpoint of the innocent bystander so often adopted by members of the intelligentsia.

I am deeply convinced of the fact that, in the last analysis, everyone is responsible, collectively, for social affairs. Once one assumes this standpoint of social responsibility, there can be no doubt that metanoetics is indispensable for each person at each moment. Therefore metanoetics, like morality, can provide the way to a universal philosophy. Furthermore, when metanoetics is viewed in relation to the *Kyōgyōshinshō* of Shinran, our guide in metanoetical thinking, his profound idea of "returning to this world from the Pure Land" (*gensō-ekō*) suggests a distinctive theory of religious society established on the ideal of "fraternity"— an ideal of equality within the social order which at the same time recognizes the ranks of elder and younger in the religious sense. This is somewhat different from the equality that emerges from love of neighbor in Christianity. There is no disputing the fact that freedom based on democracy has led to forms of socialism that run counter to the ideal of freedom. The unity of freedom and equality is not a self-evident fact but a project difficult to achieve. In order to achieve this goal of unity, is it not necessary that the idea of fraternity, restored to its original meaning, mediate in the concrete the conflict between freedom and equality? The idea of "returning to this world" in the Shin sect thus offers a concrete suggestion for a basic principle of social structure, and opens broad vistas in the philosophy of history insofar as it represents the ideal of the compassionate way of the bodhisattva in Mahāyāna Buddhism. We may therefore conclude that metanoetics is more than a mere exercise carried out in the realms of abstract thought.

During the fall of last year I devoted myself assiduously to developing metanoetics into a form of philosophy. From the point of its very inception, metanoetics needs to developed metanoetically. That is, it should not be a "philosophy of metanoesis" in the sense that it treats an object called metanoesis. Neither should it be a phenomenological or *lebensphilosophisch* interpretation that applies its own established methodology to the investigation of metanoesis. Metanoetics is a philosophy that has to be erected at the very point that all prior philosophical standpoints and methods have been negated in their entirety. It is a philosophical method of "destruction" more radical than even the methodical skepticism of Descartes. It cannot be treated on the same level as philosophy up to the present inasmuch as it is a philosophy achieved through a death-and-resurrection process of transformation. Only one awakened to Other-power who practices metanoetics in "action-witness" (*gyō-shō*) can witness its truth in self-consciousness. In this sense I gain personal conviction of the truth of metanoetics by means of my own action-witness, and thereby deepen my metanoetic self-consciousness.

In the course of my reflections, I discovered a logic that functions throughout metanoetical thinking, which I call "absolute criticism."

Philosophy based on reason can with good cause be described as a philosophy of self-power: the reason it presupposes as its basis is bound to fall into antinomies in the encounter with actual reality. Kant's remedy, as laid out in the *Critique of Pure Reason*, was to narrow the scope of reason to make room for faith. The solution is clearly incomplete. In the radical self-consciousness of being driven to the extreme, reason can only be torn to shreds in absolute disruption, after which such self-affirming reason is no longer of any use to us. Absolute criticism means that reason, faced with the absolute crisis of its dilemma, surrenders itself of its own accord. In the course of this critical task, the subject that is undertaking the critique of pure reason cannot remain a mere bystander at a safe remove from the criticism. The subject of the critique cannot avoid getting tangled in its own web and exposing itself to self-criticism. It cannot avoid dismemberment by the absolute dilemma of its own thought. Yet in the very midst of this absolute disruption and contradiction, the power of contradiction is itself negated: the absolute contradiction contradicts itself. At this point an absolute conversion takes place and philosophy is restored, through the power of the transcendent, as a "philosophy that is not a philosophy."

Thus metanoetics includes within itself the logic of absolute criticism. We arrive at metanoetics by way of the critique of reason—reason in both its theoretical and practical aspects—if the critique is pursued radically. This is in fact how the Kantian criticism of the *Critique of Pure Reason* developed into the Hegelian critique of the *Phenomenology of Mind*. The transcendental dialectic of the former was transformed into the true dialectic of the latter. Still, Hegel maintained that the absolute disruption and contradiction in reason could be overcome by the unity of reason, and that the state of reason prior to the antinomies could be recovered in its simple self-identity, because reason is able to embrace in self-consciousness its own death and resurrection by means of infinite thought in the form of the concept (*Begriff*). This led him to neglect the important fact that the resurrected life of reason is not the same as the former state of reason prior to negation, but comes about only through the activity of absolute transformation—that is, through the activity of absolute nothingness, which is neither life nor death. In the resurrection into new life, self-consciousness is only a temporary axis of transformation posited as a subjective center accessible only through action-faith-witness. But Hegel thought that the identity of absolute contradictories could be grasped in the form of the concept quite apart from any such temporary subjective center, that infinite thinking provided the unity of an infinite circle that could embrace the whole within itself.

Here we see why Hegel's concept of reason was unable to break through the constraints of the Aristotelian logic of identity completely. His failure is itself a negation of the dialectic in that the practical transformation of the self is uprooted at the core under the sway of the objective concept. And since the nonobjectifiable and nonmaterializable subjective self ceases to exist, concept turns into substance and absolute idealism into materialism. We are left with a nonexistentialism that denies the practical transformation of the self any mediating role. Not surprisingly, instead of self-consciousness in absolute nothingness we have only substance as being. As a result, Hegel's thought, which shows an affinity here with the thought of Spinoza, could evolve into Marxism.

In contrast, metanoetics remains grounded entirely on a standpoint of practical transformation and thereby open to the Great Nay–*qua*–Great Compassion. It is a standpoint on which the transformative unity of the death-and-resurrection of the self is practiced and witnessed by means of a radical criticism leading to transformation by Other-power, which I would argue is the final culmination of the Kantian critique of reason. The dialectic of absolute mediation that Hegel aimed for but was unable to attain is carried out in practice-faith in a way that was closed to Hegel's contemplation of reason. Here metanoetics is akin to Schelling's theory of freedom which, in opposition to Hegelian reason, probed deeply into Kant's notion of absolute evil. There is also a similarity here to Heidegger's existential philosophy, which, under the influence of Kierkegaard's opposition to Hegel's intellectual philosophy, strove to maintain the authentic self as the center of practical transformation. At the same time, metanoetics is critical of Schelling's speculative philosophy of "construction" insofar as it claims a standpoint of self-consciousness in absolute mediation. It likewise stands opposed to the existentialism of Heidegger which, by diverging from Kierkegaard's "existentialism of faith" to assert the freedom of the self, has affinities with the atheistic thought of Nietzsche. In contrast with these positions, metanoesis seeks throughout to maintain a standpoint of action-faith through Other-power, and thereby to insist on a relationship of reciprocal mediatory transformation between the absolute and the self. Moreover, the redeeming truth that the absolute can function only as the power of absolute mediation can reach self-consciousness by way of reciprocal mediatory activity between relative selves. In this sense, the transformation through vertical mediation between the absolute and the self (Thou and I) must also be realized in horizontal social relationships between my self and other selves (I and thou). Thus metanoetics is able to overcome the deficiencies of individualism common to both

Schelling's doctrine of freedom and Heidegger's existential philosophy, and to make the abstract truth of each more concrete through the realization of responsibility in "social solidarity." Shinran's idea of "returning to the world" (*gensō*) referred to earlier recommends such a doctrine of social solidarity. It gives the idea of a "logic of species" (*shu no ronri*), which I have long advocated as a theory of social existence, a new and deeper basis.

In light of the above considerations, I was confident that metanoetics, as a philosophical principle, would provide sufficient grounds for a new philosophy. This is why I was able to return to philosophy with peace of mind. With this idea of a renewed philosophy in mind, I ascended the platform to deliver my final series of lectures at Kyoto Imperial University. Although a new Cabinet had been formed at the time, in accord with the long-suppressed wish of the Japanese people, it proved no less ineffective in improving the situation. Fears and anxieties grew stronger by the day, as the destitution and disaster continued to spread. While I shared in the deepening pessimism of the people of Japan, I had at least one source of consolation and encouragement. And thus, with a sense of gratitude to Other-power, I presented my lectures, which began in October of 1944 and ended in December, under the title "Metanoetics." During this period I also offered an outline of my lectures in the form of a public lecture with the same title sponsored by the Kyoto Philosophical Society. Such is the history of how my philosophy of metanoetics came to be.

In preparing this last lecture, I developed the logic of "absolute criticism," and through the "destruction" of the Western philosophy in which I had been trained for many years, I attempted a reconstruction from a metanoetical point of view. It was for me a great joy to discover in the course of reconsidering the thought of such figures as Meister Eckhart, Pascal, and Nietzsche that problems I had never been able to penetrate deeply now grew clear to me—at least as far as my limited abilities would allow. Naturally, I concentrated my energies in the main on a metanoetical reading of the *Kyōgyōshinshō*, the results of which filled several notebooks. In order to make a coherent whole of my lectures, I was able to work only on the essentials. A single three-month term was too short; if I had had a year to lecture, it still would have been too short. At any rate, I was approaching the retirement age set for university professors, and on top of that, weak of constitution as I am, I fell ill in November. But so ardent was my desire to complete the lectures at all costs that I left my sickbed just long enough to deliver them. It was with a great sigh of relief that I completed the final lecture in December, after which I spent the rest of the winter in bed. I have no words to express my gratitude for the kindness shown me by my students and colleagues at that time. Since February of this year I have been legally retired from the university professorship. Looking back over my career of twenty-five years at Kyoto Imperial University, I felt regret for the personal inadequacies that inhibited the performance of my duties, but at the same time I was full of thanks to Heaven and to all those whose help enabled me to see my academic career to its end despite my poor health.

But once I had turned my attention away from my private life to focus on the destiny of our nation, my regret and sadness were without bounds. Even after a second change of Cabinet, there was still no improvement. The mainland of Japan was under attack, and the ravages of war were beyond description. Notwithstanding these calamities and even though the situation was considerably worse than before, I was no longer sunk in despair but endeavored to concentrate on the problems that lay before me. In this I could feel the power of metanoetics. Far from relinquishing myself to despair, I was transformed, converted, by the absolute and elevated to a spirit of detachment. This confirmed my conviction that metanoetics is as strong as we are weak. After a thorough-going and humble assessment of my own powerlessness, I experienced the grace of resurrection through the compassion of Other-power.

Toward the end of July I decided to move out of Kyoto and into a rural area, the increasing severity of the air raids having made it impossible for me to remain in a large city. It was entirely through the kind assistance of my close friends that I was able to make the transition in safety. Living here in these quiet surroundings refreshed me in mind and body, though I remained quite as weak as before. My spirits rose during the following two months as I began to order my notes into a longer study, the results of which are contained in this book. At first I had no clear idea of how to pursue its publication, though I did consider serializing it in the pages of the *Journal of Philosophical Studies* (*Tetsu-gaku kenkyū*) as I had done before with other works.

Then, in mid-August, Japan met with the unhappy fate of uncon-ditional surrender, plunging the entire nation—myself included—into deep sorrow. We the Japanese people have to perform metanoesis when we reflect on how this catastrophe came to be. Looking back, I have come to realize that my own metanoesis of a year earlier was destined to prepare the future for my country. The thought of this coincidence brought me great sorrow and pain. Of course, I despise the shamelessness of the leaders primarily responsible for the defeat who are now urging the entire nation to repentance only in order to conceal their own complicity. Metanoesis is not something to be urged on others before one has performed it for oneself. Still, it is clear that we the nation of Japan, having fallen into these tragic and appalling circumstances, should practice metanoesis (*zange*) together as a people. Since I am one of those who believe in the collective responsibility of a nation, I am convinced that all of us should engage in collective metanoesis (*sō-zange*) in the literal sense of the term. I feel compelled to conclude that metanoetics is not only my own private philosophy but a philosophical path the entire nation should follow.

Since metanoesis implies remorse and sorrow, it is necessarily accompanied by feelings of shame and disgrace. This is true both in the way that Shinran used the word and in the connotation of the Latin word *paenitentia*, which originally carried a sense of "pang." * There can be no *paenitentia*, no *zange*, without pain. But the heart of metanoesis is the experience of conversion or transformation: sorrow and lament are turned into joy, shame and disgrace into gratitude. Hence when I say that our nation has no way to walk but the way of *zange* (metanoetics), I do not mean that we should sink into despair and stop there, but that we can hope to be transformed through resurrection and regeneration. It is true that metanoesis is the activity of conversion and transformation performed by Other-power (*tariki*)—I can personally attest to the truth of this through my own "faith-witness" (*shin-shō*)—and I cannot but recommend it to all our people. It is as an act of gratitude that I offer metanoetics (*zangedō*) as a philosophy that belongs rightly not only to me but to all of you. With this thought in mind, I felt I ought to publish this work as quickly as possible. Of course, in making this recommendation I have no intention of forcing others to accept this philosophy. Nonetheless, it is my sincere desire to offer metanoetics to those of the Japanese people who seek a philosophy at the present time.

In spite of the suffering that goes along with defeat, the suppression of thought that we had to endure for many years has now come to an end through the intervention of foreign powers, and freedom of thought is being extolled as an ideal to which we can all aspire. As is evident to all of us, emancipation from state control has led the people of Japan to rally

---

*Tanabe's etymology is misinformed. The root word *poena* has to do with punishment or indemnity.

behind the development of culture as the sole means of rebuilding our nation. I find it a rather curious phenomenon that intellectuals in a country that has just suffered defeat should be stimulated by their freedom of activity to embrace belief in culture. So heavy was the oppression we endured for so many years, at first I am tempted to join them. But can a nation compelled to surrender, with liberalism being forced upon it from without and the development of culture urged from within, be expected to come up with the spiritual resources needed to create a new culture simply because the oppressive controls of the past have been removed? True freedom is not something one receives from another; one has to acquire it for oneself. Even should there be a flowering of new culture in such circumstances as ours, it would be like blossoms on a hothouse plant: beautiful to the eye but too weak and shallow of root to survive in the open air.

Here we see the paradox that true and living culture is not something that can be made by culture worshipers; if anything, their "culturism" is a symptom of the decadence of culture. In general, I have always been critical of abstract ideals like culturism and culture-worship, and I am especially reluctant to approve of the present stress on "culture" since I place no faith in its future. It must be said that the very ones now optimistically espousing the cause of culture are mere onlookers who have no sense of social responsibility to the nation. A moment's glance at some of the current social problems—the hunger and poverty of the vast majority of the people in sharp contrast with the luxury enjoyed by a very few owing to the maldistribution of food and goods, the stagnation and paralysis of industry despite the large number of soldiers returning to the ranks of the unemployed—shows how difficult it will be to rebuild our war-devastated nation. One step in the wrong direction, even one day's delay, may be enough to spell the total ruin of our land. Unless we all undertake the new way of *zange*, free ourselves from the evil institutions of the past, and collaborate in carrying out whatever changes are necessary in the social system, there is no possibility of reconstruction. The only course open to us at present is metanoetics, not culturism. Does not the Old Testament prophet Jeremiah show us the way?

Speaking frankly, I would say that the occupying powers themselves have yet to achieve a harmony between democracy and socialism, and that this will remain a difficult problem for them in the foreseeable future. But so long as that problem is not resolved, it is inevitable that these nations will be beset by a host of difficulties both internal and external. All nations, be they democratic or socialist, have their own need to perform metanoesis. If there is any vocation of significance for world history in the reconstruction of our nation, it lies in the search for a middle path between these two ideologies, a middle path that is neither democracy nor socialism but moves freely between the two systems to make use of the strengths of both. And if this is so, then metanoetics must become the philosophy not only of Japan but of all humanity.

Will not the true meaning of humanity be found when people enter into absolute peace with one another, helping one another in a spirit of reconciliation and cooperation, seeking mutual emancipation and salvation in the conversion of the self-affirming ego into no-self through the mediatory activity of absolute nothingness? For it is the self-affirming ego that is the cause of all conflict among people, while in the life of absolute peace all contribute their best efforts to deepen the joy of fraternal love. For this reason, all people everywhere need to perform *zange* collectively. I do not think I am arguing from a self-centered point of view in making the claim that world history has reached a turning point at the present moment in which all philosophy of any significance should be grounded in metanoetics. Naturally, I have no intention of offering myself as a guide for the world; that would run counter to the very spirit of metanoetics. "Shinran had not a single disciple," wrote Shinran in the *Tanni-shō*. His idea of a horizontal fellowship, not of a vertical or authoritarian teacher-disciple relationship, laid the foundations for an "equality" in which no one enjoyed any special privilege. What Shinran said of invoking the name of Amida—"It is a matter of your decision whether you accept *nembutsu* or reject it"—I should also say of metanoetics. And this, too, confirms my belief that metanoetics, carried out in this spirit of freedom and equality, can become a philosophy for all people.

In a spirit of gratitude for having been able to see this work to its completion, I would like, in the first place, to express my sincerest thanks to all those who have assisted me. Their kindness is something I shall never forget. I should also like to mention my gratitude to my wife who, despite her illness, has served me faithfully these many years and enabled me to devote myself entirely to my work. And finally, I would beg the indulgence of my readers for having been made to endure so lengthy a preface as this.

Kita-Karuizawa
October 1945   Tanabe Hajime

Chapter 1

The Philosophical Meaning of Metanoetics

The meaning of the term "metanoetics" · *The metanoetical development of metanoetics* · *Metanoetic transformation* · *Contemplative self-identity and the unity of active self-consciousness* · *Metanoetics as a philosophy of absolute Other-power (tariki philosophy)* · *The dialectics of absolute mediation* · *Socratic irony and dialectics* · *Metanoetics and Shinran's Kyōgyōshinshō* · *Philosophy as metanoetics* · *Metanoetics and radical human evil* · *Philosophy's mediation of science and religion* · *Metanoetics, the self-consciousness of mediation through action* · *The death-and-resurrection of philosophy in metanoetics* · *The inspiration of Shinran in metanoetical resurrection* · *Absolute critique as the outcome of the critique of reason* · *The historicization of nature in the new physics* · *The radical historicism of metanoetics*

The term "metanoetics" (*zangedō*), as I shall be using it here, has yet to receive general acceptance as part of philosophical terminology. I for one have never come across the word in the area of philosophy. Someone may object at this point: Are you not merely trying to disguise an obsolescence in your own thought and claim originality for your philosophy by coining a new word? To this question I do not intend to respond with an apology. Since it seems to me an absolutely undeniable fact that philosophy is possible only as metanoetics, it no longer matters to me if my views arouse such suspicions. If there be some selfish motive in my thinking which distorts the objectivity of my approach, it is I who am responsible for it, and it is I who must reflect on myself and perform *zange* for it.

To my shame I must confess that I am far from being noble-minded and totally free of fault in this regard. The temptation is ever lurking in my heart, and indeed if I examine my motives carefully, the very fact of raising the question myself may turn out to be a symptom of it. Be that as it may, metanoetical reflection urges me to examine myself completely, to recognize this shameful tendency within myself and to perform *zange* for it. Once I have submitted myself to this requirement and devoted myself to the practice of *zange*, I am met by a wondrous Power that relieves the torment of my shameful deeds and fills me with a deep sense of gratitude. *Zange* is, as it were, a balm for the pain of repentance, and at the same time the source of an absolute light that paradoxically makes the darkness shine without expelling it. The experience of accepting this transforming power of *zange* as a grace from *tariki* (Other-power) is, as we shall see shortly, the very core of metanoetics.

Hence the claim that metanoetics is the only way to my philosophical revival, and that no other philosophy is conceivable to me than one based on such metanoetical self-consciousness, points to an objective reality beyond all possibility of doubt, despite any arbitrary, subjective, or dishonest motives I may harbor in my breast. So powerful is metanoetics that it sweeps aside all doubt about itself. This may, it seems to me, be taken as evidence of its truth. I can therefore confess frankly and with conviction that metanoetics is, as a matter of necessity, my philosophy. As far as I am concerned, no philosophy is possible without such confession (ὁμολογία) and *zange* (repentance, μετάνοια). It is precisely the self-awakening which comes to one on the way of *zange* that constitutes metanoetics, or *zangedō*. Intrinsic to the way of *zange* is the self-awakening of those who follow it and the wisdom thus attained. It is for this very reason that metanoetics can be designated a philosophy.

There is another reason for using a word derived from a Western language, "metanoetics," together with the Japanese term "*zangedō*." "Metanoetics" carries the sense of "meta-noetics," denoting philologically a transcending of noetics, or in other words, a transcending of metaphysical philosophy based on contemplation or intellectual intuition achieved by the use of reason. "Meta-noetics" means transcending the contemplative or speculative philosophy of intellectual intuition as it is usually found in the realms of thought based on reason. Here we have a very important characteristic by which metanoetics is distinguished from ordinary mysticism or philosophies of intellectual intuition: it is not a philosophy founded on the intuitive reason of *jiriki* (self-power), but rather a philosophy founded on action-faith-witness (*gyō-shin-shō*) mediated by the transformative power of *tariki* (Other-power). If I may introduce at this point two key concepts[1] characteristic of the teachings of the Pure Land sect of Shin Buddhism—*ōsō* or "going toward" the Pure Land, and *gensō* or "returning to" this world from the Pure Land—metanoetics may be described as a philosophy of action following the path of *gensō*, while ordinary mysticism may be described as contemplative speculation following the path of *ōsō*. The doctrine of *gensō* is thus of special significance in enabling metanoetics to bring about a revival of philosophy. The term "metanoetics" helps to express these ideas clearly in that metanoetics implies, on the one hand, a self-awakening through a "way" of repentance, a "thinking-afterward" (μετάνοια), and on the other, suggests a self-conscious transcending of intuition and contemplation (μετανόησις). This is why *zangedō* can be termed a Μετανοητική or "metanoetics." The full meaning of metanoetics will be explained in detail later as this work develops, but at least these few comments seemed in order here at the outset.

As mentioned before, the very fact that I advocate metanoetics as a philosophy itself expresses my option for the way of *zange*. Only through metanoetics can I reflect on its philosophical significance. In other words, I discuss "philosophy as metanoetics" metanoetically. Therefore, I am not concerned with how others will take it. All criticism of my standpoint I willingly accept as a further opportunity to perform *zange*. Being evil and untruthful by nature, I feel a deep sense of shame and fear that my confession, or *zange*, must needs contain insincerity and impurity. Worse than that, I find myself unable to overcome the ingrained evil of feeling proud over performing *zange*. However severe the criticism against me may be, I cannot possibly excuse my vanity, folly, perversity, and wickedness. I am prepared to accept such criticism with humility; I am determined to reflect upon myself as thoroughly as possible and to perform *zange* for my dishonesty and shamelessness. This, I believe, is the only way left open to me. Indeed my power, by itself alone, is so ineffective, and my folly and wickedness so tenacious, that if left to myself, I could not perform even this *zange*. Nevertheless, the *tariki* (Other-power) that acts within me exercises its power in a way so overwhelming that it obliges me to perform *zange*. Thus it is that I perform this action of *zange* solely by following this power. And this is the reason, as I stated before, that metanoetics forces me to treat it metanoetically. In this sense, I may say that the evidence, or witness (*shō*), of the existential truth of metanoetics comes to light. Metanoia is not confined to "meta-noia," that is, a "thinking-afterward" or repentance that implies a painful recollection of one's past sins, or a feeling of remorse accompanied by the profound wish that those sins had not been committed. It is rather the "breaking-through" (*Durchbruch*) of a self that hitherto had moved exclusively within the realms of discursive thinking and reflection. In reality, as long as the self affirms its being directly, true repentance is by no means possible. This is the reason that although repentance is an act of the self, it is at the same time a breaking-through of the self, a forsaking of the self. As Hegel says, when we acknowledge our responsibility for those of our actions that inevitably result in sin, this recognition of our own sin implies the tragic downfall of our own being and a submission to the judgment of fate and destiny. So, too, does *zange*, or metanoesis, imply the downfall and the forsaking of the self. As such, *zange* means simply following a disciplined way toward one's own death.

Moreover, human sin and evil are not accidental phenomena; nor do they signify merely the evil acts of individual persons. They constitute rather a negative determination of our being itself that lies at the foundation of human existence in general, something like what Kant speaks of as "radical sin." As long as Existenz is established by determining the existence of the self spontaneously by oneself, one is endowed with a freedom analogous to the freedom of the absolute in order to respond to the transformative power of that absolute. But at the same time, as a consequence of this freedom there is a concealed tendency to forget one's relativity and presume to be the absolute. This clearly is human arrogance and shows how prone we are to extend the "analogous" structure of our being into the extreme assumption of being directly "identical"—namely, to confuse our role of mediatory activity executed in absolute negativity on behalf of the absolute with an immediate affirmation of our freedom, oblivious of the very fact that our existence can be founded only on a principle of transformation, or conversion, that presents itself through self-negation as the result of standing in contradictory confrontation. An "existence" whose principle is freedom cannot by itself eliminate the sort of latent evil we see produced by an innate tendency toward arrogance, the evil most accurately termed "original sin."

Human freedom in its true sense is rooted solely in the grace of the absolute. This grace negates our being in order to convert us to a new being by awakening in us a consciousness of the unfathomable depth of our sin and thereby leading us to recognize that this innate freedom is, in reality, the very cause of our lacking freedom in the true sense, and that only the negation of the former assures us of the latter. It is only when we forsake ourselves and entrust our being to the grace of *tariki* (Other-power) that our existence can acquire true freedom. In short, life consists of the continuous practice of "death-and-resurrection." Metanoesis is practicing, and also being made to practice, this "death-and-resurrection" according to criteria of the value and meaning of our existence, or, more correctly, of the valuelessness and meaninglessness of our existence. It must begin with a casting away of the self that is no longer qualified to exist because it is forced to recognize, through suffering and sorrow, that its being is valueless.

This means that metanoesis (*zange*) is the exact opposite of despair in the ordinary sense, which consists of getting discouraged at ourselves, asserting our negative self, and growing increasingly vexed to the point of forgetting the fact that we have been condemned to original sin. In contrast, *zange* is a true self-surrender that consists not in a recalcitrant despair but in a submissive one, a despair in which we renounce all hope for and claim to justification. Submissive despair thus preserves the permanent wish that our being be as it ought to be. Through such despair we suffer from the serious discrepancy in our being between that which "ought to be" and that which is "as it is." Through *zange* we regard ourselves as truly not deserving to be, and thereby enter fully into a state of genuine despair leading to self-surrender.

Amazingly enough, however, the power urging us to forsake ourselves is at the same time the very power that reaffirms our once negated being. After the submissive acknowledgment and frank confession of our valuelessness and meaninglessness, of our rebelliousness in asserting ourselves despite our valuelessness, we rediscover our being. In this way, our being undergoes at once both negation and affirmation through absolute transformation. In other words, the being that performed metanoesis (*zange*) experiences resurrection by salvation. Moreover, even should this resurrected being sin again, the result would not be to add further negativity to the nature of its new being. For as long as we perform *zange* continuously, there is no change whatever in the process of our being—that is, in the transforming of the negation into affirmation through *tariki*. One who truly performs continuous *zange* is made to surrender self-affirmation, and yet always experiences the wondrous power through which negation is continuously transformed into affirmation. This constancy in one's *zange* is what is called "unshakable or irreversible faith." In this sense the structure of metanoesis is one of infinite spiral process. It is, so to speak, an "eternal returning" (Nietzsche's *ewige Wiederkunft*) in the true sense of the term, namely a genuine "repetition" through the power of the transcendent, and is therefore the fulfillment of the moment by eternity. Accordingly, an increase of finite, particular sins never threatens the fundamental structure of metanoesis in any way. On the contrary, repentance of such sin, the metanoetical awareness of the accumulation of sins, is the true mediating force between our being and the activity of the absolute; it is the infinite element within our finite being. For this reason, we confirm in ourselves the fact that the sins of our being, including even the insincerity of our *zange*, are forgiven, and our being thus is resurrected.

This affirmative aspect of *zange*, as opposed to its negative aspect, is conversion (transformation). Hence the term "metanoia" (μετάνοια) can, as I have stated before, imply both conversion and repentance. *Zange* should be as infinitely continuous as conversion and should, therefore, envelop within itself the infinite repetition of "eternal return." Conversion, however, is transformed negativity, the negativity of metanoesis turned into affirmation through the transforming act of the absolute. This is why we explain them as two aspects of the same thing. The power of salvation through which the self-surrender in our *zange* is transformed into affirmation or conversion inevitably impels us to faith in such power as the absolute power of transformation.

Not only is *zange* accomplished by salvation through *tariki* (Other-power), but *tariki* itself is realized in this world through the mediatory operation of *zange*. Thus the way of mutual transformation and reciprocal interpenetration of *tariki* and *zange* is open to us, and by practicing this religious way of self-consciousness we are able to realize the truth that the activity of *jiriki* is at the same time the realization of *tariki*. In short, religious faith (*shin*) and practice (*gyō*) are one. This means that although *zange* leads to salvation, it should not be considered the same as "repentance," which is the necessary condition for one's entering into heaven, since *zange* is the "practice-faith" (*gyō-shin*) attained in and through *tariki*. It therefore involves both joy and gratitude, which are the very witness (*shō*) of its truth. In a word, *zange* is simply a trinity of action, faith, and witness (*gyō-shin-shō*).

The self-surrender effected as well as performed by one's own free will produces the grace of a resurrected self that brings with it the joy of a regenerated life. Needless to say, the suffering of *zange* is accompanied by the bitterness of repentance and the sorrow of despair. This profound pain, however, is at the same time the medium of joy and the source of bliss. Joy abounds in the midst of pain, not because we are able to participate in the joy of entering into heaven, having reformed ourselves by repentance, but rather because *zange* turns us toward the bliss of *nirvāna*, however sinful and perverted we may be. The joy and gratitude that stem from our being included in the compassion of the absolute and thus redeemed from our original sin arise neither apart from the pain of *zange* nor after it. The joy and pain of *zange* interpenetrate each other. Since *zange* itself is not caused by *jiriki* but by the grace of *tariki*, we have only to surrender to the latter, and in our surrender to experience both the pain of negation and the joy of affirmation. Further, the joy thus brought about by *tariki* necessarily leads to gratitude, the expression of which in turn leads to cooperation with *tariki* in assisting others to share in one's joy. Therein lies the proof and witness for the truth of *zange*.

Moreover, since absolute *tariki* (Other-power) itself must rely on what, from its vantage point, is "other-power" (namely, human freedom), it functions only when relative beings recognize the mediatory role of their independent self-consciousness. Thus absolute *tariki* manifests itself in horizontal relationships between relative beings, and the witness and evidence (*shō*) for the truth of *zange* is realized as a "return to" the world from the Pure Land (*gensō*).

In other words, *zange* is a trinity of action, faith, and witness (*gyō-shin-shō*), so that *zange*, faith, and joy coupled with gratitude for grace become inseparable. This results from the fact that *zange* is a transforming force whose structure may be characterized as *tariki-qua-jiriki*.[2] *Zange* comes about as an absolute transformation by *tariki*; it is not caused by *jiriki* alone. *Tariki* is the power of salvation itself that affirms the relative being of the self that has been negated, regenerating it through "death-and-resurrection." We might say that our salvation is realized through the medium of *zange*. One should not think that the transformation or resurrection we are speaking of here implies a mere return to the routine life of former relativity. It is rather a transcending of the opposition between negation and affirmation, a conversion into a new dimension that is neither life nor death—the realm of absolute nothingness—for the sake of salvation. At the same time, *tariki* performs its salvific function through the mediating activity of relative selves, and thus becomes immanent in them. Here we see the true nature of *tariki*. Although *zange* is an act of the self, it does not belong to the self but is an act of self-surrender and must be an act of absolute nothingness. Thus *zange*, as distinguished from the despair of arrogance, includes the despair of submission in which no self-assertion of the ego performing *zange* remains.

The original vow by Amida Buddha, it is believed by those who profess Pure Land Buddhism, symbolizes this power of absolute transformation or conversion. The compassion of the original vow manifests itself as the Great Nay (*daihi*). It is the quintessence of pure faith in Other-power (*tariki*), one may legitimately maintain, that the Great Nay, performed in an act of absolute negation or in the activity of absolute nothingness, becomes the Great Compassion (*daihi*) of salvation through the realization of faith and witness in mature religious consciousness. That "Great Compassion–*qua*–Great Nay," or, in other words, "love–*qua*–absolute nothingness," is realized by one's action-faith-witness (*gyō-shin-shō*) is the very essence of this religious consciousness. It is clear that the Great Compassion should be the Great Nay, or that true love in a religious sense should be grounded in nothingness, since both the Great Compassion and true love must come from the heart of the no-self. But this is only an ontological consideration. Religious consciousness consists in its genuine experience, or precisely in the self-consciousness realized through this experience.

Were someone to ask how one can become religiously conscious of "Great Compassion–*qua*–Great Nay," I should not be able to answer satisfactorily through theoretical discourse. I could only say: "You must, at least once, perform *zange* yourself."

To be sure, insofar as the *zange* we have been speaking of does not belong to the performance of *jiriki* (self-power) but is based on *tariki* (Other-power), one cannot practice *zange* by oneself alone. It is realized only according to the prompting of Other-power. At the same time, because the absolute subject of Other-power is absolute nothingness (which is, therefore, the real subject of the activity of the absolute transformation), it must be mediated by the relative self. Instead of having its ground in "the self-identity of absolute contradictories," absolute nothingness must be grounded in the absolute mediatory activity of one's religious existence through "death-and-resurrection." Hence, absolute nothingness can also be called *tariki*, since it is experienced through faith-witness (*shin-shō*) as the principle of the negation and transformation of the self. In this sense, *tariki* inevitably depends on *jiriki* as its mediatory "other." This is why it is written, "Ask, and you shall receive; seek, and you shall find" (Matt. 7:7).

This reciprocity is also the core of *tariki* faith. Since the Buddha is the one who seeks nothing, one falls into self-contradiction if one *desires* directly to become the Buddha. But if one does not seek at all to become the Buddha, one will never be able to awaken to one's Buddhahood. The way of self-contradiction involved in residing in a spirit of detachment from the desire to become Buddha in spite of a deep aspiration to become Buddha—in other words, of seeking Buddhahood earnestly without seeking it—is the only path open to everyone by virtue of being closed. This is not to say that the contradictions will be solved once and for all. This critical but contradictory way remains forever impassable to any who aspire to traverse it as a being without self-negation; and even if one succeeds in passing through it, one cannot avoid being cut to pieces by the blades of antinomy. This impassable barrier of antinomies, even as it remains closed, will become passable if the contradictions are recognized as penetrable though still unresolved, if one throws oneself into this difficult situation and surrenders oneself in absolute submission to its requirements without any resistance on the part of discursive (dis-criminatory) thinking, for in so doing one has abandoned oneself thoroughly to the situation and decided to die in the depths of the dilemma of its contradictions. This means that what is impossible with *jiriki* becomes possible with *tariki*, though both *tariki* and *jiriki* remain complementary to one another. The practice of *zange* by *tariki* thus includes within itself at the same time the action of *jiriki*.

On the same grounds that the pivot enabling the transformation of self-*qua*-other or other-*qua*-self becomes self-conscious through the experience of faith-witness (*shin-shō*), we can explain what takes place there as an absolute transformation founded on absolute nothingness. Taken on its own, apart from this experience of faith-witness, absolute nothingness is an unmediated transcendent that in fact remains being even though we call it nothingness. Considered as self-identical, ab-solute nothingness approaches being insofar as it lacks the mediatory functions necessary for absolute nothingness. Thus it comes to be seen as the content of contemplative intuition, not that of self-consciousness in action. On this view, there is no longer any metanoesis, since there is no need for transformation when one can be confirmed to the absolute identity encompassing the discrepancy between self and others. On the contrary, what characterizes metanoesis is the fact that although it is my own action, at the same time it is not my own action; or conversely, that the absolute transformation that is not my action nonetheless is my action. There is therefore sufficient reason to maintain that we can recommend to anyone the practice of metanoesis. It is in this sense that I recommend following the way of metanoesis as the only way along which we can experience, in our faith-witness, the absolute truth of the Great Nay–*qua*–Great Compassion.

Were one mistakenly to suppose that the fact of the Great Compassion–*qua*–Great Nay, which is based on faith, can itself be demonstrated by logic as well, one would have to conclude that the content of action-faith-witness could be subsumed by logic. In the course of such logical reasoning one would inevitably lose sight of pure faith, since logical thought, in complete contrast to mysticism based on the logic of self-identity, leaves no room for faith in Other-power. From such a mystical viewpoint, the idea of "returning to" this world (*gensō*) is not yet clearly self-reflective (*für sich*). Rather the Great Nay, as an undeveloped state of *an sich* and a stage in "going to" the Pure Land or the absolute, unfolds into a philosophy of the self-identity of absolute contradictories. In that case there is no need to recognize the deeper significance of the transformation that occurs in *zange*, the mediatory activity of which brings us to a realm in which we correctly experience the absolute on "the way of returning." Properly speaking, the absolute as a "returning to" this world is the motivating force behind our performance of *zange*. But mystical thinking remains far removed from the true standpoint of faith that Shinran stresses in the *Kyōgyōshinshō*:

> Never discuss whether Amida Buddha accepts you or not: The decisive question is whether you have changed your heart or not.[3]

Similarly, the story is told of the Protestant theologian Karl Barth that he was once approached by a skeptical inquirer and asked to produce proof of the saving power of Christ. He replied by pointing to the fact that the one who was asking the question was not yet saved. Here we see how the same mysteries touch the hearts of great religious teachers both East and West. While I cannot presume to be on a level with these people, there may be some similarity in my motives for introducing *zange*.

It is not possible through the logic of the self-identity of absolute contradictories to determine concretely in what direction the process of absolute transformation is moving or to plot the precise course of its spiral development. That logic remains in the realm of noetics, tied to abstract equations. It has yet to attain the concreteness of absolute mediation, wherein the absolute grants relative selves their freedom, making them the axis around which the absolute itself rotates, serving and assisting in the independent mediatory role of absolute transformation. There each relative self, through its conversion and transformation, becomes in turn the temporary axis of the transformative rotation that we call conversion by the absolute. In this way, the center of the self, which is at the same time the axis of absolute transformation, is located in the decision of each religious existence that constitutes it as a true self. From this standpoint any point can be viewed as the center of mediation from which coordinates can be drawn to determine the transformative movement of the absolute in time and space. This origin of these coordinates may be likened to the existence of self-consciousness, an existence concretized here and now from among an infinite number of possible points. To claim some other universal *topos* apart from such points would be to diverge from the authentic standpoint of action-faith (*gyō-shin*).

For those who perform *zange*, there is no need to presume the *topos* of absolute nothingness to be an abstract universal—that is, some space with no specific orientation or direction at any particular point within it. Such an idea of *topos* belongs to noetics. One may define its standpoint as one of "action-intuition," based on an experience of the "life-expression" structure of our being, as is the case with aesthetic intuition. This aesthetic consideration, however, does not serve to overcome the abstraction of intuition but is a mere development and extension of intuitionism. It neglects the deeper significance of the role of the axis in absolute transformation. From such a standpoint it would be more correct to claim, with Plotinus, that intuition (contemplation) is prior to practice since the latter exists for the sake of the former.[4]

We cannot determine the special orientation that the transformative process takes at each point of a mere topological deduction, because a special orientation is produced only as the result of the negative transformation through "death-and-resurrection." This means that a philosophy with such a standpoint lacks the idea of "returning to" (*gensō*) as well as that of a "mediation by *species*," which together provide the social determination of our being through ethical action performed in community. By reciprocity in species, species (society in its immediate state) can surpass the state of struggle among forces in competition within it, thus elevating species to a concrete universal. Each individual can then represent this concrete universal by bringing together various antagonistic forces within species and channeling their opposing orientations in one particular direction. The focus of the dynamic unity of this process is the metanoetical axis around which scattered and opposing forces are organized to work together.

In short, my metanoesis—my conversion—consists in a shift from *jiriki* to *tariki*. Put in positive terms, metanoetics represents the philosophy of Other-power. But in deference to the negative way I have been following so far, I should first like to make clear its negative aspect, that is to say, the transformative power of its negativity.

The methodical skepticism advanced by Descartes represents a formal transformation of reason, even though his true intention with the *dubito* was to gain sufficient evidence for adopting a new starting point for philosophy. The method is not yet free of subjectivity in that its *dubito* is a mere postulate lacking either content or force by itself. In order to supply the formal transformation implied in the *"cogito ergo sum"* with real content, and thus to establish it as the true ground of his entire philosophy, Descartes had to rely on background motivations— supplied in his case by his own faith in God. (In this connection, it is not without reason that in their interpretation of Cartesian philosophy, Milhaud and Chevalier link the *cogito* with Descartes's faith in God and seek the ground of the ego in the existence of God.)

True self-consciousness cannot come about through one continuous medium joining God and the relative. The real awakening of self-consciousness in its religious or existential dimension comes only through the "death-and-resurrection" of a negative transformation that takes place between the absolute and the relative. A transforming mediation between self-surrender in metanoesis and resurrection by Other-power can, together with the evidence of self-consciousness, provide philosophy with an objective ground. As the sole self-mediating realization of philosophy, it seems to me that metanoesis is, therefore, open to everyone. There is no other way of providing philosophy in the future with a sufficient transcendent ground for its absolute independence than to take the experience of action-faith-witness (*gyō-shin-shō*) as the starting point of our philosophy.

When we consider metanoesis as the path of philosophy, the salvific power of the "Great Nay–*qua*–Great Compassion" mediated by the absolute transformation of nothingness prevails. But is this not what is called "*honganbokori*" (assurance of one's own salvation and pride in one's trust in the vow of Amida Buddha)? Is there not a clear contradiction involved here in such an expression of self-affirmation? Does this not deny the self-abandonment at the core of metanoesis? If we could have direct assurance of salvation, there would be no need for mediation by metanoesis, and no reason for philosophy to start anew as metanoetics.

When I maintain that the task of philosophy is to bring about the self-realization of salvation through the transforming mediation of *zange*, I do not mean to make either metanoesis or salvation independent and self-sufficient, and the other derivative. On the contrary, I mean that metanoesis, which belongs to one's self-power in the relative sense, is a necessary mediatory element in the work of salvation—that the relative self of metanoesis serves absolute Other-power in a mediating capacity, as a result of which the self experiences a wondrous, transcendent resurrection, a conversion from the metanoesis of self-power to the salvation of Other-power. Through the self-consciousness of reason that results from the logic of mediation, philosophy therefore attempts to participate in that wondrous transformation, and thus to perform its task of understanding concrete personal religious experience through the abstract and negative mediation of concepts. Seen from the viewpoint of action-faith, and based on its own evidence, philosophy performs its proper task of logical mediation by explaining how metanoesis and salvation neither belong to an original identity nor simply oppose each other, but rather exist in a dialectical relation based on the principle of "neither-one-nor-two," "neither-identity-nor-difference."

If salvation were something that could be secured without any mediation by metanoesis, it could never signify a spiritual relation of one's spirit to the absolute, but could only be an invariable natural objective relation that exists quite apart from the action of the self. It would no longer be a salvation based on action-faith-witness of spiritual conversion. Moreover, if metanoesis were only an experiential or psychological fact with a limited connotation, of mere relative significance like repentance and regret, it could not be regarded as a transcendental, spiritual experience of converting the relative to the absolute through action-witness. If metanoesis were no more than a faculty of the discriminating mind or nothing more than personal psychological experience, it would have no mediating role in the transformation or conversion of the self; it would have no role in salvation.

Spiritual events raise questions requiring philosophy, questions lying beyond the pale of the sciences and the grasp of the principle of identity. Insofar as events are not all mystery and incomprehensibility, some degree of rational mediation can be adopted to make them understandable. Concepts, as determinations of action through the negations and transformations of thought, serve us in assimilating events whose clarification requires the self-consciousness of reason as well as the logical mediation of philosophy. Anything that can simply be reduced to the principle of identity is not a problem for philosophy. For a problem to belong to philosophy there must be something inconceivable in it; and yet by the same token, something altogether inconceivable and mysterious cannot become a problem for philosophy.

To eliminate the mediation of logic and the self-consciousness of reason from our consideration of such spiritual events poses no problem for philosophy. A problem is posed only when there is some clue of a mediation leading to its solution. This is why both repentance—which is not mediated by salvation—and mere salvation—which is simply dependent on the principle of identity and not mediated by metanoesis—cannot furnish philosophy with problems. Philosophical self-consciousness takes its clue for solving problems only from the mutual mediation of metanoesis and salvation that takes place in one's action-faith: the absolute and the relative form a unity through absolute mediation, whereby transcendence and immanence interpenetrate each other in one's action. The soul, mediated by metanoesis, relinquishes its demand to exist and thus abandons all hope of resurrection through salvation. And only such a soul can be transformed and transcendentally reborn by the transformative power of the Great Compassion into a new existence.

This event is something quite incomprehensible, belonging as it does to both the Great Compassion and the Great Nay, which in turn fall outside of any natural necessity grounded on the principle of identity. If I commit the sin of *honganbokori* referred to earlier, I am presuming on the Great Nay–*qua*–Great Compassion contained in the Vow of Amida Buddha, considering it to be a matter of natural necessity—that is, something within my control—and mistakenly supposing, through the vanity of self-assertiveness, that what is beyond my power is actually within my capacity. It is nothing less than a sin of profanity against absolute compassion. It is a betrayal and abuse of holy truth: an act of disobedience against all the Gods and Buddhas.

It is impossible to be saved from such sin without passing through metanoesis. Amida pronounced the Eighteenth Vow of *shōjōju*, the "correctly established state for the new birth," promising that all who have genuine faith in Amida Buddha are, without exception, to be born in the Pure Land, as we read in the Larger Sutra. Yet in the very same vow of absolute salvation the Buddha excludes from his mercy five forms of betrayal and blasphemy on the grounds that it is impossible to bestow salvation on traitors and blasphemers seeking to substitute their self-power for Other-power—which is the content of the Vow of Amida Buddha's absolute compassion—so long as they are not converted from their former ways.

Only through the mediation of metanoesis, wherein one renounces oneself as unworthy to exist, can one find entry into the realms of salvation. At the same time, metanoesis allows one who performs it to experience the incomprehensible fact that even the sin of blasphemy can become a mediatory moment in service of salvation. In that case, of course, *honganbokori* ceases to be an obstacle; one experiences only awe and gratitude before the inconceivable power of the Great Nay. In my case, it is not only that I possess a tendency to *honganbokori* in virtue of the radical evil I harbor within me. It is a real and inextricable part of me that continues to exist even after metanoesis and salvation. I must perform *zange* and feel ashamed for the fact that, behind my awe and gratitude before the incomprehensible nature of salvation, there lies so much evil and sin that I cannot escape from the tendency to *honganbokori* that survives my conversion and transformation. Through the incomprehensible power of salvation into which the Great Compassion is poured we are redeemed from evil passion and lusts (*bonnō*) without their being extinguished. Since grave sin and the tendency toward it still remain in *zange*, fear, gratitude, and blasphemy flow together and penetrate one another. It is here that a mediatory relationship is set up among metanoesis, salvation, and sin, a circular process wherein the blasphemy and sin of *honganbokori* can be transformed, through metanoetical mediation, into a moment of salvation without the tendency to sin having been extinguished. This infinite structure of metanoesis causes fear and trembling and yet leads one to rely on salvation, since even the betrayal and profound sin of *honganbokori* are transformed into salvation through the mediation of metanoesis. Whatever passions, lust, and sin exist, they are all converted into salvation by metanoesis without being extinguished.

No salvation of any kind can be realized without the mediation of metanoesis. Salvation and metanoesis stand opposed to each other and negate each other. The two never become one, and yet at the same time are inseparable, flowing into each other without duality. They maintain their dynamic unity by virtue of the dialectical tension of nonidentity and nondifference that exists between them. It is in the nature of their relationship to stand in correlation with the constant risk of separation. The very unsteadiness of this bond excludes any unity founded on the principle of identity seen in *honganbokori*.

As mentioned above, it is the same with self-abandonment in metanoesis mediating a conviction of salvation in spite of—or rather, precisely *because* of—the fear and trembling intermingled with awe and gratitude. By completely giving up one's desire to exist and performing *zange* with head bowed, confessing oneself to be a miserable being, a person encounters through faith-witness the wondrous grace of salvation that turns the negation of the self into an affirmation. Still, such a one remains caught in the fear of not being destined for salvation because of the evil passions of self-attachment that are never eradicated despite one's confidence of salvation. The same can be said of the betrayal implicit in the self-affirmation of *honganbokori*, which remains even though it has no place in a standpoint where one is conscious of the dynamic correlation between metanoesis and salvation.

Thus salvation, as the Great Compassion of Amida's Vow, is accomplished through the power of the Great Nay of absolute transformation. This absolute transformation, whose internal dynamic sets up a serious tension in one's mind between affirmation and negation, shows why absolute mediation and the oneness of salvation still require the relative as the affirmative element that coordinates the spontaneity of the metanoetic self with absolute negativity and thus promotes the element of negative mediation.

In short, the mediation between metanoesis and salvation is established by the truly dialectical correlation of the two. In this way it is clear to us that metanoetics opens a way to salvation for ordinary people. It is a way of dialectical logic, in the sense that any affirmation that takes place in the absolute mediation of absolute transformation includes negation and is transformed into negation, whereas negation is converted into affirmation without being simply eliminated. There can be no doubt that through metanoetics philosophy is opened up for ordinary people.

Socrates, the most authentic of all Greek philosophers, pursued the way of metanoetics through the irony of "the knowledge of ignorance." Although in his case faith in a religiously salvific Other-power was not present, the most important point of the Socratic irony, that the confession of ignorance mediates the way to a positive wisdom, is similar to metanoesis. The voice of warning of the Socratic *daimon* liberates self-assertiveness and self-attachment from all adherence to immediate affirmation without negation and nonmediation. The mind, thus disciplined, arrives at an absolute negativity totally free from all obstacles. If we take this to mean that complete freedom cannot be attained by self-power but requires the warning of a *daimon* to convert self-power toward Other-power, we can understand Socrates' attitude to the warning of the *daimon* as a consciousness of self-abandonment in metanoesis. This shifts our reading of Socrates from the ethical stage to the religious, as an implicit development from irony to metanoetics. That dialectics originated in the logic of Socrates is only natural, since he was the first to realize philosophy as a self-consciousness of subjective existence. (It is easy to understand here why Kierkegaard entitled his dissertation *The Concept of Irony with Constant Reference to Socrates.*)[5]

Although Socratic ethical intellectualism did not develop as far as the self-reflective (*für sich*) stage of metanoetics mediated by salvation of Other-power, metanoesis is already implicit in its ironical dialectics. In contrast, Shinran's teaching in the *Kyōgyōshinshō* establishes a religion almost completely reliant on salvation by Other-power (*tariki*). In this doctrine, *zange* does not figure as a special mediating element in salvation, but only functions in the background or is used to introduce Shinran's doctrine of salvation. Given that the subject matter is treated from a religious point of view, this is hardly surprising. At the same time, there is no doubt that this has contributed to the degeneration of Pure Land Shin doctrine away from what Shinran taught, and to its failure to preserve the sincerity of the founder's spirit. In this way, so-called believers lack the very ethical, rational element of metanoesis essential to the mediation of religious salvation.

While *shōdōmon*, the self-power "Gate of the Sages," retains some elements of discipline and practice, Pure Land believers (those who follow the way of *nembutsumon*) relax in the indolence of worldly life, believing that they will be saved merely by invoking the name of Amida. These have lost Shinran's profound and severe metanoesis, together with his consciousness of how, without the mercy of Amida, humanity is predestined for hell. Their lives are thus empty of all religious significance, and that—one may say without exaggeration—by reason of having lost the way of metanoesis.

I cannot help but think here of the mediatory role linking ethical reason inseparably to religion, each confronting the other and yet maintaining its independence from the other. Salvation through the Great Compassion of Other-power is not bestowed on indolent, shameless persons who, frustrated with the impotence of self-power, turn in admiration to the omnipotence of Other-power, forsaking any further ethical effort on their part. Salvation through Other-power is achieved only by those who have used every means at their disposal to seek the truth, who have felt the shame of their own impotence, and finally turned to the practice of metanoesis. It is only through the negative transformation wrought by the Great Nay that the Great Compassion comes about. The joy of salvation is bound as closely to the grief of metanoesis as light is to shadow.

Philosophy begins from a consciousness of the self in conformity with the autonomy of reason and from there extends, through the limitations and determinations of the world, to an awareness of the fact that the self exists through the mediation of absolute nothingness, which sets up a relationship of mutual transformation between self and world. Therefore, philosophy must be carried out in the faith-witness that the self is being-*qua*-nothingness, that is, being (*rūpa*) as a manifestation of emptiness (*śūnyatā*) or absolute nothingness. In this way the self is resurrected to an existence beyond life and death; it receives the gift of a new life. The action mediating this faith-witness is nothing other than metanoesis.

The absolute that philosophy seeks does not exist apart from absolute nothingness. All being thought to be in opposition to nothingness cannot but be relative. Only true nothingness, an absolute nothingness capable of surpassing being and nothingness, can be absolute. Absolute nothingness establishes being as mediatory for nothingness, and permits being to exist independently so that it exists as being-*qua*-nothingness beyond being and nothingness.

To practice metanoesis means to be negated and transformed into such being-*qua*-nothingness. The philosophical subject comes into question only after one has been converted in metanoesis. This does not mean, however, that there is some special acting subject that turns us around and effects a conversion in us. When we speak of Other-power, the Other is absolute precisely because it is nothingness, that is, nothingness in the sense of absolute transformation. It is because of its genuine passivity and lack of acting selfhood that it is termed absolute Other-power. Other-power is *absolute* Other-power only because it acts through the mediation of the self-power of the relative that confronts it as other. Only to that extent is genuine, absolute Other-power mediated by self-power. In this way, the absolute becomes absolute mediation. The relative cannot be the relative merely because it stands against the absolute. The absolute, as absolute mediation, not only has to mediate with regard to the relative that stands opposed to it but also to mediate between one relative and another. The relative stands opposed to the absolute only by virtue of the fact that one relative stands opposed to other relatives; and the relative is called relative only insofar as it stands opposed to some other relative. The mutual dependence of relatives brings the absolute into existence to mediate their correlation to one another. For mediation to be absolute it must have this dual character.

At first glance, absolute mediation seems to be an equalizing function lacking any focus within itself, a *topos* where the activity of mediation takes place as a mere transcending and encompassing of the relative by the absolute. While absolute Other-power may appear to function as such a determining force apart from the (relative) self, it would in that case no longer be absolute Other-power but only a relative other-power, since it would no longer be effecting absolute mediation but only an immediate action mediation.

True absolute Other-power has to be made part of one's faith-witness through the mediatory activity of relative self-power. The activity of the absolute with regard to the relative comes about only through the mediation of other relatives which, as relatives, also stand in opposition to the absolute. Thus, the effect of the absolute on the relative only becomes real as the effect of the relative on the relative.

Not even the *topos* of absolute nothingness exists immediately. Such a *topos* means only that a field belonging to the "being of *species*" where relatives relate to each other is elevated to the level of universal nothingness because of a mutuality-in-equality that obtains within it. Its transformation into nothingness is an absolute transformation resulting from mutual mediation. The *topos* is symbolic of being transformed into nothingness. Precisely because nothingness is mediated by being, and the absolute is mediated by the relative, absolute nothingness is able to be both absolute and nothingness. This nothingness must in turn be realized in the depths of relative mind through action-faith-witness— that is, through metanoesis. Metanoesis, which is the activity of self as well as the activity of Other-power, provides the particular content for absolute mediation: the "here and now" of absolute mediation in the self is metanoetics. It is, of course, possible for simple religious faith to be based on a theism of Other-power in which grace is experienced directly and without mediation. Indeed, this seems to be a universal form of religious expression. But such simple faith cannot mediate the absolute knowledge of philosophy because the immediate determination of faith in the myths or revelations of theism negates the independence of philosophy and obstructs the freedom of reason. From a philosophical point of view, only in metanoesis can the nature of the mediation of truly absolute Other-power be practiced, believed, and made real through philosophical thinking in action-faith-witness. Metanoesis alone preserves the full autonomy and freedom of reason, brings reason to its own limits, and thus prompts reason to self-abandonment.

Contrary to what Kant thought in his critical philosophy, it is impossible for the autonomy of reason to provide its own foundations. Reason endowed with the capacity for self-criticism cannot evade the ultimate predicament of the antinomies of practical reason, since it is caught up in original sin stemming from basic human finitude. The critique of reason needs to be pressed to the point of an absolute critique through "absolute disruption" and absolute crisis, which constitute the self-abandonment of reason. It is precisely this absolute critique through "absolute disruption" and absolute crisis that constitutes the self-abandonment of reason. It is precisely this absolute critique that makes up the rational aspect of metanoesis and provides it with a logic, as I shall explain in the following chapter. I would conclude, therefore, that metanoetics is not merely one possible way among a variety of philosophical ways: it is the *only* way, the ineluctable way. It is the ultimate conclusion to which the critique of reason drives us.

Given the viewpoint set forth above, it is natural to find in Shinran a source of great encouragement and enlightenment. I would argue that the philosophy of religion expounded in the *Kyōgyōshinshō* shows a depth whose counterpart is difficult to find in the Western world. I do not, however, intend to expound a philosophy based on the Shin sect by offering a philosophical interpretation of the dogma of "salvation through invoking the name of Amida Buddha with pure faith in Other-power" as it was propounded by Shinran. My real intention is rather to reconstruct philosophy itself through metanoesis in a way corresponding to faith in Other-power. In other words, instead of interpreting Shinran's teaching in a philosophical manner, I have it in mind here to remold philosophy as metanoetics, to start afresh along the way of philosophy by following Shinran's religious path. This is precisely how we may learn from Shinran in the true sense of the word, and it is only in this sense that I consider him to be my teacher.

Objections may be raised against the claim that Shinran's *Kyōgyōsh-inshō* is a philosophy of religion based on metanoetics. One may well ask where metanoetics is propounded in the six volumes of the *Kyōgyōsh-inshō*. In fact, there is no volume in the work that deals with *zange*, nor can we find the concept of metanoesis treated as an element of the religious system set forth in the *Kyōgyōshinshō*. Yet even though *zange* is not a formal part of the *Kyōgyōshinshō*, it constitutes its whole basis and background, only occasionally breaking through the surface.

For example, in reference to the three kinds of repentance discussed in the section entitled "The Transformed Buddha and Land of Expediency," Shinran quotes from Shan-tao (Jap., Zendō, 613–668):

> Although there are differences among the three sorts of repentance, those who have practiced *zange* throughout their lives are all accumulating merit. If one

has respect for this virtue and respects one's religious master without concern for one's own life, and if one performs *zange*, with compunction in one's entire soul and body, even for the most insignificant of his evil deeds, one will be released quickly from one's sin.[6]

And further, in arguing that *zange* is an appropriate practice, especially in the eschatological time propounded by the Pure Land sect, Shinran quotes from the *An-lo-chi* (Jap., *Anrakushū*):

Those who practice *zange* and wish to do good deeds and to attain happiness should invoke the name of Amida Buddha. Those who invoke Amida even once can be released from the karma performed during eighty kalpas. Even one such invocation has this merit. How much more merit will those receive who invoke his name as long as they live! They are truly ones who have realized *zange*.[7]

These passages make it sufficiently clear that *zange* is universal enough to include the practice of *nembutsu* (invoking the name of Amida), to stand in essential relationship with it, and finally to become one with it, even though *zange* has a negative connotation in contrast with the positive connotation of *nembutsu*. One may say without exaggeration that *zange* both represents the beginning of the practice of *nembutsu* and functions as an element in its actual process.

The sincerity and self-torment of Shinran's confession pours out of the pages of the *Kyōgyōshinshō*, as we see in the following hymn:

Indeed, how miserable am I, Shinran, who sink deep into the sea of love and lust, and lose my way within the forest of riches and fame, and do not wish to attain true faith, and do not feel joy in approaching the truth of Buddhahood! Truly, I am filled with shame and remorse![8]

Passages like this leave no doubt that the whole of the work is grounded in and sustained by *zange*. Unless one undergoes the same kind of sincere repentance that Shinran had, one will never achieve a profound understanding of the work. At the age of eighty-six—more than thirty years after having established his own faith as expounded in the *Kyōgyōshinshō*—Shinran felt compelled by inner necessity to write another hymn filled with the same spirit of repentance; it begins with these words:

Even though I have surrendered myself to faith in the True Pure Land, there is no truth or sincerity in me. I am false and dishonest, and have no pure and undefiled heart.[9]

Only one who could write such a hymn, springing from the depth of his heart, could be the author of the *Kyōgyōshinshō*.

Without metanoesis, there can be no salvation through *nembutsu* or faith in Other-power. Metanoetics is indeed a philosophy based upon Other-power. But, as is evident from the preceding, I do not mean to speak of Other-power as operating in me objectively, nor to describe the structure of metanoesis through self-reflection on how one is transformed by Other-power. The action-faith-witness (*gyō-shin-shō*) in which I myself practice metanoesis is undertaken for the sake of absolute mediation, and pursues the true path of philosophy which seeks absolute knowledge.

Philosophy as metanoetics implies taking the path of metanoesis self-consciously. This is what I understand by philosophy. It is not a philosophy of metanoesis that seeks to describe metanoesis as an object, but a philosophy based upon Other-power enabling me to practice metanoesis subjectively. Indeed, the metanoesis of philosophy is itself metanoetics. Metanoesis does not remain a mere objective presented to philosophy from without as a problem to be solved or a method to be pursued. As stated above and as will be explained in the next chapter, a philosophy for which the critique of reason forms an indispensable moment gives birth to metanoetics when that critique results in the concept of absolute critique. Metanoetics emerges from the core of philosophy itself. Philosophy achieves its ultimate end only when it becomes the metanoesis of philosophy itself.

Being is always relative and cannot be absolute, since the absolute must be nothingness, as I have stated before. Nothingness means transformation. Being, as that which mediates nothingness, can therefore be likened to its axis of transformation. But because being is the mediator of nothingness, it, too, must be reduced to nothingness. A reciprocity-inequality exists among the various pivots of being, each of which serves as an axis of transformation for the others. As I shall explain later in discussing the three stages of transformation (*sangantennyū*), the world exists for no other reason than that of *upāya* ("skillful means"): it is the world of mediation through which such a reciprocal transformation enables relative beings to move toward nothingness and to return to the world to serve as a means of enlightenment and salvation for others. Metanoesis is the mediatory activity of transcending being in terms of "being as *upāya*."

The relative self, then, as being that serves as the medium—or means (*upāya*)—of absolute nothingness and yet remains opposed to nothingness, contains within itself the relative independence of being independent of the absolute. The self, as relative being brought to existence as the medium or expedient of absolute nothingness, contains implanted within itself the possibility of securing its existence in opposition to nothingness and adhering stubbornly to its independence. This is what is termed the "radical evil" of human existence.

Evil does not consist merely of committing evil acts. As Hegel's profound interpretation shows, acts that come to fulfillment in "the true ethical world" (*die wahre Sittlichkeit*) as the synthesis of opposing elements in the form of *both/and* are never brought to out consciousness in the form of an intention or goal. There are always elements hidden in conscious acts that do not reach consciousness, which is why each and every act of ours cannot avoid the stain of sin. Not only are all our acts therefore foredoomed to sin, but the independence of our being itself is infected with radical evil. The essence of relative self consists in the fact that it is a nothingness for mediating absolute nothingness; it is emptiness, void (Jap., *kū*; Sanskrit, *śūnyatā*). This self deceives itself, grows forgetful of its own finiteness and relativity, and comes to mistake itself for absolute existence by absolutizing the finiteness of its existence. What is more, it shows an innate tendency to cling to this delusion. This what we are calling radical evil: the self-assertion and rebellion of the relative vis-à-vis the absolute.

Since the absolute, as nothingness, must act as an absolute mediating force, it presupposes relative being as its medium. In contrast with the doctrine of the creation of the world maintained by the theist, or the theory of emanation propounded by the pantheist, historical thinking must begin from present historical reality in order to reconstruct reality in practice, thus producing a circular process of "revolution-*qua*-restoration." For historical thinking, the absolute and the relative, nothingness and being, are interrelated each with the other as the indispensable elements of absolute mediation. Theirs is a simultaneous and reciprocal relationship in which neither can be derived from the other. The relative as the medium of the absolute comes into existence simultaneously with the absolute. The existence of the relative is a *sine qua non* for the absolute as nothingness. And precisely because the absolute *is* nothingness, the relative can exist as being. Conversely, because the existence of the relative is "being as *upāya*" (*hōben*) in the sense that it alone serves a mediatory function with regard to nothingness, and because it is absolutely relative in the sense that it is a being related to other beings in relative reciprocity, it is able to serve as the medium for the absolute mediation of nothingness and thus enable nothingness to realize itself.

That having been said, however, there is no doubt that the relative which serves as the medium for the absolute cannot be derived from the absolute, but must be an independent being in order to function as a self-negating and self-transforming activity within nothingness. The fact that the relative comes into existence as the relative, serving as an element in the mediating work of the absolute, makes it possible for the relative to contain within itself the independence of a finite being, by means of which it can stand in opposition to the absolute. It is here that the roots of evil lie. For the fact that the absolute makes use of the relative for the sake of its mediation also implies that the absolute, as absolute mediation, is a self-negating principle, for which reason the absolute allows the relative—as the negative aspect of the absolute—to possess a relative independence. This is why the relative is disposed toward evil. Since the absolute allows for such a disposition toward evil in relative beings, the latter in turn are able to arrive at the bliss of salvation by confessing the guilt that is theirs as a result of their misuse of the freedom allowed to them and their actualization of this deep-seated penchant for evil. In this sense, the absolute is one with the Great Compassion. This is precisely what I mean by the term "Great Nay–*qua*–Great Compassion."

In this way the self-awareness of one's guilt, or of one's radical evil and sin, as utterly unavoidable provides metanoesis with a necessary and concrete way to become conscious of the finite self. Suffering arises within a relative being because it is driven into a desperate cul-de-sac by the conflict between the consciousness of past *karma* (unavoidable guilt) and the consciousness of the aspiration for future emancipation from guilt. It is this suffering that characterizes present consciousness as anxiety. Further, the absolute transformation of nothingness leads to equality among relative beings, since the reciprocal conversion and transformation performed by relative beings result in "being as *upāya*" (*hōben sonzai*), where each axis of transformation is freely changed into others with nothing to cling to, and becomes "elect" in the sense of being something previously chosen by the absolute. The self-consciousness of relative beings that "being as *upāya*" can exist only insofar as it is one temporary axis of transformation, taking its turn like every other being at being the axis and thus serving as the medium of nothingness, brings to actuality the solidarity of a religious society in the sense of a "returning to the world" (*gensō-ekō*).[10] Here relative beings are all able to exert religious influence on one another, so that they can all be saved through the Great Compassion. In this process relative beings, as pure passivity presupposing no substantial agent other than themselves, surrender themselves obediently to Other-power. This surrender is metanoesis. At the same time, such Other-power is nothing other than self-power; and conversely, self-power is nothing other than Other-power.

Although the sin inevitably produced by one's action is always condemned from an ethical viewpoint, from a religious viewpoint it is always forgiven by the boundlessness of metanoesis. Hence consciousness of the forgiveness of one's sinfulness returns one to the relative. Filled with gratitude, one is brought back to "the action of no-action" which establishes the relationship of the relative to the relative. In this way metanoesis functions as a mediating force through which the evil of sin, without disappearing, is transformed into the bliss of forgiveness and salvation grounded in absolute nothingness. This is the self-mediation of the absolute in and through the relative, for which metanoetics, as the self-awareness of this self-mediation, provides absolute knowledge. This is why the true path of philosophy is to be sought in metanoia.

In contrast with the usual philosophical attitude adopted toward Pure Land Shin doctrine with its notion of faith based on salvation through *nembutsu* (invoking the name of Amida), I am attempting here to take another approach to the core of that faith. In my view, those who try to interpret the doctrine of Pure Land Shin from a specific philosophical standpoint do not follow the course of salvation by *nembutsu* to its ultimate conclusions. Theirs is an attitude bearing the unmistakable marks of salvation by the self-power Gate of the Sages (*jiriki-shōdōmon*), and has no connection with that faith in Other-power which is the faith of those who perform *zange*. This latter means confessing one's philosophical impotence and, driven to the humble recognition that as an ordinary ignorant and sinful being one has nothing to rely on, letting go of oneself completely. But those who interpret the doctrine according to their own philosophy make their understanding of Other-power conform to self-power and never come close to a positive realization of the truth of philosophy through action-witness—that is, according to metanoetics and in a manner befitting salvation by Other-power. They remain in the philosophical position of sages trying to save themselves by their own efforts or merits. There is nothing surprising about this, given the common understanding of philosophy as an activity based on the self-awareness of the autonomy of reason. As for myself, I no longer share this attitude because I can no longer accept its underlying ideal of philosophy. The experience of my past philosophical life has brought me to realize my own inability and the impotence of any philosophy based on self-power. I have now no philosophy whatsoever on which to rely. I now find that the rational philosophy from which I had always been able to extract an understanding of the rational forces permeating history, and through which I could deal rigorously with reality without going astray, has left me.

I feel especially obliged to share in the corporate responsibility for irrationalities like the injustice and prejudice evident in our country. I feel responsible for all of the evils and errors committed by others, and in so doing find that the actual inability of my philosophy to cope with them compels me to a confession of despair over my philosophical incompetence. More than that, I find that this predicament obliges me—the ordinary person, ignorant and sinful, that I am—to admit that such a confession applies not only to me but to all persons everywhere who are similarly ignorant and sinful.

I hold the view that philosophy consists in the autonomy of reason. In this respect it is similar to science, the difference being that philosophy claims to offer knowledge of the absolute, not of the relative as is the case with science in general. The claim is an impossible one, however, for the simple reason that as beings who are not absolute but relative, not saints or sages in communion with the divine but ordinary humans wrapped up in ourselves, we remain bound to self-satisfaction and arrogance, try as we may to assume the standpoint of reason. The claim of reason amounts to no more than an ideal that can never be fulfilled completely so long as we maintain the standpoint of self-power. Even if it were somehow possible for this claim to be fulfilled, if we were to acquire knowledge of the absolute and put it into practice, this could not be attributed to an "ascent" of self-power but only to a "descent" of Other-power transforming the relative into the absolute and thereby causing the absolute to be mediated through the relative.

In other words, whatever leads the relative self to salvation in religion should also function in the case of philosophy, whose origins are the same as those of science, so that the basic nature of philosophy should undergo a total transformation. And yet philosophy, which, like science, is based on the autonomy of reason, cannot forthwith abandon its basic principle and turn itself into religious belief. The only way for philosophy to achieve this goal of total transformation is for the autonomy of reason, the motivating force of philosophy, to become deadlocked in the self-awareness of its own incompetence. In its despair of self-power— that is, in metanoesis—reason can be led to self-surrender by Other-power, until at last it revives as a philosophy of "effortless naturalness" (*musa-hōni*), beyond all opposition between self and other.

If it is possible for me to resume the way of philosophy, there is no alternative left but to start anew in metanoesis. Surprisingly enough, I have already been walking this path. I made a new beginning from the very moment that I began to perform metanoesis. This is not to say that I set out on this way of philosophy of my own will. All such activity based on self-power had already been abandoned; I was able only to perform metanoesis, which consisted in the dissolution of my philosophy. This forced me into a dilemma that left me no choice but metanoesis. My entire existential self-awareness turned to the practice, reflection, analysis, and pursuit of metanoesis. There was no other way for me to philosophize except the self-awareness of metanoesis in metanoetics. No sooner did I begin this metanoesis, as I said, than my philosophical thinking started anew, yet not as my own doing but as the doing of Other-power in me.

The fact that metanoesis is going on within me is not to the credit of self-power. Indeed, I have to admit that even the self-power implied in my practice of *zange* is itself already mediated by Other-power, which effects the absolute transformation of my self-surrender and self-negation into self-affirmation. Self-power and Other-power converge here and thus penetrate each other. At the same time that I practice metanoesis I am being transformed—converted—into someone who can make a fresh start in philosophy without any intention of doing so. There is no attempt here to continue my old philosophy or to reconstruct it on my own power. The philosophy I am concerned with here is rather a philosophy of the "action of no-action" or "action without an acting subject" (*musa no sa*), because it is mediated by metanoesis and transformed by Other-power. I affirm myself only insofar as I, who am a being emptied (*kū-u*) through absolute transformation, can serve as a negative mediator of the absolute. All I can do is submit myself to "naturalness" (*jinen-hōni*) and let the absolute do as it will. My philosophy is simply action-faith-witness in the sense of a self-consciousness of this naturalness. Furthermore, once the standpoint of this metanoetical self-awareness has been acknowledged for what it is, the antinomy mentioned above, which leads to absolute critique because it involves contradiction beyond the capacity of the self-power of reason to resolve, is allowed to remain as it is and to mediate the absolute. From this standpoint the active, subjective moment in historical necessity is made clear, and every attempt of scientific theory to approximate truth is furnished with a necessary meaning relative to its stage in the development of the history of science.

Once reason, relying on self-power, has failed in its attempt to establish a solid foundation on the critique of reason, philosophy falls into a crisis from which there is no escape: the absolute disruption of being torn to pieces by antinomies and cast into the pit of contradictions. But if reason lets go of itself in this predicament, and if this self-surrender in turn leads to metanoesis in the form of self-conscious impotence, reason is lifted up out of the abyss and transformed into the action-faith-witness of absolute Other-power. In this state, the crisis of contradiction that was judged insurmountable from the standpoint of the self-power of reason is allowed to remain just as it is. What happens as a matter of necessity at each stage of history is thus made the result of action-faith-witness. The "way without a way" is opened up by Other-power, and philosophy is transported from the standpoint of reason based on the self-power of the Gate of the Sages (*shōdōmonteki jiriki*) to the standpoint of action-faith based on the Other-power Gate of the Pure Land (*jōdomonteki tariki*).

I do not mean to imply that this was how the Pure Land doctrine set forth by Shinran effected a conversion in my philosophy. It is only that when the critique of reason that takes place in philosophy progresses to the point of an absolute critique and thus reaches the end of its tether, a way to the suprarational "death-and-resurrection" of reason is necessarily thrown open, and a corresponding shift takes place from the world of nature to the world of history. This is just what happened when the critical philosophy of Kant opened out into the dialectical thought of Hegel. The difference between the concepts of reason of the two philosophers is the very process we are talking about here. Moreover, the reason that Hegel had to undergo the criticism of Kierkegaard is that Hegel had failed to bring the process to consummation and to emancipate himself completely from the Kantian view of reason. The "death-and-resurrection" of reason necessarily leads to the standpoint of faith in Other-power. In other words, metanoetics, as the transrational resurrection of reason, is a reconstruction of philosophy. Viewing matters in this light, one would not be mistaken in the claim that Kierkegaard's existential philosophy also developed a kind of metanoetics.[11]

In short, it has been the destiny of my life philosophy that it necessarily develop into metanoetics. It is not that I mean to graft Pure Land Shin faith in Other-power onto philosophy, but rather that the confrontation of philosophy with my personal experience of reality has forced me to develop my thought in this direction. Nevertheless, the fact remains that this my philosophical destiny has given me a new admiration for Shinran and opened the way for me to understand his faith and thought. This is so because, unlike attempts to apply traditional ideas of philosophy to Pure Land Shin doctrine, the development of metanoetics follows closely that of Shinran's Pure Land doctrine. If we assume either philosophy or religious doctrine to be fixed, and then use it to define and interpret the other, we end up in familiar theological dogmatism. In my case, philosophy as metanoetics does not come about exclusively under the guidance and influence of Shinran's thought, but is a necessary logical consequence of the critique of reason pursued to term as absolute critique; but at the same time, my interpretation of the *Kyōgyōshinshō* is not an attempt to interpret Shinran's thought from the viewpoint of an established philosophy. Of course it is true that my reading of Shinran's religious results is an interpretation peculiar to my philosophy as metanoetics. But the philosophy I am developing here is not intended as a fixed system, since metanoetics grows out of the very destruction of philosophical systems in the traditional sense due to antinomies of reason that usher in the self-surrender of reason's autonomy.

What I am attempting here, therefore, is not to interpret Shinran's thought but rather to walk the way of metanoesis through action-faith-witness together with Shinran, which is a prerequisite for a true interpretation of his thought. To the extent that this opens up the unexpected possibility of understanding and appreciating Shinran, I can then make progress in metanoetics under the guidance of his thought in a way previously closed to me. Of this I have no doubt, and can only express my gratitude to Shinran for being my precursor and teacher in the philosophy of metanoetics. In fact, I firmly believe that Shinran has returned to the world—performed *gensō*—to teach me this truth.

Philosophy and faith are thus independent of each other and at the same time correspond to each other. They develop spontaneously in reciprocal rather than one-way determination, with the activity of metanoesis serving as the center of mediation. I find the unification of philosophy and faith here—and indeed, speaking more generally, life itself—to be based on metanoesis through action-faith-witness. Not only in philosophy but in life itself, the self-negation of metanoesis is transformed into self-affirmation: my death in self-surrender restores me to a new life where despair turns to hope. Because my life cannot exist apart from philosophy, nor my philosophy exist apart from my actual life, philosophy as metanoetics becomes the basic principle of my life, the ground on which I can live a life of "death-and-resurrection."

I assure myself through faith that absolute self-negation and pure passivity—in absolute death—is the turning point at which I live in dying and live in being brought to life. This is not a negative self-assertion, as is the case with suicide, but a letting go of oneself in despair, where one forfeits altogether the ability to decide by one's own will whether one should live or die. The process of mediation at work here is metanoesis carried out through "despair in obedience." But when I am moved by Other-power to the point of total passivity and obedience, the agent of this absolute transformation is nothingness, which means that nothing confronts me in the way of "being." As agent, being is always relative being and cannot possibly be absolute. Absolute Other-power is pure passivity with nothing in the way of "being" as an agent, and therefore consists entirely of the pure negation of the self, of the mediating character of absolute transformation, that is, of a "naturalness" (*jinen-hōni*) beyond the opposition of self and other.

From this line of argument, it is obvious that transformation does not mean merely that I have found a way to make a new start in philosophy or recovered the ability to develop my thought in new directions. If this were the case, there would be no room for absolute Other-power. Instead, I remain as powerless as ever, and under the constant compulsion to surrender myself to metanoesis because I am driven incessantly to despair. At the same time, I continue to live insofar as I am brought to life as a mediator of absolute Other-power. Wherever absolute Other-power functions, it makes use of the relative, which is opposed to the absolute, as a mediator for bringing about the salvation of relative beings. This means that salvation by the absolute is realized only through the reciprocal influence of relative beings on one another. In this sense, I have to speak of Shinran as returning to the world as my teacher to guide me on the path of metanoetics, for there is no doubt that absolute Other-power, in the attempt to lead me to metanoetics, makes use of Shinran as its mediator and representative. The fact that metanoesis makes the *Kyōgyōshinshō* understandable to me awakens me in turn to the fact that Shinran is continually teaching me and guiding me, and has returned to the world for that purpose. It is not a matter of a causal relationship in the temporal order, according to which a preceding cause produces a succeeding effect, but of a reciprocal relationship in which each element mediates and influences the other.

In this way, philosophy—once closed to me—finds a new beginning through self-abandonment. A new philosophical task and its solution are given to self-consciousness through the negation and transformation of the absolute in actuality. For me, philosophical self-consciousness does not mean becoming conscious of the spontaneity of freedom motivated by self-power. On the contrary, it means letting go of myself in obedient despair because of my powerlessness and impotence. In other words, the philosophical awareness in question here is a realization not of life or of one's ability to live, but of obedient surrender to absolute death or of one's unworthiness to live.

Since it is through such self-consciousness that I am urged to begin philosophy again in metanoesis, it follows as a matter of course that all pride of supposing I might offer my own philosophical interpretation of the doctrine of Pure Land Shin, as if I were some sort of sage, is swept away. The only thing that happens is that I am allowed to make a fresh start in philosophy, following the path that Shinran once trod to reach the truth of Pure Land Shin. This is why the reconstruction of philosophy in the spirit of Shinran provides a new beginning in philosophy rather than a new philosophical interpretation of Shinran's teachings. It hardly bears repeating that I do not mean thereby to compare myself to Shinran. I mean only that since I am deeply convinced that the metanoetics I am now practicing coincides, as a matter of ineluctable fate, with the spirit of Shinran, I sense the force of his influence and encouragement and revere him as my teacher and guide. At the same time, if I accept him as my teacher and guide, I must have a true understanding of his thought in order to develop my own way of thinking. This is the sense in which I shall be offering interpretations of doctrines like that of the Three Minds and the Three Stages of Faith in the *Kyōgyōshinshō*. It is by discovering my own independent philosophy that I come under Shinran's influence and guidance.

The path of the sage is closed to me. I am but an ordinary person groping my way through dark tunnels and moving in directions diametrically opposite to those of the sage. Metanoetics must only be developed into philosophy *metanoetically*. Metanoetics becomes philosophical self-consciousness when it is mediated by the performance of metanoesis through one's faith-witness. Hence the posture of *"credo ut intelligam"* is also applicable here. This posture may be of no use for the absolute standpoint of the sage, which is essentially identical with that of God, but it is indispensable for an ordinary person such as I.

If faith is defined directly in terms of revelation and further determined by dogma, philosophy cannot claim the autonomy or self-determination of reason as grounds for its necessity and universality. This is why the theology of theism leans toward a dogmatism that clashes with the critical spirit of philosophy. Metanoetics, however, is able to avoid this difficulty because it consists in a transformation that can be mediated by faith. Apart from metanoetics, it is impossible to establish a standpoint from which philosophy can be mediated by faith in such a way as to attain evidence of absolute truth without leaving its own standpoint. In spite of this, metanoetics has gone all but unnoticed throughout the history of philosophy up to the present for the simple reason that philosophy has developed essentially on foundations of the autonomy of reason. On the one hand, to be sure, philosophy has made great advances because of its reliance on reason and the self-confidence of the intellect. Yet on the other, as the history of philosophy clearly shows, it is far from being the case that this self-confidence of philosophy has never been shaken. Doubt is philosophy's constant companion.

Though it is hardly necessary to repeat it, the transcendental dialectic set forth in Kant's *Critique of Pure Reason* has made it amply clear that this fundamental predicament is not due merely to some accidental weakness or flaw in the human condition, but derives from a primordial limitation built into the structure of human knowledge and affecting the very nature of human reason itself. For Kant, the way to overcome such doubt is to admit the essential limitations of reason, keep human knowledge strictly within these limits, and thus avoid all pretense of surpassing or transcending these limits. As is well known, Kant argues that human knowledge must be confined within definite limits in order to make room for faith, whose validity falls outside the bounds of knowledge. Thus faith and knowledge coexist in Kant's transcendental philosophy with a boundary line drawn between them, so that each is assigned its own domain without interference from the other. In other words, theirs is an external relationship where each is distinguished in terms of its content: the one absolute, the other relative. Furthermore, Kant claims that faith transcends knowledge and secures it a validity only on a transcendent plane inaccessible to human knowledge.

There is no reciprocal mediation to be seen here, no process of transformation intrinsic to the mutual mediation of both terms so that either, having arrived at its limits, is transformed into the other—so that both, in spite of being independent of each other, stimulate and develop each other. Such a reciprocal mediation I regard as characteristic of metanoetics. But I wonder whether the sort of harmonious reconciliation of faith and knowledge that Kant works out on the basis of the self-limitation of each can be brought satisfactorily to fulfillment. In fact, I am convinced that Kant's thought, as developed in the chapter entitled "Metaphysics as a Natural Disposition" in the section of his *Critique of Pure Reason* dealing with the transcendental dialectic, shows beyond doubt that such reconciliation cannot provide a final solution. I shall reserve a detailed examination for the next chapter. But even a moment's reflection on the matter in its broad outlines should suffice to show that recent developments in mathematics and natural science, which Kant regarded as prototypes of all forms of knowledge, are frustrating this sort of reconciliation.

In the attempt to avoid the antinomies in which traditional metaphysics had become entangled, Kant confined human knowledge to the phenomenal world as a limited relative world and denied the possibility of knowledge of an unlimited absolute. That is to say, according to Kant, natural science, whose scope is coterminous with human experience, leads to valid knowledge, while metaphysics, which aims at acquiring knowledge of the absolute in such a way as to objectify the idea of the infinite merely in order to bring to completion the ordering of a system of concepts beyond the scope of experience, cannot be admitted as scientific knowledge. This is the sense of his so-called negation of metaphysics as science.

But insofar as human reason, in the sense of the capacity for inference, demands a deductive system of concepts, Kant thought it unavoidable that human nature would conceive of an infinite whose function is to make it possible for such a system to arrive at a final conclusion, and that it would not only provide this infinite with the formal regulative capacity of an ideal but also posit it as an objective concept with a given content. This is the sense of his "metaphysics as a natural disposition."

In order to protect this subjective metaphysics from the presumptuous claim to constitute an objective metaphysics, Kant drew a distinction between the *regulative* unity of the system fashioned under the formal guidance of the ideal and the *constitutive* unity of objective knowledge, which cannot be acquired through experience but only imposed on thinking as a problem to be pursued. Mere formal ideals, however, do not exist by themselves. An ideal does not determine reality one-sidedly; it is also mediated in turn by reality. The unity of ideal and reality is not based on an analogy with experience set up in terms of a ratio between rational numbers, such as we find in Kant's "analogy of experience" concerning categorical concepts. It is rather based on an analogy with experience in the sense of dialectical mediation.

In a hypothesis, analogy is mediated through experiments. Being independent of experience, the hypothesis works on the one hand as its regulative principle; on the other hand, it enters into experience as a heuristic concept in order to establish the experience through experimentation (action). Thus the hypothesis mediates experience precisely because it is mediated by experience. In this sense, it can rightly be called an ideal that constitutes an "analogy of experience" on a higher level and functions as a mediator through action.

One of the remarkable things about the new physics of our day is that ideals whose function is to bring a theoretical system to completion enter into the content of physical experience as a mediator of experiments, so that the notion of the infinite comes to form a constituent element of physical theory. It appears in the theory of relativity and in the new quantum theory as a mediation of physical subjectivity. What we have here is nothing other than an intrusion of the Kantian notion of "metaphysics as a natural disposition" into the realm of natural science.

Contrary to what Kant mistakenly supposed, in arriving at a definition of metaphysics as subjective through his critique of human knowledge, it is impossible for the subject to be considered as the transcendental ground of the object, while the object—within the subject-object opposition—is firmly established by means of the subject's formal independence. In truth, subject and object stand in a dialectical relationship in the sense that each mediates itself by making the other mediate it. This is the structure of active reality whose essence, we may say, consists in "subject-*qua*-object" and "object-*qua*-subject." This is also the structure of history. What the new natural science makes clear to us is that nature is also in fact historical.

It is therefore impossible for philosophy to stand apart from science in such a way that it presupposes science as a fact for which only a formal basis has to be found. To repeat: the essential feature of contemporary science, the understanding of which was not available to the age of Kant, is that philosophy enters into the content of scientific theories, indeed that science cannot stand on its own ground apart from philosophy and therefore must include philosophy within its own theories. Typical examples of this phenomenon are to be found in basic mathematical theory as well as in the new theories of physics referred to above. Seen from this viewpoint, we have no alternative but to conclude that Kant's critique of science has been refuted by science itself. The *Critique of Pure Reason*, the principal section of which is devoted to a critique of science, was unable to resolve the problem of the relationship between science and philosophy. If we also take into consideration the structure of historical reality itself, which poses further obstacles to the critique of reason, we find that it is not only the critique of theoretical reason—taken in the sense of the critique of science—that is doomed to unavoidable antinomies, but the critique of practical reason as well. This confronts the critique of reason with a crisis that threatens to undo it altogether. This is what I have been calling absolute critique, which I take to be the logic of metanoetics. Metanoetics is the logical consequence of conducting philosophy through the critique of reason to its final consequences. Only when science is led to religion, and knowledge transformed into faith, will the standpoint of *credo ut intelligam*—that is, the restoration of philosophy—be open to us. This is what takes place in metanoetics, as I shall discuss at length in the next chapter.

Chapter 2

Absolute Critique:
The Logic of Metanoetics

From the critique of reason to absolute critique · The subject of the critique of reason · The action of absolute Other-power · From ri to ji · The mutual circularity of riji · The circularity of the critique of reason · The transforming mediation of riji in action · The historicity of nature · The interpenetration and correspondence of science and philosophy · History as the ground of the mediation of religion and science through philosophy · The role of the self-consciousness of historicism in metanoetics as upāya · Symbolism of the ideal · The active "empty being" of symbols · The divided self of reason · Absolute critique as absolute crisis · Metanoetics as the absolute transformation of absolute critique · The active intuition of the self-power confidence of the sage and the metanoetics of the Other-power faith of the ignorant · Goethe's spirit of resignation · The integer of intuition and the differential of action · Rational faith and self-contradiction · Having-no-thing-by-nature · The absolute criticism of Hegel's Phenomenology of Mind · The standpoint of Kierkegaard · The illuminatio of Augustine · Hegel's rational view of religion · The Gate of Master Wu-mên · The discrimination of nondiscrimination and the unity of absolute contradictories

Metanoetics is not a product of my subjective feeling; nor is it simply a matter of my having been so overpowered by the Pure Land Shin doctrine expounded by Shinran that I was forced to mold my thought in conformity to it alone. I would argue that metanoetics is the inevitable result of philosophy pursued as the critique of reason. Accordingly, I refer to metanoetics as *absolute critique*. Absolute critique constitutes the theoretical side of metanoetics, and as such it may be termed the logic of metanoetics.

What does absolute critique mean? Admittedly the concept is every bit as unusual in philosophical language as is that of metanoetics. But does not the very fact that an idea like absolute critique has been commonly considered unnecessary in Western philosophy betray a lack of thoroughness in philosophical thinking and point to the very quandary that has characterized it up to the present?

Hegel's *Phenomenology of Mind* is itself a product of this absolute critique. In fact, we may rightly view the work as an account of the historical development of absolute critique from Kant to Hegel. In laying out the stages of development in Western intellectual history, Hegel confused logical developments, which might have led him to absolute critique, with the historical elements of social and human situations, and thus failed to develop absolute critique in its authentic form as the crowning accomplishment of the critique of reason. Consequently, he inherited the structural defects of German idealism from his predecessors, explaining "absolute knowledge" in the final chapter of his *Phenomenology of Mind* as if it were something that could be attained by reason alone. In this sense Hegel's absolute knowledge is not sufficient to carry the idea of absolute critique through absolute disruption. It is this defect that occasioned the criticisms of the later Schelling and more notably of Kierkegaard.

Philosophy stands in need of the rigor and unwavering spirit to push on beyond life and death that we see in the discipline of Zen Buddhism in the East. It is worth noting here that the faith in Other-power attained by Shinran reveals something in common with Zen in terms of the rigorous posture it takes toward the critical present in sharp contrast to the past and future. That any standpoint of faith can be attained only by practicing and then breaking through ordinary discursive modes of thought would seem to force philosophy to reflect seriously on its own nature. Like religious faith, philosophy, too, is a standpoint of "death-and-resurrection." This is the very absolute knowledge that philosophy seeks. The dissatisfaction that Kierkegaard felt with Hegel's philosophy lay chiefly in its failure to see this standpoint through to its final consequences. In this sense, what Zen calls "the decision and practice of the Great Death" must also be the first prerequisite of philosophy. Absolute critique is the equivalent of this Great Death in critical philosophy. The critique of reason must needs arrive at this point. Detailed treatment of the historicity of nature, as well as of the structure of the objects of knowledge in general—which, as mentioned at the end of the preceding chapter, can be understood only as historical realities in a concrete sense—shall be left for later.

To begin with, it should be noted that Kant never faced the problem of the critique of the critique of reason itself, nor indeed even considered whether such self-criticism is possible. As is well known, in his preface to the first edition of the *Critique of Pure Reason*, Kant characterized the world of his times as, "in especial degree, the age of criticism," [1] insisting that religion, for all its sacredness, could no more exempt itself from criticism than could the law of the land, for all its sovereignty; and that metaphysics, as the self-criticism of reason, was likewise liable to criticism. But even though Kant considered the emergence of critical philosophy to be the distinguishing mark of his age, he did not expose his critique of reason itself to criticism. Though a critical philosopher, he did not venture into criticism of the very possibility of criticism. It would seem he was convinced that if criticism is the proper task of reason, as he believed it was, philosophy becomes possible only when we presuppose and admit criticism; and moreover that the possibility of criticism itself cannot be called into question without negating reason and abandoning philosophy. In this he was from first to last a philosopher of reason. Yet it takes no more than a moment's reflection to locate the problems with such an idea of criticism.

First of all, when reason criticizes reason, does the reason doing the criticizing stand outside of the critique as a criticizing subject, without becoming an object of criticism? If this is the case, the critique of reason cannot be a thorough critique of reason in its entirety. Or if this is not the case, and reason and criticizing subject is later to become the object of criticism, then we end up in an infinite regress where each critique gives rise to a critique of itself. We would then be forced to conclude that the thoroughgoing critique of reason in its entirety is simply an impossibility, involving a contradiction beyond the means of analytical logic to resolve because of the antinomies into which the infinite process of self-awareness is doomed to fall.

Just as self-awareness must break through itself by awakening to a consciousness of nothingness, so must the self-criticism of reason run aground on the impassable antinomies of the one and the many, the whole and the individual, infinity and finitude, determinacy and spontaneity, necessity and freedom. Criticism has no alternative but to surrender itself to this crisis of self-disruption, and to overcome it by allowing itself to be shattered to pieces.

What concerns us here, in making the assertion that the possibility of criticism must itself be criticized, is not the problem of analytical logic: whether or not there are, in terms of the law of identity, any contradictions in the system of reason, and if so, how to eliminate them. Nor is the question of the critique of the possibility of criticism the problem of transcendental logic: whether or not there are sufficient grounds for the principles of synthetic reason, and if so, what kind of system they constitute. For here, too, the possibility of criticism would end up face-to-face with the antinomies of reason and sink into a nothingness in which neither "yes" nor "no" could be spoken. It is both a matter of destiny and ultimate truth that in the pursuit of full autonomy, reason must finally break down. But where can reason, shattered and sunk into sheer nothingness, find a foothold from which to break out of its crisis by breaking through itself, from which to be transformed and resurrected from nothingness into new being? Only in actualizing the self-criticism of reason. For, as we saw in the last chapter, the depths of reality as a whole can be fathomed only when we are convinced that the absolute consists solely in the transformative power of absolute nothingness.

Insofar as reason has been shattered in the experience of breaking through reason, without as yet being formally aware of its crisis, we may speak of "fact-*qua*-act," that is, of fact as *genuine action* (*gyōteki-ji*) resurrected from nothingness. This fact-*qua*-act (*ji*) is based on a higher reason (*ri*) that transcends reason in its former sense. In concrete terms, this means that we are converted entirely to "being as *upāya*" through the transformative power of absolute nothingness, and thus can effect that genuine action that is an "action of no-action"—or "action without an acting self"—since our activity no longer belongs to ourselves alone and cannot be based on the autonomy of reason. Indeed, the standpoint of fact-*qua*-act presupposes the metanoetic awareness that our human predicament cannot be explained by reason alone, and that genuine action always has something of a transrational character. In this fact-*qua*-act (*ji*) which makes it possible to establish the rational (*ri*) in spite of the negation and transcendence of the rational, the dynamic structure of being-*qua*-nothingness, or emptied being, forms the ground from which reason is resurrected by breaking through itself.

All this is nothing more than a circularity resulting from the necessity of reciprocal mediation between *quid facti* and *quid juris*, which brings us to a second difficulty involved in the self-critique of reason: a circularity in reasoning itself. As noted before, the first contradictions (antinomies) of reason are broken through by the fact or facticity (*ji*) of the circularity of critique: *ri* is transformed into *ji* and the critique is reduced to the reciprocity of critique, that is, to criticizing the criticizing.

Critical philosophy starts from fact—the actual existence of pure science—in order to justify itself. Kant's so-called transcendental deduction is of course concerned with this question, and makes up the most difficult section of the *Critique of Pure Reason*. In his preface to the second edition, Kant likened the transcendental method of his critical philosophy to the experimental method of natural science, pointing out that the purpose of experimentation is to test whether the law-regulated structures that reason has constructed in advance of experimentation can actually be realized in nature. Insofar as this is also what Kant had in mind with transcendental method, his transcendental principles must mediate (construct) empirical fact on the one hand, and on the other, their validity must be mediated (attested to) by empirical fact.

Ri, presupposed as transcendental to experience, finds the basis of its verification in being confirmed by *ji*. This reciprocal mediation between *ri* and *ji*, which constitutes the true meaning of transcendental deduction, shows an obvious circularity. The experimental method of natural science clearly displays its circularity as a reciprocal mediation between rational construction (*ri*) and factual verification (*ji*), but this is no mere repetition of a formal identity. There is no doubt that this reciprocal mediation opens up ever deeper levels of the dynamic structure of being, and that nothingness, as mediator of being, reveals ever more of its inner depth in accordance with the "practical" development of being.

This being so, is it not natural that the transcendental method of Kant's critical philosophy should show the same circularity as the experimental method? Even if the aporia of the above-mentioned contradictions involved in the critique is solved from the standpoint of *ji* by reason breaking through reason, we are still left with the second difficulty, namely, the circularity between *ri* and *ji*. This second difficulty in turn is overcome by being drawn down deeply into the vortex of circularity and sinking into the depths of nothingness, so that one is transformed into a manifestation of nothingness and restored in a "return to being as *upāya*." Contradiction and circularity coexist to the extent that the contradiction based on *ri*, or the contradiction between *ri* and *ji*, is transformed into absolute negation through practice in accordance with *ji*, and establishes the action-faith that effects an interpenetration of *ri* and *ji* (*ri-ji-sōnyū*).

From the viewpoint of *ōsō*, intellect-based reason is heightened to action-faith by being made to break through itself by means of the antinomies. At the same time, from the viewpoint of *gensō* it is brought back again to the mediated intellect of witness to the absolute truth, resulting in religious communication between one being and another. This is the self-criticism of breaking through the self that I call absolute critique, that is, critique without a criticizing subject. Here, in self-consciousness grounded in nothingness, action-faith-witness represents the very self-transcendence of reason. Free and autonomous reason transcends itself in the absolute critique of performing action, faith, and witness through the nothingness of reason. This is what I call the death-and-resurrection of reason. It is metanoetics as the manifestation of absolute nothingness, the way of salvation through Other-power–*qua*–self-power. For what is called absolute critique in intellectual terms is possible only in action through metanoesis.

As I have stated above, the experimental method of natural science implies a "historicity-through-action" mediated by absolute critique, since the experimental method itself is based on the reciprocal mediation-through-action of *ri* and *ji*. But to the extent that historicity is present in the structure of a natural science only nonexplicitly (*an sich*)— that is, to the extent that it has to do with the theoretical construction of science and the historical development of its hypotheses—the methodology of science remains bound to this view of historicity. But once one becomes conscious of the antinomies that arise in the context of the systematic unification of the total, fundamental requirements of reason, one's being is transformed into a manifestation of absolute nothingness as a *neither/nor* that occurs on the standpoint of *ji*, established through the self-transcendence of *ri*. Here the problem of historicity is brought to the stage of explicit awareness (*für sich*) through action-faith-witness. It is seen as the circularity of nothingness in which *ri* and *ji* mediate each other. In other words, philosophy appears as absolute critique.

Philosophy may be said to come into being when the experimental method of science, having passed through the transcendental method of the critique of reason, arrives at antinomies and is transformed into the absolute critique of metanoesis consisting of the metanoetical action-faith-witness of absolute nothingness. That is, at the very point that science is transformed into religion, philosophy makes its appearance. The milieu of this new philosophy is history, and its method is metanoetics. Reason is transformed from science through religion into philosophy; and the practice of religion, insofar as it involves the element of a return to the world, makes use of the actual objective knowledge of science. Precisely because this practice consists in the absolute negation of self-reliant ethical action and provides "the returning aspect" (*gensō*) of nothingness, ethics is transformed into a mediatory activity that makes possible one's contribution to the historical world, insofar as the two aspects of moving toward the absolute (*ōsō*) and returning to the world (*gensō*) coincide with each other in one's ethical action. In the breakthrough of the self (metanoetics), reason arrives at a transrational emancipation by means of the reciprocal mediation of science, religion, philosophy, and ethics.

Such emancipation is not a mere critique of reason that stops with negative resignation, as is the case in Kant's critique of reason. Evading the antinomies, Kant abandons metaphysical knowledge and limits the idea of an unconditional absolute, which reason requires, to the role of a postulate for moral action. The standpoint that concerns us here is one of "death-and-resurrection." It entails throwing oneself boldly into the crisis of antinomies so that one is restored, by the transformative grace of absolute nothingness, to a standpoint of absolute submission—so that one is enabled, by one's action-faith-witness, to participate in the realization of a *ji* that is "*ri*-without-*ri*" (that is, a *ri* that contains *ri* by surpassing it). In this way, theory and practice, mediated by nothingness (the breakthrough of the self), come to penetrate each other through one's action-faith. Reason and practice are thus exalted to the standpoint of religion in which one's witness produces knowledge as it returns to the world (*gensō*). This may be said to provide a means of overcoming the abstraction inherent in Kantian philosophy, whose fall into the formalism of "a two-world theory"—distinguishing the phenomenal from the noumenal world—inhibits its ability to provide a philosophical foundation to history. Concepts based on the standpoint of absolute critique are not "ideals" or mere formal "oughts," as is the case with Kant's rational concepts. Rather, they denote "emptied beings," that is, "beings as *upāya*." More precisely, although they come into existence as *ji* (actual transitory reality), they exist as "ideal-*qua*-reality" and always remain as mediators of nothingness. Once we lose this self-awareness, our relative being can only be negated entirely as mere phenomenal being entangled in radical evil.

Ideals are symbols of the mutual transformation of being and nothingness. A symbol does not remain in the realm of expression-and-formation, even though it originates as an expression of historical life. Through this inner antinomy—that it is a formation of expression and yet should be a realization of nothingness—the symbol is transfigured from expression-formation into a self-contradictory emptied being (that is, into being-*qua*-nothingness). More precisely, it is through the metanoesis of our powerlessness that we realize that mere expression-formation cannot afford a solution to our "pro-blem."[2] A symbol does not designate a consummation of the formation process, as an ideal does. A symbol implies that the final result of formation consists in the self breaking through the above-mentioned antinomies, and signifies what is transformed into nothingness and then restored again as something returning to "a temporary emptied being" (*hōbenteki kū-u*). The ideals in Kant's philosophy, such as freedom, immortality, and God, are all truly symbols in this sense.

As we have said, the *Critique of Pure Reason* cannot provide the ultimate standpoint for philosophy that Kant claimed for it, since his solution of separating the phenomenal world from the noumenal is a mere compromise incapable of bringing reason to an ultimate state of peace. Quite to the contrary, reason is left exposed to antinomies that can only rend it asunder and cast it into a state of absolute self-disruption. As far as the critique of pure reason is concerned, reason as the criticizing subject always remains in a safety zone where it preserves its own security without having to criticize the possibility of critique itself. Yet precisely because reason cannot thereby avoid self-disruption, the reason that does the criticizing and the reason that is to be criticized must inevitably be separated from each other. Reason thus forced to recognize itself as self-disruptive because of the critique must finally admit that the very reason that has come to think highly of itself in virtue of its capacity for critique must be shattered. Reason must recognize that it lacks the capacity for critique; otherwise the criticizing reason can only be distinguished from the reason to be criticized. In either case, there is no avoiding the final self-disruption of reason. In other words, reason that tries to establish its own competence by means of self-criticism must finally, contrary to it own intentions, recognize its absolute self-disruption.

I understand this sort of absolute self-disruption as an "absolute crisis," since crisis means disruption. Thus the self-consciousness of reason that leads to the absolute crisis of absolute self-disruption is absolute critique. What the absolute critique of reason aims to do is not to provide a safety preserve for the criticizing subject by assuming criticism to lie beyond all criticism, but rather to expose the entirety of reason to rigorous criticism and thus to a self-shattering. The critique of reason cannot avoid leading reason to absolute critique. The absolute self-disruption brought about in absolute critique is unavoidable for reason awakened to consciousness of itself. The self-consciousness that all things are in absolute disruption because of antinomies and self-contradictions is the final result of the demand for self-identical unity in reason. Pure self-identity is possible only for the absolute. Insofar as reason forgets its standpoint of finitude and relativity and erroneously presumes itself to be absolute, it is destined to fall into absolute contradiction and disruption.

Nevertheless, if we submit obediently to this destiny, choose this death willingly, and throw ourselves into the very depths of these utterly unavoidable contradictions, reality renews itself from those depths, and opens up a new way, urging us to head in the direction in which actuality is moving and to collaborate with this movement. Accompanying reason's option for its own death, the gate of contradictions, which was barred as long as reason clung to self-reliance, is thrown open. Contradictions do not thereby cease to be contradictions, but restore reason to a transrational dimension, where it can serve as a mediator to, or collaborator in, the transformative activity of the absolute. The "Great Nay" of absolute nothingness as absolute transformation becomes "Great Compassion" in that it takes us ourselves into itself and brings us to salvation by death-and-resurrection. Herein lies the structure characteristic of the "Great Nay–*qua*–Great Compassion" of the absolute.

Metanoetics consists in submitting to this transformation obediently, in ceaseless joy and gratitude. Reason is restored to salvation through transcendent grace so that, in its metanoesis, it repents for its sins, acknowledges itself as presumptuous and guilty of self-reliance, and awakens to its own finitude. Since that which leads us to the metanoesis already comes forth from the Great Compassion, metanoesis is an action we cannot perform by ourselves. It is action based entirely upon Other-power in spite of being our own action; we are but the subjects of a mediatory activity. Reason, once fallen into absolute disruption, is now restored to salvation in and through action based on absolute Other-power, which altogether transcends reason. This does not mean, however, that reason, having recovered from its disruption, is restored to its original unity, an idea to which Hegel's concept of reason still adheres. Taking the standpoint of reason, Hegel defines religion as the recovery of a former unity, from which humanity had become separated, through the reconciliation of God and humanity by means of God's love. Clearly Hegel's theory of religion never leaves the standpoint of the self-identity of reason. As Kierkegaard correctly argues, Hegel cannot free himself from the realm of the intellect. By remaining within the immanence of reason, Hegel cannot cope with the absolute paradox that Kierkegaard proposes.

In genuine religious faith, absolute disruption is itself a unity even as it goes on being a disruption, and contradictions are resolvable even as they continue to be unresolvable. The contradiction that is unresolvable so long as we are caught in self-reliance becomes resolvable without thereby ceasing to be a contradiction when we decide to die our own death and voluntarily abandon ourselves by being forced to abandon ourselves. Hence the barrier of contradiction turns out to be surmountable and ceases to be an obstruction. This is why the disruption is defined as a unity while still remaining a disruption. This is also what Shinran has in mind when he writes, "We participate in *nirvāna* during life, without cutting ourselves off entirely from our lusts."[3] If it were a matter of a return to self-identity, we could not speak in such terms. Hegel assumes such a self-identical subjectivity when he maintains that self-consciousness is the self-identical subject of religion. But in truth there is no self of which we are conscious, for the self is so utterly shattered that nothing remains. The very situation in which the self is transformed into nothingness makes unrestricted freedom possible. The self is abandoned and there is no self left to act. It is only restored to a temporary axis of absolute transformation when it cooperates in the realization of absolute (historical) reality and thus serves as a mediator for absolute nothingness. Once we grant an all-encompassing, self-identical totality that makes up the unity of the self, there is no room for absolute mediation through action. This is why Hegel's Absolute Mind cannot finally free itself from the self-identity of reason.

Some may imagine a self-identical totality directly accessible to the grasp of intellectual intuition, but the nothingness we are speaking of here cannot be intuited at all. In the case of "action-intuition"— intuition, for the sake of action, into the content of one's formative (creative) activity, in contradistinction to Plotinus's concept of intuition[4]—action is understood as the functioning of self-power that is at work in aesthetic expression-and-formation. It has nothing at all to do with action based on the Other-power of absolute nothingness. This latter both is and is not an action of the self: it is action based on nothingness, and to that extent contains everywhere within itself "openings" to nothingness, through which being and nothingness, like front and back or inside and outside, ceaselessly interpenetrate each other. It is by no means possible to intuit such a totality. What can be intuited is superficial being, not its reverse aspect of nothingness. What is in absolute disruption because of a reciprocal mediation between being and nothingness cannot be intuited. Transformation can indeed be realized by self-consciousness through action, but this is only a negative mediator of action so that intellect and action can interpenetrate each other, so that being and nothingness can mediate each other. Insofar as this is true, there can be a self-consciousness of action but not of self-identical intuition. Self-consciousness does not mean a self coming to awareness of itself by considering itself to be self-identical. Rather, precisely because the self is negated for the purpose of becoming a mediator of nothingness, the only mediation in action there can be is that of a self practicing "the action of nothingness;" and the only dynamic unity, that of a reciprocal transformation between being and nothingness.

The self-consciousness of nothingness must be the nothingness of self-consciousness. But because the nothingness in question is not a relative nothingness opposed to being, but rather absolute nothingness, self-consciousness is continually converted and transformed into a mediator of nothingness without either being deprived of itself or getting caught in self-attachment. Since nothingness as absolute nothingness surpasses the opposition between relative being and relative nothingness, it opposes itself to the self transcendentally to become the unifying basis of self-consciousness, which in turn transcends the relative opposition between being and nothingness. The unity inherent in the transformation of nothingness cannot be intuited as the content of formative activity. What we are concerned with here is rather a transformation based on the Other-power of transcendent nothingness, which is absolutely inaccessible to intuition and even negates it. It is not intuition for the sake of action, but the self-consciousness of action in and through nothingness in the sense of a "disruption-*qua*-unity" that transforms intuition through its negation. The self-awareness of nothingness is not concerned with practice wherein one acts by oneself in order to construct something, but with the self-abandonment to which the self is forced to surrender in the sort of desperate situation to which the self in action-formation is doomed. What is meant here by the self-consciousness of nothingness is one's action-faith-witness which is attested in such a way that—or better, precisely because—the self that abandons itself is transformed and restored to a temporal, transitory being that acts in reliance on Other-power through faith. That is, in breaking through intuition and moving out of being into nothingness, action becomes action worthy of the name. If it remains intuition, it is being but not nothingness. The self-consciousness of action is not an intuition of being but a self-consciousness of nothingness. If I may speak in stronger terms, it is self-consciousness of death and self-destruction, but not an intuition of life and self-formation.

In regarding action as formation, action-intuition is clearly seen to be only a matter of continually extending the self but not of negating it—in other words, it has to do not with death but with life. Nor is it concerned with "being as *upāya*," that is, with the void as transitory, temporal being mediating nothingness. Such action-intuition displays itself rather as the content of aesthetic formation and as the product of self-expression. That it has nothing to do with action-faith—which arises from the transformation that takes place through self-abandonment in metanoesis to which ordinary people submit themselves in coming to awareness of their powerlessness—is perfectly clear. It is simply the self-assertion of sages or mystics presumptuously convinced of having achieved union with the absolute. This is why the content that this self-identity takes on in its formation is based on an intuition of the absolute. The action of expression-and-formation belongs entirely to self-power; it is the operation of the relative striving for unity with the absolute. As such, its orientation is quite different from that of the self-consciousness of the Great Action (*taigyō*), which, as a symbolic existence allowed only in order to mediate the absolute nothingness of Other-power, is itself mediated through its own self-negation.

I should like to illustrate my position through one more example, though in doing so I fear it will involve a further detour. The usual way of understanding Goethe, it would seem, is to look on him as a poet of life, or more precisely as a poet of the self-transcendent life. Few regard him as a poet dwelling in the serene light of resignation. In my view this is why "The West-Easterly Divan" and Part II of *Faust*, which characterize his maturity as a symbolic poet, often tend to be neglected. Even if great weight is given to his concept of resignation, its significance cannot, it seems to me, adequately be appreciated from the standpoint of the self-transcendence of life. Of course, what Goethe means by resignation is throughout a negative attitude, nothing so positive as what I call action out of joy and gratitude for the Great Compassion, the action of *zange*. And yet the characteristic structure of Goethe's resignation is that of a unity-in-transformation through (absolute) negativity, which is similar to *zange*. It is not the result of a mere affirmation of life unfolding and transcending itself. On the contrary, it points to an attitude of death-

and-negation wherein one completely abandons direct affirmation, wherein the assertion of life is transfigured into its resurrection and affirmation. It signifies a spontaneous recognition of the determinations of a given destiny as one's own choice, a living hope of the future without getting trapped in grief over a lost past, and a free and tranquil acceptance of present reality as it is.

Therefore, even though the state of mind that marks Goethe's resignation cannot be compared to the radiant joy originating in the Great Compassion—as in the case of faith based on Other-power, where gratitude issues in an enthusiasm to act on behalf of others (*gensō-hōon*)—there is nevertheless something of the same resigned tranquillity of mind in Goethe's contemplative life. While it is devoid of the positivity inherent in a bodhisattva's return from *nirvāna* to this world, it is nevertheless colored by the peace of mind that characterizes enlightened Buddhas (*pratyekabuddha*). Here we see a certain negative tinge congenial to the Eastern concept of nothingness. Indeed, I have no doubt that the "West-Easterly Divan" was inspired by the spirit of the East. The peak of Goethe's maturity is also reflected in Part II of *Faust*, whose symbolism sets it off from Part I. The death of Faust reveals a self-consciousness characteristic of "a return to the world through conversion and transformation" that is wholly unrelated to the death of the so-called tragic hero. In fact, true self-transcendence cannot be attained by mere affirmation of the self. It must be a negative transformation mediated by such a death.

Is it appropriate then to term the self-consciousness and resignation of this death "intuition"? I think not, for the self-consciousness of negation is an assertion of detachment from the self and a self-consciousness which abandons everything that can be thought of in terms of "mine." The affirmation that is restored through the mediation of this negation is in no sense a direct affirmation. It is rather a symbol of the serene light behind which always lies—nothingness. It is a way of realizing a self-abandonment that can never be intuited in terms of being. In other words, it reveals a new vista at every "moment." This is the sense of Goethe's statement, "Everything is allegory [*Gleichnis*]." The speech of Zen masters is full of such allegory. It is comparable to what Baudelaire calls *correspondance*, and it is the very mark of Goethe as a symbolic poet. Part II of *Faust* and "The West-Easterly Divan" can be likened to two great treasuries of his symbolism. It comes as no surprise that his famous saying, "*Stirb, und werde*" (Die and become), is to be found in the latter.

Is there anything in Goethe's concept of resignation that can be intuited as self-identical? If there is anything self-identical in such resignation, it cannot be considered resignation. The self-consciousness of self-abandonment is by no means self-identical. Furthermore, if absolute contradiction could be reduced to a self-identity, the contradiction itself would have to be considered as having vanished at the same time. For it is not a matter of contradiction being *overcome* from a standpoint that envelops and transcends it, but of being *recovered*— pardoned and redeemed—through metanoetic self-consciousness, without thereby ceasing to be contradiction. Just as when we intuit the content of resignation, resignation ceases to exist, the unity of resurrection resulting from our obedient self-surrender to a transformative power in the very midst of absolute self-disruption cannot be said to be based on Other-power if we consider it as self-identical.

Absolute critique, insofar as it is action based on Other-power, is restored in and through absolute nothingness only by submitting obediently to the latter. Reason is not restored here to what it once was, namely reason grounded on the principle of self-identity. Negatively speaking, one who abandons oneself through resignation, forsaking independence and freedom, is brought to a self-consciousness in action-faith characterized by the submissive awareness of having been restored to life while dying to oneself. The Japanese Zen master Bunan (1602–1676) once wrote:

> If one can die to oneself completely
> While one is still alive,
> One can excel
> At whatever one wants to do.

Here, the words "wants to do" signify "no-mind–*qua*–mind." In other words, the mind that "is in accord with things can encounter things in order to change them into what they really are, even though there is no body-and-mind since the body is shattered and the mind has so completely disappeared that there is no longer anything that can be called mind." In this context the sense of "things" is that of the phrase "having-no-thing by nature" (*honrai-muichimotsu*). It is a question of an activity that can at any moment and any place be transformed into a new creative phase. Nothingness consists in constant transformation and thus transcends self-identical intuition. By means of "direct seeing which is no-seeing and direct hearing which is no-hearing," seeing and hearing become possible in the true sense, and as such witness to "having-no-thing by nature." There is nothing here that can be intuited as something self-identical. The realization of "having-no-thing" requires an act of negation to make it genuine; only then is the resurrection of self realized through one's faith-witness. Here we see the positive aspect of absolute critique. Even though I speak of the self-consciousness of resurrection, I do not mean to use a mathematical analogy and imply that there is some intuition of an integral whole consisting in an all-embracing self-identity of contradictions; I mean only that the act of transformation through action-faith is such that one's "death-and-resurrection" can be performed at any differential point in the world of time and space.

This, then, is how reason is transformed through absolute critique into an action-faith-witness directed toward Other-power. The critique of reason, through which reason strives in vain to establish itself on a solid basis, terminates in an absolute critique that brings reason to destruction. But absolute critique renders reason capable of being restored to "emptied being" (*kū-u*), insofar as it is thereby transformed into a mediatory moment of transrational absolute nothingness and thus allowed to exist as transitory "being as *upāya*." All we have to do in this transformation is bear witness to our own nothingness through action-faith, and this is what I call the self-consciousness of nothingness.

In using the term "resurrection" to describe the transformation that occurs, I do not mean merely restoration to a former life. It is rather that the self is restored to a new life so that, though dead to itself, it can still act perfectly. Moreover, in speaking of a "restoration," I do not mean that reason is restored to its former state, but rather that reason is brought to the self-consciousness of an action-faith-witness that transcends reason. Kant proposed a "religion within the limits of reason alone," but in truth there can be no such religion. The principle of absolute goodness which furnishes a basis for religion and is able to overcome the radical evil in humanity belongs only to God. Religion consists in the faith of those who participate in the work of establishing the Kingdom of God on earth and who, as members of the Kingdom of God, submit to the supremacy of divine providence. The faith in God to which Kant was pointing was rational and universal, as distinct from faith based on God's revelation as a historical event. Genuine faith, however, is an absolute negation of reason, worthy of being termed religion only when it transcends mere rational thinking.

As I understand it, therefore, "rational faith" does not signify a faith *based on* reason but a faith *mediated by* reason. In other words, "rational faith" is a concept to be defined not by means of self-identical determination but by means of negative dialectical mediation. A rational faith must be transrational; it must be the negation of reason. Reason, whose very nature it is to be dialectical, is self-negating and can exist only in the mediation and resurrection effected through its self-negation or self-destruction.

This process of transformation-and-mediation, which constitutes the essential core of reason, is rightly designated as "having-no-thing." Here we are in accord with Hui-nêng (Jap., Enō, 638–713), the Sixth Zen Patriarch, who describes human nature in terms of "having-no-thing." But this process is witnessed to only in and through the workings of absolute nothingness, which effects the death of the self and can in no way be conceptualized as a self-identical idea.

It was on this very point that Kierkegaard criticizes Hegel for basing his dialectic on intellectual thinking and regarding the self-identity of reason as capable of synthesizing contradictory oppositions by reconciling them with each other. At the same time, the fact that Hegel's dialectic, by pursuing Kant's theory of transcendental dialectic to its conclusion, passes through reciprocal negation to arrive at absolute disruption, accords well with the idea of "absolute critique" I have been describing, and shows the extent to which he carried philosophical thinking through to its radical consequences. In particular, I cannot but admire the theory of dialectic based on absolute nothingness that is developed in the *Phenomenology of Mind*. Of course, the unique quality of this work and its original contribution stem from the fact that Hegel develops a historical approach to the problem: in dealing with an absolute critique based on individual consciousness, he takes into account the concrete development of mind in history. Since history involves social and human aspects in addition to rational criticism, it is inevitable that Hegel's *Phenomenology of Mind* should have been affected by trends of thought unrelated to the critique of reason and that it should get tangled up with things secondary to the logical development of absolute critique. Still, the essence of the work lies in absolute critique, and, in my opinion, in an absolute critique whose historical development runs parallel to the concrete stages of development of the history of Western thought. It is to Hegel's great credit that he did not consider absolute critique as something that could be carried out once and for all (non-historically), but pursued the self-deepening process of the consciousness of contradictions. Moving successively from the most abstract stage of "sense-certainty" to the concrete stage of the ethical view of life which culminates in the "Beautiful Soul," he clarified the process of the mind's unfolding, describing how it sinks into its own destruction (negation) and rises up restored to new life. The *Phenomenology of Mind* may be called the historical development of absolute critique.

In saying this, we should not overlook the defect in Hegel's abstract thought resulting from the fact that he regarded religion as belonging to reason and as consisting of mere representation (*Vorstellung*) rather than of concept (*Begriff*). By arguing that reason is provided with a positive side by speculative reason, which is also the apex of its development, he makes his philosophy into a complete system. At the same time, he cannot avoid falling into a nondialectical, self-identical philosophy, which is simply a return to Kantian reason and to Schelling's philosophy of identity. In other words, we come here to a loss of the paradox that characterizes the dialectic, a point on which Kierkegaard sharply criticized Hegel. The paradoxical dialectic advocated by Kierkegaard belongs properly to dialectic in action, which forms part of the authentic standpoint of action-faith. The standpoint of intellectual reason grounded on the principle of identity is a degeneration away from authentic dialectic.

While following Hegel in his pursuit of absolute critique to the final conclusion to which Kant's critique of reason leads, we need not stop at his tenacious but inconsistent attachment to reason. We must take the further step of dying to self in the depths of absolute disruption and, through the practice of acting as though dead, be restored to a new life. In this way we come to the positive aspect of absolute critique. Insofar as one is conscious of this as a faith-witness to the "Great Nay–*qua*–Great Compassion," one is engaged in metanoetics. Hegel arranged a system of reason in which both the negatively rational—the dialectical—and the affirmatively rational—the speculative—are brought into a synthetic unity of identical reason consisting in "negation-*qua*-affirmation." This is why his science of logic turns out to be a metaphysic in the form of an ontology. With its completion, Hegel's system deprives the dialectic of its vitality, leaving behind only a skeleton of logic. Dialectics, deprived of its paradoxical character, can no longer be authentic dialectic; it degenerates into a mere logic of identity. Nevertheless, since such dialectic attempts to become the self-identity of absolute contradictions, it has no alternative but to set up mysticism as its basis, which is why Hegel's logic is considered mystical.

Nor can Hegel's philosophy avoid the criticism that it does not conform to practice and results in an impersonal pantheism, as Schelling and Kierkegaard argue. His logic, in addition to being bound to the standpoint of reason, is bound to an immanentist teleology that has been maintained ever since Aristotle. In contrast, Schelling, particularly in his later period, emphasizes the freedom of evil and insists on the positivity of revelation as a necessary condition for salvation. Kierkegaard, too, based himself on the paradoxical dialectic, emphasizing that faith in the genuine sense is entirely a matter of the salvation of the individual self and is unrelated to universal reason. It must be said that both of them, in contrast with Hegel's philosophy, which does not depart from the standpoint of reason that characterized Greek philosophy and thereby cannot avoid being pagan, are attempting to clarify the biblical faith of Christianity. There is no doubt that in their efforts to develop a thoroughgoing existential historicism they became the forerunners of contemporary existential philosophy.

My absolute critique and metanoetics leave me no alternative but to follow Kierkegaard. Even Augustine's concept of *"illuminatio,"* interpretations of which have produced a great deal of ambiguity, shows how reason's fall into self-contradiction is transformed into absolute passivity in the negation brought about by the transcendent. This means that with the transformation of reason, or intellect (*ri*), into fact (*ji*) "in the due course of nature" (*jinenhōni-teki ni*), free and formless truth is crystallized into the content of "idea." Accordingly, the structure that characterizes Augustine's doctrine of illumination may be said to conform to absolute critique and metanoetics.[5] Indeed, we have here the essential feature of Augustinianism, which transcends Aristotelianism to become evangelical. As such, it is marked by a "return to the world" (*gensō*), whereas Aristotelianism, by assimilating *ji* to *ri*, moves toward the absolute (*ōsō*). It is no exaggeration to say that the fundamental tone of Augustinianism as a whole is in complete accord with metanoetics. In fact, Augustine may be called the pioneer of metanoetics in the West.

Of course, Hegel, too, takes the stance of evangelical Christianity and considers Christian revelation to be the supreme form of religion. Numerous coincidences between his thought and terminology and those of metanoetics or absolute critique can be found in the transition from section IV, "Mind" (*Geist*), to section V, "Religion," of the *Phenomenology of Mind*. Yet even where he uses concepts corresponding to those of my metanoetics, he develops his own thought and belief in a quite different manner and from his own philosophical standpoint. There is logical necessity in the fact that his thought is similar to mine, insofar as it results from carrying the critique of reason to its conclusions, not to mention the fact that evangelical Christianity exerted a great influence upon him. In his idea of the necessary existence of evil within the acting self, Hegel tries to clarify the concept of radical evil expounded by Kant by bringing more profound reflection to bear on it and shifting its focus from the propensity of the will to ethical action in the world. According to Hegel, because of human finitude, action performed in the world in conformity with one's individual character is destined to be particular; that is, one cannot avoid one-sided action that cannot but incite rebellion and opposition in others. The more one heeds one's conscience, the more one must recognize one's sin as the inevitable result of one-sided action. On this point, we have to acknowledge the depth and keenness of Hegel's thought. In his view, the self-disruption or self-contradiction of reason necessarily comes to hold sway not only over theoretical reason but also over practical reason; and since the acting self that becomes conscious of the contradiction or opposition in the self through recognition of its sinfulness is redeemed and purified from its particularity as a one-sided acting subject, thereby returning to the universal whole, the limitations and determinations imposed on the mind as the result of action disappear completely. This "confession (*Bekennen*) [of sin] and recognition [of others]" belongs to one who abandons the abstraction of the "Beautiful Soul" that presumes itself to be supreme and good, to one who knows the self intuitively solely in and through the other, only by recognizing the other. Only thus can one reconcile oneself to others and live in harmony with them. In other words, at this stage of mind the acting subject has been restored to universality through self-estrangement and has returned to the totality. Absolute mind is thereby achieved through reciprocal recognition or reciprocal reconciliation. This brings about the unity of a universal self that overcomes the distinction between self and others, so that selfhood arises as a genuine individuality with the universal as its substratum. Here God becomes manifest in the conviction that the self exists through the mediation of that which opposes it in others, and mind arrives at its totality in religion as the self-consciousness of such a divine self. Religion brings to self-awareness a totality which, as the absolute, provides the basis for the self in its relative existence. Therefore religion is that which leads the development of mind to its consummation and gives it ultimate unity.

In this sense, we may say that Hegel's phenomenology of mind leads us to reflect on how, by returning from religion to each previous stage of mind that marked the way of death taken by absolute critique, the content of each stage is now transformed into, or restored to, a way of life. According to Hegel, therefore, absolute knowledge comes about because of the fact that in this transformation each stage of mind is preserved as a moment constitutive of the absolute mind of religion. The philosophy that consists in absolute knowledge is the self-consciousness of rational religion, and the science of logic that comprises the theory of categories is the logical self-consciousness of each of the stages in its development. The science of logic thus reflects knowledge within itself in the form of categories.

Hegel's *Phenomenology of Mind* is essentially absolute critique, and the restoration of mind to its universality by means of religious confession is similar to conversion through metanoetics. In spite of that, Hegel holds firm to the self-identity of reason, confuses it with the unity of the transcendent action-faith of religion through the transformation of nothingness in absolute critique, and clings throughout to a logic based on self-power in line with his efforts to establish a system similar to Greek ontology.

In contrast, metanoetics employs absolute critique in order to achieve witness in an action-faith based on the Great Compassion of Other-power. Its essential feature consists not in the self-identity of reason but in a voluntary submission in faith to absolute nothingness. We can, I think, draw a distinction between the related concepts of confession and metanoesis by seeing the former as belonging to reason based on self-power, and the latter, to faith based on Other-power. At any rate, the reason that dies in the depths of absolute critique is not resurrected in the same form as before, as reason whose principle is self-identity. When we speak of the resurrection of a rational being, we mean that one who has died is restored to life *as one dead*, situated at a point that is neither "death" nor "life"—the standpoint of "having-no-thing by nature"— and free to enter either death or life without becoming attached to either life or death, past or future.

This does not mean, of course, that reason adopts a universal viewpoint that synthesizes contradictions by negating them, but that it is transformed into a mediator of nothingness which is no longer hindered or restricted by contradictions, even though they remain as they were. This truth is something to be realized only when each of us performs his or her own unique role by being motivated to do so in the transcendent present of absolute nothingness in accord with absolute Other-power. When the famous Chinese Zen master Wu-mên (Jap., Mumon) claims that the genuine essence of Buddhist truth is a barrier, what he means by the term "barrier" is, I think, comparable to what we have been calling the way of death-and-resurrection. For Wu-mên, such truth is not accessible by the way of reason open to all, like a gate through which horses and vehicles can pass freely; it is a barrier which horses and vehicles can pass through privately, even though officially it does not allow even a needle to pass. That is to say, it is passable only for the individual person whose practice accords with nothingness: one is restored to life only in the form of one who is dead, having pursued the way of reason to the end in the depths of absolute critique to face the death that awaits one as one's destiny. The secret entrance to this gate—the transformative action of each individual self—is discovered only through the witness of the individual, who cannot pass through the public way of reason but is allowed to pass through the barrier as a private individual. This would appear to be why the Japanese Zen master Daitō (Myōchō, 1282–1337), who had attained enlightenment by passing this "checkpoint" *kōan* given by Wu-mên, added the comment: "How many can take this same route?" What we have here is a mysterious, lonely way unpassable and yet passable, passable and yet unpassable. There is no way to understand this as an intuition of self-identity, which would obviously make it a publicly accessible passageway, the way of reason.

In an attempt to clarify the logic of Zen, one authority on Zen Buddhism has characterized it as the "discrimination of nondiscrimination." I find the term altogether appropriate, provided it is understood that the words may not be turned around. At first glance, it would seem to make no difference to speak of the "nondiscrimination of discrimination," but in fact the two are far from the same. As the phrase goes, "A hair's difference at the start, worlds apart at the end." For me, "nondiscrimination of discrimination" looks to be the equivalent of the self-identity of absolute contradictions. What at first seems close to the logic of Zen in fact deviates greatly from it. For the "discrimination of nondiscrimination" characteristic of Zen is a *neither/nor*—as in the phrase "Neither do I say that it is life, nor do I say that it is death"—and always shows up in such a way that "nondiscrimination" lies behind it only as the nothingness that holds it together. In contrast, the sense of self-identity spoken of in "the self-identity of absolute contradictories" sets up a "nondiscrimination of discrimination" in the form of *both/and*. Were this not the case, self-identity could not be stated in positive terms. Even though the term "absolute contradiction" is used, insofar as it is also considered self-identical, it is this latter that is meant, however vaguely it is hinted at, and the absolute contradiction in question ceases to be a *neither/nor*. The result is simply an intuition similar to artistic creativity, and therefore distinct from the faith-in-practice of Zen. It may be termed dialectic, but like Hegel's dialectic it is bound hand and foot to Aristotelian self-identity: it cannot shake free of the standpoint of *both/and*.

It is for this reason that the notion of the self-identity of absolute contradictories is liable to objections like those of Kierkegaard, who set forth his standpoint of *neither/nor* in terms of a practical and paradoxical dialectic. If the "discrimination of nondiscrimination" is characterized as a "return to the world" (*gensō*), the self-identity of absolute contradictories may be characterized as a "moving toward the absolute" (*ōsō*). That is, the self-identity of absolute contradictories posits an ontological "contradiction of contradiction"—or identity—but lacks the existential witness of action-faith. Only the "nondiscrimination" of nothingness, which provides for an absolute return to this world through the negation and transformation of the self, can provide discrimination with transcendent unity on practical and paradoxical grounds. This is why Kierkegaard sets up his own practical and paradoxical dialectic in opposition to Hegel's speculative and intellectual one. As the logic of my metanoetics, absolute critique follows the same course as that of Kierkegaard's practical and paradoxical dialectic; and as a self-consciousness in action-faith, it is similar to his standpoint of faith. This unified structure of action-faith-witness gives philosophical consciousness its particular distinctiveness.

I trust the thread of the preceding argument has been clear, even if there is still much wanting in the explanation. As we saw, Kant's critique of reason inevitably leads us to the absolute critique that in turn breaks through the transcendental dialectic to arrive at absolute dialectic. While Hegel's contribution here is highly significant, he did not see the process to its conclusion, namely the point of what I call absolute critique. I have therefore had to reject Hegel's identical reason but also to give special importance to Kant's idea of practical faith, since it is my aim to mediate knowledge and faith by action. Metanoetics is precisely the concrete performance of such mediation in action, which is why my position shows a marked similarity to that of Kierkegaard in terms of its approach to history.

Chapter 3

Absolute Critique
and Historicity

The historicity implicit in the critique of reason · The historicity of the notion of transcendental synthesis · The reciprocal circularity of history · The fundamental structure of history · The triune mediation of the logic, critique, and history of science · Circularity and antinomy · Absolute criticism in history · Contingency in history · The laws of nature and history · The contingency and "thrownness" of the past · The free "project" of history · The "project" of the future · The transforming mediation of contingency and freedom · Freedom as the core of history · Absolute mediation in time · Freedom and the asymmetry of time · The structure of self-consciousness as transformation through action · The metanoetical structure of time · An analytical critique of Heidegger's ontology of time · The freedom of the relative and the absolute · The unity of the absolute through action and contemplative identity · Heidegger's view of history · The philosophy of history and metanoetics · The historicity of metanoetics · The absolute mediation of dialectics and the despotism of theism · The circular unfolding of history and immanent transcendence · The obstacles of pantheism and theism to history · The inadequacy of the dialectic of Hegel's Phenomenology of Mind · The mediatory relationship of religion, history, and philosophy · The abstractness of history in Hegel · Nietzsche's will to power and view of history · A metanoetical interpretation of Nietzsche's thought

In the preceding chapter I endeavored to explain what I mean by the absolute critique wherein the critique of reason brings its principle to consummation. Before embarking on the absolute critique of history referred to there, I should like first to consider how the historical element implied in the critique of reason necessarily leads us to absolute critique, and why history and absolute critique are therefore inseparably related.

Kant's critique of pure reason, as is well known, presupposes the fact of scientific knowledge or the transcendental synthesis of reason in general. From there he goes on to inquire into the question of justification (*quid juris*). What he calls transcendental method is simply the procedure he adopts to answer this question. Science and morality, of course, belong to history, but Kant worked within a rational framework that neglected the historical. He took the transcendental synthesis as something eternal and unchangeable in form, even though its matter is susceptible to change; for him, it was something possessed of necessary and universal validity. As theoretical knowledge, however, the categories or forms of the transcendental synthesis are *not* eternally unchangeable. Their development follows the course of science in history, as the history of science clearly teaches us.

Consider the notion of number, thought to be the simplest and most universal of concepts. It was through Arabian mathematics in the Middle Ages that the concept of natural number first became systematized. In Greek geometry, arithmetic did not develop into a complete system because it lacked a method of symbolization. The systematization of natural numbers cannot in principle exist apart from the development of arithmetic as science, since the concept of the natural number cannot achieve a precise scientific determination without the assumption of mathematical induction. In other words, the concept of number is a historical product whose appearance had to conform to the historical development of mathematics.

The same can be said of the category of causality. It would appear that one of the main purposes of Kant's critique of pure reason was to defend this category—which is fundamental to natural science in general and to physics in particular—against Humean skepticism in order to provide a basis for Newtonian physics. The notion of causality is bound inseparably to that of force or the cause effecting change in things in a state of motion or rest. Newton, who saw force as the potency of remote action, constructed his physics on the principle of universal gravitation. But even in his time there was never any lack of doubt concerning the idea of remote action; quite to the contrary, it gradually came to gain the ascendancy. It was the tendency to deny remote action by admitting only direct, contiguous action that led to the physics of "field" which separated the concept of force from that of causality by a geometrization of physics. At the same time, positivism, which may be viewed as a restoration of Hume's idea, worked to expel the concept of force from physics. In this way both the concepts of causality and of force were all but eliminated from physics. Recent neo-quantum theory, it should be noted, has demonstrated the unsuitability of the category of causality for dealing with micro-phenomena, as a result of which the scope of its validity has come to be further restricted in present-day physics. From all of this, it is clear that even so fundamental a category as causality cannot enjoy unalterable, universal validity.

The category of substance, which is taken to be as fundamental as that of causality, is also of limited applicability since it has been shown to be incompatible with the geometrization of physics. In place of the Kantian understanding of material substance, a "functional" approach has taken hold. By replacing substance with energy, this approach recasts substance in terms of energic dynamics and brings it closer to the notion of causality, endeavoring to conjoin the two concepts by means of the mathematical concept of function. Given the basic orientation of the new physics of our own day, with its synthesis of relativity theory and quantum theory, it is inevitable that the two categories will be related to each other. Indeed, we may go so far as to predict that the principle of this combination will be the principle not of identity but of dialectics. In my view, the action-witness of absolute nothingness, verified through new experiments, will render such a unity possible. At any rate, there can be no doubt that the categories need to be understood as historical in accord with the development of science.

In the case of Kant's moral theory, his doctrine of formal, subjective morality appears at first sight to contain truth of the same invariable universality that characterizes transcendental principles. But such fundamental concepts as personality, freedom, autonomy, and so forth, which he takes as constructive principles of moral subjectivity, are not mere formal synthetic concepts like the formal, logical categories of the theoretical realm. Rather, they determine the contents of the moral subject, and thus can never exist apart from the historical environment of the subject. It is now taken for granted that these concepts, including Kant's theory of formal morality itself, are part of the history of moral thought in modern Europe. Kant's ahistorical rationalism, like the idea of natural law, is a historical product of his time.

In the realm of science as well as in the realm of morality, the whole array of transcendental synthetic ideas have thus to be seen as historical facts. Yet Kant's transcendental method presupposes the existence of the transcendental synthetic ideas and focuses its inquiry on the transcendental ground (*quid juris*) of their validity. This search for a basis to distinguish truly valid concepts from those that lack validity is what makes the transcendental method a critical method. The transcendental deduction expounded in the *Critique of Pure Reason* is the working out of this method. In contrast with what is known in ordinary logic as the method of inference—the derivation of the particular from the universal—the deduction referred to here assumes the synthesis as an actual fact and seeks the *ground* of its existence, which must then in each case accord with the fact to be grounded. It is never merely a matter of the particular being derived directly from a self-determining universal. Following juristic terminology, deduction is taken to mean "justification" for what is factually given—a propositional *quid juris*—and presupposes the transcendental thesis as fact—the propositional *quid facti*. At the same time, this latter becomes the ground because the former is inferred from it by logical deduction. In other words, transcendental deduction is not a simple derivation like general logical deduction, but a reciprocal one.

Obviously this has nothing to do with the fallacy of circular reasoning proscribed by formal logic, but it is a sort of circular reasoning nonetheless in the sense that it consists in a reciprocal mediation. Strictly speaking, even the deduction of ordinary logic, insofar as it is a method for obtaining concrete scientific knowledge, can take place only when it is bound reciprocally to inductive inference, and thus amounts to another version of circular reasoning. Pure deductive inference is no more than hypothesis, incapable of yielding any real knowledge. The historicity of reality contains an element of historical contingency that cannot be inferred deductively. We can do no more than recognize it for what it is, just because it *is*. Deductive inference must be mediated by and answer to the reality it presupposes. Deduction based on such a presupposition is therefore circular in its reasoning. Indeed, no knowledge of historical reality can avoid this circular reciprocity: in history, everything constitutes a reciprocal circularity. The same holds true also for the relationship between reality and our knowledge of it, since the relationship of subject and object is also reciprocal and needs to be mediated by practice. This is why theoretical knowledge cannot avoid circular reasoning mediated by action.

The circularity in transcendental deduction thus turns out to be one mode of a more general circular reasoning. As mentioned above, in his preface to the second edition of the *Critique of Pure Reason*, Kant compares the transcendental method to the experimental method in natural science, noting that experimentation assumes essential structures that have been previously imposed on objects by our imagination in accord with the laws of reason, and only later demonstrates these structures to be attested to by real objects themselves. But if this is true, there is no room for *creatio ex nihilo*, no scientific discovery to which experiments might lead when mere theories fail or lead us up a blind alley. Seen this way, experimentation remains a process of continual verification and reformation, with no prospect of any qualitative leap to epoch-making discoveries in the history of science. For such developments to take place, human reason must be driven through the impasse of contradiction to its own death. And there, mediated by the transformation of absolute nothingness, it must be restored to a middle way that belongs to neither pole of the contradiction but develops into a new theory as a synthesis of both. This is the circular movement of creativity, a "revolution-*qua*-restoration" that forms the basic structure of history. The task of the critique of reason as a critique of science is to trace the history of science in order to bring this fundamental insight to self-consciousness.

The structure of historical reality referred to above represents the foundations on which Kantian deduction is forever engaged in circular reasoning as a process for the justification of scientific values. Values are to be investigated not in connection with the facts of nature but in connection with concrete (historical) subjectivity, that is, in connection with self-consciousness as the subject that justifies scientific knowledge. The knowledge of history or the self-consciousness of the practical construction of history cannot be derived merely from universal principles. The ideal toward which it is oriented is one in which the circle of reciprocal reasoning leads to an increased tenseness of opposing forces, until any remaining slack is finally removed. Thus the knowledge of history advances to the realization of the core of historical reality by constituting a circularity of "evolution-*qua*-involution." In other words, history is not a rectilinear process but a circular one that has to be seen as a "conservation-*qua*-development." This is the fundamental dynamic of history.

To explain this fundamental structure of history in terms of the structure of time, we would say that it constitutes a circularity in which a continual reformation directed at the future is carried out practically in such a way as to effect a deeper return to the past and a restoration of original sources to a more genuine form. The eternal present serves here as a pivot around which "revolution-*qua*-restoration" moves in our faith and witness, thus making history possible. So long as transcendental deduction remains only the projection of this triadic structure in the self-awareness of human theoretical consciousness, it is only natural that it should bring about a reciprocal circularity.

But once the transcendental deduction is taken as a reciprocal mediation in circularity, we must abandon the autonomy that Kant proposed for reason in his *Critique of Pure Reason*. Our approval of circularity implies an abandonment of the logic of self-identity in reason and an overcoming of its law of contradiction. The authentic circularity of the dialectic consists in this, that our outward progress toward distinction and opposition is already an inward return to a unified self. To shun this kind of circularity on the grounds that it is incompatible with the demands of reason is to opt for disruption and inconsistency. It is to forfeit the sort of close relationship among the various stages of circular process that "repetition" can furnish, and to end up with each of the stages disjointed from the others.

This is precisely the conclusion to which absolute critique led us in the last chapter. Circular reasoning and the antinomies of reason are two sides of one and the same thing: to flee the one is to fall prey to the other. The unfolding of the circular reasoning of the *Critique of Pure Reason* into the antinomy of absolute critique follows as a matter of course. The limitations built into the very structure of the transcendental method destine it for absolute critique. Even if we retreat before the antinomies inherent in human reason, as Kant did, and consequently abandon metaphysics as an exact science, we have still to recognize metaphysics as a natural disposition. As soon as we try to satisfy this demand for metaphysics by means of the postulates of practical reason, the antinomies of practical reason rise up unavoidably before us. The only way to escape the problem is to call upon the principle of religion which supersedes reason from within the limits of reason. Such are the self-contradictions into which reason inevitably falls when it tries to elude the absolute critique of metanoetics.

The limitations of the transcendental method just referred to—in particular, the circularity of transcendental deduction, where the limitations are most apparent—belong to the essential structure of history, as explained above. In other words, the circular structure of the absolute reciprocal relativity that marks historical reality in general, and the overall antinomies that constitute two sides of the same reality, make their appearance in accord with the requirement of reason to criticize itself, to bring its antinomies to final consummation, and to have assurance of its autonomy. Hence the absolute disruption of absolute critique. To continue, I should like to clarify the broad outlines of the absolute criticism of the structure of historical reality.

Among the fundamental characteristics of history, we may begin with contingency. We have just seen that transcendental deduction cannot derive historical fact from universal principles, but must seek in historical fact a clue to universal propositions presupposed in the deduction. This led inevitably to the introduction of circular reasoning into Kantian deduction, since it is particular historical facts that prompt us regarding the correct use of deduction. The particular historical fact cannot be deduced from universal principles. This is its absolute contingency: it must be recognized as being simply because it is. The impossibility of deduction is what makes history what it is at core. This primordial contingency—the fact that what might possibly not have existed now exists—is one of the main things that sets history off from nature. As far as nature is concerned, the fact of its being determined by universal law is its distinguishing feature, as we see clearly expressed in Kant's critical philosophy. This means that no contingency in the proper sense of the term is allowed to exist in nature, that the particular can be grounded in universal and necessary law by deductive reasoning. This is why the concept of freedom, which always entails the contingency that its opposite might exist, is regarded as diametrically opposed to nature. Furthermore, insofar as the world of morality expounded in Kant's moral philosophy takes nature as its model, and in spite of the fact that it is aimed at achieving freedom, its final state shows it to be a world determined by laws and necessitated by reason. This is why the Kantian moral world is to be seen as a world controlled by natural law, and why Kant was prevented from grasping the proper meaning of history.

At the beginning of the nineteenth century, the historical method enjoyed ascendancy over natural-law theory in the field of jurisprudence. Indeed, it was advocated as the proper method for the science of culture in general, resulting in the rise of the historical school. According to the view of historicism, as this trend is known, the state of culture characteristic of a particular nation cannot be deduced from universal natural law. Historical reality is to be taken as it is, and its individual characteristics clarified on that basis. Where history is concerned, therefore, the first thing to be acknowledged is its contingency. All particular evaluations of historical content aside, it is in the contingency of history itself that formal grounds for the opposition between particular knowledge of historical facts and universal knowledge of natural science are to be found.

Turning from historical facts to our own existence, contemporary existential philosophy speaks of the contingency of historical facts as our "thrownness" (*Geworfenheit*), a term used to express the past of Dasein. We must accept actual facts for their contingency and their inability to be grounded on reason; they are simply something into whose midst we are "thrown." The past is given to us and, therefore, is contingent. It is not something we can determine at will; we are "thrown" into history and have no alternative but to accept it as it is. This is the primordial contingency of our being. And since our being arises in this way, it points by its very nature to the past. The past, therefore, must embrace part of our being that we are entirely incompetent to dispose of and can only acknowledge as our destiny. This is the contingency of the past; or put the other way around, it is in the nature of the past to be contingent.

Suppose that there were no contingency in the past and that it fell entirely under the sway of natural law. Nothing would have come to pass. Everything would be in the present, repeating itself over and over again (or rather, all things would be simultaneous), and nothing would take place without rational explanation. History, whose essence consists in temporal process, would disappear.

Hence recognition of the contingency of past history is already implied willy-nilly in the commonsense notion that history has to do with the past. The fact that we are interested in past history and seek to know its particulars presupposes, first, that the element of contingency in history is outside our control; second, that we have no choice but to regard it as given to us from without; and finally, that it determines our existence in such a way that our existence has to avail itself of its mediation in order to achieve authenticity. Because the determinative role of the past in our existence mediates our existence, it provides a ground for the being of the self to become authentic through free decision.

In actual history, however, there is another aspect in which the being of the free self, aware of the mediation of the contingency of the past, can crystallize intention into practice and action: the aspect of the future that contemporary existential philosophy refers to as "project" (*Entwurf*). Whatever lacks the element of free action does not belong to history but to nature. History consists in the transformation of contingency into freedom. And freedom, of course, presupposes contingency in the sense that contingency stands opposed to natural necessity, yet cannot of itself be free since it lacks subjectivity. For in addition to containing contingency, freedom belongs to the self-consciousness of the subject which transforms contingency into determinative decision. Contingency implies the equal potentiality of opposites and lacks any principle for determining which one will be affirmed in actuality. Lacking such a principle, it is not liable to the control of human reason, since there is no subject capable of making a choice between the possibilities. In short, contingency means a complete absence of any subjectivity that might control its undetermined status.

Freedom, on the contrary, means turning contingency into the choice and decision of the subject. It means transforming "having no principle" into "having its own principle." Insofar as freedom lacks principle, it is contingent; but freedom cannot merely remain contingent. It becomes real when the subject turns this lack of principle into principle by taking over the determination (destiny) of contingency as its own will, changing it into the content of its own decision, and rendering itself capable of overcoming contingency by submitting itself to it. Freedom makes it possible for the subject to identify itself with contingency through its decision. It is through this subject that contingency is transformed into freedom.

As to the question of how such freedom arises, there is no answer and can be none. For if there were any reason to be given, it would no longer be a matter of contingency but of necessity, and freedom would cease to be. Being that does not arise spontaneously cannot be called free. This is why there is no demonstrating the freedom of being. Freedom exists only in the subject's self-consciousness of being free. Only the subject that realizes freedom through its action has freedom. Contingency, too, is understood to be contingent only through the free subject that experiences its susceptibility to being the opposite of what it is. No contingent being as such can determine its own contingency. Only the subject, which is able to experience opposites, can come to an awareness of the mode of contingency.

Attention should be drawn here to the fact that, in general, the category of modality belongs to the free reflection of the subject. There is no distinction of modalities in nature. It is only in virtue of a freedom conforming to the facts of history that modalities come to be distinguished from one another. To arrive at self-consciousness and subjectivity, freedom has to be seen as preceding contingency, and the latter as no more than one element abstracted from the former. Contingency is brought to self-consciousness only when it is mediated by freedom. The same holds for the temporal modality of the past, since it is only through the mediation of a free "pro-ject" into the future that the modality of the past comes to consciousness. There is no self-consciousness of "thrown-ness" as such. Since self-consciousness belongs to the activity of the free subject, there can be no thrownness without a subject that projects itself into the future in order freely to determine its own being. Were this not so, consciousness of time itself would be impossible, and the thrownness and contingency of the past could never reach consciousness. Freedom, not contingency, is the principle of history and the essence of reality. Without a self projecting itself and freely making plans, there is no history of reality. History is the trail of footprints left by freedom.

To carry the argument a step further, we need to inquire as to how the "thrownness" of the past can be combined with the "project" of the future to give a single unified sense of time. Obviously, without contin-gency there can be no freedom. An individual completely determined by the necessity of universal law is not a historical individual. Insofar as history is possessed of contingency, it does not consist of anything created in conformity with law, nor does it admit inquiry into the ground of its being. In other words, history is not something we determine on our own, but rather something through which we are determined, some-thing given to us from the past that precedes us. This is why history is regarded as belonging to the past and as diametrically opposed to free-dom, which relates to the future.

As a spontaneity that cannot be deduced according to laws, freedom has similarities with contingency. Indeed, as we have just noted, without contingency there could be no freedom. Yet freedom is diametrically opposed to contingency: it is not something given by which we are determined, but something we ourselves determine and transform into necessity by voluntary choice. The fact that the contingency of the past and the freedom of the future have something in common and yet oppose each other creates a conflict of forces in which the exertion of the one implies the expulsion of the other. In short, they form a *real* contradiction and not a merely formal logical contradiction; or in other words, theirs is a dynamic opposition, not a static one. Freedom and contingency stand in a relationship of conflict and contradiction. They "consume" one an-other. Such is their correlativity that if only one of them "consumes" the other, both must disappear. The reason is that, dynamically speaking, opposites are always correlative; one can only exist because its opposite also exists. That is to say, dynamic opposition is marked by the fact that even though—or rather, precisely because—opposites are contradictory and incompatible, they require one another.

But how do the conflict and correlation of contradiction relate to each other? And how is the contradiction between contradiction and unity to be resolved? Already in the formulation of the problem we see the infinite regress to which it leads. From a finite standpoint, there simply is no solution. The only thing we can do is awaken to the realization that in absolute contradiction the contradiction contains a unity within itself, even though the contradictories do not cease to be contradictory; and that absolute unity contains within itself a contradiction (of contradictories), even though it does not cease to be a unity. In other words, we have to see that both the contradiction and the unity are maintained by being negated, and that each corresponds so profoundly to the other that the more it asserts itself, the more it denies itself. Absolute contradiction restores contradiction back to unity by bringing it to the point of a contradiction of contradiction. This is an essential feature of reality itself, whose fundamental structure is time. It is the dialectic inherent in the logic of reality that transcends the principle of identity of formal logic. This is the structure of the actual being of the self, the source of its existence. Further, the fact that we become conscious of something or think of it is based on this principle. As to how contradiction and unity can be brought to unification, we cannot say. All we can do is acknowledge the fundamental fact that it does. This acknowledgment itself is what is meant when we speak of contradiction as unity. To be determined is to determine; negation is affirmation, and affirmation can be affirmation only because it mediates negation within itself. The principle of being is nothingness, and being exists only as a mediative moment of absolute nothingness.

To judge merely on the basis of the formal determination mentioned above, since all that is being asserted is that a contradiction and a unity give rise to the further unification of contradiction and therefore constitute an infinite series, it would seem at first glance that the opposition between contradiction and unity is merely reciprocal and symmetrical. The same thing can be seen in the modalities of time. Past and future are opposed to each other as contradictories: they are equal in the sense that both are nonexistent in the present. However, insofar as they are nonetheless able to establish the unity of time, it is not enough simply to stress their nonexistence. It must also be seen that the negation—their nonexistence in the present—serves the mediating function of grounding the assertion that they "exist" in the present in the true sense of the word. To the extent that this is true, we may conceive of "the presence of the past," which makes it possible for the past to exist, and "the presence of the future," which makes it possible for the future to exist, as brought to a unity-in-contradiction in the absolute eternal present as "the presence of the present."

As is well known, Augustine's theory of time developed this structure ontologically. In his analysis, however, the future and the past appear equally determined as the existence of the nonexistent, and in that sense are symmetrical. This is clearly seen in his characterization of the eternal present as a *nunc stans*. But if time means simply that in the eternity that transcends and comprehends the past, the present, and the future, the nothingness (nonexistence) of the past and the nothingness of the future are juxtaposed symmetrically and brought to unity in the center point of the present, then time falls out of the picture. It is degraded into space. The stream of time ceases to exist; the process of time which goes from the past through the present to the future disappears.

Time is never horizontal; it is always sloped. Unless its process is so conceived, it cannot be called time. It is not enough to juxtapose symmetrical foci on a conical curve to indicate the contradiction of time. The contradiction of time is closer to the asymmetry of a parabola than to the symmetry of an ellipse or a hyperbola. That is, time is determined by the past and breaks through this determination toward the future. This is what characterizes the spontaneity of action and establishes freedom.

As noted earlier, time consists in being determined by the past and being free toward the future. The unity of being determined and determining, of being determined and breaking through determination, represents an awakening of self-consciousness without which there could be no such unity. The very structure of self-consciousness is such that the self that is determined, and therefore negated, breaks through its determination to an affirmation—a negation of negation, or a disruption of opposition—which brings about the unity of self.

In effect, this means that time can be grounded only in a phenomenology; ontology alone is not sufficient. In attempting to treat time and its flux ontologically, ancient philosophy missed the essential feature of time. It is only with Augustine that its basic structure is illuminated. This is related in turn to a shift in Augustine's standpoint from ontology to phenomenology, wherein he begins to treat the modalities of time phenomenologically in terms of the intentionality of consciousness, allotting the past to memory, the present to perception, and the future to anticipation. In so doing, he is hardly in complete accord with the tradition of metaphysical psychology and its ontological notion of the soul. His shift of standpoint represents a shift from being to the self. Time, he saw, cannot adequately be understood from the standpoint of being, but comes to consciousness only through the standpoint of the self. In other words, the concept of being belongs to the being of self-consciousness.

It is interesting to note here that Heidegger, who belongs to the circle of those pursuing existential philosophy in terms of the ontology of self-consciousness, entitled his major work *Being and Time*. In defining the past in terms of "thrownness" (*Geworfenheit*) and the future in terms of "project" (*Entwurf*), Heidegger bases himself entirely on an ontology of self-consciousness. The crux of the distinction between the definitions of Heidegger and Augustine lies in the fact that whereas Augustine's begins from the intentionality of consciousness, Heidegger begins from a definition of the being of self-consciousness that goes beyond psychology. Despite its phenomenological nature, Augustine's standpoint is like Husserl's transcendental phenomenology in its failure to free itself completely from psychology. It is only with Heidegger's hermeneutical phenomenology that a new ontology of self-consciousness is established that makes it possible to explain the essential structure of time. It seems to me that it was mainly in order to provide a solid foundation for his "being of self-consciousness" that Heidegger abandoned the concept of eternity that serves as a fixed point of mediation in Augustine's philosophy, and that he took his start from the fact that in self-consciousness the determined is at once the determining, thus defining the contradictory unity between the past and the present as a *geworfener Entwurf*, a "thrown project." Clearly the structure of Augustine's "eternal now" as "the presence of the present" whose essence it is to unify the three modalities of time—as "the presence of the past" and "the presence of the future"—belongs to ontology rather than to phenomenology. Heidegger's concept of "thrown project," on the contrary, refers to the contradictory unity of the being of self-awareness, and as such can never possess an identity determined after the manner of "substance-quality." "Thrown project" signifies a transformation wherein the negative determination of self-consciousness as "thrownness" is willingly embraced as a matter of necessity, and is thereby broken through to a freedom that affirms the self. Accordingly we are dealing here with a concept that is to be realized practically through action, in contrast with the identical substance-quality determination of being, which is grasped from a standpoint of mere contemplation.

Although existential philosophy shows this practical nature of self-consciousness, its principal difference from metanoetics is that it regards self-consciousness as an activity based on self-power, whereas for metanoetics self-consciousness must be a transformation based on the great activity of Other-power. The need for conversion and transformation is already suggested by the negative affirmation of being "thrown," but is fully realized only through the mediation of nothingness. Self-consciousness is a unity of contradictions occurring in a process of transformation where the negation of self comes to mediate an affirmation, where the determined becomes the determining.

Because self-consciousness arises from such a transformation of the self, it must at least be practical. This is why self-consciousness is referred to as "inner action" (*innere Handlung*), although it is impossible to imagine action as purely inner. Action is always a unity of the inner and the outer. When we speak of ourselves as *being determined*, we necessarily presuppose something outside of ourselves, whereas when we speak of ourselves as *determining*, we are referring to something coming from within. This being so, it is clear that there must be a unity between inner and outer, insofar as the two are brought to unity in transformation. Action is the unity of the inner and the outer in the process of transformation that constitutes self-consciousness.

Self-consciousness, then, cannot be understood simply as the inner moment of action, but implies a reflection, or a return, of action to the self. Posed against this orientation of action returning to the self, or self-consciousness, is intuition, which is oriented outward, toward the other. When the content of some past event is preserved in memory and brought to recollection, it undergoes a change, mediated by the spontaneity of the self, and turns toward the future. In thus being submitted to a synthetic decision in the present, it becomes intuition. Self-consciousness may be called a unity of nothingness, because the spontaneity of the decision involved in determining and acknowledging the conformity of the past and the future with the contents of memory represents the unity of the aspect of action that is oriented to nothingness, through whose mediation the process occurs. In contrast, intuition represents the aspect of action that is oriented toward being, and as such manifests the variety of the contents of memory. Action therefore means accommodating the spontaneous decision of self-consciousness to intuition and thereby altering the content of the latter. This action, it goes without saying, needs to be self-conscious. Without self-consciousness, movement may be possible, but not the action of a spontaneous self.

Further, the being of self-consciousness must be practical, arising as it does in the self-consciousness of a free being. Whereas the genealogy of the ontology worked out by Heidegger can be traced directly to Husserl's transcendental phenomenology, there is no denying its close kinship with Kant's philosophy of freedom. Just as Heidegger related his theory of time to Kant's transcendental scheme, so also his notion of the being of self-consciousness—that is, of *Existenz*—corresponds to Kant's conception of practical reason: both are the subjects of freedom. It is only natural that his treatment of the being of self-consciousness should also show close ties to Fichte's science of knowledge (*Wissenschaftslehre*). In his existentialism, however, Heidegger breaks through the idealism propounded by Kant and Fichte to arrive at transformation through action that goes far beyond the self-identity of consciousness, bringing him to a nihilism close to Nietzsche's *amor fati*. In this sense, Nietzsche is the real precursor of Heidegger's philosophy.

There is no doubt that the practical subject of thought, even though it is determined by the past, breaks through this determination and possesses an infinite opening oriented toward the future that turns the determined into the determining. Heidegger refers to the unity of the conversion out of which the self-consciousness of existence arises as "ecstatic horizon," but to speak of horizon is to speak of limits on all sides. What is devoid of limitation cannot be a horizon. Since a horizon signifies a movable boundary that expands and contracts as one moves forward or backward, up or down, from a given standpoint, it cannot be free of all limitation. The horizon of time, however, differs from an ordinary spatial horizon, which is limited on all sides. A spatial horizon, however far its outer limits are extended, cannot possess the ecstatic character of time. Ecstasy signifies a going beyond or overcoming (*ek-stasis*) of a previously determined self. It is a breaking through the self, a transformation from the determined to the determining. Action, as we have been speaking of it here, is ecstatic in the strict sense that the realization of a higher and deeper self is based on a breakthrough, an overcoming of the self in action. This is why action becomes the mediator of self-consciousness.

The horizon of time must be ecstatic because time breaks through and overcomes the free and spontaneous acting self. The asymmetrical, dynamic, and ecstatic character of time is conspicuous here for the

contrast it presents to the symmetrical, static, and comprehensive character of space. The horizon of time is not a "bad infinity" (*schlechte
Unendlichkeit*) that forces its outer limits ever wider and wider like a
circle expanding its circumference horizontally in space; nor is it a "bad
infinity" like the "indefinite" (the *indefinitum* in contrast with the *in-
finitum*) that abolishes all boundaries once and for all. It is rather a
"thrown project" that conforms to and mediates the determination of
the past, a transformation of the determined into the determining, and
therefore has to be seen as an opening up to nothingness.

In attempting to explain the structure of time, I took as a metaphor
the asymmetry between foci or between focus and directrix in a parabola
in contrast with the symmetrical foci in an ellipse or hyperbola, and also
drew attention to the infinite distance between foci in the latter in
contrast with those in the former. Naturally, this sort of metaphor is far
from adequate to describe the characteristic features of time. They do
not permit us to express the unity and correspondence between determination and the breaking through of determination. They are incapable
of drawing attention to the concrete dialectic at work in the transformation of nothingness whereby the negation of determination produces
its affirmation, or conversely, whereby the affirmation of determination
breaks through it and thus negates it. But then again, no form of expression that remains within the realm of being can fully describe what
takes place in the transformation of nothingness. It is impossible to
substitute the spatial terms of being for the temporal symbols of
nothingness.

Still, I would like to suggest that the "structure of reciprocal negation" we have been speaking of as the breakthrough of ecstasy—
wherein the negation of a limit turns around to mediate its affirmation—
can more properly be expressed in terms of a circularity. In this way,
light is shed on the principle of reciprocal mediation according to which
the determinations of the past are never simply fixed without any mediation from the present, but are correlative to the self that affirms them
and are therefore mediated by freedom.

There is more to the temporal past than contingent determinations
that we have simply to acknowledge and reconcile ourselves to as given.
Past determination itself is correlative to how and in terms of which
beings we affirm it. There is therefore a sense in which the past already
holds the future and is mediated by it. In fact, our experience accords
with how we as subjects affirm the determination of the past, which in
turn fixes the nature of our being. In this sense, the determination of the

past depends on how we mediate it and is endowed with meaning according to its relation to the future.

This is why metanoesis can be spoken of as a principle constituting the fundamental form of action. In metanoesis the past is not merely a "thrownness" that has passed away and is out of our control, but a present incessantly renewing its meaning and caught up in an unending circularity in accord with the future that mediates it. We might say that "thrown projection" is transformed into a "projecting thrownness."

Self-consciousness arises in a circular development-*qua*-return, where the orientation of the development is contradictory and negative, while that of the return is affirmative and unifying. What is here called "self" is no more than the center of the circularity, moving outward by being continually negated and at the same time forever returning to unity. Moreover, since the return to the past to mediate it to the future and affirm it is a manifestation of the freedom of the self in action, there is nothing immovable like an "immovable now." Only absolute motion is brought to self-consciousness by this circularity.

Some question still remains as to whether the self-consciousness of pure movement is itself immovable and whether motion can be brought to self-awareness without immovability, just as the many can be brought to self-awareness only through a one, and contradiction can be brought to clarity only from the standpoint of an identity. But the being of self-consciousness becomes conscious of the self not as being but as nothingness. It becomes conscious of the self not as self-identical but as contradictory. That is, it does not set up the self as something unmoved, but puts it into action and practice as a flux of activity. The self is affirmed not as a self-identical acting subject, but always and invariably as something that is negated.

When I speak of "action," I do not mean that the being (or substratum) of the self changes its qualities, but that being is converted into nonbeing and nonbeing into being, that the very character of being itself is transformed in the process. In other words, action means that absolute nothingness emerges to work in such a way that being is converted into nothingness and nothingness into being. The notion of a self-identical immovable posits a substratum that sustains the movement or qualitative changes in a thing. Here, on the contrary, "action" points to pure movement without any immovable substratum, an incessant conversion in which being is transformed into nothingness and nothingness into being. What is continual in this process (that is, what is not annihilated) is discontinuity (or annihilation itself) and transformation into nothingness.

Nor does the self-consciousness of this fact mean an awareness of a conversion or change occurring in some substratum of the self that continues to exist without being annihilated. If that were the case, we could speak of movement and change, but not of action. There is simply no self-identical something lying beyond and outside of the transforming process of action in order to bring a self-identical unity to action. Were such a unity to ground action, action would not be spontaneous and free; we could not call it action. Thus it is not self-identity but the negation of self-identity that brings unity to action. In other words, since the negation of unity ends up with nothing in the way of an "other," the negation of unity is brought to unity through the mediation of nothingness as other. If there were something general that served as a ground of unity, action would lose the free and spontaneous mobility that makes it action. Action allows for no such ground in being. To suppose a mere incessant motion without any mediation of being would make the question of how transformation and conversion can reach self-awareness still more difficult to answer. The clue to the resolution of this dilemma can rest only with nothingness, which cannot be taken for the sort of "general something" that being is.

For Augustine, eternity is not nothingness but being, which means that it becomes an encompassing, *comprehensive* something that "envelops" all modes of time within itself as an "eternal now." Time thus encompassed makes a breakthrough of time impossible and leads to its establishment as an immovable substance incompatible with negation. Such a time, since it is no longer time, can readily be transformed into space. It was only natural that Heidegger should be led to deny such eternity in his attempt to achieve an awareness of time whose principal characteristic lies in a transformation and a breakthrough of the self. We cannot be permitted to regard eternity as a being that comprehends (*umgreift*) time. As finite, we are incapable of achieving awareness of such an eternity. The demand that the "eternal now" be immanent in us is equivalent to the presumptuousness of making the self one with God. The "eternal now" must be transcendent, and therefore is incapable of being intuited.

Those who dare to demand that such a transcendent be immanent have no alternative but to submit themselves to mysticism, for mysticism is nothing other than a body of assertions meant to confirm an experience of the transcendent somehow made immanent in our finite beings. It maintains that we can have an intuition of the self as transcending itself to become one with that transcendent. In the attempt to satisfy the self-contradictory demand of transcending the absolute in spite of the fact that the relative is completely separated from the absolute, mysticism affirms an intuition of ecstatic union which goes beyond ordinary knowledge. But in the relationship between God and the soul—which can be compared to the relationship between the source of light and the light that emanates from it, as we see for instance in the philosophy of Plotinus, which is one of the historical sources of Western mysticism and may even serve as its prototype—mysticism shows itself incapable of constituting the structure of time wherein God is the pure movement of absolute nothingness mediating a transformation between being and nothingness, while the soul is the acting subject of this transformation mediating absolute nothingness. Reduced to a mere shadow of eternity, time is denied its reality. It is taken as no more than a diluted form of the transcendent eternity of absolute being.

Of course, we also find the view expressed in Plotinus that time is one of the characteristics of soul, a view that prepared the way for a transition from the Aristotelian ontology of time as motion to a phenomenology of time. In this connection, mention is also made of the dialectic whereby, on the one hand, the concentrated unity of beings in eternity is destroyed by the multiplicity of souls, while on the other such unity seeks its own restoration in order for time to produce a fragmented image of eternity. But in approaching the nature of time as an image of eternity rather than attempting to understand it from the viewpoint of action based on absolute nothingness, Plotinus missed the essential core of time: the absolute mediation of the conversion from being to nothingness. Consequent upon his view of eternity, which comprehends time as its substratum, time cannot but be deprived of its independence. From the standpoint of mediatory thinking, which would hold that there is eternity only because there is time, such a conclusion is impossible. Plotinus shares with religion a *Weltanschauung* in terms of which time is seen as the root principle of life and death, of coming to be and passing away, or the source of metempsychosis, and according to which one must make emancipation from the bondage of "life and death" one's ultimate concern. It is only natural that the modern spirit, which puts great stock in the history of present actuality, should attempt to locate the meaning of existence in the freedom of its constructive action. It follows, too, that the theory of time presented by Heidegger should reject the notion of a substratum of eternity.

Are we correct in thinking that the present, as a modality of time, is satisfactorily explained in terms of "facticity"?[1] In Heidegger's view, facticity constitutes a point of contact between the past and the future, from which the organization of "care" (*Sorge*) gets its orientation in actuality. This conception of the present may be explained as a product of the positivistic spirit of historicism, which emphasizes the aspect of the fixed fact in actual reality. According to Heidegger's existential analysis, facticity combines the past as the thrownness of an "already-being-in-a-world" (*Schon-sein-in-der-Welt*) with the future as the project of a "being-ahead-of-oneself" (*sich-Vorweg-sein*) into a "thrown project" (*geworfener Entwurf*).[2]

As noted earlier, however, since "thrownness" and "project" are mutually contradictory, opposing moments, the former can never proceed to the latter as potentiality to actuality. Moreover, I have just been arguing that the dynamics of time, which consist in the reciprocal transformation of being and nothingness, cannot be explained in terms of movement grounded on a substratum of identity. In Heidegger, however, the negation and transformation of "thrownness" through "pro-jection"—breaking through the previously fixed determinations of the past inherent in "thrownness" by means of "projection"—still lacks dialectical development.

The definition he offers for "project," namely the self-consciousness of can-be" (*Sein-können*), is suspiciously close to that of potentiality or possibility in the Aristotelian sense. On the one hand, there is no doubt that his idea of *Sein-können* points to a breaking through of self to beyond the self (*über sich hinaus*),[3] which belongs to the capacity of subjectivity and is voluntary and spontaneous. On the other hand, he fails to distinguish it clearly from the Aristotelian potentiality for identity that constitutes one moment in the movement of a changing process. As a result, his idea of the breakthrough as negation and transformation is apt to be misunderstood as change occurring in a self-identical being.

In fact, there is no possibility that is not mediated by previously fixed facticity. At the same time, as noted above in connection with "thrownness," the fixed facticity of the past is determined in accord with how it is mediated by the free possibility of the self; that is, it is affirmed in correlation to "projection." Therefore, we are speaking not merely of a one-sided determination of projection by facticity but also of the free possibility of projection to determine the nature of facticity. In other words, we might say that absolute nothingness, which is neither facticity nor freedom, determines both of them to exist in correlation, even as it mediates both to itself. The negation whereby nothingness comes into contact with being and vice versa exists in the present. Conversely, since the present divides and separates the past and the future from each other, it renders mutual transformation of past and future possible through the mediation of absolute nothingness and the action of conversion and breakthrough.

Great emphasis is placed on this in Heidegger's philosophy as well,[4] where the dialectic of conversion and transformation is worked out in careful detail. Still, one cannot avoid the impression that the logic of identity prevails in his thinking as far as the transition from the past to the future, or from thrownness to projection is concerned. The reason is that Heidegger's existential ontology remains in the realm of hermeneutics and fails to attain a self-consciousness based entirely on action or practice. Hermeneutics comprehends self-consciousness in action in terms of the interpretation of linguistic expression. As a result, Heidegger's existential ontology falls short of the standpoint of the self-consciousness of absolute nothingness, wherein the action of mediation can truly transform thrownness into project. For him, self-consciousness in action is merely changed into an ontological self-consciousness grounded on a substratum of identity and circumscribed by the interpretation of expression.

In such a scheme, the limitation of the thrownness that lies at the bottom of the being of the self—an "empty nothingness" of the ground of being in terms of which the self does not attain to perfect possession of its ground—turns out at the same time to be the empty nothingness of the ground itself, since the self now can become its own ground through existential projection. The ground ceases to be ground, or rather, the self is its own ground. For in willing the empty nothingness itself, the empty nothingness of the ground becomes the ground. Heidegger terms this sort of "not" (*Nicht*) an "existential nihility" (*Nichtigkeit*), and considers the nihility of the ground as the fundamental guilt (*Schuld*) of one's being (*Dasein*). The awakening to consciousness of this guilt is called conscience, and the resolve to preserve conscience, the freedom of one's being. Hence, projection means turning away from the everyday world of the ordinary person (*das Man*, the "they") to the conscientious freedom of shouldering responsibility for oneself.

As far as its fundamental structure is concerned, I have no doubt that Heidegger's thought is in complete accord with my idea of conversion in and through absolute nothingness. But for Heidegger, the mediation of nothingness through action is taken as a mediation of being in the realm of the interpretation of linguistic expression; he has not realized how absolute nothingness, as the principle of absolute transformation, functions as ground. For this reason, the present for Heidegger lacks the character of "being-*qua*-emptiness," by means of which the present mediates absolute nothingness. In the final analysis, the present becomes the *being* of self-consciousness.

The self of the present, according to Heidegger, does not get beyond the being that bears the burdens of conscience; it does not make nothingness *für sich* through the breakthrough and negation of absolute nothingness. His idea of nihility, which may well be called the Great Nay (*daihi*) since it transcends all forms of negation, is responsible only to the self and lacks the assurance and support of Great Compassion (also pronounced *daihi*) that it is accorded in metanoetics. To this extent, his idea of freedom remains a postulate immanent to the self. It has not the assurance of Great Compassion breaking through facticity in the leap of action and turning being into nothingness.

In other words, Heidegger is not yet aware of the fact that only absolute nothingness can affirm being and transform it into the free project of the self by means of a conversion in action. That Heidegger has little concern for this idea of transformation by means of absolute nothingness is clearly shown in his 1929 inaugural lecture, "What Is Metaphysics?"[5] He does not probe Kant's critique of reason deeply enough to arrive at the standpoint of absolute criticism wherein the criticizing subject itself is abandoned to "absolute disruption," but rather maintains the self as the subject of self-consciousness and interprets being from this point of view. Although he mentions radical nihility, it remains an immanent postulate, not yet the realization of nothingness as transcendent manifestation. His standpoint keeps to the realm of ethics and does not bring him to religion.

In Heidegger's case, the absence of the mediation of absolute nothingness keeps him from providing an adequate ground for temporality in his attempt to replace Augustine's notion of eternity with the self-consciousness of time. His idea of transcendence through ecstatic states of temporality (*Ekstase*) does not get beyond the mere possibility of the self transcending itself in the direction of an absolute. As a result, the autonomy of the relative as mediator of the absolute is not assured. Heidegger's way of thinking belongs to the idea of ōsō (going to the absolute) but not to that of gensō (returning to the relative). In a word, Heidegger cannot get beyond the postulate of idealism which maintains that what "ought" to be should also be possible. But insofar as the ought transcends the mind, the appeal to the "immanence of transcendence" as a "principle of existence" remains incomprehensible.

In order not to consign comprehension of the incomprehensible to mysticism, it is necessary, in the first place, to consider the absolute not as being that reaches from existence to transcendent existence but as absolute nothingness; and second, to understand the reciprocal relationship between the absolute and the relative as the action of absolute mediation. It is necessary to avoid any attempt to interpret the absolute contemplatively as a union of the absolute and the relative in the identity of being. The contemplative unification of the absolute and the relative is based on a demand for supreme identity that is beyond our human ability, and can only end up in the dissolution of the mind into mystical unity. Mysticism does not allow us to regard what is relative as free and autonomous. Similarly, if we take as our starting point the immediate experience of freedom, we are driven to the conclusion that the absolute, insofar as it is transcendent, is an abstract universal with no connection to relative.

I see no way to avoid these difficulties but to adopt the viewpoint I have been setting forth here. In being mediated by the practice and action of the individual, and becoming itself the mediator of absolute transformation in the present, absolute nothingness transforms the thrownness of the past into the project of the future and affirms the facticity of thrownness in the present to the extent that it is mediated by the freedom of projection. Thus transcendent nothingness, which is neither the past nor the future but transcends both of them, mediates the present by transfiguring the being of facticity in the present into a mediation of nothingness and hence into a relative grounded in the absolute. This is what I understand by the immanence of transcendence.

As nothingness, the transcendent absolute mediates the relative through and through and demands its autonomy, thereby securing the freedom of the relative and setting up the unification of the contradiction between the development and the breakthrough of its given facticity as the practice of the relative in the present. Only through an awareness of this transformational mediation can what for Heidegger remains at the level of a mere postulate of possibility be guaranteed and supplied with a transcendent ground.

Since the mediation we are speaking of here is bound irrevocably to the action and practice of nothingness, and is not a contemplation that results in an absolute-*qua*-being, it does not run the risk of leading to the kind of freedom to which Augustine's notion of eternity leads. Because absolute nothingness is the ground of human freedom, to submit oneself to the absolute and serve as its mediator means to be free in the true sense of the term. It means to set one's feet squarely on a ground where one can realize the spirit of detachment referred to in Zen Buddhism as "having-no-thing" (*muichimotsu*), which is the self's own "original countenance." In this way, the transcendent becomes immanent and eternity transforms the present into a state of *ek-stasis*[6] in which the self is broken through. Action no longer belongs to the self in the usual sense of carrying on one's own work according to one's own plan. Instead, a higher spontaneity is made manifest—we may call it "transcendent facticity" or "absolute reality"—wherein the plans and doings of the self are mediated, subsumed, and negated. This is "naturalness" (*jinen-hōni*) in Shinran's sense of the term, an "action of no-action" or activity without an acting self in which action ceases to be merely the doing of the self.

What has hitherto been understood from a Heideggerian standpoint as the action of Existenz must in fact, as already pointed out, be understood as the transformation of absolute nothingness. That is, the former is nothing other than a relative manifestation of the latter, grounded on it and established through its mediation: mere being as "empty being." Even though the coming to be of the present can be interpreted as facticity, its absolute ground is to be found only in the unity of transcendent eternity as absolute nothingness, which can achieve self-consciousness only in and through action. Action is simply the manifestation of being as a medium for the absolute. In Shinran's terminology, it is the Great Action (*taigyō*) that reaches beyond the doings of the self in virtue of the very fact that the self is allowed to practice and act freely and of its own accord. Great Action is not a deed of the self, but a conversion of self-power into Other-power.

To approach the question from another angle, ethics cannot avoid the self-contradiction wrought by the antinomies inherent in the concept of human freedom, its basic principle. Pursued to its final end, ethics is transformed into the absolute nothingness of religion. And yet, in order to function as a mediator of absolute nothingness, human action must be resurrected as empty being by what transcends it. This is the outcome of faith (*shin*) in which the self abandons itself and submits obediently to absolute nothingness, the faith of a self-conscious action based on total self-abandonment. Just as action is not a mere doing, but an obedience to absolute nothingness that signifies conversion of the self to a new realization, so faith is not self-consciousness in the ordinary sense of an immediate affirmation of the self, but a self-consciousness of the annihilation of the self. More than the mere possession of beliefs, faith must be seen as action-faith (*gyō-shin*), a self-consciousness of action carried out in complete reliance on Other-power. In Shinran's words, faith is a "gift from the Tathāgata." Because having faith thus means being made to have faith, the self-consciousness of faith may be said to consist in the self-consciousness of the annihilation of the self; it is the nothingness of self-consciousness.

Since absolute nothingness is always a transformation and a mediation, it can never exist immediately. It cannot exist in the nonmediated existence that Heidegger characterizes as "ontic" (*ontisch*) to distinguish it from the "ontological" (*ontologisch*). Nothingness is by no means immediate. Its truth is realized through one's action and witness (*gyō-shō*), and thus provides a transcendent ground for the mediatory activity of self-consciousness. Since transcendent nothingness confronts the relative self as wholly other and annihilates the self, the human existential freedom that remains a mere postulate or possibility at the level of the ethical self is actualized at the standpoint of religious belief in Other-power as action and witness (*gyō-shō*). Heidegger's ontology is grounded in an ethical self-awareness of freedom as self-power, and thus cannot break away from the hermeneutic standpoint of being with its principle of self-identity. But it is necessary to go further than this, to pass through the antinomies of self-consciousness and the self-contradictions of freedom all the way to absolute critique, to pursue self-consciousness in action all the way to its conversion into religious action and faith (*gyō-shin*) in metanoetics.

Although the influence of Kierkegaard, and indeed of Christian tradition in general from the time of Augustine, is easy to recognize in Heidegger's thought, he develops his philosophy of freedom from the standpoint of "a theology without God," an approach whose contradictions reach back to deeper, ineradicable difficulties in his philosophy. The decisive influence on his atheistic standpoint, as I have stated before, is clearly Nietzsche, who proclaimed himself Antichrist. Thus both Kierkegaard and Nietzsche, whose systems of thought are diametrically opposed despite certain common elements, have left their mark on Heidegger's thought.

In place of Kierkegaard's conception of the "moment" as an atom of "eternity" through which eternity manifests itself in time, Heidegger proposed a nihility which he considers to be the ground of what Nietzsche calls *amor fati*. His fear is that unmediated being—for instance, the will of God that undergirds theism—would make human freedom impossible. Of course, if we identify the will of God with the love of God, and divine grace with the working of divine love, then grace, far from destroying human freedom, only draws it out as it fosters and sustains the activity of human will. This is the solution at which Augustine arrived late in life, after having pondered the problem for many years. It means that the eternity of God and the freedom of the human person are united through mutual mediation.

In this approach God closely resembles nothingness as the principle of absolute mediation. To carry this idea to its logical conclusion, the notion of God as a personal being, as theism understands it, would have to be abolished. Conversely, to avoid this conclusion by positing God as a positive and immediate being, human freedom would be thwarted to the extent that God transcends the determinations of absolute mediation. Here we see the consistency in Heidegger's attempt to establish human freedom by denying theism and adhering to Nietzsche's nihility as the ground of human freedom.

In this connection, one may note that the notion of freedom expressed in Spinoza's "intellectual love of God" (*amor Dei intellectualis*) —an attractive idea despite the unresolvable contradictions in his system—has something in common with Nietzsche's *amor fati*, in that both have to do with a love directed at something by its very nature necessary. Consequently, Spinoza's God of absolute being must be a mediated state embracing within itself absolute nothingness. Both Schelling and Hegel regarded Spinozism as the presupposition of their philosophical systems, both of which were based on dialectical unity.

Nietzsche's affirmation of the past "it was so" in the form, "I willed it so and shall so will it forever,"[7] points to a freedom and liberation resulting from a love of fate. His insistence that the "will to power" can hold sway over necessity by affirming it as its own will is grounded on a nihility that is close to that of Heidegger, who also defines the ground of human freedom (pro-jection) in terms of a radical nihility. In this sense, it is clear that Heidegger's absolute nihilism has something in common with nothingness as the principle of absolute transformation which grounds absolute critique, the logic of metanoetics. Still, his *Nichtigkeit* is the principle of a *Nicht* that is quite different from absolute nothingness. The reasons are obvious. Whereas Heidegger's "not" stops at awareness of the responsibilities of one's conscience, and hence remains an immanent postulate concerning what one ought to be, the nothingness of metanoetics is practiced and witnessed to (*gyō-shō*) as a transcendent principle that converts the self by annihilating it.

In "What Is Metaphysics?" Heidegger speaks of nothingness (*Nichts*) as the principle of the "not" (*Nicht*)—that is, as the principle that precedes all forms of negation in judgment. The result is that his idea of nothingness becomes more static, no more than a setting within which to understand being, a setting which he characterizes in terms like "the bright night of the dread of nothingness." Because our being hangs suspended over the abyss of nothingness and is permeated by anxiety, Heidegger argues, the phenomenon of anxiety shows our being as it is; free Existenz is made possible by our awakening to the opposition between nothingness and being. On this final point, Heidegger's notion of nothingness still has something in common with absolute nothingness, but it is not a principle for the absolute conversion of the self and its restoration to life in death-and-resurrection. His nothingness belongs to being as a category of self-consciousness for interpreting the self.[8] In spite of the negation of nothingness, Heidegger's being, as the subject of self-awareness, remains the same as before, just as the rational self that functioned as the subject of Kantian critique was preserved and sustained through the critique of reason. Existential philosophy seems incapable of overcoming the defects inherited from the standpoint of the critique of reason.

In absolute critique, however, the nothingness of the self becomes a matter of one's action and witness (*gyō-shō*) through the transformation of absolute nothingness, and nothingness is believed to be transcendent. We might express the distinction between Heidegger's existential philosophy and that of absolute critique by saying that the former is a process of going toward the absolute (*ōsō-teki*), whereas the latter is a process of returning to the world (*gensō-teki*). In other words, the former remains immediate (*an sich*) whereas the latter is mediated (*für sich*). Nothingness cannot be realized in its truth from a standpoint of mere immediacy, because a nothingness that is not mediated is immanent in the realm of being, and hence cannot be nothingness in the true sense of the word. Strictly speaking, insofar as Heidegger's nothingness points to a possibility, it remains a postulate, an "ought." It is not true nothingness but a concept of nothingness belonging to being.

Despite the fact that Nietzsche regarded nothingness as the basis of his will to power, his Dionysus is a representative of being, not of the nothingness of the self. Only by exhausting the fullness of life and arriving at death can Dionysus witness to the nothingness of the self. Only by demonstrating the absolute transformation of a passing away in death and a returning in resurrection does absolute nothingness become fully *für sich*. This is what takes place in the death-and-resurrection of absolute critique.

Heidegger's nihility is not a principle through which this death-and-resurrection can be realized in action and witness. The fact that the death with which he is concerned in his work remains a limit-situation bringing to awareness the "possibility of being-as-a-whole," and the fact that awareness of oneself as a "being-toward-death" requires only that one accept death and face it resolutely, together show that it does not have to do with the manifestation of absolute nothingness witnessing (*shō*) to resurrection in the practice (*gyō*) of death. A sharp distinction needs to be drawn here between a merely hermeneutical ontology of self-awareness and the absolute critique that characterizes metanoetics.

We do not necessarily break through and transcend death itself and witness to resurrection merely by facing death resolutely. While this may be possible for sages and heroes, it is not the way of ordinary ignorant people. It is a death interpreted entirely from the standpoint of life, a nothingness interpreted from the standpoint of being. Its standpoint does not get beyond the postulation of the possible, in contrast with the standpoint of action-faith in absolute nothingness at which a true breakthrough of the self occurs. Absolute nothingness supersedes all forms of negation that remain within the domain of the immanent; it entails a turnabout of the self through the transcendent power of the Great Nay–*qua*–Great Compassion. In this sense, existential philosophy may be likened to the doctrine of the sage which teaches a way to salvation through self-power, a way that is closed to the ordinary and the ignorant. For these latter, the absolute critique of metanoetics is the only way. Theirs is the "easy way" (*igyōdō*) which may be likened to the Pure Land path of reliance on Other-power. In this connection, Nietzsche and Kierkegaard, who otherwise stand at opposite poles, share a common religious orientation.

Freedom cannot be constituted from a standpoint that affirms the self immediately. The view that freedom belongs immediately to the limited, relative human self involves a contradiction in the very use of the words "relative" and "limited." For that which is absolutely free cannot be found except in the absolute—that is, in God. At the same time, it must be admitted that we humans enjoy some degree of freedom. Self-consciousness itself arises from freedom; without freedom, there would be no self-consciousness at all. Still, how can the self, which is relative, possess freedom? How is it possible that the relative has a freedom of its own without becoming absolute? Is it possible for so-called human freedom to exist autonomously, apart from the freedom of God, to depend on it without being destroyed by it? Freedom is not something that can be established as a mere fact of direct experience, but a problematic to be faced and solved. At the same time, the antinomies it embraces within itself render it impossible for us to regard it as a mere postulate; the aporia inherent in the notion of freedom stubbornly blocks the way. How much discussion and argument have been focused on this problem since the time of Augustine!

By removing God from the picture, Heidegger attempts to see freedom as a fact of self-awareness and refuses to admit that there is any problem involved. At first glance, and judged from the standpoint of phenomenological self-awareness, this would seem to work. But insofar as his freedom does not get beyond the level of a postulate about possible Existenz, it is clear that his freedom is only a matter of the "ought," not something to be realized in practice through faith (*gyō-shin*) in the transcendent. His is a notional freedom immanent in the self, open to hermeneutics but not to understanding as a fact actualized in a process of transcendence. The self-transcendence or breakthrough of the self which is the basis of Existenz can never be realized so long as freedom remains a phenomenon within the self immediately accessible to consciousness.

Freedom is in need of the ground of transcendent nothingness in order that the self may break through itself without destroying its spontaneity in the process. That is to say, freedom is in need of a transcendent absolute which, in spite of its absoluteness—or rather, precisely because of it—both enables the relative to stand on its own and makes use of it as a medium for realizing its own absoluteness by allowing the relative to exercise its independence and to cooperate with the absolute. For the relative to serve in such a mediating capacity, it must be both immanent and transcendent. Self-consciousness in action shows us this process at work.

This means that the essential feature of the finite relative, seen as a mediator of absolute nothingness, consists in an autonomy determined by the transcendent and lying beyond the self-power of the relative on its own to refuse, and that the conquest of the radical evil latent in the autonomous existence of the relative requires as its ground the transformative power of the transcendent, or absolute nothingness. Accordingly, hermeneutic self-conscious existence must be brought to the point of a self-conscious existence of action and faith (*gyō-shin*) based on Other-power. This change of standpoint takes place when the relative self, lacking the power within itself to break through the antinomies, is forced by absolute critique into the ultimate predicament of finding contradiction itself driven to the point of absolute nothingness (in a negative sense). At this outer limit of "absolute contradiction," contradiction brings itself to unity, as it were, through a contradiction of contradiction; the absolute disruption is made whole again in nothingness; and the powerlessness of the self—the metanoetic practice of self-abandonment—restores the self as a mediator of nothingness. In this conversion to the metanoetic self, the hermeneutic self is led from the ethical self-consciousness of self-power to the religious self-consciousness of action-faith in Other-power. Absolute critique comes to term in the unity of nothingness in the sense that the bringing of unity to absolute disruption and absolute contradiction through nothingness affirms and restores the self that has abandoned itself in metanoesis, so that it may serve as a mediator of nothingness. It is this Great Nay–*qua*–Great Compassion that makes freedom possible.

Understandably enough, Augustine looks to grace for the possibility of freedom. In his view, grace prompts the will but does not force it, and therefore does not destroy freedom. The problem with his theism is that he considers grace to be predestined by the will of God. With good reason Heidegger seeks to avoid this difficulty. His nihilism insists that the ground of human existence is the abyss of empty nothingness, and that human freedom consists in the essential groundlessness of "project," making it clear that his nihility is not a mere void but implies a sense of nothingness as absolute transformation.[9] This is clearly seen in his treatise "On the Essence of Ground,"[10] a short piece into which he has packed many of his basic ideas. There he argues that awareness of the bottomless nihility of Dasein liberates self-consciousness from the being of the past and opens it to the freedom of projection into the future.

As noted before, as long as the task of nothingness is presented in terms of the "will to power" to perform *amor fati*, there is no assurance of its being fulfilled. Only sages can have that sort of assurance. For us ordinary and ignorant ones, vindication must come through the action-faith of Other-power, the Great Nay–*qua*–Great Compassion. In my own case, I commit my freedom back to the Great Nay–*qua*–Great Compassion of absolute nothingness, and as a result a new way opens up through the aporia of freedom spoken of earlier. But it is only by means of metanoetics that I can realize this truth.

As I have tried to make clear, metanoetics is not an awareness of one's own mere self-power but an awakening to the Other-power of the Great Nay–*qua*–Great Compassion. Thus the overcoming of absolute disruption through absolute critique achieved in metanoetics takes place without removing the disruption. The resurrection of the self by the Great Compassion—that is, the process in which the absolute disruption of the self is converted into an affirmation through the mediation of the unity of absolute nothingness, so that it can then cooperate to mediate the absolute—can be confirmed only in the action of metanoetics which involves dying in the Great Nay of absolute critique. The fact that the Great Nay can also be confirmed in metanoetics as the Great Compassion implies that the nothingness of the Great Nay confronts the relative self as absolute, as that which is believed to be an "Other," as a transcendent that turns out to be immanent.

Here we see the essence of absolute mediation. There is no saying which of the two, faith (*shin*) or witness (*shō*), comes first. They arise simultaneously as complementaries, which is why the transcendent is at the same time the immanent. In other words, action based on Other-power is also brought to religious self-consciousness as a trinity of action, faith, and witness (*gyō-shin-shō*). In the *action* of negation the self, driven to absolute disruption in metanoesis, breaks asunder and dies to ordinary life; but at the same time, this action *witnesses* to a change, a conversion in which the self is resurrected by the Great Compassion and reaffirmed in passive, obedient reliance on Other-power. The fact that absolute nothingness, in spite of being an absolute transformation, can be realized as a unity of absolute contradiction, stems from the self-transcendence of *faith* in this Great Compassion.

Since that which the self obeys in faith must transcend the self as an "Other," and since the Great Nay of absolute critique transcends the relative self by virtue of its being absolute, the Great Nay of the transcendent power of negation, even though it is nothingness, is believed in as that over against which the self is posited and through which the self is mediated. It is a transcendent nothingness that serves as a unifying basis and support for self-consciousness. The reason that the unifying force of absolute nothingness, or absolute transformation, remains from first to last nothingness and is not equated with the being of self-identity, is that as Great Compassion it must resurrect the self to being and make it self-conscious of its unique role of witnessing as a mediatory being.

The view that regards this process as the self-identity of absolute contradictories fails to account for this trinity of action, faith, and witness. Its notion of "action-intuition" does not include self-consciousness of the interpenetration of faith and witness through action, nor self-consciousness of the dynamic unity of transcendence and immanence. Instead, it reverts back to the aesthetic contemplation involved in producing a work of art, after the manner of Plotinus who treats action only in terms of its relation to contemplation.[11] A mysticism that lacks the action-faith of the Great Nay and the witness of the Great Compassion cannot furnish a religious standpoint. How can it witness to the absoluteness of its "absolute contradiction"? The attempt of the self to regard itself as absolute without thereby performing metanoesis may lead to a view of the unity of the divine and the human in which the self becomes deified, which would end up in being, the opposite of nothingness.

The dialectic of absolute transformation through which absolute negation—the absolute's complete and utter self-negation—is transformed into an affirmation as the negation of negation, is not the result of the contemplation of self-identity. It is made accessible to faith as the Great Nay that forever remains nothingness even as it bears witness to the Great Compassion. In this faith, the contradictions are brought to unity in spite of the nothingness that keeps them just as they are. Affirmation is not direct affirmation. Nor does resurrection mean restoration to a former state. Without ceasing to be nothingness but precisely because of its nothingness, nothingness becomes the object of our faith-witness vis-à-vis a transcendent unity.

Once nothingness is intuited as the One of Plotinus, however, it ceases to be nothingness and turns into being. It becomes affirmation instead of negation. In its authentic sense, nothingness must remain bound to absolute transformation in action, and in order to perform its mediating role in this transformation, it must be witnessed to in faith through action. The absolute One that Plato deals with in the *Parmenides*, and from which the One of Plotinus derives, corresponds exactly to the transcendent One of absolute nothingness which mediates the transformation of the relative one (the individual self). It is not merely contemplated as self-identical Being, like the One of Plotinus, but is always "practiced" in action.

At first glance, Plato's transcendent One and Plotinus's One would appear to be the same. Actually the two are qualitatively different. Since I am convinced that the extreme position adopted by Plotinus ultimately diverges from the truth, I shall adhere to a standpoint of the self-consciousness of action-faith that follows Plato in proscribing aesthetic contemplation. Even so, Plato's practice of the transformation of the One and the many in the formal categories of existence will not suffice where actual historical reality is concerned. We shall have to concretize the theoretical and practical critique of reason until it is transformed into absolute critique, lest any doubt remain that the Great Nay–*qua*–Great Compassion is revealed through the action-faith-witness of metanoetics.

Unfortunately, in trying to elude the obstacles that theism places in the way of a theory of freedom, Heidegger fails to recognize the transcendent that lies at the ground of time as nothingness-*qua*-eternity, and as a result he falls into atheism. No less unfortunately, and despite the influence of Kierkegaard on his thought, Heidegger has failed to grasp Kierkegaard's regard for repentance as the ineluctable essence of ethics. It is also regrettable that his philosophy does not pursue the spirit of the Kantian critique of reason to its logical conclusion of absolute critique, and that his ethics does not contain the treatment of metanoetics that would develop it in the direction of religious faith. The anthropology that stems from Augustine emphasizes the finitude of the human to distinguish it from the divine, placing human beings in an intermediate state between God and animals. In contrast, Heidegger's anthropology restricts humanity to the realm of temporal being with no reference to eternity. In this regard, his thinking falls short of clarifying human finitude. On the one hand, we see his notions of freedom and death-awareness tremble with a Kierkegaardian anxiety, while on the other we see him longing for the repose of a Nietzschean will to power. Is he not attempting the impossible? Instead of a metanoetic development of the mutual mediation of anxiety and repose as they interpenetrate each other and are transformed into each other as a pure unity in contradiction, Heidegger seems to me ultimately to revert to the mysticism of Eckhart.[12] If this is indeed the case, we are forced to conclude that whereas the dialectic of metanoetics is a philosophy suited to ordinary, ignorant persons such as I, Heidegger's existentialism is a philosophy meant for the sage.

In order to point out the problems involved in Heidegger's theory of time and to clarify the shortcomings of his standpoint, it has been necessary to venture rather deeply into his philosophy. The results of our treatment may be summarized as follows: The dialectic underlying Heidegger's theory of time has been developed insufficiently because of his standpoint of hermeneutics; accordingly, the transcendence of absolute nothingness which provides a basis for the ecstatic unity of time cannot become the action-faith-witness of eternity. The conversion of the past into the future, and the interpenetration of the two that takes place in the present, remains a postulate that is assumed immediately by the hermeneutical self without the self being conscious of it as a manifestation of eternal, transcendent nothingness; accordingly, ethics based upon self-power remains bound to the closed standpoint of human existence and fails to open a new vista on the eternal. His atheism suppresses religious faith and remains from first to last a philosophy of finite freedom, and instead of pursuing the critique of reason to its logical conclusion so as to arrive at absolute critique and its accompanying absolute disruption as the inavoidable consequence of ethics, it prevents the critique of reason from entering the path of metanoesis; accordingly, his philosophy may be characterized as a philosophy for the intelligentsia that gives assurance of unity with the absolute.

Heidegger himself believes that by taking this approach to time, he has clarified the structure of history.[13] And indeed, there is no denying that one of his most important contributions lies in his approach to the problem of history from the aspect of the transience of Dasein, in contrast with usual philosophical approaches that attempt to interpret the historical in terms of a commonsense, popular idea of time. Heidegger acknowledges as the ground of history a subject who confronts the future by appropriating the past and, by embracing historical facticity as its destiny, freely resolves to accept the finitude of the self. While the idea owes much to Nietzsche, Heidegger's contribution is an important one. Nevertheless, according to Heidegger's ontology of time, projection toward the future belongs to the realm of "interpretation" and "understanding"—categories characteristic of hermeneutics—and is not truly action based on absolute nothingness; similarly, his idea of resolve and decision in the face of death remains a self-awareness of mere finitude, and does not achieve the level of faith-witness of the eternal Great Action (*taigyō*) in which the self truly practices "dying its own death."

As a result, Heidegger's philosophy tends toward a revival of the master-disciple pattern of transmitting tradition rather than toward the continual revolution-*qua*-restoration involved in the leap to the religious decision of "dying one's own death."[14] He correctly interprets the notion of "repetition" as the restoration of the past to self-consciousness by means of the decision of the authentic subject—which he takes from Kierkegaard—and therein locates the essence of tradition.[15] For Kierkegaard, repetition does not point to a self-identical being but to eternity through a death-and-resurrection in which dialectical negation must affirm being (through repetition) as mediating the manifestation of nothingness. For Heidegger, repetition shows rather the tendency to become the repetition of self-identical being. Kierkegaard clearly asserts that repetition belongs to the category of transcendence,[16] an assertion made possible by his standpoint of faith. But the sort of idealistic transcendence that Heidegger's approach recommends cannot shake free of the limitations of the identity of relative being, and this means that he cannot completely overcome historicism in the sense of a traditionalism or revivalism.

Hermeneutics is always accompanied by historicism. But history cannot get free of the relativism involved in "historicism" if it is deprived of the unity of transcendent nothingness in the "eternal now." To the extent that history, as the manifestation of absolute nothingness, provides a basis for transcendent unity while being correlative with each moment of the present, a mediation is established in the form of a relative-*qua*-absolute, thus guaranteeing the unity of the historical world. Repetition is authentic repetition insofar as it is also the negation of repetition. Unity is nothing other than the transcendent quality of nothingness. Absolute mediation effects a circularity (of the past and the future) not in the identity of being but in the unity of nothingness. But this has nothing to do with the repetition of hermeneutics. As far as hermeneutics is concerned, the absolute unity of nothingness disappears from the picture precisely because it is not immune to the relative identity of being. Hermeneutics is too historical to be authentically historical.

The fact that the philosophy of history since Augustine has been inseparable from the philosophy of religion cannot be unrelated to the concomitant persistence of a notion of time as based on eternity. Heidegger seems to break this relationship. His hermeneutics appears at first glance to stand on the side of the positivistic reality of history, but in fact it has not escaped idealistic subjectivism. In particular, what Heidegger designates as the common world represents a mutuality of human persons mediated by a common environment, in which people relate to one another through the medium of tools. It does not take into account the religious world of Existenz communicating with Existenz. The common world is a product of abstraction bound to atomistic liberalism. From such an abstract standpoint, it is impossible to understand the political vicissitudes of societies or states, which make up the main content of history. This limitation is understandable, given the fact that hermeneutics has developed from a method of interpreting the history of culture. But of course, the history of culture is only one aspect of history; the history of politics is another. And the dialectic between culture and politics mediated by ethics demands religion as an ultimate basis of unity. That is, the reciprocal circularity of the movement to the absolute in ethics (ōsō) and the return to the world in religion (gensō) constitutes the historical world. In order to understand the structure of the historical world, therefore, mere temporality does not suffice. The historical problem of the spatiotemporal world issues from the facts that the spatial limitation and exclusivity found in a society of "species" underlie the struggle for political domination and the power of cultural tradition, and that the reciprocal determination of these two is mediated both by the past and the future.

I cannot go into further detail on this question here, except to note that the finite, relativistic viewpoint that marks Heidegger's theory of time clearly makes it difficult for him to understand history, as he claims he does. The being-in-the-world of Dasein is not only the transcendence of an *ascent* from within but also the transcendence of a *descent* into immanence from without with the world as mediator. The present can achieve a practical unity in contradiction only as the manifestation of eternity. As noted above, it is not only a matter of "going toward the absolute" but also of "returning to this world." The mutual transformation of these two diametrically opposed orientations is not possible for finite beings except through the metanoetics of absolute critique. Only metanoetics can pave the way for a philosophy of history that is also a philosophy of religion.

After the foregoing clarification of the notion of absolute critique— that is, the logic of metanoetics—which is necessary for understanding the nature of time and history, it must now be demonstrated how absolute critique and metanoetics possess an indelible character that leads to a philosophy of history. In effect, this is to urge a confrontation between metanoetics and Hegel's phenomenology of mind. As noted in the previous chapter, Hegel's phenomenology of mind not only opens up the way to absolute critique in the sense of deepening Kant's critique of reason but also displays a remarkable sensitivity to historicity lacking in Kant's work. Still, viewed from the standpoint of metanoetics, Hegel's treatment of the problem remains incomplete in that it develops into a kind of absolutism which actually negates the dialectical method and thus, ironically, results in having his own system negated by authentic dialectic.

The basic reason behind the failure of Hegel's dialectic is that he understood the personal God of theism as having created the world through unmediated, absolute will. If one conceives of the absolute as absolute nothingness, however, and engages in action-witness in utterly dialectical fashion—that is, in the sense of absolute transformation and absolute mediation—the absolute necessarily requires relative beings for its own mediation, and the process of mediating this relativity ceases to be a direct one in virtue of the requirement that it be mediated in turn by mutual activity between one relative being and another.

In assuming such a standpoint of absolute mediation, the absolute and the relative become simultaneous: there can be no temporal priority of one to the other, since the priority at issue is one based on the principle of absolute and relative, not one of time. This is why Augustine has it that the creation of the world does not take place in time, but that time is created together with the world. Since he conceives of the will of God in terms of perfect love (as distinct from the selective love of human beings) and interprets the creation of the world as the self-revelation of that love, he naturally comes to think of the ongoing revelation of love as a process of making the world contemporary with God.

It is no coincidence that Christian theology since Augustine has embraced Platonic dialectics as a way to understand the Gospel logically. But the deepening of dialectics through absolute mediation and the positing of God as absolute nothingness does not accord with theism's idea of a personal God. In the view of theism, God is an absolute existence transcending absolute nothingness and a unified will embracing the mediation of dialectics. Thus it is clear that the ground of the world and its being are seen not as a mediation of revelation in the self-negation of love but rather as an unmediated, direct activity of God's will which determines the mediation of love. But, speaking metaphorically, God is the principle of democratic organization among people—not lording it over humanity but appearing only in a mediatory function—and therefore the divine activity may be considered as one of mediating among human beings. If we think of the relationship between the divine and the human as based on a democracy of cooperative relationship in mutual mediation, we may rightly speak here of an absolute mediation of dialectics; thus, even if the opposition between the absolute and the relative is symbolized as a master-subject relationship, it will not necessarily be an autocratic bond but one of mediation and cooperation.

Are we not correct in assuming here, incidentally, that the imperial ideal at work in the political system of our nation is also democratic in the same sense, at least in principle? Democracy, as a *sine qua non* of politics, may be a necessary condition for the establishment of a state, but it is certainly not of itself sufficient. The sufficient conditions are constellated only through the mediation of the special characteristics of particular racial and social groups. Even the United States of America, for example, is not entirely lacking in the "specific" foundation of a racially corporate body, since the Puritan immigrants were in part a natural grouping of English people and their principles were not limited to those of democracy. Conversely, the establishment of a political state by the Japanese people was not, in principle, contrary to democracy.

Theism, however, does not allow for a deepening of the principle of democracy in the relationship between God and human beings. The selective, spontaneous will of God always remains the ultimate principle, like the will of an autocratic monarch, and this does not accord with the principle of democracy just referred to. This is not something peculiar to Christianity, but may be seen as a carry-over from Judaism, the historical womb out of which Christianity came to birth. In this sense we may say that Christianity realizes its truth through the ongoing process of mediating Judaism—that is, through the activity of transforming the theism of Judaism into its own expression of the absolute mediation of love, and of witnessing to its absolute truth—"God is Love"—through faith. This, we may say, is the historical establishment of the truth of Christianity: the historical realization of the facts that being is mediated by nothingness and that existence is grounded in the Great Compassion. This is the very structure of historicity that we have been considering in this chapter: the historicity of being is witnessed in action-faith which, through the *amor fati* stemming from the transformation of absolute nothingness, changes the contingent, direct, and imposed determinations of being into the autonomous plans of a free "project." Even the historical establishment of the state does not come about apart from this process of action-faith.

I do not mean to point here to some kind of goal for history in the eschatological sense, or to efforts exerted to reach that goal in a direct, linear fashion. As nothingness, the absolute is absolute mediation, and therefore permanently correlative to being; it is a circularity of unceasing mediation. The absolute is not an ideal or goal that ultimately sublates the relative; it is, rather, a principle that supports us continually wherever we stand and makes it possible for us to engage in authentic action. It is not a point that lies forever beyond the reach of our advance, but the very force that moves us here and now. Wherever the relative exists, the absolute is there as its correlative. In the realm of being, nothingness always mediates and is mediated. The absolute coexists with the relative and becomes manifest through its confrontation with the relative.

Similarly, self-consciousness of the absolute does not exist apart from the faith and witness of authentic action. Yet even when the content of relative being is mediated by absolute nothingness, and is practiced in the eternal present as an "action of no-action," it loses its temporally structured mediation and becomes something burdened with the defect of direct nonmediation: our actual existence simply cannot avoid its destiny of being enclosed within the thrownness of the past. Hence, even if one practices the mediating action of nothingness as an "action of no-action" and a free project toward the future, and even if one bears witness to "being as the manifestation of nothingness," this gives no cause to sit back and relax. For the being that is witnessed to in action as the manifestation of nothingness quickly recedes into the past as an established fact, which then needs to be mediated again so as to renew itself as being, and already implies and foreordains the possibility of further future action based on the mediation of nothingness. Hence the circularity of the future being mediated by the past while the past is being mediated by the future. In a word, the nothingness that is the principle of this absolute mediation turns on the eternal present as its axis, manifesting itself unceasingly in its unfolding and transformation of time.

This is the nothingness that is believed in and witnessed to in the self-consciousness of action. It is something we can seek but not attain, but also something that is attained even if we do not seek it. As nothingness, the absolute is the principle of this absolute mediation, yet paradoxically transcends us even as it remains forever immanent in us. Our very awareness of its unattainability already witnesses to its having been attained; the fact that it belongs to an established past as something already attained requires the action of constant renewal as something not yet attained. The eternal self-consciousness of such circular development, based on absolute nothingness, is history. And the absolute of which we become conscious through practice—that is, in the absolute disruption of absolute critique—is believed in and witnessed to only in this history.

The process of conversion in which absolute critique, the consummation of the critique of reason, forces us to the extremity of disruption, causes us to die in its depths, and transforms us into resurrected beings through the action of Other-power, is certainly not something that takes place once and for all. In the realm of theoretical reason, for example, scientific theory arising from knowledge of nature may often fall into absolute disruption in its opposition to and estrangement from the irrationality of actuality, bringing us to a standstill where we can neither remain in the past nor advance toward the future. But at the profoundest depths of the contradiction, where the self is made to die, if one performs a new scientific experiment passively and obediently on the "roadless road" where the self still exists even though it cannot be seen and does not appear, one may be able to break through the crisis and advance a step further. In such a case, the metanoetic breakthrough of the self takes the form of the death-and-resurrection transformation of absolute critique.

Even when this takes place, however, it is no more than a first approximation; it does not mean that a complete theory has been achieved at a single stroke. Indeed, time and the contingent irrationality and temporality latent in actual history make it impossible for that to happen. Experimentation aimed at producing theory transforms reality, and thus requires in turn a reformation of theory. Consequently, even if the circularity of history be dismissed as beyond the limits of natural scientific knowledge, the very theory that dismisses it gets reentangled in historicity. The structure of reality makes the complete removal of that circularity impossible. We have no choice but to acknowledge the fact that it is there, inevitably conditioning the structure of theory. There is no way out of the relativity and circularity of history. We can only affirm it, or rather allow it to mediate our belief-witness of absoluteness and eternity.

Scientific theory, the critique of science, and the history of science do not exist separately, nor are they simply united externally. They interpenetrate one another and mediate one another, bringing about a transforming unity based on authentic action in experimentation. A critique of reason that assumes the factual existence of the theory, and in which the contingent establishment of the facts is taken as a preliminary assumption for an eternal theory, is no more than an abstract view lacking this mediation between history and experimentation. Such lop-sided logical moorings must be rejected in favor of the circular historicity of absolute critique.

Therefore, as we advance from the knowledge of nature to the knowledge of history, and from there proceed to the realm of practical reason, the absolute critique emerging from transformation of the critique of reason necessarily takes the form of a circularity. The present, which manifests absolute nothingness through death-and-resurrection, is unified by transcendent nothingness to become an axis of unceasing transformation. Eternity, meantime, is not some absolute being removed from the continuous rotation of that axis. Even though as an absolute it transcends the relative, as nothingness it is manifest only in the mediation of being, and therefore can be found only as something immanent in the development of relative being. Unity is brought to history through nothingness, which functions as a principle of absolute mediation in the sense of an immanent transcendence. Although it mediates the absolute in the sense of belonging to an established past, it is also mediated by the absolute in the sense of belonging to authentic action oriented toward the future.

Even the absolute we term God cannot in principle exist apart from this absolute mediation of nothingness. To imagine an absolute apart from this historical mediation, a being that transcends and encompasses the relative, is to end up either in the submersion of the autonomous individual in the vile equality of pantheism, or in the dominion of the unmediated, selective divine will of theism. Obviously, in either case the freedom of the individual personality is extinguished.

Both tendencies are undeniably present in Hegel. Evidence for the former may be seen in the frequent proximity of his position to Spinozism, which he cites with praise; the latter appears in the compromise he struck with orthodox belief in affirming the unmediated, absolute being of God. Here Hegel contradicts his own standpoint of dialectical mediation and involves himself in a position irreconcilable with the mediatory existence of the state as the relative-*qua*-absolute. The inconsistency and vacillation this brings to his idea of relations between religion and the state are clear to see. The basic and unfortunate underlying mistake is Hegel's positing of an unmediated, absolute being beyond the transcendental unity of dialectical nothingness, locating it outside of the practice of nothingness as self-identical being, and entrusting it to a heretical logic of substance.

The legacy of medieval theology, which is a hermeneutics of the Gospel based on Greek philosophy, endures in Hegel's philosophy and prevents his dialectical historicism from being carried out radically in action. As Heidegger has pointed out,[17] the transcendent existence of God—who is seen as a subject of an unmediated, selective absolute will—keeps religion in Hegel's thought at a distance from historicity in action, and leaves him no means to escape from the vulgar view of eternity descending into time. In his *Phenomenology of Mind*, Hegel notes that when Kant's moral worldview loses its critical nature and becomes dogmatic, it immediately tends to consider itself alone as morally correct and to fall into the self-righteousness of a "beautiful soul" (*die schöne Seele*) that affirms itself, but negates others by refusing to recognize them. For Hegel this self-righteousness is what constitutes the self-alienation of the spirit. Reflection on the evil of the escape from reality implied here, however, awakens the self through suffering and anxiety to its deep-rooted sinfulness, and leads it to a standpoint where, in the very midst of the inevitable sinfulness of action, it can abandon itself metanoetically and find forgiveness and reconciliation with others. In doing so, the spirit converts toward a religion of absolute spirit marked by mutual recognition and a cooperative soul.

I cannot refrain here from expressing my admiration for the profoundness with which Hegel has carried through the critique of reason and brought it to the level of absolute critique and metanoetic action. It goes without saying that his thought has given me considerable guidance, both directly and indirectly.

Just as the spirit loses its relativity and acquires absoluteness when it has arrived at the standpoint of religion, the transformation of time attains the unity of its transformation when it awakens to consciousness of eternity. From the standpoint of the absolute mediation of religion, we can see in hindsight how each stage of the relative consciousness of this mediation is a partial realization of the absolute and participates in the absolute. In other words, religion absolutizes the relativity of history. Accordingly, religion itself becomes historical in proportion to the intensity of the historical consciousness of relative beings as being themselves mediators of the absolute, and thus renders itself concrete as historical religion. For Hegel, this process reached its peak in the spiritual consciousness of the Protestant church, and consciousness of the death-and-resurrection of the divine-human Christ as universal truth unfolds completely in the absolute mediatory nature of religion as individual consciousness annihilating itself and returning to the fundamental, universal self-consciousness that provides a common ground for basis of the self and others, thus bringing the manifestation of absolute spirit to consummation. This can be understood, no doubt, as absolute mediation revealing itself and fulfilling the circularity of history. But because the standpoint of religion is directly representational, it is unavoidable that this truth should harden into a creed. In this way the truth of absolute mediation itself forfeits its mediatory quality and falls into contradiction. What negates this contradiction and fulfills the role of mediating absolute truth to relative reality is conceptual philosophy, which is nothing other than absolute knowledge. Absolute knowledge may be understood as the dynamism of absolute spirit of religion mediating itself in history and becoming self-conscious of the mediating activity of the relative-*qua*-absolute. This being so, it may be said that absolute knowledge itself, in order to achieve its goal, prompts the organization of the various historical stages of spirit to an "internalization" (*Er-innerung*) in "remembrance" (*Erinnerung*), and takes the path of conceptualizing history.

In short, absolute knowledge may be called the self-consciousness of the historically mediatory nature of a religious absolute spirit. But as mentioned previously in connection with Heidegger's critique of Hegel's view of time, the latter fails to get beyond the vulgar view of time and to develop a structural awareness of the concrete nature of history. As a result, the absolute knowledge that Hegel unfolds for us loses the historicity that mediates the movement of ideas, and is transformed instead into the logical development of an eternal, divine substance antecedent to the creation of nature and finite spirit. Hence his simple reliance on the vulgar idea of eternity as something falling into time. Or put the other way around, since Hegel fails in his understanding of time and historicity as the mediation of time by eternity, the historical mediation of absolute knowledge, which is the heart of the whole process of determination, turns into something external, loses its internal basis, and falls into self-alienation. Absolute knowledge can preserve its true absoluteness by mediating itself in connection with the relativity of history. But when it takes leave of this mediation, it becomes alienated from itself; when it seeks absoluteness in abstract nonmediation, it loses its true absoluteness and sinks to the level of the relative, where it is replaced by other relative forces and thus left exposed to the relativity of history.

History has not come to term in the spirit of the modern Protestant church, nor has the movement of spirit ended with a philosophy that Hegel envisaged as the self-consciousness of that spirit. But Hegel's absolute knowledge in effect makes it look as if the history of spirit had indeed reached its fulfillment at that point. As has been said, this is due to the fact that he did not stop with self-consciousness of the subjective unity achieved in the action of absolute mediation, with its correlative understanding of eternity as the permanent mediator of time, but went on instead to conceive of eternity as ancient philosophy had conceived of it: a substance whose essence is ahistorical and trans-temporal, and which can be made into an object of logic in the form of a pure essence that precedes the fall into temporality and historicity. In this way absolute knowledge became at once a logic and an ontology. In place of self-consciousness achieved in action, there is a shift to a standpoint of speculative reason.

On the one hand, the various realms of circularity, whose unending circular movement mediates the relativity of history, form the various stages of history; on the other, they realize the unity of transcendent nothingness. To this extent, the truth of absolute knowledge, whose absoluteness is preserved in historical mediation, falls out of the picture and the demand arises for absoluteness in an unmediated state. When this happens, absolute knowledge is exposed to the relativity of history, and assertions regarding the absolute fall prey to antagonistic trends of thought. In the process, absolute knowledge of itself witnesses to the truth of the dialectic of absolute mediation. In this way, Hegel's absolute knowledge cuts itself off from the truth of absolute critique and retires once again to the direct self-affirmation of reason. Indeed, it may be said that he lets go of the spirit of the critique of reason itself, to leave the stamp of dogmatism on his thought. Is this not a result of Hegel's lack of a thoroughgoing metanoctics and, as Kierkegaard claims, of his lack of religious practice and faith?

In contrast, absolute critique, which is the logic of metanoetics, is necessarily accompanied by historicity. Just as the structure of temporality and historicity requires the absolute transformative quality of absolute critique, so too, conversely, does the transformation that occurs in absolute critique, as absolute nothingness, necessarily require relative being to realize the eternity of its absolute in the circular unity of history. Hence philosophy as metanoetics cannot but make the "action" of the philosophy of history its object, and religious faith its core. In truth, it *is* nothing other than the self-conscious witness of action and faith.

There is no longer any room for doubt: for us ordinary and ignorant people, the way of *zange* is the only way; only in metanoetics can a philosophy of history that is also a philosophy of religion—which is the heart of philosophy—become a subjectivity of self's action-faith-witness, and be mediated by the self-consciousness of an existential philosophy.

At the same time that Heidegger's existential philosophy shows an affinity with metanoetics in terms of the Christian aspect it gained through the influence of Kierkegaard, the penchant for the way of the sage or "superman" it picked up from Nietzsche makes it diametrically opposed to metanoetics. While Nietzsche's character is similar to

Kierkegaard's for its strong ego and extremely impressionable, sensitive, and nervous temperament, in matters of religiosity his anti-Christian and self-affirmative manner cuts a sharply contrasting figure. Still, it seems to me that the only way that ordinary, ignorant people like me can appreciate Nietzsche is through metanoetics. Not without reason, his thought had long been a locked treasure house as far as I was concerned. Now that metanoetics has given me a key, it seems worthwhile to try to open it up and have a look inside. After the manner of Heidegger, then, let us consider briefly what Nietzsche has to say.

It hardly bears repeating that Nietzsche's will to power, as an absolute affirmation of life, is diametrically opposed to the absolute negation of reason and hence, at first glance, would appear to represent a standpoint diametrically opposed to metanoetics. Yet, as we see clearly from his concept of *amor fati*, what constitutes the core of his thought may in fact be interpreted as a spirit of absolute negation. The absolute affirmation that greets joyfully and unreservedly everything inevitable about life—especially the fate of death by ruin and destruction—and goes still further to choose and will the inevitable, is actually mediated by an absolute negation that brings about the death of the self in the midst of such inevitability.

We may understand this as a transformation of Goethe's sense of resignation into something positive and active. In formal terms, of course, absolute negation and absolute affirmation are direct opposites that can be viewed as identical only at the price of causing confusion. And yet, to the extent that absolute negation, in the sense of the negation of negation, no longer undergoes negation no matter how many negations are added to it, we may also speak of it as absolute affirmation. Absolute affirmation is therefore simply a perspective on absolute negation that views it not in terms of its process of coming to be but in terms of its results. This is why we can say that there is no absolute affirmation apart from absolute negation. For direct affirmation that does not include the mediation of the negation of negation, however strictly one may determine it as absolute, has no way of avoiding a confrontation with negation: it fails to escape completely from relativity because that which we usually term affirmation, or being, exists only in opposition to negation, or nothingness. Only something in the mediated state of absolute negation-*qua*-affirmation, wherein even nothingness and negation must be negated, can truly be called absolute. Accordingly, Nietzsche's absolute affirmation, in its basic structure, is nothing other than absolute negation.

In a self-critical essay composed as a preface to *The Birth of Tragedy* sixteen years after he had completed the book, Nietzsche sets forth clearly the dialectic whereby Dionysus, suffering from an excess of life, seeks the negation and pain of life, a pessimism that in turn enhances the self-confidence and abundance of life. His proclamation of nihilism and his comments on nothingness gathered together in *The Will to Power* express the same view. There is no denying, of course, that what he called nihilism involved a historical critique aimed at showing the inevitability of the collapse of the highest established values, and that in this context nothingness was meant above all to imply meaninglessness and valuelessness. Yet neither can we deny that, seen from the point of view of formal structure, his brand of nihilism, with its emphasis on the inevitable collapse of values, was essentially directed at laying bare the destructiveness and insecurity inherent in all immediate Dasein. Is not an absolute affirmation that makes no attempt to avoid but welcomes with joy all vicissitudes and change, including destructiveness and extinction, and that further, by accepting them, changes them into the content of one's own will, exactly what absolute negation is all about?

In the affirmativeness of negative mediation, an absolute affirmativeness is given to active nihilism that contrasts sharply with the negativity and world-weariness of a passive nihilism. The latter is no more than an endurance of negativity, of which Nietzsche considered Buddhism the paradigm. While the point may apply to the Hīnayāna tradition, it ill accords with the positive spirit of Mahāyāna altruism, where the endurance of negation and suffering itself already contains the positive dynamism of a negation of negation that is likewise and at the same time an affirmation. Surely this is more than mere passivity. In fact, the "nihilism of passive endurance" can properly be called a nihilism only when it contains a negation of negation, when it corresponds to the "empty being" (*kū-u*) of the "action of no-action" (*musa no sa*) or "doing of not-doing" (*mui no i*). Indeed, all *gensō* action, the action of *tariki-qua-jiriki*, may be considered nothingness to the extent that it is passivity-*qua*-activity. As "absolute negation-*qua*-affirmation," nihilism is the standpoint of absolute affirmation; apart from it no other standpoint of absolute affirmation is possible. This must be why Nietzsche himself, in his treatment of Sophocles' *Oedipus* in *The Birth of Tragedy*, stresses the fact that a purely passive attitude attains a sublime level of activity that far surpasses life itself.

Nevertheless, the reason that Nietzsche disliked the concept of negation and failed to acknowledge adequately its mediating power is that the goal of his philosophy was to save Europe from the degeneration into which it had fallen, a position to which his study of the spiritual history of Europe and keen sensitivity to the need of a critique of his age had led him. His notion of negation generally refers to the normative "ought" of morality forcing the restraints of reason on the power of nature and the activity of life. The constraints and limitations thus imposed by reason—the "Apollonian" element in human nature— gained strength after the Greek philosophers Socrates and Plato, and as Christianity came to respond to and embrace this attitude from the standpoint of popular faith, eventually took control of the spiritual history of Europe. As a result, the will to power, which is the very core of the primordial life-energy of human beings, was weakened, and the envy and hatred of the weak for the strong, of those who suffer for those who are happy, of the ordinary individual for the extraordinary, came to motivate the generation of moral values. As this natural life-force grew more and more feeble, sympathy for the weak became the morality to replace the control of the strong; humanity suffered a deterioration and corruption. It was in this context that Nietzsche proclaimed the doctrine of the will to power as an active nihilism that could redeem Europe.

Nietzsche's call for the return to the tragic spirit of ancient Greece— to the strong life-force he termed the Dionysian spirit, which joyfully greets the destruction of death and which affirms and loves all the vicissitudes of fate—is a plea for an autocratic morality in which one controls everything without being controlled or enslaved by anything, in which one transforms everything into the content of one's own positive will and is able to use all things freely. For Nietzsche, this meant not only that the individual truly would be elevated above the degeneracy of the vulgar masses to the level of a noble and superior being but also that a new species of "superman" would evolve to surpass humanity itself. Armed with this hope, he stressed a sort of vitalism and naturalism and launched an all-out attack denouncing reason and morality.

Of course, this precludes all appreciation or sympathy for the notion of negation. Nietzsche considered the use of reason in philosophy to be a kind of obsession peculiar to philosophers, and attacked them for their hatred of all change and their lack of a sense of history, which issued in the mummified notion of the entirety of being and a zealous reverence for the idol of unchanging being. He rejected the antinominalist position that makes a primordial being out of the abstract universal as no more than a hypostatization of words. To this metaphysics of words he attached the German word *Vernunft*, and from there went on to negate the reality of the thing-in-itself which that reason takes as its object, maintaining that only the empirical sense-content of this phenomenal world is reality, and that this is both infinitely varied and under continual transformation, so that it is impossible even to say that it "exists."[18]

Nietzsche's philosophy is therefore not an ontology but a living philosophy of transformation and becoming. To conceive of an eternal, unchangeable world as an object of reason abstracted from this world of change is an abuse, an insult, and a slander against the life that is ours. For Nietzsche, such a "two-world" view is a sign of degeneracy. To this he opposed an absolute transformative power that assimilates the world of sensation, which is exposed to transformation and becoming, into the stuff of life and controls it freely. This is the "Dionysian" spirit that Nietzsche links to the hope of a transcendence of humanity, an expectation of the superman who stands beyond good and evil. That he did not pay much attention to the concepts of negation or mediation from this standpoint is hardly to be wondered at.

There is no need to mention the passion of the poet that flows like an undercurrent through Nietzsche's thought. Nor is there any need for elaborate arguments to sense how inappropriate it is to try to organize his philosophy logically and understand it rationally. In spite of this, it is definitely philosophy, not a mere emotionality but the interpretation of a profound personal experience of life. Even for someone like me who is unable really to enter into his poetical thinking or appreciate his prophetic genius, it is hard not to be struck deeply by his sincerity and to feel deep sympathy for the sense of loneliness it brought him.

At the same time, I have to admit that I fail to understand fully how he can be the most popular philosopher among the intellectuals of our younger generation. Perhaps it is just that his thought is so very different in character from my own. As I progress along the way of *zange*, however, I find to my surprise that my understanding of Nietzsche has also progressed, and I have the sense that I have drawn closer to him emotionally. It is, of course, rather embarrassing for me to speak of my personal feelings in this way, but I do so nonetheless because the foundations of Nietzsche's thought are in fact related to absolute nothingness, and because there are points of unity between the absolute transformation and becoming of the Dionysian spirit, which he proclaims from a standpoint of life that has rejected reason, and my own notion of absolute transformation. Since the reason he is rejecting is really no more than what the logic of self-identity calls discursive thought, and thus is altogether different from reason viewed as the essence of the self that appears in the breakthrough of the self, and since the negative self-transcendence of this latter type of reason is really a self-consciousness of the negative mediatory structure of what Nietzsche calls "life," I am further prompted to clarify the sense in which our two paths of thought run parallel.

I realize that the question of whether Nietzsche does full justice to the spirit of tragedy is an important and difficult one that merits special attention. It is, nevertheless, difficult to deny that he has grasped a profound truth in viewing the core of tragedy as a spirit of absolute affirmation that welcomes even destruction and downfall with joy, and thereby makes it an object of one's own will. He is right not to treat the spirit of tragedy as directly identical with the Dionysian spirit, but to base the emergence of the artistic nature of tragedy on the primordial and fundamental nature of life only insofar as it is mediated by the purifying power of the Apollonian spirit and collaborates with it. Only when the Dionysian is mediated by the negativity of the Apollonian can it lay bare the foundation of the world in symbolic form and bring eternity to self-conscious realization.

If this represents the core of Nietzsche's thought, it is nothing other than the mediatory, factual standpoint of reason set forth above as the breakthrough of the self through absolute critique. The critique of the age that he wraps around this core is woven in a prose whose distinctive emotional outbursts of poetic passion preserve the ecstatic abandon and exuberance of what he terms the Dionysian (Bacchic) hymn of praise, and make many of his statements and ideas look contradictory at first.

This is true particularly in the case of his emphasis on the autocratic control of the will to power and his attempts to tear away the enslaving restrictions of moralism. In assimilating the absolute *gensō* action—the "action of no-action" (*musa no sa*)—realized *beyond* the opposition of good and evil to the standpoint of a life *prior* to the opposition of good and evil, he confuses his thought with antimoralism and naturalism. Most of the misunderstanding and distortion of his thought, it would seem to me, has arisen at just this point. Actually, it is a result of his option for an ongoing creation and transformation of life in place of a transformation of nothingness that breaks through reason and morality in absolute negation and performs *gensō* to attain the transcendent position of the fact-*qua*-reason (*ji-soku-ri*) of religion. A philosophical standpoint that lacks the concepts of nothingness and negation naturally fails to produce a sense of true discontinuity or authentic transcendence, and cannot escape direct, ongoing immanence. This is why, despite similarities in motivation and structure, there are inevitable differences between the orientation of Nietzsche's thought and the way of metanoetics, which I must follow.

Nietzsche is right to point out the abstraction of analytical logic and take leave of it. In fact, this has been the general task of philosophers since the time of Kant's transcendental logic. Kant was too attached to the autonomy of reason to take the autonomy of reason still deeper. His fear of this antinomy and his attempts to restrict the use of reason in order to avoid it seem at first to be an exercise of self-control aimed at rescuing the autonomy of reason, but in the end all his efforts betray a lack of rational courage.

Viewed as the capacity for death-and-resurrection, reason is a function of *jiriki-qua-tariki*, established in the transformation and mediation of obedience to absolute Other-power and arriving at a manifestation of absolute nothingness. In reason the self casts itself into the contradictions of rationality (*ri*), abandons itself to the crisis of absolute disruption, and is transformed into absolute nothingness. It destroys the self confronted with the inevitable antinomy of the affirmation and negation in *ri* as well as the antinomy latent within the universality of *ri* and the particularity of "fact" (*ji*); and it resurrects the self from the ashes of the fire in which the old self has been consumed.

Thus authentic reason appears only in the mediatory process of being transformed into what lies beyond reason, and the knowledge that comes with authentic reason bears witness (*shō*) to action-faith (*gyō-shin*). So long as one does not take this absolute transformation of death-and-resurrection as the basic principle of reason, reason cannot but present its self-identity as the basic principle of life. But this means that it avoids the contradictions of antinomies, rejects circularity, and shows a lack of courage in the efforts it makes to rescue itself from them. Since it is incapable of risking the breakthrough of the self, reason sinks to the level of formalistic and moralistic abstraction.

Assuming reason to enjoy a self-identical unity and unwilling to submit to its restriction, Nietzsche saw the circular development of death-and-resurrection as belonging to the very essence of a *life* far more concrete than reason, the life of the subjectivity of a creative and transforming force surpassing mere being and therefore able to replace reason. Thus in place of absolute nothingness, he tried to make absolute being the basic principle of philosophy. He took the "idealistic" standpoint of reason represented by Kant and converted it to a "factual" standpoint of life. In place of the metanoetic negation of reason that sees

reason as the manifestation of absolute nothingness, he offered an affirmation of life whose basic essence consists in the will to power that seeks
to place all things under the control of the self.

We may also sympathize with the sensationalist empiricism he
opposed to reason to the extent that it is an expression of his positivistic
spirit, and we must admire him for having exposed the true face of
religious idols in his desire to bring deeper sincerity to the scientific
mind. Yet we must conclude that he did not attain, as Kant had, a true
appreciation of the experimental method which understands the cognition of the laws of natural science to come about only by the cooperation of experience and the conceptual constructions that precede it.
That he did not depart from the dogmatism of a dated form of empiricism and sensationalism represents a definite bias on Nietzsche's part.
From a strict hermeneutical standpoint, he recognized that the historical
facts of the actual world are accessible only through interpretation (he
proclaimed his theory of the will to power as an interpretation of history); but with regard to the knowledge of nature, he adhered to a
sensationalist position, a contradiction that shows a lack of consistency
on his part. How did such an indefatigable thinker as Nietzsche interpret
the fact that, even in the primordial experiences of life, cognition cannot
be established without the very rational thinking he was rejecting on the
grounds that it was no more than a faculty for abstraction and formaliza-
tion? Without the very thought and language he naturally despised and
rejected, is it not impossible to interpret life at any depth and shed light
on it?

Cognition is not directly life. Mere vital instinct, however strong,
lacks the clarity of insight. Life attains the clarity of cognition only when
it mediates the abstraction of the very thought that negates life in its
immediacy. If thought stops with abstraction, it has not fulfilled its basic
mission. The function of thought does not lie in performing abstraction
for the sake of abstraction. Abstraction does not have as its object the
negation of life; instead, it mediates the reconstruction of life. Once
established, a concept enters into dialectic movement in virtue of the
contradiction it necessarily incurs because of its very abstraction. (Such
contradiction appears in the form of a disruption within the concept
stemming from the alienation of the conceptual from the actual.) At
every stage of its synthesis the concept seeks a self-consciousness that
reconstructs life in its entirety. Indeed, it is abstraction and negation that
carry out the self-consciousness of life. This is precisely what Nietzsche
forgets in his zeal to reject them.

Much the same is true in the case of Bergson, who had a keen eye for recognizing and making use of the findings of science, but grew overly eager to criticize the conceptual fixation and homogeneity of science as he came to stress more and more the intuition of life, the personal experience of flux, and the heterogeneity of the contents of consciousness. In so doing, Bergson overlooked the important fact that his own metaphysics, which was based on the intuition of life and the personal experience of reality, could be reconstructed as self-conscious cognition only through the negative mediation of these scientific concepts.

Just as Bergson's philosophical position got tangled up in patent contradictions, so did Nietzsche's when he rejected reason in favor of instinct, laid excessive emphasis on the expulsion of morality in favor of nature, and set up his own morality as something transcending morality. He forgot that the philosophical position he was espousing is possible only through the *absolute* negation of reason. Simply to negate reason and reject the abstraction of concepts results only in doing away with philosophy itself. Nietzsche makes the word *Wechsel* (transformation or exchange) synonymous with *Werden* (change in the sense of becoming in general).[19] But a conceptual distinction needs to be drawn between the general notion of change as alteration or mutation (*Veränderung*) on the one hand, and change as becoming, on the other. In contrast with the change of becoming, which is the completely unmediated ebb and flow of becoming amidst the continuity of life, the change of mutation refers to the fact that an unchangeable substance undergoes a change of the state or accidental condition of its being. In contrast with both of these, the pure change of transformation may be understood as pointing to a replacement of the "one" of autonomous subjectivity with an "other." At least when I speak of "transformation," it is this kind of exchange and transformation of subjectivity that I have in mind.

The change of transformation is discontinuous and sharply disjointed; what is required for its mediation is not continuous being, the transcendent "existence of life," but absolute nothingness. Being here is "being as *upāya*," that is, being as a mediator of nothingness. Moreover, human existential self-awareness, which realizes the compassion and altruism of the bodhisattva through the equality of mutual transformation, must be a mediation of nothingness in the sense of just such a transformation of subjectivity.

It is certainly not the case, as Nietzsche supposes, that mere becoming or change can describe the basic structure of human existence exhaustively. The "life" of which becoming and change may be predicated can hardly be elevated thereby to the level of authentic subjectivity. In Nietzsche the self is not treated as *für sich*, and consequently not as *für anderes* either. It is equated with life and transformed into the subject of the will to power, the instinctive self-assertion of life. Though called a subject, it is nothing more than ego that does not recognize other subjects. If the will to power completely lords it over others this way and without mediation, if it remains at the level of a self-affirmation of egoism that does not acknowledge the autonomy of others as beings that are its equals, it fixes itself on a standpoint from which self cannot become *für sich*, a self that mediates the other.

Since the self did not entail this sort of problematic for Nietzsche, it ended up becoming absolutized. As a matter of course, Nietzsche's atheism not only negated God but deified the self and required the emergence of a superman who would surpass the human. But what will happen in a world of such supermen when each attempts to gain dominion over the others? Obviously, it would end up in the destruction of the species of supermen. If one understands Nietzsche's theory of eternal recurrence as the cyclical circularity of generation and extinction, it does not seem unreasonable to conclude that the evolution and progress of life to the point of the appearance of the superman would mark the beginning of the devolution and retrogression of life as soon as that goal had been attained. The notion of eternal recurrence is itself a product of the abstractions of natural science that overlooks the process of deepening that goes on in the mediation of spirit, an idea deduced from premises marred from the start by their failure to take into account the infinity of space together with the infinity of time.[20] Moreover, the theory of the emergence of the superman is based on the analogy of the emergence of a new species by the natural selection of biological evolution, and therefore represents the sort of abuse associated with scientism.

Of course, the concept of eternal recurrence is important in the sense that it points to the unending repetition of human weakness, puniness, ugliness, and defilement, and to the negating mediation of the will to power that accepts these things, affirms them, and assumes responsibility for them. The nature of the superman is determined by the absolute negativity of this mediation, as we see most clearly in Nietzsche's atheism, which sets up a radical transformation in the form of *edo-soku-jōdo* ("this corrupt world"–*qua*–"the Pure Land" or *mundus sensibilis–qua–mundus intelligibilis*), and which, as the final chapter of Part Three of *Thus Spoke Zarathustra*, "The Seven Seals," shows unambiguously, is being presented as a new religion.

On first encounter, his description is strange and easily leads to confusion; moreover, as I have stated above, the scientific model that stands behind it is mistaken. But the core of eternal recurrence, as Nietzsche himself explains, lies in the eternal unalterability and infinite preexistence of the past;[21] and their conquest by the will to power means the redemption and overcoming of yesterday.[22] If we include in eternal recurrence the acceptance of today (the present),[23] we have to admit that it has grasped the truth of our human condition.

What makes the past the past is this: on the one hand, it has already passed us by and we can do nothing whatever about it; yet on the other, it continually returns to the present, usurps the present, coerces the present. Is this not the very sense of Nietzsche's eternal recurrence? According to the Buddhist notion of *karma*, which sees the karmic links of the past as reaching back to an infinite past, there is no escape from *karma*: each present moment is ordained by the *karma* of the past. If we interpret the core of Nietzsche's eternal recurrence in terms of *karma*, the idea takes on a meaning of still vaster proportions. But even in that case, by proceeding to accept the past, to negate the self and break through the self within it, the past itself can be broken through and transformed into the free content of the self.

For Nietzsche, it is the will to power that effects this process. Through it the present overcomes the past and attains freedom: it becomes an *amor fati*. The joy of freedom becomes greater as the pressure of the past, which is eternal recurrence, becomes heavier. As this pressure reaches its peak, the wheels of time grind to a halt and finally cease to turn. Life passes into a state of stagnation and suffocation. But if life, faced with this outermost limit, can move beyond itself, abandon itself, and accept death, the time of the present, which has stopped, will be transfigured into the fullness of a moment possessed of the weight of infinity. Here is the manifestation of infinity transcending life and death. In it the present is replete with the joy of a past redeemed and the hope of a future to be created. Filled to overflowing with such joy and hope, we are enabled to affirm and accept any pressure of the past as a means to intensify the dynamism of life. Just as eternal recurrence uses the pressure of the past to make all that is pettiest and ugliest in the human condition recur over and over again without end, so too does it make all that is greatest and noblest recur eternally.[24] This is precisely what is meant by the eternal present.

In similar fashion, there is no denying that the strongly resistant functioning of *karma* in the present enters into the pulsation of infinity as the transforming stuff of creation that gives birth to the stars, and that this fact is the very core of religious enlightenment and salvation. And yet at the same time, there is no doubt that this power belongs to the will of the sage and is not something open to the ordinary and foolish. Ordinary and ignorant individuals like me can participate in and receive the deliverance of the sage as the unmerited grace of salvation only insofar as we "work while being worked upon by Other-power" and perform metanoesis. Only to that extent can we understand the transformation of negation-*qua*-affirmation that Nietzsche speaks of as the pressure and liberation of eternal recurrence.

It seems to me that Nietzsche's attempt at complete and utter sincerity has helped him to touch the secret mechanism of this transformation. Behind his words, which profess atheism and antimoralism, stands an uncommonly high and noble spirit that reveals a deep interiority and purity. Perhaps it was his sufferings that drew him close to the realm of the sage. In essence, his thought is no more than religious thought located at a point beyond good and evil. To be sure, the notion of the superman situates the person who, from the viewpoint of values, is thought to be a sage, at a point *prior* to the opposition of values, so that its own transcendent structure can be understood only as an absolute negation. But the Dionysian spirit, which is its basic determining element, is simply a grasping of reason breaking through reason as life in its *an sich*, or recurrent, stage. Nietzsche's sister relates how, to close relatives and friends, he seemed like a sage pretending to be evil.[25] This would mean that once the satanic disguise is removed, the Dionysian spirit should disclose its true form as the reason of absolute nothingness that breaks through the self and overcomes the self. The will to power should no longer seem to be the mere egoism of seeking direct dominion over others, but the process of regaining dominion over the self that has been negatively determined by others, and totally negating it. It should mean making negation impossible: nothing less than a total renunciation of negation wrought through the negation of negation.

In other words, the free will which is mediated by negation and which, through self-control, converts control of the self by others into nothingness, is the true state of the will to power, and hence may rightly be called transcendent will. What Buddhism calls the "supple mind" that overcomes others by its very suppleness must be a will to power in this sense of the term. The egoism that lies directly on the surface of Nietzsche's will to power is actually nothing more than a disguise. Though the mask be that of a devil, the reality is that of a sage. Here lies the secret of Nietzsche's Dionysus: on the outside we see a strong and heroic figure who does not shrink even from a religion of Satan; but on the inside, beneath the exterior garments, lies the heart of a sage overflowing with infinite love. For this very reason, the world of the superman is not the devil's world full of struggle and destruction, but the sage's Pure Land of love.[26]

The world of conflict and struggle that appears at first glance to lead to mutual destruction and ultimately to one's own destruction is not the true world of the superman. If the will to power is understood not as the desire for unmediated control over others, but as a mediation of absolute affirmation that freely considers determination by others inevitable and freely wills its own self-negating nature, the world of the superman has to be a world of love in which coexistence without struggle is guaranteed on the basis of a mutual negation-*qua*-affirmation, a mediation of absolute negation performed by oneself and others collaboratively.

Might we not say that when Zarathustra—the mouthpiece for Nietzsche's own thoughts—proclaims the appearance of the superman, calmly "under-goes" his destiny as a forerunner of the superman who "over-comes," and considers it his nature to sacrifice himself for the sake of the emergence of the superman, he is practicing a kind of self-interest-*qua*-altruism (*jiri-soku-rita*) that reminds us of the Buddhist bodhisattva-ideal? The whole tone of *Thus Spoke Zarathustra* clearly points in this direction. As teacher of the doctrine of the superman, Zarathustra despises the weakness and ugliness of humanity but is not one to forsake humankind. Instead, he elevates the human and thereby mediates the birth of the superman.

It is said that Nietzsche himself was possessed of the attributes of a teacher which make him comparable to Socrates.[27] Along this line, I should like to interpret him as a saint who rejected debilitating sympathies to preach a strengthening evangel of suffering and overcoming. No doubt, his is a sainthood not attainable by ordinary men and women—indeed, one that he himself did not fully realize. Even Zarathustra remains an intermediate figure relative to the superman eagerly awaited in the future. Although fundamentally a sage, Nietzsche was not without his imperfections, a finite historical individual forever denied the fullness of his sagehood. We would do better to say that he was not an actual sage but only a potential one. The way of Zen, which seeks to awaken people to the Buddha nature latent within them, is close to the thought of Zarathustra here in its teaching of the will of self-power.

All of this helps us to understand why Nietzsche's thought was an exception in not opening into metanoetics. As is well known, it was because of its notion of *ressentiment* that Nietzsche accused Christianity of practicing the most conspicuous form of masochism and self-torture, worthy only of his detestation and denunciation. To be sure, metanoesis seems to be completely opposed to the idea of a superman. The sense of repentance he addresses in his chapter "On the Higher Man" in the closing section of *Thus Spoke Zarathustra* clearly remains at the level of the ethical rigors of self-power; it does not rise to the level of self-abandonment to the transformation of Other-power. I do not mean to imply that the sympathies and dissatisfactions expressed in Nietzsche's critique of metanoesis are without reason, but only that they are the result of his own failure to reach the turning point of religious metanoesis.

For ordinary and ignorant persons like me, there is no choice but to walk the way of metanoesis. The exceptional path that Nietzsche followed is out of the question for me. Nevertheless, overcoming the past through the action-faith-witness of metanoetics, which is more suited to me, actually provides proof of his ideas on the liberation of the past, the eternity of the present, and the creativity of the future. What is more, my confrontation with Nietzsche has not only demonstrated a common structure of absolute negation but also crystallized the distinct forms to which our different viewpoints inevitably give rise. And here, conversely, I find indirect proof of the truth of the authentic subjectivity of metanoetics. Is it not true that in opposing the truth of Zarathustra to the illusion and falsehood of the poet (exemplified by Wagner), Nietzsche recognized that only the moment of metanoesis can be pure and true?[28] Surely he realized that for those who were not the exception like him, eternity is mediated by spiritual metanoesis. It is here that I find myself having to believe that Nietzsche's thought witnesses indirectly to the truth of metanoetics.

At the same time, I would insist that for Heidegger, for Nietzsche, and even for Kant, the so-called independence and autonomy of the Northern European spirit did not go deeply enough into the human to achieve the denial and breakthrough of the self. In the end, they all cling to a kind of self-centered elitism that makes it impossible for them to pass beyond into the freedom of absolute nothingness by renouncing and letting go of even the noble self. Of course I, too, am not without reverence for the nobility and dignity that certain individuals achieve. At the same time, I know that I, weak and insignificant as I am, have no assurance of ever being able to realize such a state myself. Hence, the level of confidence in self-power that such sages enjoy is closed off to me.

I can do no other than seek my salvation in the metanoetical action-faith-witness of Other-power. Yet it is precisely because I find myself in this situation that I feel an unbounded respect and love for the teachings of these sages, and especially for Nietzsche, who penetrated the depths of human suffering to reach a "religion without religion."

Actually, what this amounts to is reading Nietzsche's thought as a doctrine of *gensō*. For years *Thus Spoke Zarathustra* had been a closed book to me. No matter how many times I tried to read it, I could not understand it. But now it has become one of my favorite books, and this is due, strangely enough, to metanoetics. In the doctrine of the superman, which at first seemed so contrary to my own way of thinking, I found proof of metanoetics and could hardly contain myself for joy. I say this resigned to the fact that sages of self-power and young admirers of Nietzsche might not take kindly to the interpretation of an old and foolish man and might dismiss it as altogether wide of the mark.

As Heidegger has pointed out, Nietzsche's distinction of the three approaches to historiography—the monumentalistic, the antiquarian, and the critical—provides profound insight into the historicity of Dasein,[29] offering a critique of the present age that gets beyond historicism. The fact that he takes as the foundation for his critique of history a sort of nothingness[30] akin to the nothingness of absolute critique suggests that Nietzsche's nihilism and my metanoetics can interpenetrate each other as opposing orientations of self power and Other-power.

Nietzsche's view has close affinities with the Kierkegaardian "moment," the point where eternity touches time, in the sense that it forms the ground of a death-and-resurrection. The fact that Heidegger's notion of the "present," which takes a stance close to both of these, establishes the existence of free self-consciousness in the nothingness of Nietzsche rather than in the eternal faith of Kierkegaard is an expression of the German people's worship of the sage and the hero, which stems from a convergence of his character with the spirit of his age. Conversely, the fact that my metanoetics coincides with Kierkegaard's faith may be said to be an inevitable consequence of the standpoint of the ordinary, ignorant individual, which also is ordained by individual character and the spirit of the age. That metanoetics, despite its opposing orientation, should be able to open a way to the understanding of Nietzsche is hardly surprising when considered from the standpoint of absolute transformation. It shows us the dialectic of paradox. It would not be going too far to say that the only way for old fools like me to becomes disciples of Nietzsche is to walk the way of metanoetics.

Chapter 4

Metanoetics and the Philosophy of Freedom

Freedom as the will to nothingness · The symbolism of absolute reality-qua-nothingness · The freedom of reality-qua-self through the mediation of nothingness · The limits of self-power will · Metanoetical freedom · Divine freedom · Zazen and the kōan · Reality as kōan · The kōan-like quality of metanoetics · "Nembutsu-Zen" · Nothingness as the ground of freedom and time · The ethicoreligious nature of the kōan and everydayness · The relationship to history of Zen and metanoetics contrasted · The essential role of action in dialectical unity · The elimination of opposition through love (compassion) · "Dialectical synthesis" · The nullification of being as the mediation of nothingness · "Empty being" · The duality of the present and the two dimensions internal to freedom · An outline of Schelling's theory of freedom · Schelling's views contrasted with metanoetics · Freedom and metanoesis · The mediatory nature of freedom · From theories of freedom to metanoetics · The relationships among Hegel's phenomenology, Schelling's idea of freedom, and metanoetics · Love and Great Compassion · Nothingness and Ungrund · Ungrund and Grund · The position of metanoetics vis-à-vis Schelling's view of freedom and Heidegger's philosophy of existential hermeneutics · The significance of Kant's view of religion

The idea of taking freedom as the principle of history does not so much solve the problems of history as raise them anew. Indeed, so many are the problems contained in this idea that few concepts in the history of ethics, religion, and philosophy have given birth to so many theories.

In ancient Greece, the problem of freedom was not a matter of great concern. Its philosophy was primarily concerned with nature and hence grew into a philosophy of nature or metaphysics, the main purpose of which was to investigate the principle of being and their structures of meaning. Later it came to deal with the problem of the human, but even there its chief concern was with humanity in the polis. It did not give much attention to the human individual, that is, to the person as the subject of freedom. Even in the final stages of Greek philosophy, when the focus had shifted to human emancipation, it was still unable to bring into question the idea of freedom itself. This in turn had a profound bearing on the fact that the philosophy of history was not able to come into its own in Greece. The "being" thought to be the primary element or purpose or principle of order in nature was viewed in terms of unchanging essences, while only the appearances of nature were seen to be in a constant process of flux and change. As a result, the notion of history as creative development, in the double sense of a *reformation* that represents a radical thrust into the future and a *renovation* that returns to past origins, did not reach full consciousness in the Greek mind. It was only natural that the notion of freedom as a subjective—existentially self-conscious—principle of history did not become one of the major concerns of Greek philosophy.

The issue of freedom came to the fore with Christianity. One of the distinguishing features of Christianity is its view of history as a human process that begins with the Fall (occasioned by freedom), continues under the shadow of divine judgment against the sin of humanity, and leads to the reconciliation of humanity with God through the redemptive death of Jesus Christ. The doctrine of freedom and the philosophy of history produced by Christian thought effected a radical revolution in the Greek spiritual tradition. Later, when the emphasis that medieval thought had put on the authority of the church was replaced by modern liberal thought, and freedom came to be recognized as constitutive of the essence of the human, the theory of freedom was made to occupy a central position in the world of philosophy. The philosophical standpoint of general ontology that had marked the late Middle Ages shifted to one of subjective-existential self-consciousness. In this way, the inquiry into the nature of freedom came to represent a central problem of modern philosophy.

Proof of origins of freedom, however, remain as elusive as ever. It is not a matter to be solved by deductive inference since knowledge by its very nature has to do with being; and freedom, as I have already explained in speaking of the notion of contingency, is not concerned with preexistent being. Freedom is realized only through creative action initiated in nothingness and located in the future; it is absolutely spontaneous action developing out of nothingness. Put in formal terms, freedom is the spontaneity of human will mediated by nothingness; or the spontaneous decision of the self voluntarily submitting itself to nothingness; or the spontaneity of relative being voluntarily submitting itself to the absolute and thus being transformed into a mediator of the absolute; or the self-determination of the human person obedient to God. Since God, as the absolute, is not being but nothingness, the act of submission or obedience that belongs to freedom represents a spontaneous and self-determining choice on the part of the human person, with no external restrictions. The human individual gains freedom through the mediation of God, while God in turn is realized and made manifest through the mediation of human freedom. It is out of this absolute mediation that freedom arises. All specific theories of freedom elaborated since the time of Augustine contain some such mediation of nothingness at their core.

It is not being, then, but nothingness that provides a foundation in the human for freedom, a locus at which the will is constituted. The main problem with theories of freedom is the usual tendency to pass over the whole question of nothingness. Nothingness is not something to which immediate experience can attest; whatever can be experienced immediately, or intuited in objective terms, belongs to being, not to nothingness. To suppose therefore that freedom is capable of being grasped in an act of comprehensive intuition is tantamount to turning it into being and thus depriving it of its essential nature as nothingness.

Kant's theory of freedom was marred by just such a tendency, prompting Schelling to develop a theory of his own in critical response. Under the influence of the Platonic dialectic of nothingness, Schelling modified Kant's position of immediate personal experience to produce a doctrine of freedom that ranks as one of the most remarkable in all of Western philosophy. Nevertheless, his idea of freedom swung so far in the direction of the speculative that it tended to forfeit the true self-consciousness of the subject, the authentic personal experience to which Kant had drawn attention. As a result, it was inevitable that the dialectic of nothingness would grow weaker in Schelling's theory of freedom and that an understanding of nothingness based on the ontology of being would rise to a position of dominance.

In clarifying his own position, Schelling too often refers to mythical allegory and poetic symbolism to the neglect of dialectical mediation, even though this latter is necessary for any method aimed at philosophical reflection on nothingness. Insofar as dialectical mediation is a stand-point that involves the negation of objective thinking grounded in the principle of identity, it cannot avoid the paradox peculiar to dialectics. That is to say, it is a matter of an absolute transformation (or conversion) in which the self that has been torn asunder by contradiction and antinomies is resurrected in new being from the depths of nothingness, to become like "someone dead returned to life," and in which the self is enabled to perform the genuine activity of nothingness, even though it is the force of absolute nothingness that does the enabling by turning the self into a mediator of nothingness. Thus any claim to know nothingness "objectively" or to grasp it in an act of self-consciousness, insofar as it involves some thing called "nothingness" or some self that is aware of it, is misguided. From the standpoint of dialectical mediation, knowledge or self-consciousness of nothingness is possible because there is no object that is known nor any self that knows, no self to be self-conscious or to become the object of self-consciousness. In this sense, even though it is said that we are conscious of our action or aware of our will, authentic action and true will become possible only when the so-called acting self has been annihilated and our ordinary willing self brought to naught.

Here, true knowledge is knowing in ignorance, and authentic self-consciousness is without self. And yet the religiously awakened consciousness is said to "perceive clearly at every place and time." When there is neither any object of knowing nor any act of knowing, and yet there exists true knowledge, or when there is neither any self present in self-consciousness as agent or as object, and yet all beings are regarded as self-conscious realizations of their true nature, it is then that there is "clear witness at every time and place." What is at stake here is not a knowledge of being but of nothingness. We become aware of the activity of nothingness by exerting ourselves to become nothingness and at the same time by being made to become nothingness.

The will *of* nothingness is not a will *to* nothingness that wills nothingness as its goal. The will *to* nothingness may be a will to being, but this is not the case with the will *of* nothingness, since this latter is not a will engaged in the quest for nothingness by itself. It is a will that seeks "no-thing" by simultaneously *abandoning* its own immediate will and *being made to abandon* its every immediate desire. This is the very process that takes place in the awakening to Buddhahood. To consider the Buddha as one who seeks "no-thing" means that Buddhahood is inaccessible to those who make it the object of their search, since their efforts drive them in the exactly opposite direction. Only those who can resign themselves to accepting the total annihilation of all objects of desire as well as all desiring subjectivity—only those whose desire is free of all desire—can face their own death with "naturalness" and be restored to life as one who has died to the world and to self. Only for such "living dead" as these can nothingness be truly willed, and the self that wills nothingness be brought to self-realization as "will without willing."

Such is the will that arises out of true freedom; only such a willing subject is fully free. Perfect freedom belongs not to being but to nothingness, since freedom itself is the activity of nothingness. It is also, as noted earlier, an "action without an acting subject" in the sense that it is performed by a subject that has been annihilated. This is what is meant by "naturalness" or "action of no-action." Such truly free activity takes place unhindered and everywhere at once.

If freedom is the activity of nothingness, a pure activity without a concrete subject, does not this land us in mere idealism? This is what happens with Fichte, for instance, whose notion of the pure ego reduces the subject of freedom to a mere abstract universal devoid of concrete individuality. Is it possible to identify the self-consciousness that is the subject of nothingness with such an ego? The question in fact arises only because we are still trying to think of nothingness directly, to gain an immediate experience or intuition of the subject of nothingness. Because Fichte himself was stuck at such a standpoint, he failed to rid himself of the abstract conceptualism of his pure ego and to bring the problem of freedom to a satisfactory solution, despite the strenuous efforts he exerted in that direction. His free self is finally nothing more than what any of us could bring to self-awareness merely by acknowledging the experience of intellectual intuition. Because this sort of unmediated freedom exists only in the personal experience of a subject devoid of the mediating negation of a particular object, it can only collapse when it confronts the oppositions and contradictions that prevail in the world of actuality. To the extent that we cling to the pure ego, we cannot but get tangled up in attachments that entail nonfreedom and thus end up at the opposite pole of unrestricted freedom. The early Fichte was unable to extricate himself theoretically or practically from this predicament. The only way out is through metanoetics. Practically speaking, we must first be driven to a total negation of self by confronting the depth of the contradiction of radical evil and then be restored to life through the spontaneous decision to accept death in metanoesis (*zange*). In this performing—or being made to perform—the conversion of death-and-resurrection, we come to realize that our true self is the self of nothingness whose being consists in acting as the mediator of nothingness.

Theoretically speaking, the logic of absolute transformation according to which nothingness is defined as absolute mediation requires relative being as the medium of negation. That is, in this process of transformation and mediation, nothingness manifests itself at the center of relative being as it exists here and now, so that our being can be constituted only as the actuality of "living, or being restored to life, as one who is dead." Nothingness cannot become actual except by way of the absolute mediation of a resurrection repeatedly realized at the particular core of relative beings by means of a circular movement between the absolute and the relative. Such a truly religious self-consciousness is confirmed only in the paradox of nothingness-*qua*-being and universal-*qua*-individual. It has nothing to do with any act of subsumption on the part of a universal that permeates the individual with universal being in accord with a principle of identity. The element of "clear witness and perception at every time and place" is an instantaneous realization. It is more like a differential limit than an integral whole, since the latter is not nothingness but being. Because nothingness emerges at the point that the conversion and transformation of the individual takes place, the individual has to be regarded as a being that mediates nothingness. Nothingness cannot function apart from the cooperation of being, which is why self-consciousness of nothingness consists in nothingness-*qua*-being and arises wherever the center of the relative self is established through death-and-resurrection. The Zen saying, "Light and darkness, side by side" (*meian sōsō*), seems to point to just such a reciprocal penetration and correspondence between nothingness and being.

Further, for nothingness to perform its mediating role, the real world must first be destroyed, sunk into the abyss of antinomies, in order later to be restored as part of the subjective experience of death-and-resurrection that takes place in the knowing self. Alternatively, we may say that the acting subject and objective reality correspond to each other and presuppose each other, so that, on the one hand, the death of the self is brought about by the antinomies that arise out of its confrontation with reality and, on the other, the antinomies of the real world are brought into being with the free action of the self serving as the determining factor.

Because history is a product of the interaction between actual reality and the human subject, reality and the subject bring destruction upon each other so that both sink into nothingness. At the same time, through the circular movement of nothingness referred to above, reality is rendered capable of restoration after its destruction, and of destruction after its restoration. This is what is meant by speaking of history as "reformation-*qua*-renovation." It is not that either actual reality or the subject destroys the other unilaterally. Such one-sided determination would mean that the one that did the destroying would never come to its own destruction. Or again, if the one were to reach self-destruction by sinking into nothingness, it could not negate the other.

From the standpoint of nothingness, these opposite forces are used to create an axis of reciprocal negation and transformation so that they can achieve mutual destruction. In other words, nothingness leads to (mediates) the complete and total destruction of both elements in such a way that the self-destruction of the other is at the same time the self-destruction of the first. In its radical mediation, nothingness brings into being the death-and-resurrection of being: "being as *upāya*" (*hōbenteki-sonzai*) or emptiness (*śūnyatā*). Both the self and the actual world are realized as unrestrictedly free and empty—void of self in the sense of the selflessness of the thing-in-itself and of one's own self—on the basis of nothingness. Nothingness is brought to awareness subjectively as the free and "selfless" self and is symbolized objectively as emptiness. That is, actual reality is transfigured into emptiness as a symbol of nothingness, thus mediating freedom and revealing its divine nature.

To put this in the context of Buddhist wisdom, the emphasis is placed on self-awareness because "mind, just as it is, is the Buddha himself." In other words, the absolute mind of absolute idealism is already the standpoint of religion, which is why Hegel defines religion in terms of absolute idealism as the self-consciousness of absolute knowledge. But to say that "mind, just as it is, is the Buddha himself" implies at the same time the opposite: "neither mind nor Buddha." Absolute idealism symbolizes the viewpoint of the "absolute idea" in the sense that just as self is at the same time actual reality, so too every objective being in the present is directly identical with self or mind. Apart from this identity, there *is* no mind and no consciousness. Because objective being is transformed into emptiness as the symbol of nothingness, it is likewise crystallized into the core of the subject, manifesting the content of the "selfless self" and united to the self-consciousness of the absolute idea. This self-awareness is the "mind of the Buddha that is no-mind." It is based on nothingness, where what is Buddha is at the same time "no-Buddha."

The free self is determined by present reality, but in accepting this determination and submitting devoutly to it, reality itself becomes an element of subjectivity. Objective reality thus becomes the realm of unrestricted freedom. In this way present reality, seen as a symbol of nothingness, is transformed into a mediator of freedom. Or put the other way around, there can be no free self so long as reality and the self are set over against each other.

In dying obediently to itself in the face of reality, in voluntarily giving itself over to the determinations of reality and accepting these determinations, the self achieves that realization of "having no thing" which is the essence of the "selfless self." This voluntary abandonment to nothingness on the part of the self signals a transformation into the unrestricted freedom of "naturalness." This is precisely what authentic freedom is all about: the self-awareness of nothingness consisting in the fact that reality is self and self is reality.

As long as the self is presumed to exist apart from this process of mediation and transformation—that is, as long as it is regarded as the self's immediate and spontaneous determination and construction of reality—its freedom must forever elude our understanding. Indeed, that sort of freedom is not only paradoxical, it is impossible. From ancient times, difficulties inherent in theories of freedom stem from this approach and the concomitant failure to reflect on freedom as a medium of nothingness, which would provide foundations for appreciating its real meaning. This is not to say that the philosophical position being presented here is altogether free of paradox, since it too requires an act of death-and-resurrection on the part of the one who would gain self-awareness of free existence. For it is only through an act of voluntary submission that the self can achieve the faith-witness (*shin-shō*) of its freedom; and, at the same time, it is only when the way of action-faith-witness (*gyō-shin-shō*) opens up before us that freedom becomes manifest to us.

But then the question arises: Is this not a freedom reserved for saints and sages, inaccessible to ignorant people like us? As I have stressed before, unrestricted freedom does indeed belong only to those who have realized nothingness in themselves; and only those who are able utterly to negate themselves by submitting to objective actuality—to arrive at nothingness by letting go before the abyss that swallows up them and all of reality—can be restored through this self-negation to life as "emptied being" (being-*qua*-nothingness). But does such experience come only to the enlightened who can bring themselves to nothingness and to the recognition of their essence as "having no thing"? Is it only for those who would become one with absolute nothingness by embodying Buddhahood in themselves? Let such as these participate in unrestricted freedom as they may. For the unenlightened, such freedom must be said to remain no more than an ideal state that can be aimed at but not achieved.

The lofty words and noble deeds of the Zen masters recorded in various accounts can fill us with admiration, but lie beyond the reach of our own learning and practice. To the Zen master who might rebuke me with the claim that I hold this view because of my "lack of faith in my own innate Buddhahood," I should reply that it is precisely because this lack of faith is so characteristic of us ignorant persons that we, in our folly and sin, know not what to do in the way of self-power (*jiriki*). What we need is rather a recognition of the limits of self-power. In saying this, I in no way mean to deny the possibility of unrestricted freedom to those who, "having passed through the gate set up by the Zen master Wu-mên, have found the road to open up in all directions with no further hindrance whatsoever."[1] My own limitations give me no grounds for denying the existence of saints and sages of that sort. Quite the contrary, the profound disturbance I have felt over the stubborn tenacity of my unenlightened state has led me all the more to long for that noble state of mind, inaccessible as it is. Whatever personal experiences I have had of such states of mind have lasted no more than a moment; and I can only deplore the fact that I remain stuck in the miserable condition of attachment to my own ego and to the world. All this I have to admit.

Thus the ultimate state of absolute nothingness and acting "naturally, having no thing" by self-power are still no more than mere concepts for me. Yet when, in the profound experience of this suffering, I am forced to confess my own lack of enlightenment and my unworthiness to exist for all the shame I feel, I find that in spite of it all and without any of the grounds for my shame being removed, I am graced with a personal experience of emancipation from the eternal darkness of mind, as if a serene light had poured forth from eternity into my mind. Indeed, I am able to have such moving personal experiences precisely because I am unable to free myself from ignorance and satisfy my longing for wisdom and freedom, because I recognize that self-assertion is denied me and that I must voluntarily submit myself to despair. In this way I am made to see that the gate that does not officially (by objective logic) allow even a needle to pass through, now turns into a wide road which privately or personally (in a state of existential awakening) horses and vehicles can traverse. I now see that what *is opened up for me*, as one whose "lack of faith" inhibits him from relying on self-power and even drives him to renounce it altogether, is similar to what the saints and sages *open up for themselves* through the self-power of their faith. I see that through the roundabout path of negation I am permitted to arrive at a point comparable to the summit achieved directly by the saints and sages. This is what I call metanoesis (*zange*).

Whether or not the occurrence of this positive event through *zange* is identical with the *satori* of the saints and sages I cannot say, since I lack experience of the latter to make the comparison. Be that as it may, I have no doubt, relying on my faith-witness, that my position and the enlightenment of the saint are analogous. As far as I am concerned, I am convinced that their qualitative structures are comparable, however lacking in vitality and strength the former may look in the comparison. Even should I be mistaken in this view, I can still perform the act of *zange*, trusting in the standpoint of metanoetics and bearing witness through faith (*shin-shō*) to what is revealed through the experience. For all the anxiety and doubt that remains, I find that from such a position I am at last able to achieve a certain peace of mind, to interpret the lofty state of the saints and sages, and to attempt a clearer analysis of their free existence in nothingness.

The communication of existential thought comes down finally to the analogy of being. The self-consciousness of the individual cannot be known directly by means of universal reason, since it cannot avoid the limitations of being individual through and through. Even the saint and the sage can only communicate individual truth interpersonally, and only to those with whom they have established an intimate spiritual relationship. Moreover, since we must admit an affinity between the analogy of being present in reciprocal relationships among relative beings and that found in the relationship between the absolute and the relative, the attempt to interpret the unrestricted freedom of the saint and the sage in terms of nothingness seems justified. I have also sought to explain the structure of the enlightened mind by the indirect route of the analogy of being. While myself lacking any direct experience of enlightenment, I can still know something about it through negation and the indirect way of *zange*—that is, through the light of my action-faith-witness. Thus, if I am allowed to extend the analogy a bit further, I would argue that, structurally speaking, the coincidence between the metanoetics I have developed in terms of action-faith-witness and the way of the saints and sages reaches all the way to the core of *satori* itself.

The way of Zen is, of course, a way of meditation and concentration. In contrast with the doctrine of "gradual enlightenment" found in other Buddhist schools—namely, that *satori* is sought through a logical, systematic, and theoretically developed study of the *sūtras* and *sāstras*—it holds up *zazen* as a method of practical mental discipline that enables one to achieve the "sudden enlightenment" of awakening to the nature of the true self as "having no thing." In particular, we may mention here the Rinzai sect, which places emphasis on wrestling with paradox through the *kōan* and uses this mental discipline in *zazen* to guard against falling into the vanity of a meditative introspection that closes the mind in on itself. Even the Sōtō sect, which represents this latter tendency, includes the likes of Dōgen, who practiced the *kōan* no less than members of other Zen sects that valued the practice. Indeed, it was Dōgen who transcribed and brought back to Japan the anthology of *kōan* known as the *Blue Cliff Records (Hekigan-shū)*, a work that had earlier been burned by the great Zen master and exponent of *kōan*-Zen, Daie (1089–1163).

As a Zen method, the discipline of the *kōan* is on a par with *zazen*. Unlike the physical practice of *zazen*, however, the *kōan* seems to be indispensable as a form of mental meditation and intellectual awakening. As its original meaning of "official document" suggests, the word *kōan* implies the sense of a key to open the gate to enlightenment. Accordingly, we may think of it as the antinomy of the contradiction involved in the transformation of being into nothingness. Viewed in terms of logic, the *kōan* is generally constructed on an antinomy, though there are obviously many *kōan* that rather use the antinomy as a symbolic form of expression for nothingness. Even in these latter cases, the *kōan* preserves its basic role of opening up a way to nothingness by means of contradiction and paradox, a role that it could not fulfill if it were no more than mere poetic metaphor. In a word, the function of the *kōan* is to force the ordinary, discriminating mind into a blind alley through paradoxical antinomies, to leave it hanging precariously at the edge of a cliff where it can practice the Great Death of letting go in order to be restored to new life. Of course, the *kōan* also helps to clarify the inner workings of one's practice, as well as the various transformations that take place there, in a way that the conceptual and propositional language cannot. Furthermore, as Dōgen's famous phrase has it, we can "realize reality as *kōan*" (*genjō-kōan*): the whole world of actual realities can become a *kōan* because of its structural contradiction of being determined by the past and shaped by the future. This shows us how deeply *kōan*-Zen is rooted in the real world. Because everything can become a *kōan*, the *kōan* is present always and everywhere, not only in the traditional methods of Zen.

The ethical practice of taking one's place in historical actuality makes encounter with the *kōan* inevitable. The pangs of conscience drive us headlong into confrontation with antinomies and, ultimately, bring us to the metanoesis (*zange*) of self-abandonment. It is as Kierkegaard had said in arguing that repentance is the result of ethical existence, in contrast with the enjoyment that characterizes aesthetic existence: the confrontation of ethics with radical evil cannot avoid facing antinomy and arriving ultimately at *zange*. The self that has been forced to let go of itself in metanoesis is then restored to itself; the "action in gratitude" that had been impossible at the ethical plane of self-power becomes possible through Other-power. In this way the antinomies are resolved without being dissolved, and the roadless transit of the "action of no-action" becomes manifest as a "naturalness" (*jinen-hōni*)[2] that surpasses all opposition between good and evil. The gate impassable for *jiriki* becomes passable through *tariki*.

The ethical death-and-resurrection that takes place in *zange* belongs to the "return to the world" (*gensō*) of religious action-faith-witness. I used to speak of the antinomies of ethics as a consequence of logical necessity, and of the conversion or transformation that rescues us from them as a religious *gensō* consequent upon a submission of oneself to the utter disintegration of the antinomies. At the time I had not yet come to the metanoetical standpoint of Other-power. All I could do was try to clarify the logical dimension of the transformation, which I conceived as a sort of resurrection, albeit a resurrection still bound to the principle of self-identity and far removed from the complete serenity of life *sub specie mortis*, of "living as one who had died."

In any event, the contradictory structure of reality as both a "thrownness" and a "project," as well as the "destruction through negation" at work in the reciprocal determination of reality and the self, transforms reality as a whole into a *kōan*, and thus demonstrates the deep moorings of *kōan*-Zen in reality. The *kōan* are constructed from elements in reality that serve to point out the sharp contradictions within reality or to disclose its marked paradoxical character. To be sure, they take shape in the workings of the Zen master's imagination. Moreover, only a comparatively small number of well-known *kōan* have come down to us from the past, and practitioners of Zen are always trained to meditate on the same *kōan*. Nonetheless, from everything that has been said so far, it should be clear that the ethical metanoetics I am proposing may also be considered a "total *kōan*" rooted in the essential structure of reality. It is not restricted to saints and sages, but is one *kōan* in which ethics and *zange* are made directly accessible to anyone possessed of conscience. It is a gate to the religious life for ordinary, ignorant persons so long as they strive sincerely to avoid all self-deception and to pick themselves up when they trip and fall, as it is our lot to do.

Even if our sinful nature is so deeply rooted that it is not easy for us to practice continual *zange*, and if our arrogance invariably gets in the way of our every attempt at heartfelt repentance, these very defects themselves give rise to the *zange* that helps us to penetrate them and see through them for what they are. In this sense, *zange* is a storehouse of unlimited possibilities, and there is no cause to worry over the imperfect way in which we practice it. Simply by touching our imperfection, *zange* passes through it. In other words, it is through the grace of the Great Compassion that the gate of *zange* is open to all. This I have been made to feel in a personal way, for which I cannot but be grateful. This is what encourages me to address my explanation of conversion through *zange* in terms of Great Negation–*qua*–Great Compassion to the ignorant and the ordinary person, knowing full well that what I have to say cannot be compared to the teachings of saints and sages. This is what the philosophy of metanoetics is about.

If, in virtue of the structural similarities of the two ways, we may refer to the action-faith-witness of pursuing the path of metanoetics—believing in the Other-power of the Great Compassion, entrusting oneself to it, and accepting the determinations of reality in obedient submission—as the way of the *nembutsu* (invoking the name of Amida Buddha), it would not seem unreasonable actually to call metanoetics, which treats *zange* as a *kōan*, a form of Nembutsu-Zen. Historically speaking, the term "Nembutsu-Zen" designates a degenerate stage of Zen Buddhism. In the time of the Ming and Ch'ing dynasties, Zen Buddhists forsook the lofty and unshakable spirit of their discipline and began to adulterate *jiriki* (self-power) with *tariki* (Other-power), substituting prayers and invocations of the Buddha's name for the *kōan*. Be that as it may, I am persuaded that the standpoint of metanoetics gives us good reason for referring to Other-power *nembutsu* as Nembutsu-Zen, since it possesses the structural characteristics of the *kōan* practiced in Zen. In any case, I would insist that freedom constituted as the awareness of the nothingness of the self is not necessarily limited to saints and sages, but is open to all of us. By following the way of *zange*, we ordinary fools can participate in that freedom just as we are, with all our ordinariness and folly. Once we have set foot on the path of *zange*, access to freedom through the Great Compassion is ours.

If the understanding of the essence of freedom laid out in the previous pages is correct, we are able to comprehend not only the future, which is the main concern of freedom, but also the past, through which the future must needs be mediated, and the present, where past and future come together. As has been pointed out, in contemporary existential philosophy the past is viewed as a "thrownness," the future as a "project," and the present as a "thrown project" that unites the two aspects into one. This means that the project of the future is thoroughly mediated by the thrownness of the past, that the "potential for being" (*Seinkönnen*) of the former is also determined by the latter, that the very possibility of project arises in conformity with thrownness. In other words, the "forerunning" (*Vorlaufen*) of the potential for being, which constitutes the projection of the future and takes it beyond the thrownness of the past, is already implied within that thrownness. Project is nothing other than a self-consciousness of the fact that Dasein not only bears on its shoulders the preexistent thrownness of the past but also contains the freedom of spontaneous decision as its own potential. The notion of "thrown project" signifies that the "forerunning" of the potential for being cannot come about except through that mediation.

The fusing of the two elements of thrownness and project, which stand opposed as contradictories, is not as smooth and simple as the above description might make it seem. Simply to speak of a *geworfener Entwurf* might lead one to suppose that there is no contradiction at all between them, that the notion of "thrownness" is added to the notion of "project" as a species is added to a genus under the principle of identity. If this were true, "thrown project" would represent no more than the state of being bound to the fallen and inauthentic world of everydayness, the realm of *das Man*. One should not speak of "project" where there is unawareness of the determinations of the past as determinations (that is, where the determination by the past has been forfeited together with the freedom toward the future). As existential aspects of authentic existence, thrownness and project cannot be united by the principle of self-identity but must oppose one another as contradictories. "Thrown project" must remain a dialectical notion whose elements are not to be conjoined as distinct determinations of being after the manner of the specification of a genus, but united in a transformation of negation wrought through the mediation of nothingness.

Although it is just such a dialectical structure that Heidegger has in mind, I find his treatment of the transformation of negation unclear, at least to the extent that his hermeneutical standpoint glosses over the "action" of transformation and leaves the dialectical structure of the problem to recede into the background. His conception of a *Selbstsein* whose possibility is projected into the future as a result of the decision to affirm the determination of having been "thrown" into the present from the past, is not even worked out to the extent of Goethe's notion of resignation referred to earlier. Consequently, the project of being a self is not a symbolic content illuminated by the serene light of unrestricted freedom, but a fixation of the self on itself, confronted with the harsh and gloomy decision of accepting its own death. It is only natural that *Angst* is singled out to disclose the structure of human existence or Dasein. For the hermeneutical approach to self-conscious existence, which is far removed from the approach of "action-faith," there may be nothing strange about this. But it means the eclipse of nothingness from the ground of dialectics. Nothingness is interpreted mainly as a nihility, like an abyss over which existence hangs suspended, and its positive element of absolute transformation is almost entirely lost. As self-consciousness of Dasein, nothingness is reduced to an abstraction. Moreover, since the present in which nothingness is manifest is completely deprived of its transcendent and bottomless quality, it is no more than the facticity of "being according to one's moods" (*Sein bei*). The deforming effects this has on an analysis of the structure of time are serious.

Ever since Augustine, the duality of the present as an infinity made finite, or the eternity of the present as ranging over the three worlds of time (allowing us to speak of the present of the past, the present of the present, and the present of the future), has been accepted as a necessary premise for the establishment of time. The dialectical mediation of nothingness, which is indispensable for the analysis of temporality thus understood, resists penetration by hermeneutics and the intuitive contemplation of phenomenology; it can be witnessed to only from a standpoint of faith-witness. To overlook this fact is to forego understanding the structure of time.

It is regrettable that the theory of time presented in Heidegger's *Being and Time*, a work of great acuteness and subtlety, lacks metaphysical depth in this regard. Despite its explanation of human self-transcendence, we are still left with the question: Without this ground of nothingness, where can one transcend *to*? The mere disclosure of "horizon" does not suffice for the fulfillment of true transcendence. What is disclosed from the standpoint of "potential for being" actually belongs to the realm of being; it cannot become true nothingness. The standpoint of hermeneutics cannot embrace action and faith. Action and faith are transcendent states that supersede the immanent scope of hermeneutical explanations; they do not belong to being, but arise only with nothingness. The girth of eternity that binds time together is nothingness, and can be witnessed to only through action-faith. The facticity of the present seen as a mood-bound existence cannot supply the eternity of nothingness to mediate between the mutually contradictory opposites of past and future. Hence the union of past and present cannot be dialectical either, but must slip into hermeneutical self-identity.

It is altogether unfortunate that the abstractness of the present moment in the existential theory of time deeply scars the metaphysical depth of this philosophy. To avoid this problem, we have no choice but to take leave of hermeneutics and move on to a practical standpoint of action-faith. Only through metanoetics can this transition be realized. Only this standpoint allows us to achieve comprehensive understanding of time, and hence also of the structure of history that is based on time.

The Zen Buddhist path of enlightenment or *satori* makes us of *kōan* drawn from the experiences of everyday life. Because of the mediation of the *kōan*, the way of *satori* is not ethical in nature but remains completely at the everyday level. Its ideal of "the ordinary, everyday mind is the way" implies that the awakening of enlightenment occurs in the everyday activities like dressing and feeding ourselves. But history, as objective and common "social reality," is not assured in this way. In Zen, reality unfolds from the standpoint of everydayness, with the emphasis on the "nothing" of its "empty being." At the same time, it is devoid of ethical seriousness and neglects the significance of the objective historical world whose being should be "being as *upāya*." This tendency points to a general flaw in Buddhism itself, but is particularly prominent in Zen. By way of contrast, because metanoetics views ethics as the "*kōan* of reality," the affirmative standpoint to which it is restored through its transformation-in-negation represents an ethical world in the sense of a "return to the world" (*gensō*) in gratitude, and through the construction of that world gives shape to history. Metanoetics *is* philosophy become conscious of the foundations of history. Given that the basis of metanoetics is history, this follows as a matter of course.

Thus far we have seen how the critique of reason worked out by critical philosophy comes to term in absolute critique, and I have shown how this latter actually characterizes the structure of history. In explaining the absolute criticism of history—that is, the absolute crisis or disruption of its structure—I pointed to the absolutely contradictory opposition between the past and the future in the form of "thrownness" and "project" or necessity (contingency) and freedom; I showed how the deepest ground of this absolute contradiction is overturned in a conversion to unity, manifests absolute nothingness, and is witnessed to as action-faith revitalized through the Great Compassion. The absolute present or "eternal now" appears in an eternal circularity of conversion and transformation within the unity of love wrought by the Great Compassion. This absolute present is not something that unifies past, present, and future in integral fashion, as the "present of the present" does in Augustine's theory of time; as nothingness, it is only the circularity of the dynamic of transformation. If Augustine's "eternal now" is a static contemplation bound to an integral locus, the present of transformation and conversion comes about momentarily and differentially; the moment is repeated in circular fashion and eternity is established in the infinite structure of that circularity.

Even though we speak of a circularity, it is not a circularity that goes round and round on the same track. Its repetitiveness is rather such that each new movement deviates from the course of the preceding movement, so that even though they are analogically identical, one circle never coincides exactly with another. It is thus not through static identity but through dynamic analogy that unity is brought to the whole process. To adopt the precision of a geometrical metaphor, the circularity we are speaking of here may be likened to a series of ellipses, each of which enjoys its own variable eccentricity, unlike the repetition of concentric circles drawn one on top of the other. Just as it is impossible to determine the enveloping curve that embraces the whole series of ellipses like a universal concept, so, too, the "eternal now" is not an integral locus to be grasped by intuition but something infinite to be realized only through one's action. That is, the unity of time in the present is not a static, self-enclosed unity, but a dynamic, open unity that holds within itself a contradiction of opposites: a return-*qua*-departure.

Here dialectical unity is both a unity and an opposition. It is not the sort of unity that brings contradictions into synthesis by way of negation and sublation, but a unity that leaves contradictions just as they are. Insofar as dialectical synthesis contains the idea of sublation or sublimation, it necessarily implies the removal or dismissal of the opposition between thesis and antithesis, and therefore cannot get beyond the realm of rational identity. But such a synthesis is different from the unity of the dialectic of love or the unity of the Great Compassion. In these latter, contradictory opposites are never abrogated. Rather, because the subject dies in the depths of the contradiction, the opposition ceases to be an opposition, but the contradictories are left as they are.

In the case of a love that forgives evil or a compassion that redeems one from sin, it is not that the evil and the sin cease to be what they are, but only that they lose their force of opposition. The negation or eradication of sin and evil is altogether different from forgiveness of sin or salvation from evil. In love, as in compassion, there is no opposing and no negating; things are left just as they are. The opposition remains, but evil and sin lose their power to oppose. As long as love and compassion stand opposed to sin and evil, the opposition itself is not truly extinguished. But the annihilation of opposition in the former becomes a mediator for the annihilation of opposition in the latter. Synthesis or the negation of negation does not mean extinguishing negation and embracing it in a unity; that would be a unity of being, a sort of "all-encompassing." The unity of nothingness, in the proper sense of the term, does not dismiss the opposition of an other but only detaches itself from it.

It is not as if there were some "locus" capable of comprehending contradictories in a greater synthesis. The only locus is nothingness, transformation itself. Since all things are transformed there, what appears there is not the *being* of individuals completely opposed to one another, but a manifestation of the *emptiness* of nothingness. Emptiness does not signify the mere negation of being, but the mediation and nullification of being through realizing nothingness in one's own existence. Being that is transformed by the absolute into a mediator of nothingness loses the "being" that requires opposition and is nullified. It is "empty being." The synthetic unity of dialectics is a *neither/nor* that rejects the synthesis of a *both/and*. It is a unity of nothingness that renounces the unity of being.

Thus love or compassion that annihilates the self provides the unitive aspect of the dialectic. To submit oneself to one's own death without reserve is, dialectically, to live. In dialectical synthesis, opposition is by no means directly abrogated, but is retained to the end. The renunciation or submission to extreme opposites that leads to death is turned about into an affirmation of new life, surpassing the opposition. This is what is meant by absolute transformation or absolute conversion. This transformation could never be intuited as a self-identity. For what would be intuited would not be nothingness but being, not a transformation but a tranquillizing, not action but contemplation, not a dying but an immediate affirmation of life, not a symbol but a direct expression. But the witness and self-awareness of dialectical unity through action-faith in the Great Compassion belongs to nothingness. The self-consciousness of nothingness is not the intuition of the existence of a self aware of itself, but action-faith in the Great Compassion wherein the self dies in the abyss of contradiction and makes nothingness manifest. It is not a self-consciousness of the fact that "my" self exists, but an action-witness of the fact that "my" self does not exist.

From this standpoint, the very notion of "self-consciousness" itself may seem inappropriate, but since there is no other more suitable notion, we are forced to remain with it. Dialectically, it means nothing more than the action-witness of the fact that the self is not being but nothingness. There is no doubt that such notions as love and renunciation are always accompanied by a clear self-consciousness of the self as selfless. Self-consciousness of nothingness is not a consciousness of the being of the self in some state of existence called "nothingness," but rather a consciousness of the nullification of the self that dies in the abyss of contradiction. The word "self-consciousness" simply indicates the action-witness of a transformation of the self in which it becomes nothingness even as existence itself comes to no-thing.

The transformative mediation of the present where freedom is made concrete is a dynamic, transforming unity of absolute contradictories—the thrownness of the past and the project of the future—that refuse analogical identification; and as the faith-witness of action, it maintains this immanent duality within itself at all times. This is of great importance for understanding the notion of freedom. A few paragraphs earlier, I attempted to illustrate the structure of this dynamic unity based on nothingness by likening it to a series of ellipses drawn about two foci. Unlike concentric circles, ellipses run on quasi-circular courses that deviate one from another, each according to its own particular eccentricity. This is precisely what Schelling had in mind when he spoke of the inner duality of human freedom.

For Schelling, an essential distinction is to be drawn between *Wille des Grundes*, which has to do with the ground of existence, and *Wille der Liebe*, which relates to actual Existenz. He characterizes the opposition as a contrast between light and darkness. Just as light becomes visible only through the mediation of darkness, and love through the mediation of hatred, the will of love is actualized only through the mediation of the will of the ground. Thus only a dual principle, or dual center, can make possible a concrete freedom that includes the freedom for evil. God, as spirit, is the eternal unity of love that surpasses the relative opposition of light and darkness. Nevertheless, the principle of darkness is required as the ground of Existenz disclosed in divine revelation. This is what he terms *Natur in Gott*, since it is in God but is not itself God. Here is where Schelling lays the foundations for the freedom for evil: because there lies hidden within God a principle which, as the ground of Existenz, stands opposed to God and negates God, it is possible to rebel against God and set oneself up in place of God by exercising this principle or *Wille des Grundes*. The origin of evil can thus be traced back to a principle of darkness: *Natur in Gott*. There is no way to cast out this principle by the light of reason for the simple reason that this principle is what grounds the continued reality of that light itself.

The principles of light and darkness may be compared to the two foci of an ellipse which are separated from each other and can never converge as the centers of circles can. Provided they have identical diameters, concentric circles will coincide; but this is not possible in the case of ellipses, even if the lengths of the long and short diameters are equal, because of the deviation between the positioning of the foci expressed in their eccentricity. Still, we can speak of a series of ellipses forming an analogically similar group. In like manner, the synthesis of the present in history cannot take the form of concentric circles drawn about a single focus because the congruence between the past and the future is one of analogical similarity and can only yield a whole of partially similar circularities: the two centers, or twofold essence, are unified without weakening the opposition between them. This is also the internal, dual structure of freedom, whose unity is a personal unity of love, not a synthesis of identity based on reason. This sets Schelling's thought apart from rational philosophies built on the principle of identity.

To understand the development of this approach, we should recall that Schelling's idea of freedom was worked out after the publication of Hegel's *Phenomenology of Mind*, which had attacked the abstract unity of Schelling's philosophy of identity and leveled the famous critique against its absolute as "a night in which all cows are black." In reply to this charge, Schelling abandoned the philosophy of identity which Hegel was criticizing, and threw himself more deeply into the problem, adopting an approach that would neutralize the criticism.

While it is no secret that Schelling's theory of freedom was greatly influenced by Jakob Boehme both directly and indirectly, there is no denying the fact that his contribution to this core problem of Western philosophy was of epoch-making proportions. For my part, I have found his thought illuminating on not a few points. In particular, I find him preferable to Hegel in terms of the concreteness with which he treats the mediation of negation.

For Schelling, the "will of love" does not negate the "will of the ground" (which would entail negating the Existenz of its own revelation), but gives it leave to operate independently of itself and upholds it in this state. This is the essential characteristic that distinguishes the unity of love as nothingness from the unity of being based on reason. Instead of opposing and negating the will of the ground, the will of love negates itself, and through this self-negating mediation annihilates the power of opposition inherent in the will of the ground. It surpasses the ground, becoming a groundless, bottomless *Ungrund*. To the extent that eternity in the present does not negate the opposition of the past to the future but preserves it, it must be something like this bottomless unity of love.

But in order for the will of the ground to be permitted and upheld throughout the unity of love, it is not enough merely to acknowledge an independent "nature in God." The will of the ground must be let go to function positively on its own, to assert its egoity, to set itself up like a living replica of God in place of God. This rebellious attempt to assert egoity against God is radical human evil. While "nature in God" can be considered the *potential ground* of evil—the principle that belongs in essence to God, yet stands opposed to God as something independent and not God—this radical evil is its *actual ground*. The former belongs to nature, the latter to the standpoint of spirit. The inner duality of love versus will does not remain a mere static polar opposition, but develops into a dynamic opposition in order that the power of love may transform its opposite into a mediator of love's own power. Such is the unity in a love based on personal freedom, a love of spirit that surpasses the immediate identity of nature. It is here that history truly becomes history, not merely as something that belongs to nature but as something constituted by a twofold movement: the Fall that followed from freedom and the Redemption and reconciliation with God that comes through *zange* and atonement.

The centrifugal movement of humanity away from God and the centripetal movement back to God make up the two aspects of history that Schelling likened to the *Iliad* and the *Odyssey*. The former, obviously, belongs to the past and the latter to the future, or more precisely to the period that extends from the present into the future. In dividing history into stages, Schelling took as his principle the eschatological doctrine of Judeo-Christian religious tradition—a principle, incidentally, whose absence represents the main deficiency of the philosophy of history found in Greek thought. Pointing to the inner duality that such a view sets up at the core of history, and laying the ground for a distinction between the actuality and potentiality of evil, Schelling deepened the notion of radical evil on which Kant's theory of religion had hinged. For Schelling, radical evil can be seen as a positive, active principle of negation surpassing nature. It is the ground for the very existence of love, and as such mediates spiritual reality. The self-negation of love leaves room for radical evil only in order to transform it into a ground of divine love, thus making it the cause of an actuality that exceeds its own potential.

The idea is a profound one. It sees hidden in the ground of reality an intelligible act that conforms to the intelligible essence of the self. Through this act selfhood is realized as the functioning of an ego allowed by God to work independently of God. Thus, like the *karma* of a former life essentially prior to this life, the intelligible act of selfhood is stimulated by the inclination to evil. The self-positing of the ego results in the arrogant self-assertion of the ego, and this self-centeredness of the ego is deeply rooted, in turn, in the creation of nature. Already in its creation, the powers of nature are discriminated one from another and yet bound together in the form of various distinct species. The appearance of the individual self breaks this bond between nature's powers by forming a discrete point at which the powers of nature are rejoined. The emergence of the individual self therefore represents a displacement of the primordial center of unity in nature, and in its place a position of the self-centeredness of the ego. In one sense, the character of each human being may be said to be predestined, but this predestination is the result of the intelligible act of the self, not of a direct decision on the part of God. One's character is the outcome of what the self freely chooses to be as an individual. That is, in its intelligible act a human life belongs not to time but to eternity; in its own free choice it finds itself at the beginning of eternal creation. In the "eternal now" the human subject enters perpetually into eternity. The groundless abyss of love is nothing other than eternity.

In this manner Schelling thought it possible to solve the perennial problem of reconciling human freedom with the predetermination of all things in God. The overcoming of Spinoza's rational realism seemed to provide him with a solution to the incomprehensibility of the relative independence that individual modalities enjoy from substance. Furthermore, Schelling's interpretation sought to explain without contradiction the origin of the evil and untruth of relative being, as well as the mystery inherent in intellectual emancipation (that is, how it comes about that the self-consciousness of a relative being of its dependency upon the absolute unity of substance actually turns into a realization of a freedom able to determine itself spontaneously within substance), both of them problems that represent aporias in Spinoza's system.

In all these ideas, Schelling bases himself on a principle of absolute mediation, a radical pursuit of mediation that he is no doubt right to stress. If his theory is flawed by a certain abstractness, it is because he has failed to carry the principle of mediation far enough. It is worth noting here that Hegel had failed in his philosophy to see his principle of self-negating mediation to term as absolute mediation because of his adherence to the principle of reason. Midway in the development of his system, the dialectical principle degenerated into a principle of identity, a point on which he was criticized by Schelling and openly attacked by Kierkegaard. Where Schelling's own theory of freedom fails on similar grounds, it is no less open to attack.

Hegel's philosophy of history was toppled by the materialistic philosophy that succeeded it for reasons of its inherent tendency to rely exclusively on a rationalistic principle of identity. In this regard, if it is to be revived for our age, it needs the corrective of a standpoint of trans-rational mediation of practical action. Given this historical situation, we see an increasing tendency at present to give importance to Schelling's philosophy of history and to reevaluate him as a precursor of the philosophy of the future. His *Philosophical Inquiries into the Nature of Human Freedom*, a work that contains the core of his philosophy of history, stands out here as a masterpiece.

With his theory of freedom, Schelling developed Kant's relationship between ethics and religion in a new direction. Where Kant had argued for the primacy of ethics over religion, Schelling turned the tables to set religion before ethics. Such a reversal was already implied in Kant's notion of radical evil, but he failed to pursue it radically enough in his theory of religion because of his commitment to reason. According to Schelling, the good as such cannot be established merely in terms of the autonomy of reason but is the victorious outcome of a conversion wherein the freedom of the will, even though disposed toward evil, submits obediently to the unity of love and thus becomes one with a higher necessity. The arrogance of evil is transformed into the spiritual unity of pious belief.

In taking this position, Schelling does not lose sight of the truth of the autonomy of ethics by falling into a position of the heteronomy of will, which would be the undoing of freedom; but neither does he disregard the limitation of radical evil by insisting on a wholly autonomous freedom. Accordingly, the idea of transformation or conversion that marks his philosophy is one that preserves the independence of ethics within the transcendent unity of religion. At the same time, the limitation of ethics is brought to awareness through an absolute critique in which the autonomy of reason is followed through to its radical consequences. In this awareness, "conscience" ceases to be merely a matter of inspiration and becomes a solemn fact, terminating at last in a conversion of submission to a divine love that transcends the self. It is therefore through the Other-power of love, not through the self-power of reason, that ethics achieves fulfillment as an ethics of *gensō*. In this sense, Schelling's logic of conversion and transformation accords with what I have described above as metanoetics, and I can agree with it completely.

This leads us to the question of whether Schelling's theory of freedom can be identified with metanoetics. I cannot but reply: not so. The mere fact that the two are characterized respectively as a "theory of freedom" and a "metanoetics" suggests that each has its own defining traits that make complete agreement difficult. A further comparison should help shed some light on the structure of the two standpoints.

What is the fundamental difference between the theory of freedom and metanoetics? How can the two notions be distinguished from each other as standpoints? To begin with, they are diametrically opposed in principle insofar as the former speaks of self-assertion or self-affirmation, whereas the latter speaks of self-abandonment or self-negation. Freedom consists in a decision made by the willing and acting self without outside restrictions, which is why the theory of freedom is discussed in terms of self-assertion or self-affirmation. In contrast, metanoetics as I have described it so far signals the self-abandonment or self-negation of one's very capacity for existence.

The action of *zange*, while belonging to the self, is at the same time an action through which the self is forced to admit that it lacks the qualifications to exist. Even though it stems from the self, it is action in which the self is moved by Other-power to submit voluntarily to Other-power. Thus, if we may draw a distinction between "act" (*kōi*) and "action" (*gyō*), the former pertaining to self-power as the solitary assertion of autonomy and the latter issuing from Other-power, we should have to speak of *zange* as an "action" rather than an "act." As far as metanoetics is concerned, it is not that the self determines the content of its self-consciousness but that the self entrusts its decision to Other-power and becomes a mediator for Other-power. Hence, metanoetics is the content of the witness (*shō*) born to the action-faith (*gyō-shin*) through which the self is prompted by Other-power to submit voluntarily to it. As explained above, it is nothing less than a transformation of death into life, of abandonment into restoration, of negation into affirmation. This is the action-faith-witness of *zange*. Clearly all of this points to a standpoint of mediation.

In contrast, there can be no doubt that freedom—at least in the immediate sense of the term—conveys the unmediated affirmation of the self, according to the definition we have just seen in Schelling's theory. But the fact is, the self confronts its surrounding world and through the mediation of the world confronts other selves. Hence to assert the self directly and affirm it immediately is to set up a conflict with the self's environment and to enter into competition with other selves. The result is nothing less than the downfall and destruction of the self, in other words, the extinction of the unmediated self in general. This means that one can attain authentic freedom only insofar as one negates oneself in one's own depths for the sake of the world, so that through this self-abandonment all selves—one's own self as well as every other self—return from their particularity to a universality where they acknowledge one another and are reconciled to one another in social solidarity. Concretely, it is in the nation that the individual acquires true freedom, which is but another way of describing the fact that freedom establishes itself only through self-negating mediation. In this way, freedom comes about only through a conversion of self-negating mediation.

Actually it was Schelling's intention in his theory of freedom to develop just such a dialectical structure of freedom. In a sense it is a more concrete elaboration of the self-negating mediation present in the dialectic of the *Phenomenology of Mind*, where Hegel demonstrated that only when consciousness evolves to religion is it able to bring concreteness to the self-negating mediation of mind. Similarly, in Schelling's theory, freedom can adequately realize its essence only to the extent that consciousness has performed *zange* for its own radical evil and has reached a stage of mutual recognition and reconciliation with other selves. Only through such a more radical self-negating mediation can his theory of freedom unfold the fullness of its notion of transformation.

In a word, it is through *zange* that self-negating transformation is actualized as *an und für sich*. To the extent that freedom is mediated self-consciously through its self-negation, it can be transformed into authentic affirmation. Here a genuine dialectic predominates: freedom becomes true freedom only insofar as it is not the freedom of immediate self-assertion. In other words, the truth of freedom resides in *zange*. This is the relationship between freedom and *zange*. The latter is undeniably more concrete than the former, which is one of the reasons that Schelling's theory of freedom cannot replace metanoetics, however similar the two may be. Metanoetics has thus to be acknowledged as a unique standpoint, a philosophy far more concrete than theories of freedom. As long as theories of freedom remain theories of freedom, they are incapable of exercising their proper function. A theory of freedom fulfills its function only when it assumes the standpoint of metanoetics and is itself transformed into the stuff of metanoetics.

As a conceptual foundation for a philosophical standpoint, therefore, the notion of freedom is inadequate of itself. It requires the notion of *zange*. Just as Schelling's theory of freedom developed Hegel's rational standpoint of self-identity further by means of self-negating mediation, so metanoetics represents a further refinement of Schelling's standpoint. That is to say, Hegel's *Phenomenology of Mind*, the product of logical and historical thought aimed at absolute critique, was carried closer to self-negating transformation through Schelling's theory of freedom; and in the same way, metanoetics simply carries this process to completion.

Following this line of thought, it is possible to point out how Schelling's theory of freedom gets stuck in an abstract mode of thought, in spite of certain structural similarities to metanoetics. First of all, the "bottomless abyss of love" that Schelling sets up as the universal ground of freedom shows clear parallels to the Great Compassion–*qua*–Nothingness of metanoetics. But a closer look reveals a fundamental difference. Metanoetics is concerned with the voluntary self-abandonment and self-negation of the self in *zange*. Since this *zange* is wrought by a Great Compassion operating in the same self that is the subject of *zange*, the self practices *zange* as an action of voluntary submission that makes its standpoint one of action-faith. Thus even as the self entrusts itself absolutely to Great Compassion, it is cooperating with the Great Compassion in a mediatory role. The self bears witness within itself to an absolute conversion: the self that has been abandoned is now rescued; what has died once again lives. Because the self bears witness to this resurrection, the absolute can be spoken of as Great

Compassion, which is surely more than a mere construct based on the abstract notion of self-negating love.

I do not mean to call into doubt Schelling's religious experience. Indeed, without such personal experience one could not assert, as Schelling did, that the good is not a mere rational concept of ethics but belongs to religious devotion and humility. Furthermore, the depth of Schelling's ethical and religious experience shows up in his deliberate determination of freedom as the freedom of evil and his distinction between the potentiality and actuality of freedom. I have no doubt that the love of which he speaks originated in the evangelical belief that "God is love." But that having been said, it must also be admitted that when he brings love to the fore, he is not referring to his own experience of and gratefulness for divine grace, but restricts himself to an objective explanation of the content of faith. In this sense, we may say that Schelling's thought stops at a *metaphysics* of love without arriving at a *religious witness* to love.

The contrast to metanoetics, with its emphasis on concrete witness through action-faith, is striking. Although the Great Compassion to which metanoetics bears witness might be replaced with the notion of divine love, it is not a metaphysical conception of love that is meant, but the self-consciousness of an existential reality within the center of one's subjectivity. Obviously the existential self-consciousness of those who affirm a religious experience of God as love is no different from what I have called the religious witness to Great Compassion. And this is equally true of Schelling's notion of love to the extent that he assumes a standpoint of faith. But a philosophical theory of freedom can never become a genuine existential philosophy as long as it is restricted to the mere understanding of the contents of self-conscious existence.

In the attempt to construct a metaphysics of being, Schelling speculated on the idea of "nondifferentiation," which he derived from his earlier principle of identity. In forsaking his philosophy of identity for the notion of nondifferentiation, he was not only acting in response to Hegel's disparaging remarks but also pursuing a logical demand generated from within his own thought. In so doing, he overcame the identity of reason to arrive at a new standpoint based on personality originating from transrational will. His idea of nondifferentiation points to the absoluteness of love that supplies a unity in the depths of the bottomless abyss (*Ungrund*) where all differentiation and distinction disappears, where the opposition between good and evil is transcended.

Apparently still dissatisfied with this notion of nondifferentiation, he went further to claim that the bottomless abyss transcends not only identity but nondifferentiation as well. It may be that he felt the notion of nondifferentiation to be too abstract. The idea is in fact far removed from witness to love through action-faith, a mere product of speculation negating differences and not at all suited to express the concreteness of love. It differs from identity only on the conceptual level and, like it, has no alternative but to resort to the principle of the identity of reason insofar as it is a conceptual representation. In this sense, even the concept of the bottomless abyss, which Schelling regarded as absolute, would not be immune from the same criticism of abstractness. With this concept, he posited within God a principle of opposition that is not God, a ground of existence which he called simply *Grund*. Moreover, he spoke of a primordial ground or *Urgrund*, a "ground of the ground" that transcends the *Grund* as a groundlessness or *Ungrund*, a bottomlessness that is the absolute negation of the notion of ground itself.

This *Ungrund* is not, however, to be confused with nothingness. Nothingness can never be conceived of directly and without mediation, and anything so conceived cannot be nothingness. Nothingness necessarily entails the mediation of being and cannot imply the negation or annihilation of mediation. Nothingness plays its mediatory role only when it is preserved and restored to life in negation. For this reason, it is always accompanied by mediating being and becomes manifest through this mediating being. This is what is called "empty being." Furthermore, our limited self exists as empty being to the extent that it is mediated by nothingness. To the extent that it entails a positive return to the world (*gensō*) that is at the same time its "being returned to the world" as a true bodhisattva cooperating with the Great Compassion of nothingness, the self performs the action of gratitude toward the Great Compassion of nothingness. In this way, nothingness is practiced and witnessed to in gratitude for Great Compassion and reaches self-consciousness in the core of the self.

All of this must be distinguished clearly from Schelling's notion of the bottomless abyss of "love as nondifferentiation." The abyss can only signify a negation or transcendence of the ground, and as such points to the path of *ōsō* aspiring to the universal. Whereas Great Compassion consists of a subjectivity witnessed through action-faith, the love of which Schelling speaks cannot get beyond an abstract universal devoid of the self-consciousness of authentic subjectivity. The abyss that characterizes such love can only denote a negation or transcendence of the ground. It lacks the positive and deliberate quality of nothingness and does not attain the same free mediation of being. One may object that Schelling's *Ungrund* in fact means more than a mere state of privation—the lack of *Grund*—and points instead to a positive transformation and reversal of the ground as nothingness does. But the abyss remains an abstract universal concept lacking the self-consciousness of subjectivity, since the notion of *Grund* from which *Ungrund* is derived is not an existential concept but an ontological one without subjectivity. Conversely, despite the fact that the notion of nothingness stems originally from general ontology, where it is opposed to being (and is still often used in such a sense), I take nothingness as an existential concept to indicate the ground of the action of self-negation, that is, of subjective self-consciousness. Put in these terms, it seems legitimate to conclude that Schelling's bottomless abyss belongs to the path of *ōsō* moving through mere negation toward the universal, while nothingness carries the positive connotation of belonging to *gensō*. In other words, the gap between the two concepts is that between speculative ontology on the one hand and existential philosophy on the other.

The same distinction may be drawn between love and Great Compassion. Needless to say, the original meaning of love allows for subjective and existential connotations that are the same as those for Great Compassion. The same could be said of the history of a great many other concepts, but we are not concerned here with clarifying the meaning of terms by tracing them back to their origins. The general connotations that these terms carry today suffice to permit us to differentiate between those that express metanoetical content, such as nothingness and Great Compassion, and those that belong to theories of freedom, such as love and *Ungrund*. The former are subjective-existential concepts pointing to action-witness; the latter, speculative constructs. This is why I am led in the final analysis to separate myself from Schelling's theory of freedom, despite its initial apparent similarities to my own position.

Based on this distinction, further questions arise with regard to such concepts as "ground," "will of the ground," and "essence of ground" that characterize Schelling's thought. All of these concepts, together with that of "bottomless abyss," can be traced back to Jakob Boehme.[3] No doubt they are effective in distinguishing the practical philosophy of will from formal rational philosophy and in illuminating a ground of existence that is quite different from the mere potentiality of formal essence.

Schelling's idea that the ground of existence consists of a negativity, and that a being does not exist in immediate affirmation but only realizes itself through a self-negating mediation, allows his dialectic to become a logic of existence in the form of a logic of negation. Starting from the concreteness of mechanical physics in contrast with mathematics and passing on to the concreteness of the will in contrast with reason, the truth of his dialectical method is contained in its use of opposites as mediatory moments which it actualizes by converting negation into affirmation. Through this mediation, the limitations of self-identical logic based on reason, which is unable to distinguish actuality from mere potentiality, are disclosed. For the same reason, will and personality, which go beyond reason, are seen to supply the requisite concreteness of existence. The principle of freedom also constitutes actuality; through it history comes into being. The principle of self-negating freedom is what Schelling terms "ground," the indispensable mediation without which there could be no freedom. On his view, freedom stands in need of "bottomless love" as its ground. And this ground that negates itself and transcends itself as *Ungrund* is further seen as "nature in God," that is, something in God that is not itself God. This notion of "nature in God," which also comes from Boehme, forms the core of Schelling's theory of freedom and is considered, along with his notion of the *Ungrund*, to be his most important contribution.

"Nature in God," like "bottomless love," is clearly part of a speculative construct that runs counter to my own subjective-existential position. The very notion of "ground" as used here demonstrates clearly that, unlike the notion of love, it belongs to abstract speculation. Strictly speaking, since ground indicates that by which a being can be what it is, it must by nature precede such being, even though for us it is recognized only subsequently. The fact that such a ground is required and posited as a ground of what actually exists, despite its nonexistence for us beforehand, proves that it is an intellectual construct and not something witnessed through action-faith. Here we have being of an order diametrically opposed to that resulting from subjective action-faith-witness. This is not surprising, considering the fact that Boehme's theosophy, from which the idea is derived, is a speculative attempt to transfer religious experience from the human standpoint to a divine one, where divine wisdom can be brought to bear on explaining its foundations in eternal being. Such affirmations extrapolate what is inaccessible to our human existence, what we cannot possibly bring to self-consciousness. It is remarkable how speculation not only constructs something that transcends existential self-consciousness but does so in reverse order. They are no more than the assertions of a dogmatism built into the speculative standpoint.

It is difficult to gloss over the fact that whereas metanoetics seeks to carry criticism through to its final consequences, the philosophy of freedom abandons the critique halfway and sets up dogmatism in its place. The point is of great importance for philosophy, and it explains why I am reluctant to adopt the notion of ground. Actually, to speak of ground is to speak of something prior to being—not prior for us but prior in its own nature. But have we sufficient reason to posit such a thing? If not, to adopt the notion is to allow our thought to descend to the dogmatism of an ontological speculation that transmutes concepts into being. The dogmatism that puts intellectual necessity in place of being is based on the presupposition that, in terms of Aristotle's distinction between the πρότερον πρὸς ἡμᾶς (prior for us) and the πρότερον τῇ φύσει (prior by nature), the latter could be recognized apart from the former and that the two would not need to mediate each other in the sense of each preserving itself by opposing the other. The existentialist position of authentic subjectivity, in contrast, consists in opening up a way to bear witness through action-faith to the fact that because of our mediating action, what is "prior by nature" becomes identical with what is "prior for us," even though the two remain opposed to each other. To allow the opposition between the two to remain needs to be seen as an example of evil and sinful existence, deprived of mediation with the absolute but asserting itself as something apart from it. It is what existential philosophy calls inauthentic existence or the "fall" from being. In authentic existence—existence in the good—what is prior by nature must at the same time be brought to self-consciousness as that which is prior for us. Such is the case, for example, with the Great Compassion of the absolute.

Accordingly, even though the notion of ground developed in the theory of freedom is determined as the ground of evil, seen as inauthentic existence and a fall from being, evil is subsequent to God; and it is in opposition to authentic existence that the ground of evil is termed a "nature in God." Moreover, just as evil is never prior to God but always subsequent, so it is with us insofar as we are subsumed within the absolute to serve as its mediator. Thus it cannot be claimed that as our ground, "nature in God" is prior for authentic human existence. That is, it must not be regarded as the ground of existence in the authentic ontological sense but must be limited to the ground of our inauthentic being, our evil. This is what is called "radical evil." It is not to be asserted positively as the ground of being but is to be accepted in its negative implication as inducing mediatory activity resulting in the negation of being. This may be what Schelling had in mind fundamentally. But because the concept of ground came to be asserted positively as the ground of reality and affirmed as something independent of God and without mediation, the ground of existence that is explained in terms of something existing with God and yet not itself God led him unavoidably to a positive interpretation of ground that is incompatible with something whose rightful determination can come only through mediation.

The temptation is to elude the problem by claiming that it belongs to the mystery of Existenz. But from a standpoint of action-faith, this mystery cannot be dismissed as a mere speculative construct; it needs to become accessible to the subject, to be witnessed to in action-faith, and to be shifted from the realm of being to that of act. Then the mystery no longer exists in being but enters into the self. The mystery then consists in the fact that the self participates in the core of being by transforming being into the center of nothingness. This is why the self achieves an intimacy with the mystery without its ceasing to be a mystery, why through action-faith the self draws the mystery down from the heavens above to the earth below. There should be no cause for doubt about the mystery because it is brought to self-consciousness in action-faith-witness.

Here again we see what it is that sets metanoetics off from the theory of freedom. The latter is marked by its concept of ground; the former is not. In truth, concepts like the "essence of ground" or the "will of ground" are really the negation of essence and will since they come to no more than the mediatory functioning of inauthentic existence. That is, they signify only the negating mediation characteristic of the dialectic of being and could never exist in an authentically independent and unmediated state. Such a claim is altogether inappropriate, yet there is no denying the fact that it predominates in the theory of freedom. In comparison with Hegel's *Phenomenology of Mind*, which begins with a critique of sense perception in the here and now and sees the absolute critique of consciousness to its end, Schelling's theory of freedom inclines more in the direction of pure speculation and hence to the very dogmatism that the critical spirit opposes.

I cannot register these few negative impressions of Schelling's theory of freedom without reiterating that in other respects I admire his work as a major philosophical achievement. By comparing it with metanoetics, I mean only to bring to fulfillment the dialectical mediation that constitutes the genuine essence of his theory, and am therefore convinced that metanoetics supersedes the theory of freedom.

I should like to conclude this chapter by comparing Heidegger's hermeneutical existentialism with Schelling's theory of freedom, and then by contrasting both with metanoetics. I hope in this way to illuminate the relationship between the three. In *Sein und Zeit* Heidegger notes, in connection with his attempt to analyze the ontological essence of nihility (*Nichtigkeit*), that evil is brought positively to self-awareness through an awakening of conscience as being "answerable to guilt."[4] Given his hermeneutical standpoint, it is clear that he is incapable of unearthing the snarled roots of evil that lie deep within the self as undisclosed being. Radical evil is impossible to comprehend from the standpoint of hermeneutics because as *radical* it is something from which the self cannot be released by the self's own power. It is a transcendent moment of negativity for which the self will always be guilty as long as it exists. It is the dark of an abyss that cannot be annihilated by the immanent transcendence of self-consciousness.

It was for this reason that Kant had to acknowledge the need for divine grace to overcome radical evil. Precisely because it is a transcendent obstacle that an ethic of practical reason cannot surmount, Kant held that the possibility for its removal lay only in reliance on the will of God as a principle of absolute good. Even though this belief in God be termed a rational belief in contrast with belief in a revealed religion, it arises in fact in the mediation of absolute conversion wherein reason negates itself since no religion is possible "within the limits of reason alone." Religion is based solely on the absolute negation of reason.

In the hermeneutics on which Heidegger's existentialism is based, existential interpretation takes as its starting point the problem of death as the terminus of human existence. Thus death does not become a pivot on which a conversion of human existence can take place in the form of a negation-*qua*-affirmation. His standpoint of hermeneutics does not allow for an adequate treatment of religious faith in that the self is considered only as surviving on this side of death. To the extent that it seeks to illuminate the structure of being, it cannot concern itself with a radical evil based on the principle of darkness. The principle of evil does not belong to a transcendence required from within the self. To this extent radical evil cannot be explained in merely "ontological" terms.

Of everything Kant has written, his theory of religion represents his most important thinking, and yet it finds no place within the framework of his critical philosophy. Religion simply does not fit within the bounds of reason. It comes about only in a transformation or conversion of the self that is based on an absolute critique of reason itself. This is why Schelling's theory of freedom needs to be seen as a further development of Kant's theory of religion. At the same time, there is no doubt that in distancing itself from Kant's critical spirit, Schelling's position tends to sink back to the level of conceptual constructs that reintroduce metaphysical speculation. In Heidegger's terms, it is not *ontologisch* but *ontisch*. The contrast here between existentialism and Schelling's theory of human freedom is striking. The one stands fixed in immanence, the other in transcendence. As mentioned above, this is why we must withhold unconditional assent to Schelling's theory, despite its profound merits in other respects. The absolute mediation that distinguishes the approach of metanoetics cannot approve of his disregard for the critique of reason and his deviation into conceptual constructs.

As far as Heidegger is concerned, the renunciation of the ontic standpoint in favor of an ontological one is in keeping with the spirit of the critique of reason. At the same time, the fact that this impedes his deeper understanding of the problem of evil and keeps it bound within the limits of an existential analysis concerned with the awakening of conscience and the awareness of responsibility—thereby overlooking the fact that self-consciousness is the basis of religious faith—flaws his existential ontology. As noted before, this imperfection means that in maintaining the standpoint of hermeneutics, Heidegger keeps the self intact and fails to perform the Great Action—genuine religious action based on Other-power—through which the self, cast into the abyss of death, is immediately restored once again to life. This is why he does not pursue the critique of reason to the point of absolute critique. In other words, adherence to the being of the self results in his failure to venture into nothingness. This leaves him no recourse for handling the problem of evil adequately. In a word, the standpoint he clings to is a standpoint of bondage to evil.

In contrast, metanoetics, which is grounded in absolute nothingness, does not fall into an *Ontik*: insofar as it takes its stand on the transforming mediation of nothingness, it is a self-consciousness of transcendent nothingness. It never departs from ontological self-consciousness. Yet far from resting on an immanent standpoint that closes off the significance of radical evil as a transcendent negating principle, metanoetics permits a mediatory self-consciousness of evil through the action-faith-witness of nothingness. Therefore metanoetics is able to elevate the theory of freedom from the level of speculative construct to that of authentic ontology or self-consciousness.

While metanoetics must finally part company with both existentialism and the theory of freedom, it does so by taking a middle way between the two that effects a synthesis of the truth that each expresses. It is my conviction that the standpoint of action-faith-witness based on absolute critique enables us to touch the core of religion that is closed off to mere theory or interpretation. For what is inaccessible to self-power is illuminated and revealed through Other-power. Neither immanent nor transcendent, it takes its stand on the absolute mediation of transcendence-*qua*-immanence.

Chapter 5

Absolute Mediation in Metanoetics

The demand of absolute mediation that self-consciousness of evil must belong to the subject of the good · The mediation of the transcendent nondiscrimination of religion and the discrimination of history and ethics · The negation of evil from the standpoint of faith · The necessity of evil as mediator · The dialectics of "just as it is" · The ethics of Buddhism as escape from samsāra · The mediatory nature of discrimination contrasted with nondiscriminating equality · The meaning of life after death · The meaning of "living as one who has died" · Absolute nothingness, absolute transformation, absolute mediation · The mediatory relationships between good and evil · The structure of religious deliverance · The meaning of realizing Buddha-nature · "Above all else, the Great Death" · Self-consciousness of death · Living in death · Submission to contradiction · "For me, there is neither life nor death" · Intuition and action-faith-witness · Zen enlightenment · The path of sages · Metanoetics: a path between Zen and the nembutsu · The differences between the demands of the absolute and action-witness to the absolute · The characteristics of mysticism · Mysticism and metanoesis · An interpretation and critique of Eckhart's thought · A comparison of Eckhart's mysticism and metanoetics · A comparison and critique of Otto's and Oltmanns's readings of Eckhart · Eckhart's letting go of God and Dōgen's letting go of Buddha · The affinities of Eckhart with Zen · Eckhart and Zen on freedom and deliverance contrasted with metanoetics · The circularity of the self-power deliverance of the sage · The "continuous state of true mind" and fundamental evil · The differential "light and darkness" of continuous metanoesis · The concreteness of faith-witness in metanoetics

The notion of "ground" as radical evil treated in the previous chapter presupposes the authentic being of goodness, without which we could not appreciate its negative mediation. In other words, self-consciousness of the ground of inauthentic existence cannot belong to that inauthentic existence itself but only to authentic existence. It is utterly important to realize that it is not the subject of evil but the subject of goodness that comes to awareness of the structure of evil. This is equally true of the critique of religion in general apart from a critique of theories of freedom. We must take deliberate precautions against the frequent temptation to corrupt religion by neglecting the fullness of mediation. This was the point on which the critique of the theory of freedom worked out in the previous chapter hinged. Religion requires an absolute, and as a result it is prone to introduce ideas of an unmediated equality that do not discriminate between the absolute and the relative, between good and evil, or of an absolute nondifferentiation accessible to self-power and devoid of any negation of the self. From the viewpoint of the advance of the self (ōsō), such religious thinking may represent the profound conceptualizations of speculative reason. But when considered in terms of the self's return to the world (gensō), it is found to lack the ethical practicality and historical reality that mediate our Existenz.

While this is bad enough when confined to a narrow sphere, the more radical and diffuse religious thought becomes, the worse the situation becomes. The idea of unmediated, nondifferentiating transcendence can then spread its poison and corruption more widely and deeply in society. The shameless deeds of priests and monks of the Zen and Nembutsu traditions, both of which represent the very highest attainments of Buddhist thought, provide us with examples in this regard. Behind the corruption of such forms of religion frequently lies the error of presuming the truth of nondifferentiation or equality to be valid in areas where in fact it has forfeited its validity by becoming inauthentic.

For the redeemed who have been delivered from worldly passions, all is permitted. Everything is good just as it is. As the Zen phrase has it, "Nothing lowly, nothing unpleasing." The illusion of life-and-death stems from the discrimination between the lovable and the despicable. This is expressed splendidly in the opening of the *Treatise on Faith*: "The way of the absolute is not difficult to pursue. One should simply abandon discrimination. If one can cast off the mind of love and hate, one can see the way of truth."[1] Even if one aspires to enlightenment, renounces the life of illusion, and seeks to acquire a new state of mind through religious discipline, so long as one bases oneself on discriminative thinking, there is no way to attain to true *satori*. It is quite as the famous poem says:

> Returning to the world after *satori*
> I see no difference.
> Mount Rozan is dim in the rain
> and the River Sekkō flows as the rain falls.

It is a familiar Zen pattern: Mountain is mountain and water is water. "When one is hungry, one eats and drinks; when tired, one sleeps." Or again, it is said: "The mind of everyday life is the way of truth." Apart from the way things are, there is no other way to be sought for or achieved. All things are good just as they naturally are. In the Shin sect, great emphasis is placed on "naturalness" (*jinen-hōni*). The core of faith consists in leaving everything to Other-power; there is no other path to salvation than the way of "entrusting" (*o-makase*). Anything else added by the contrivances of self-power becomes a hindrance to salvation.

Seen from this point of view, radical evil is nothing more than a product of human arrogance. For those who are redeemed or have attained *satori*, there is no radical evil that cannot be overcome. Surely this is true, but only for the saved and enlightened ones. Those who have yet to be saved or attain enlightenment have no right to usurp this truth as their own. Indeed, even for those who are already redeemed, who have experienced the limit of their self-power and abandoned their own selves completely, radical evil has to be seen as an ineluctable mediating element for salvation and transformation. Those who have no self-consciousness of their own evil and no experience of repentance have no prospect of salvation.

Only for sages and saints, who are able to deliver themselves and attain *satori* by their self-power, is such an assertion true without qualification. To be strictly logical, even in the case of the wise and the saintly, the claim to have the same original nature as the Gods and Buddhas means that there is no distinction between their state of *satori* and their illusory life before attaining *satori*.

Meantime, for ordinary, finite people, the distinction between good and evil remains in full force. Anyone who tries to deny this fact or convert it into the indifference of nature is in effect refusing the existential truth of what it is to be human. The differentiation of nondifferentiation is already an affirmation of differentiation. It is not a matter of a pure and simple negation of nondifferentiation but of an affirmation mediated by its negation. It is not affirmation without mediation, but

affirmation mediated by negation in the sense that everything is transformed and restored into a new form of differentiation through absolute
negation.

Thus, the standpoint of naturalness wherein everything is allowed to
be just as it is does not mean "naturalness" or "as such" in the ordinary
sense. For us, it means the sweat and blood of religious discipline. Only
one who has really attempted to "be just as one is" truly knows how
difficult a task that is. Many of a mind so shameless and indolent as never
to have exerted themselves to seek the good and avoid evil, many who
have not wrestled with moral torment employ the terms "absolute
nondifferentiation" or "naturalness" in order to justify themselves in
staying just as they are and attributing their state to the grace of Other-
power. They misuse the terms to defend an indolent, tranquil life by
displacing the notion of "naturalness" from its rightful locus in the
realm of absolute nothingness, where it is understood as being *beyond*
ethics, to a new location *beneath* ethics. And that is surely the most
frightful damage that can be inflicted on religion. "Naturalness" or the
state of things "just as they are" is not a simple fact but a goal toward
which one must strive through the mediation of self-negation.

The real dialectic here functions in virtue of the fact that being "just
as one is" does not imply resting content with one's present state but
rather exerting oneself to become "natural." A being that is affirmed
directly falls into a pit of contradictions because of its finitude and
relativity, where it is made empty as a manifestation of a nothingness
emerging from the chaos and confusion. By becoming conscious of its
nature as nothingness, it is restored to the unity of solidarity with others.
In this, its true meaning, it is merely negated as a directly differentiated
being. Moreover, the nondifferentiation attained through this negation
should not be considered an achievement of ōsō. If that were the case,
relative beings would vanish into nondifferentiation, and their significance as mediators for the manifestation of nothingness would also be
negated. Relative beings can maintain their independence only insofar as
they mediate absolute nothingness, but this independence does not free
them from the inclination to evil, the permanent disposition to isolate
oneself from the totality of the absolute. This is radical evil. It permeates
the ground of being as the principle of differentiation. To annihilate it
would amount to forfeiting the manifestation of nothingness and further
to abandoning existence.

One may argue that religion in its essence lies beyond ethics, and
therefore that religion is free from the discrimination that characterizes

ethics. One may argue further that Buddhism is a good example of this, and that the mediation of religion by ethics in Western religions is due to a tradition peculiar to Judaism and Christianity but incidental to the essence of religion, namely the inextricable bond between the "love of God" and the "wrath of God." And yet even when it comes to deliverance from the source of *samsāra* (the cycle of life and death), which is generally regarded as the chief impulse of Buddhism, there is a difference between life after attaining the truth in enlightenment and simply continuing an illusory life without enlightenment. The difference between awakening to truth and staying caught in illusions constitutes the opposition between good and evil. Insofar as the former is taken as a goal to be sought after and the latter as an obstacle to be avoided, far from lacking a distinction between good and evil, Buddhism requires ethics as a mediating element. Indeed, it takes rational discrimination as its medium.

The practice of Zen shows extremely rigorous self-discipline and training, and a system of rigid regulations that present a striking model for the ethical life of the ordinary laity. If reason were not truly employed by them to the full, the limits of reason could not be expected to make themselves apparent. To explain nature without a sense for discriminating illusion cannot really amount to anything more than proof of a lack of ardent desire to quest for the truth.

As for the Shin concept of *jinen-hōni*, it is something that can be realized as truth only by those who, having exerted themselves to the utmost, experience despair over the powerlessness of their own being and submit themselves to it obediently. It is therefore clear that such "naturalness" should never be confused with mere "equality" in the objective sense, or with the nondifferentiation of nature, since such lack of discrimination does away with ethics, which is based on the discrimination of good and evil. Shinran uses the word *zange* (metanoesis) in conjunction with *zangi* (humility and remorse) in the sixth part of his *Kyōgyōshinshō*, "The Transformed Buddha and the Transformed Land." One's feeling of *zange* is always accompanied by a feeling of *zangi* over the ineffectiveness of self-power. But those who shamelessly insist on the ineffectiveness of self-power and, rather than put forth their own efforts, are content to boast of the strength of Other-power are far removed from the salvific Great Compassion of Other-power. The absolute, which consists solely in absolute mediation, cannot function without their mediative cooperation: it requires the self-negation of their self-power. The former is realized only correlatively with the latter. The transforming mediation turns on the axis of metanoesis. From this viewpoint, we can assert that the concept of metanoetics is characterized by its rejection of abstract nondifferentiation and the concrete realization of transforming mediation. As a philosophical standpoint, the mediation of reason constitutes an essential moment without which metanoetics could not be what it is.

Now if it is true that the element of differentiation is necessary to establish the fact that the equality of nothingness is mediated by differentiation and that one's action-faith in religion is mediated through the inner duality of ethics, are we not driven to conclude that the ultimate state of unity is unattainable even after one has reached the unitive state of enlightened deliverance? In fact, the main reason that Schelling came to his view of nondifferentiation seems to be in order to avoid that very difficulty. In his theory of freedom he consistently held to a standpoint of human freedom, but the "will of ground" became the ground of an inner duality that, given his clear distinction of human freedom from divine freedom where the "will of ground" is identical with the "will of love," actually shed light on the limitations of his own theory. In the same way, if it is true that in authentic faith one must go through life regarding radical evil as mediating faith for the sake of salvation, does this mean that it is impossible to attain absolute unity through faith? According to Schelling, as long as a human being exists in this life as a relative being, the absolute is unattainable: divine freedom lies forever beyond the reach of human achievement. That is, misery and grief are the ineluctable lot of finite beings, and the pleasures of human life must always be purified by the sufferings of life that accompany them. Schelling concludes that a human being can attain perfection of being only in the next world, that is, after death in the immortal state of a disembodied soul. Only through death can one be freed of bondage to the body and to matter. Only then can one transcend the selfishness of adhering stubbornly to "being-within-the-self" and be converted to "being-without-the-self." Kierkegaard also argues for the view that eternity can never be attained in this world but belongs to the hope of the future.

On the question of belief in life after death, religions East and West have something in common. It is remarkable, for example, that the Pure Land Shin sect (*Jōdoshinshū*), which is generally regarded as a consummate form of Buddhism, teaches the existence of the Pure Land in the West over which Amida Buddha holds sway and for which he prepares everyone to be reborn. This Buddhist belief must, in my view, be taken as a myth of particular, local origins. It does not contain the profound truth of the story of the bodhisattva Dharmākara (*Hōzō-bosatsu*), the account of whose disciplinary effort before his attainment of Buddha-hood is pregnant with intelligible symbolic content. Of course, the idea that as long as one lives in this world, *nirvāna* cannot be fully attained but only promised in a form predetermined by Amida Buddha is based on a deep insight into the interim quality of human existence. As Shinran states,

> That we in this life attain
> the Right Established State [*shōjōju*]
> And later *Nirvāna* Great
> Unfailingly we obtain.²

Moreover, it is highly symbolic that the Pure Land, to which the believer goes after death in order to attain *nirvāna*, is located in the West, where it is illuminated brightly by the setting sun. Given my high regard for science, I can find no basis for belief in either the Pure Land or the Kingdom of Heaven, nor can I believe in the continuation of a disembodied soul after death. Further symbolic significance of this religious notion appears in the idea that the solidarity of humankind is realized in accord with one's return (*gensō*) to actual history. In fact, the notion of the return carries great significance for one's witness to salvation. It says that believers who are saved and are approaching the state of complete *nirvāna* in the Pure Land must return to this world as boddhisattvas after death in order to help their followers, teaching and enlightening them by serving as a model of faith. In this way, believers in turn become mediators of the Great Compassion for the sake of the salvation of their followers. But with regard to what may be termed a negative aspect of human bodily existence—the positive aspect of which was discussed above—doubt remains as to whether one can set oneself free from the bonds of egoism that stem from radical evil or from an innate principle of darkness, as long as one lives upon earth. Further doubts remain as to whether one is capable of moving away from a limited human freedom into the absolute and unlimited freedom that belongs to God. Thus, even when one attains the unity of nondiscrimination, one may not be able to free oneself from the particularity of being (Schelling's *Grund*) because the unity of nondiscrimination is also a unity of nothingness.

These doubts must be taken seriously into account since they serve to clarify the meaning of history and to solve the problem of whether the Kingdom of God can be realized on this earth. Here we touch the core of faith, as given in such expressions as "to act as one who has died while one is still alive," "to be restored to life again once and for all immediately after dying the Great Death," or "to come to life by dying with Christ on the cross." All of this points to the same idea referred to frequently in earlier chapters as "death-and-resurrection." To be sure, terms like "living as one who has died"—not unlike Goethe's *"Stirb, und werde!"*—are often used carelessly. At the same time, there are hardly any who will claim that what such terms really mean, how such a paradoxical state is possible, or what truth it can express, is easy to comprehend. What is at stake here is nothing less than the central issue that concerns religion and philosophy. It is a problem of vital importance that cannot simply be dismissed by the manipulation of words or ideas. It should rather be the touchstone for determining how far religious belief or philosophical thinking has developed. And metanoetics can be no exception.

Let us attempt now to state the question at hand briefly and clearly: All beings that are affirmed directly must, because of their relativity, fall into reciprocal negation, lose their being, and ultimately end up in nothingness. Nothingness is an absolute and as such can in no way itself be negated. At the same time, nothingness does not exist directly. Anything that affirms itself directly is not nothingness but being. It cannot, as we just noted, escape the relativity of mutual negation. Only nothingness, which manifests itself mediatively in this negation of being and affirms itself indirectly, is an absolute free of further negation. Still, absolute nothingness is realized in actuality only by affirming relative beings, negating the immediacy of its own absolute power vis-à-vis relative beings in order to give them life. This means, moreover, that absolute nothingness can actualize its function as nothingness only through a self-negation of relative beings in the form of a reciprocal negation between beings. Thus the self-negation and transformation wrought by relative beings among themselves is made possible because they are affirmed by nothingness, whereas this self-negating act of nothingness becomes its own affirmation and its realization in the world. This absolute transformation is truly absolute nothingness and at the same time absolute mediation. This, and none other, is the only absolute that can really be considered absolute.

Since the true absolute always entails an absolute mediation, it can never dispense with relative beings but brings about their cooperation in this mediation in order to make its own nothingness real. Even though relative beings are negated in order that they may be mediators of nothingness, they are upheld in a state of "being-in-nothingness," that is, a state of "emptiness" (śūnyatā). And insofar as this "emptied being" is a mediator of nothingness, it is allowed to be independent of nothingness. For this reason such beings contain within themselves a radical evil that urges them to proclaim their own being—that is, their independence from nothingness—and to remove themselves from the mediation of nothingness which is a necessary condition for any independence they have. Unless relative beings were possessed of such a disposition to evil, they would lack the very thing that characterizes their being and hence would fail to qualify as mediators of nothingness. Therefore we cannot speak of such beings as *absolutely* autonomous, but only as endowed with a certain *mediated* quality of "empty being" as mediators of nothingness. In other words, they exist as long as they participate in absolute nothingness, which is the subject of good by means of which this self-consciousness of emptied being is witnessed through their action-faith.

Here we see a contradiction in the sense that what is allowed to participate in the subject of good is nonetheless burdened with an unavoidable propensity for doing evil; or conversely, the self that appropriates this evil as its own "intelligible act" is allowed to exist only so long as it frees itself from its evildoing and is converted to the good. The contradiction comes down to this: being is nothingness and nothingness is being insofar as being becomes nothingness and nothingness becomes being. One may try to elude the contradiction by distinguishing between the essential and the actual: evil is that which ought not to be in essence but is unavoidable in actuality, while the good is that which ought to be in essence but cannot exist in actuality. But even here there is no escaping the contradiction that essence can never be separated from actuality, because the former is the essence *of* the latter and the latter is the actualization *of* the former. Hence the contradiction that what ought to be is not, and what ought not to be is, is everywhere in evidence.

This contradiction is more than a straitjacket that binds relative, finite beings. It is also a web from which even the absolute cannot disentangle itself. Even the infinitely absolute is absolute only when it is related to the relative; it comes to self-consciousness as absolute only through the mediation of the relative. The absolute realizes its own absoluteness only through such contradiction, which is why we attempt to witness to the absoluteness of the absolute by abandoning every form of self-identical thinking and practicing the transforming mediation of nothingness. Since absoluteness is realized in our action-witness only to the extent that the absolute is provided with the mediation of the relative and conforms to it, it must follow that absoluteness cannot be realized apart from this contradiction. Nothingness is the absolute, and dialectics is the principle of its self-consciousness. The contradiction involved in living by dying, in acting in life as one who has died, is nothing more than an expression of this state of affairs.

Here a series of questions arise. So long as the contradiction survives as contradiction, is it really possible for it to be taken up into the absolute? If this is the form of religious deliverance and salvation, how are deliverance and salvation possible at all? And if they are impossible, is it not fitting to speak of religion and the spiritual history it has given rise to up to the present as no more than mere illusion? Is the fact that the blood of so many individuals and even of entire nations has been shed in the defense of faith no more than the result of a gigantic delusion? In a word, how is religious faith possible at all? Or again, how can any religious structure bring unity to this contradiction and yet allow it to be the contradiction that it is?

It seems to me that these are among the most important points to be kept in mind in attempting to shed light on central problems of faith like rebirth in the Pure Land, resurrection, and the realization of one's Buddha-nature. In order to make this treatment clear and concrete, I should like first to consider certain of these religious concepts, beginning with the notion of the realization of one's Buddha-nature.

Realizing one's Buddha-nature, or attaining to Buddhahood, is of course the goal sought by the self-power discipline of Zen. Even *satori* is desired only for the sake of that goal, or perhaps better, *is* itself the realizing of one's Buddha-nature. The spiritual life of one who has attained Buddhahood consists simply of "living as one who has died." The question at issue here is whether such a contradictory existence is really possible at all, and if so what it would mean.

It should be obvious that the problem can hardly be resolved from the ordinary standpoint of analytical logic with its basic principle of self-identity. It rather presumes that we allow contradictions to remain as they are. It is meaningless to discuss the ontological possibility of a contradiction from the standpoint of analytical logic. We have no choice but to begin by simply accepting this contradictory mode of being—that is, to take a standpoint of faith with regard to it—in order to reflect on it and bring it to self-consciousness. Where faith is concerned, logical analysis "from the outside" is altogether impossible. It has to do necessarily with the transcendent and hence involves self-contradiction. In seeking to clarify questions of faith, faith itself must first be present; the solutions are to be found only within faith itself.

Faced with the contradiction of "living as one who is dead" and before any understanding can take place, one must therefore first *become* a person who has died such a death. This is why Zen masters enjoin on their disciples, "Die to yourself once and for all!" and why they stress, "Above all else, the Great Death!" But what does such a death mean? Is it the death of the body? Or is it perhaps some sort of self-negation, a letting go of the world that has nothing to do with physical death? In a sense this sort of analysis looks like an outright abandonment of the original contradiction. A more concrete, mediated approach is called for.

What does it mean to deal with death philosophically in the first place? If death is observed as an event taking place outside of the self, then it is no more than a natural or social phenomenon. To become a philosophical problem, the question must concern the death of the self. But since death means the extinction of the self, it is self-contradictory to speak of a "self-consciousness of death." Hence, at first glance, talk of the "death of the self" would appear to be simply a manner of speaking about preparing oneself for death in the future. If this is so, does that mean that death is no more than the anticipation of something that is to happen in the future? Or again, can regard for death as a future matter be reduced to a mere anticipation of death? Surely this is not what is meant by preparedness for death, let alone the self-consciousness of death.

Self-consciousness of death cannot stop at a mere anticipation of a future event; it requires that death become *present*. For death to be made present and to determine the mode of being of the present, it must not only enter the present from the future but also determine what the present imports from the past. Accordingly, self-consciousness of death requires the "presence of the past" of death. Seen from another angle, however, the self that is in the process of dying from the past to the present cannot be self-conscious. For the self to be conscious of itself, it must be conscious as something that exists. Hence, our first consideration of the self-consciousness of death must be that of the preparedness for death in the future referred to at the start. At the same time, the self-consciousness of death is concerned not only with the future but also with the past and present, since death has already existed from the past to the present.

Self-consciousness is constituted in the moment of eternity intersecting with the present. The same structure holds true for the self-consciousness of death. Since the self exists in the present, self-consciousness of death first takes the exclusive form of a preparedness for the future and mediates that preparedness. The Zen injunctions "Die to yourself once and for all!" and "Above all else, the Great Death!" are both clearly concerned with the future in that they are expressed in the form of imperatives. In his existential analysis, Heidegger speaks of the self-consciousness of the "being-toward-death" of human existence as a potential for wholeness. Insofar as this total self-consciousness of "being-toward-death" imposes on the self the responsibility of transforming itself from its everyday, inauthentic mode of being into an authentic existential one, Heidegger's position is somewhat similar to the Zen imperatives.

To prepare oneself for death does not therefore mean indulging oneself in imagining death or merely anticipating it. In true preparedness, death is not brought into imagination or anticipated as an objective phenomenon that is bound to happen to the self at some future date. One who seriously prepares for death not only does not seek to avoid or obstruct the arrival of the limit-situation of one's own extinction, but positively exerts every effort to mediate the course of this event in such a way as to cooperate with it. This is what gives meaning to the injunction to die once and for all. It is really not so much the submission to death and acceptance of the need to prepare for one's coming death that is implied in the injunction, but a personal choice to become in a positive sense the efficient cause of one's own death. Obviously, it is not a question of suicide here; suicide is not death in the sense that it represents a partial affirmation of life. At the same time, the efficient cause of death must refer to one's actual death. This is why it is termed the "Great Death," in contrast with the partial death of suicide, which is a "small death." In other words, what we are speaking of here is not a direct death but a mediated death, a total affirmation and voluntary acceptance of one's death. This is also why it is similar to existential preparedness for death. Furthermore, preparedness for death, as I am using the term, does not remain a mere passive submission to death but implies the initiation or promotion of authentic death according to one's circumstances.

Briefly put, the terms "activity" and "passivity," or "initiation and promotion" and "voluntary submission," are complementary despite the dichotomy they suggest, because all of them refer to a state of transforming mediation. It is not unlike the transformation that takes place when the possibility of evil becomes the actuality of evil. But in this transformation, which is one of reciprocal penetration, self-consciousness of death as a "living as one dead" or a "dying as one alive" is possible. It is the self living in the present that prepares itself for death in the future, but such a self-consciousness of death is possible only when the self is already dying to itself. Without a self-consciousness in which one completely negates oneself and dies to oneself, one cannot achieve preparedness for death.

In a sense, we begin to die from the moment we are born. To live is to walk toward one's death step by step, or rather to enter deeper and deeper into death. In this sense, death comes from the past to reach self-consciousness in the present. This is not, however, a self-consciousness of nondifferentiation (in fact there can be no self-consciousness without differentiation), but is an affirmation in the sense of daring to affirm what one has been trying to deny. Hence it is possible not only to *prepare* for the death that awaits one in the future but even to *bring it about* by freely accepting it. It is here that talk of preparedness for death or dying one's own death becomes meaningful. Indeed, we may say that life is truly authentic only when one prepares oneself for one's death and accomplishes it willingly. No one can live a genuine life except through death. Living in death, acting as one who has died, becomes the way to true life.

The problem remains, however, that when one prepares for one's death, the self so prepared exists the same as before; and further, that when we speak of "acting as one who has died," the self so acting is in fact not dead. We seem to be thrown back into the same contradiction as before. Has our attempt to come to terms with the problem of death been all in vain? Not necessarily, for we have become conscious of the fact that the contradiction should not—indeed, cannot—be evaded, but that our positive affirmation of it and our voluntary submission to it enable us to transform it and thereby to live without obstructing it, through its mediation.

What does it mean to submit to the contradiction voluntarily and affirm it in this way? If it amounts to no more than falling into the contradiction aware of what is happening to us, we can hardly speak of truly affirming it or submitting to it, since the self is set up in opposition to the contradiction. It becomes something for the self to negate or, failing that, something by which the self is negated. In either case, the self can neither affirm it nor submit to it. It can only confront it in conflict. In other words, the self and the contradiction contradict one another, with the result that the contradiction remains unresolvable while at the same time the self is prevented from transcending it.

The strategy of *either/or* in which *either* the contradiction *or* the self is to be affirmed is unsuitable because it involves a one-sided affirmation or a one-sided negation, the former ending up in negation, the latter in affirmation. Nor is it any help to appeal to a relationship of *both/and* wherein both are simultaneously affirmed. The only relation left is that of *neither/nor*, in which the self does not stand opposed to the contradiction nor the contradiction to the self, but negates the self by means of the contradiction, so that at the same time as the self is extinguished in the negation, the contradiction is also extinguished as that which opposes the self. Converted into the *neither/nor* relationship, both self and contradiction cease to be contradictory opposites. "Death-in-life" and "living as one who has died" cannot survive in a self-consciousness based on a universal principle of self-identity that unites life and death into one. It is not something that can be reduced to a simple *both/and*. There is no other standpoint from which authentic action is possible than that of *neither/nor*, of neither death nor life.

The nothingness on which this *neither/nor* is grounded can never be intuited as a self-identity. Through action based on faith and performed in obedience to Other-power, one's resurrection and return to the world (*gensō*) is witnessed to, and in this the self-consciousness of nothingness is realized. This is the true meaning of such expressions as "living in death" and "acting as one who has died yet lives." Here, self-consciousness of nothingness consists entirely of action-faith-witness. It is a self-consciousness based not on the continued existence of the self but on the passing away of the self. It is a self-consciousness established in the witness of a self that lives as it dies. Even though the self has been restored to life, this does not mean that life reappears after death to replace it, as it is the wont of analytical thinking based on the principle of identity to suppose. The dialectic of death and life consists rather in this, that just as death does not follow life but is already within life itself, so is life restored within death and mediated by it. The point at which the mutual transformation of life and death takes place is not a universal locus where death and life together are subsumed into a relationship of *both/and*. It is rather in the dynamic of the *neither/nor* itself, in the very transformation itself.

If we may compare the standpoint of *both/and* to a mathematical integral, that of *neither/nor* is like a differential. In general, the differential is what determines the direction of a tangent in relation to any curve (with the exception of special cases such as the Weierstrassian curve). That is, it is common for functions in general to possess derivative functions. The presence of the integral, however, is limited only to special kinds of functions. The possession of an integral is not regarded as a quality of a function in general. Only in special cases is there a solution to differential equations. Integral sections, too, can be realized only in special cases; in general, time cannot be embraced in spatial areas. Philosophically speaking, the Dedekind cut, which constitutes the continuity of an irrational number, signifies a dynamic function of transformation combining the two parts of a complete series of numbers by dividing that series into two parts in a contradictory way. This in turn suggests that the Dedekind cut cannot be grasped through the image of space as a self-identical locus. That the continuity of an irrational number cannot be produced by a transfinite aggregate is comparable to the fact that in physics, fictional displacement cannot be reduced to a geometrical figure. Philosophically this can be interpreted as demonstrating that transformation in these two cases is based on self-consciousness in action and not on the intuition of a comprehensive locus. So, too, self-consciousness based on practice does not emerge by something past and previously existing being intuited all at once like a spatial configuration. It is rather a restoration to nothingness of a self emerging from the transformation of death into a present full of the hope of future resurrection. In other words, it is the self-consciousness of death.

The unity of nothingness here is the transformation of a *neither/nor* in which there is no *both/and* at all. It is witnessed to only as the resurrection of a believer who has truly carried out the action of death and submitted obediently to Other-power. The resurrection takes place and practice is carried out without any locus-intuition of nothingness as the self-identity of contradictories. Instead, nothingness is manifest in the self-consciousness of a self that dies to itself and passes away in becoming a medium for Other-power, yet through that very mediation is preserved in being and returned to the world as "empty being." For those who do not exert themselves in the act of dying their own death, nothingness is no more than a hollow word. In fact, it becomes being for them. This is why such as these insist on their own action-intuition as the self-identical ground of their practice. But in their case no transformation of practice takes place because the action of death is absent. Only one who carries out one's own death can witness to and become self-conscious of nothingness.

Death-and-resurrection witnesses to nothingness and is brought to self-consciousness only for persons of action-faith. Witness to nothingness is not the sort of thing that can be intuited as a ground, or locus, of practice. Such a view is pure illusion in that it interprets practice not as the action of Other-power through which the self dies and comes to nothingness, but as a function of the life of self-power that gives form to existence as an expression of oneness with existence. In such a viewpoint there is neither authentic action (*gyō*) nor nothingness. Even though it may use the words "nothingness" and "practice," this viewpoint is concerned with "making" being, fashioning it into an expression of life, and as such it remains diametrically opposed to the nothingness that practices the action of death.

If terms like "living in death" and "becoming as one who has died yet still lives" are given the meaning just described, it is obvious that more is involved than the direct negation of life through its contradictory, death; or of death through its contradictory, life. The *either/or* position that looks on life and death as opposites in order to affirm one and deny the other is not the standpoint of *neither/nor* I have been arguing for here. Whichever side one takes, there is no avoiding death. Nor is the standpoint of *both/and*, which brings life and death together in coexistence in order to effect an affirmation of life, what is called for. Only the absolute negation of "neither life nor death" will do. It is not only that life is negated by death and thereby extinguished but also that death is transformed into life through death-and-resurrection and thus ceases to be a death opposed to life.

The true meaning of absolute nothingness is contained in the famous saying of Kanzan (Egen, 1277–1360), "For me, there is neither life nor death." Living in death and dying while alive means renouncing the *either/or* opposition. Moreover, it means renouncing the transcendence of the opposition through an *both/and* in which life and death are embraced as one. This is what is meant here. It simply means performing the *neither/nor* action of transformation in which life and death cease to oppose one another. It means being able to say with Egen, "For me, there is neither life nor death." Such an experience is not a locus that can be intuited as the performance of action. Even the locus of nothingness, insofar as it exists outside of and previous to action, is not nothingness but being. The *neither/nor* is brought to faith-witness (*shin-shō*) only in accord with action (*gyō*). Belief accords with action in the sense that the performance of action presupposes it. But to be brought to faith means that the self becomes a mediator of nothingness and as such ceases to be. It would be impossible for us to have genuine faith in Other-power by maintaining the self through direct affirmation. In faith, the believer must submit to what is believed, and therefore dies in faith and is resurrected in faith. In intuition, the intuiter and the intuited are brought to unity, a unity consisting in the self-identity of *both/and*.

Even in the case of a mysticism like that of Plotinus where we see the twofold orientation of self-transcendence (*Ekstasis*)—the ascent of the soul and the descent of the One—fuse together, we remain within the standpoint of being, of "making" and "expressing," insofar as such mysticism is based on intuition and not action performed through the mediation of negation. In other words, in place of the *neither/nor* of nothingness, we are still at the level of the *both/and* of being. It may be called nothingness, but it is no more than a nothingness for reason, signaling no more than a transcendence of all predication.

An example of this is to be seen in what Christian mystics, after Plotinus and under his influence, spoke of as "godhead." What they meant was not absolute nothingness but the very opposite: absolute being. From this viewpoint all beings in the world could be considered emanations of being itself. Instead of seeing reality as "empty" (*śūnyatā*), as being that mediates nothingness yet is itself neither being nor nothingness, reality is mistaken as something relative and incomplete, part being and part nonbeing.

Even if the concept of emanation found in Plotinus is taken not as a one-directional emanation—as it usually is taken—but as a mutual mediation of two opposing orientations, it still does not bring us to the manifestation of nothingness through death-and-resurrection. For such mysticism, mediation can only indicate the fact that self-power and Other-power flow together and cooperate: *jiriki-qua-tariki* and *tariki-qua-jiriki*. This sort of mediation may be considered as belonging to a more concrete and advanced stage in comparison with the one-directional doctrine of emanation or the doctrine of creation, where individuals, which are manifold and relative, are dissolved in an absolute One, resulting in the loss of the mediative function of One-*qua*-many and absolute-*qua*-relative, so that the absolute One becomes impossible. Even so, this does not yield mediation through self-negation or death, and relative, manifold beings are not yet regarded as the subject of an egoity grounded in evil. Evil is therefore reduced to a mere privation, and the good is thought to be achieved through a restoration to self-identity rather than through a transforming negation.

As a result of this way of thinking, the death on the cross and resurrection lose their significance, and yield the ascendancy to the aesthetic standpoint of pantheism. It seems to me that the current emphasis on faith, as represented in the dialectical theology of crisis, maintains its special character through registering strong disapproval of such a tendency. Its standpoint is similar to that of metanoetics in that it pursues the *neither/nor* to its consummation and needs to be firmly distinguished from the intuitional standpoint of *both/and* with its principle of self-identity. This is the very distinction that Kierkegaard was at such pains to draw between the religious and the aesthetic. In religious faith, the defining feature rests in the Great Nay–*qua*–Great Compassion, where absolute nothingness is realized through absolute contradiction and disruption, that is, in the absolute crisis out of which relative beings are resurrected. In intuition, there is no such experience of Great Compassion. The self does not perform its own death in and through metanoesis (*zange*) but continues to live through its own "making," so that there is no cause to feel gratitude for having been resurrected. The self dwells in a state of aesthetic enjoyment. On the one hand, therefore, we have a standpoint of death and nothingness; on the other, a standpoint of life and being. Metanoetics sides with the former and against the latter.

On the basis of what has been said so far, let us return to consider the special traits of the self-power school of Zen Buddhism with its injunction, "Above all else, the Great Death!" Is it truly capable of bringing the negating transformation of faith to fulfillment? Or does its achievement of *satori* by self-power merely degrade the transformation of Great Nay–*qua*–Great Compassion into something like the intuitive union of mysticism?

There is no doubt that, among the sects that base themselves on salvation through self-power, Zen differs from other schools of "gradual enlightenment" (*zenkyō*) in that it renounces speculative ontology as a way of deliverance, whereas the *zenkyō* schools in general are inclined to pursue such a course. Convinced that the existence of the self provides the sole key to deliverance, Zen concentrates its entire effort on attaining Buddhahood in enlightenment. Its concrete approach to the problem of deliverance reminds us of the similar position taken by existential philosophy against general ontologies. Moreover, Zen is unique in its use of the *kōan* as the means to enlightenment. From a philosophical standpoint, we must make every effort to come to grips with this approach.

As noted above, the consideration of *kōan* in Zen Buddhism represents a way to absolute negation corresponding to absolute critique in the field of philosophy. Anyone who has ever come in touch with the core of faith along any philosophical or religious path can appreciate at once how the seeker for absolute truth, driven to the extremity of the dilemma of absolute critique, runs into the wall of absolute contradiction where the conversion to resurrection is experienced after the manner of the Zen saying: "Hanging from the edge of a precipice, one lets go and is immediately brought back to life."

The heart of Zen discipline lies in realizing one's own Buddha-nature. This is what is known as "seeing into one's nature" (*kenshō*). All sentient beings are in their original nature Buddha. At the moment of awakening, one becomes the Buddha that one is, while a mere sentient being is a Buddha that has gone astray. Buddha and sentient beings relate to one another as water to ice. At first glance, sentient beings seem to stand in diametrical opposition to the Buddha, but in fact both share the same nature. Death as a sentient being is none other than life as Buddha. There is nothing like resurrection here, and hence no sense of gratitude to the Great Compassion. Since the Buddha is seen to be "the self's own original countenance," there can be no question of the sort of personal relationship we find in the Shin Buddhist notion of Amida Nyorai Buddha. It does not *confront* the self because it already *is* the self.

If we may employ the notions of "in-itself" (*an sich*) and "for-itself" (*für sich*) in this context, the relationship of the Buddha to sentient beings remains at the stage of in-itself, that is, of self-identity. It is not yet at the stage of for-itself with its self-negating transformation. Where the elements of opposition and conversion are clearly present, as in faith in Other-power based on the Great Compassion, we may more properly speak of a for-itself mode of the absolute. But in Zen, which is based on *kenshō* through self-power, it seems more fitting to speak of an in-itself mode of being. Of course, Zen also demonstrates a for-itself mode in the sense that it stresses the "discrimination of nondiscrimination." Still, at the conceptual level, Zen shifts to the in-itself mode by preferring a "nondiscrimination of discrimination," leaning inevitably in the direction of the principle of self-identity.

Seen from the stance of the for-itself mode, the in-itself mode must appear debased and abstract, but this is altogether natural and inevitable, like a scale leaning toward its heavier side or water seeking its own level. Even though sentient beings are originally Buddha, Buddhahood contains within itself the inevitable tendency to degrade itself to the level of sentient being. This is precisely what radical evil means. But Zen puts the emphasis not so much on this inevitable degeneration as on the in-itself mode of the original Buddhahood of sentient beings. To be sure, enlightened deliverance is never in-itself but always for-itself. That is, *satori* belongs to the "discrimination of nondiscrimination." Zen's exhortation to others to the attainment of *satori* and its advice on progress along the path to enlightenment dispose it to see the path as open and accessible to all, and hence to lay the stress on self-identity and the in-itself.

Moreover, this tendency follows naturally from Zen's preferential concern for saints and sages rather than the ordinary and ignorant, for saints and sages belong to an in-itself mode of being that recognizes the original Buddhahood of the self and thus have no need of the love and compassion of Other-power. They are able to penetrate the self's true nature by self-power and the self's own freedom, to dwell in the tranquillity of unrestricted freedom of the authentic self. This is why the Zen Buddhist locates the most important aspect of human religious existence in the elemental fact of resting at home, eating when hungry, and sleeping when weary, which are also the essential marks of the wise and the holy.

It is not the place of ordinary, ignorant persons like me to disapprove of these higher spiritual states. I can do no more than admire them and long for them. The saint or sage may of course accuse me of a lack of faith in my own Buddhahood, but I am at a loss as to what to do about this unbelief of mine, since it is the very thing that makes me the ordinary, ignorant person that I am. Even though I can understand intellectually that the self's true countenance is none other than the Buddha himself, I cannot witness to this out of my own experience. However many tears I shed over my unenlightened state, and however overwhelmed with shame I become for my own powerlessness, I remain utterly incapable of penetrating my self's true nature. It is only in acknowledging my state without arrogance and submitting myself to it in shame that the miracle of belief in and witness to my powerlessness and ignorance are overcome by the absolute, even though I remain just as before. This is what I mean by metanoesis (*zange*), through which I feel myself allowed to participate to some extent in the spiritual state of the saints and sages.

The way of *zange* does not—as is the case with the way of *satori* of saints and sages—enable the self to be absorbed into the absolute through exaltation into an in-itself mode. But it does enable the self to be transformed into a new being within the absolute in a for-itself mode, so that one is allowed to exist by the grace of Other-power and to cooperate as the mediator of the absolute. Metanoesis is action performed by the self, but at the same time it is the practice of abandoning the self. Hence, it originates in the Great Compassion of Other-power. Nevertheless, it is actually the self that submits itself voluntarily to Other-power and performs this action. Paradoxically, metanoesis both is and is not the action of the self. As mediated by absolute nothingness, it is action without an acting self. In this we see the for-itself mode of the absolute unfold. It is a self-consciousness of the absolute through action in which the action-faith-witness of the relative is revealed.

While Zen Buddhism is based on the "discrimination of nondiscrimination," and thus belongs to the for-itself mode, its tendency to the in-itself mode is inevitable, given the limitations of the relative beings that engage in it. Still, it cannot be overlooked that the sage or the saint is apt to stay at the level of an in-itself and to adhere to the principle of self-identity without facing its original for-itself mode. Zen Buddhism, which discloses its true countenance in the fact that "Mind, just as it is, is identical with the Buddha," can immediately be converted to "Neither mind nor Buddha." Its basic characteristic, therefore, lies neither in idealism nor in pantheism, but in self-consciousness of nothingness realized in action. For this reason not only the religion of Other-power and "returning to the world" (*gensō*), with its view of the enlightenment of all sentient beings through a process of reciprocal help (this is what is referred to as the "solidarity" or "communion" of Existenz), but also the philosophy of *gensō* must acknowledge the distance of metanoesis from Zen. There is no question but that the in-itself tendency of Zen Buddhism runs the risk of falling prey to unmediated self-identity. For the fact is, the principle of "Above all else, the Great Death!" often degenerates into a mere notional slogan, and religious action fails to be mediated by the rational seriousness of ethics, lacking the mediation either of the powerlessness of the self that is awakened in the confrontation with ethics, or of the radical evil that is hidden in the depths of the self. When this happens, Zen has recourse to its affirmation of daily existence through such things as "dressing, drinking, and eating," but only rarely concerns itself with ethical questions related to society or the nation. Such expressions as "The mind in everyday life is the way of truth" and "No-occurrence (*buji*) is the noble mind" tend to become abstractions whereby religious truth is seen merely from the *ōsō* approach aimed at nondiscrimination, with the result that the *gensō* approach aimed at discrimination is easily overshadowed. The sage who stops short at this point advances no further than the aesthetic enjoyment of the Taoist hermit. Both the sage and the hermit, despite their best efforts to transcend the ethical, can only end up in a state of nature that is in fact sub-ethical.

It seems to me that what is original about *kōan* is not that they treat trivial matters of daily life or flights of imagination, but that they bring their practitioners to the limits of reason and ethics by means of absolute critique, and in this way are able to accomplish a "realization of reality" (*genjō-kōan*) and inspire a more concrete attitude toward the return (*gensō*) to historical and social reality. If the purpose of Zen discipline is the realization of practical subjectivity in actual reality, I would argue that there is good reason to regard metanoesis as one method of practicing Zen. At least this is the case for those like me to whom the path of sages and saints is closed and who must walk the way of metanoesis. But in spite of this similarity to Zen, metanoetics differs in virtue of its being a for-itself mode.

When we examine the Other-power sect of Nembutsu Buddhism, we find that its strong emphasis on the personal relationship between Amida Buddha and sentient beings, which is a relationship of "for-others," is a belief largely supported by myth where self-consciousness based on for-itself mediation is no longer possible. Metanoetics wards off this orientation, thus positioning itself midway between the in-itself of Zen and the for-others of Nembutsu Buddhism. It is neither one nor the other, and yet participates in both of them in virtue of its for-itself stance.

This stance of metanoetics is of special significance in that it makes possible self-consciousness of the absoluteness of the absolute on which religious belief is grounded. As mentioned above, the doctrine of Zen with its exhortations of "Above all else, the Great Death!" often slides into the in-itself mode of "Mind, just as it is, is identical with the Buddha." Within itself Zen harbors the constant danger of falling into a mere play of ideas and "mere talk about Zen" (*kōtō zen*). This results from a tendency to unite the absolute with the relative on the basis of the principle of self-identity. Where this is the case, there is room left for entering into death, the function of which is to separate the relative and the absolute from each other, but no room left for talk of opposition and transformation.

It is difficult to deny this propensity of Zen for self-identity in an in-itself mode. To do so, on the one hand, is to misunderstand Zen by forgetting that only when one practices Zen in its authentic form can one come to and speak of the supreme realization of its truth as we find it expressed in the poem:

> How splendid it is:
> Even as one lives, to become as one dead,
> Completely dead,
> And to work as the heart desires![3]

Yet how many pitiable and shameless deeds have been performed by people blindly imagining themselves free to do as they please, turning from the supreme truth to a secular and relative one! This results from the mistaken view that the absolute and the relative penetrate each other so fully in self-identity that there is no room left for death-and-resurrection to enter in and unite them on a level deeper than the level of their separation and mutual opposition. The relative is thought to participate in and penetrate the absolute, or even to become identified with it, so that the sense of the true absolute that is brought to faith-witness through the act of self-negating transformation, where the relative functions as the mediator of the absolute and according to which the true absolute can never be manifest in this world, falls from view. The true absolute is lost altogether not only with respect to genuine action but also with respect to the faith that arises only at the limits reached by the absolute critique of reason.

Impelled by logical necessity arising from the antinomy of human reason—that is, by the inevitable twofold need for union and repulsion between the universal and the individual—I have often maintained that the sole way to overcome this antinomy is to elevate oneself to a position that is entirely beyond all discursive thinking and consideration, and then to submit oneself obediently within historical reality to what is given and determined. I now recognize that even this standpoint, like Zen's emphasis on the Great Death above all else, still carries the defect of reliance on the principle of self-identity and thus falls into mere idealism, unable to overcome the demands of relative subjectivity. For even when relative beings are exhorted to abandon their relativity and to resign themselves to the absolute, this absolute remains only something *conceived of* as absolute by relative beings, a simple subjective postulate that we have no evidence for regarding as a manifestation of the absolute itself. In general, any absolute that is postulated on the part of relative beings cannot escape this limitation.

At the same time, to the extent that the relative and the absolute are merely opposed to each other in a "for-others" mode, the relative cannot sustain its existence as a relative, nor can the absolute manifest itself in its absoluteness. This urges on us the need for the third mode of the "for-itself," which is neither "in-itself" nor "for-others." Yet even with this third standpoint, there is no way to prove that it is the standpoint of the absolute, since human being is relative being and not absolute being. From time immemorial, mystics have sought to attain entry into and union with the absolute. The fact that Eckhart conceived of the relationship between the godhead and the soul not in terms of *unitas* but as a *unus* is simply the consequence of his longing for a concrete union that would admit of no separation between the two. This is the reason that the concept of "ecstasy"—in the sense of an *ek-stasis* or standing apart from oneself—came to signify the state of rapture. No matter how fervently one longs for union with God, of itself longing can never provide assurance of such union. (Here we may leave aside cases of pathological subjectivity such as we find in certain female mystics seized by hallucinations in a fit of abnormal physical excitement.)

The mark of genuine mysticism consists rather in this: that the demand for divine transcendence as something infinitely high and perfect, without the slightest taint of relativity whatsoever, becomes more conspicuous as the demand for union with God, which is the counterpart of the demand for transcendence, becomes stronger. The demand for the "in-itself" mode of self-identity and the demand for the "for-others" mode—where absolute and relative are separated from each other—combine warp and woof to produce the essential pattern of mysticism. Mysticism is further characterized by the fact that its demand for divine absoluteness and the demand for divine infinity and transcendence combine with yet another demand: that God embrace within himself and unify all relative beings so that all opposition between the relative and the absolute disappears. Because it involves the experience of bringing to unity these contradictory and opposing demands, mysticism abounds in mystery.

In the case of the mysticism of Plotinus, we find a successful unification of aesthetic intuition and rational speculation wrought through a dialectical logic. As a whole, his thought represents a consistent and admirably harmonious system. After its introduction into Christianity, however, Plotinus's thought underwent a change. The principle of matter, which he had taken simply as the principle of multiplicity before the One, as the being of nonbeing, was transformed into something personal and rebellious, the principle of the flesh rebelling against God. Accordingly, the existence of human beings as finite and relative beings came to be set at a greater distance from and in stronger opposition to the absoluteness of God, at the same time as their demand for union with God grew more intense.

Christian mysticism is thus marked by the same tension between negation and affirmation that we find in metanoetics. Indeed, to one degree or another, metanoesis became one of the dynamic factors in religious mysticism. It is present, for example, in the system of Eckhart, the most profound and coherent system of mysticism constructed in the Middle Ages. In his remarkable interpretation of Eckhart, Rudolph Otto has argued that the key to understanding his thought lies in grasping the idea of "possessing God." It is the possession of God and intimate communion with God that gives meaning to authentic human existence. The starting point for this cooperation and union with God lies in concentrating the mind firmly on God, to which God adds the transforming power—that is, the power of metanoesis—but only for the truly sincere. Purified and intensified, this transforming power of metanoesis becomes a power of the will, which is why the soul can be spoken of as a "second God."[4] Otto's interpretation makes it clear that the first step of metanoesis lies in conscientious self-reflection on the part of the sincere and serious soul, and that for those who lack such sincerity, metanoesis fails to provide a turning point for conversion and salvation.

At the same time, metanoesis does not come about merely as a result of self-reflection carried out under self-power. It suffices to ensure conversion and salvation only when the Other-power of the absolute is performing the work of transformation. Metanoesis is not simply a process of human consciousness, not merely an intellectual dynamic within consciousness brought about through the self-power agency of the soul. It is not through a *mere idea* but through a *real power* that the soul is converted and turned in a new direction. Accordingly, metanoesis may be termed an inner action determined by Other-power. But the real power of this Other-power does not simply function from without as a "for-others." In that case, metanoesis would degenerate from an inner activity into an outer dynamic. In order to be true inner action, what is determined by Other-power must at the same time be brought to self-consciousness through an act of self-determination: the real power from outside must simultaneously constitute the spontaneous ideal element of self-consciousness. This is why metanoesis must be a "real-ideal." This is what we have called its "for-itself" quality. Hence the concentration of the self-conscious soul is at the same time a mediating factor in the absolute transformation of the absolute which converts relative beings, through the mediation of their self-power, into a mediating element in the absolute's own self-negation, that is, its compassionate activity. In this way, the real existence of Other-power is transmitted to the ideal activity of self-consciousness.

All of this shows why metanoetics must needs arise as something on the one hand belonging to the self-consciousness of a relative being, and on the other resulting from the transforming power of the absolute (*tariki-ekō*). In metanoetics, this relationship of opposition and mediation between the relative and the absolute in which the two are neither identical nor different, neither one nor two, comes about through transformative action. This quality of *neither/nor* is something metanoetics has in common with Eckhart's practical mysticism, in contrast with Plotinus's contemplative mysticism which shows rather the quality of *both/and*. Nevertheless, to the extent that Eckhart's standpoint is a mysticism, and hence distinguished from metanoetics, it cannot free itself completely of the contemplative tendency. In addition to lacking a sense of sin, as Otto clearly points out,[5] Eckhart is unable to pursue a radical metanoesis, and in this he shows a greater similarity to the Zen way of *jiriki* (self-power) than to the Nembutsu way of reliance on *tariki* (Other-power). Distinguishing between the sacramental mysticism of traditional Catholicism and the dialectical approach of the German school of mysticism, Rosenberg and others have pointed out Eckhart's conformity to the latter in his inclination toward the free and noble human person. Clearly this suggests Eckhart's approach is closer to self-power than to salvation based on Other-power, and more sympathetic to the self-enlightenment of saints and sages than to the metanoetics performed by the ordinary and ignorant.

Eckhart's idea of soul and godhead united in a relationship of "oneness" does not amount to a mere identity of the two, even though it does set up a tension between them so that they are *neither* one *nor* two. The simplicity of "oneness" he stresses contrasts with a notion of unity that presupposes more or less separate terms. Hence his notion of "oneness" does not signify a union in identity but a oneness existing within dynamic tension, a crisis of separation and isolation.

This becomes easier to understand if seen in the light of Otto's subtle and perceptive reading of Eckhart in terms of a parallel passage from Paul's epistle to the Philippians. With the aim of clarifying the "for-itself" structure of the reciprocal mediation of metanoesis and salvation, we may cite the passage in question: "work out your own salvation with fear and trembling; for God is at work in you, both to will and to work for his good pleasure" (Phil. 2:12–13). According to Otto, the words are altogether contradictory if judged in terms of ordinary logic. For if God always acts in such a way as to redeem some and condemn others to damnation voluntarily—namely, according to a willfully predestined plan which, as Paul believes, has been established before all worldly ages—and remains immutable, unmoved, and unaffected by anything whatsoever, then what is the point of the admonition to "work out your own salvation with fear and trembling"? This admonition demands that one exert all of one's willpower and courage to the utmost. But if salvation is predestined by the voluntary will of God, then why should such an exertion of self-power be necessary?

According to Otto, what Paul really means by these words is that we ourselves should *become* what it is our eternal destiny in God *to be*, so that the fact that, in advance of our choice, we are eternally predestined, selected, called out, and justified by God alone becomes precisely what we choose for ourselves.[6] For Paul, what is eternally predestined and justified is not a matter of some purely abstract idea conceived within God, but an actual reality hidden from the world. In this enigmatic logic, we see that what is fact from all eternity in God, the eternal determination of a divine decision (no doubt Paul himself believes this fact to belong to the eternal, unchangeable essence of God), is precisely what we of ourselves accomplish through our own decision and action. Hence we are admonished to act with fear and trembling since if we did not, we would have to assume full responsibility for our failure. Those who are eternally redeemed and whom even Satan is unable to snatch from the arms of God are the truly helpless sinners who are in need of the grace of salvation.[7] By restoring compatibility to this apparent contradiction in Paul, Otto tried to explain Eckhart's idea of freedom in the "soul of the noble person" and its complete unity with God in terms of a dialectical logic wherein the two contradictory factors are charged with tension and crisis. On this point Otto's interpretation of Eckhart gives us a clue to explain the mediatory relationship of mutual self-negation that obtains between metanoesis and salvation.

The really enlightening part of Otto's interpretation consists in his location of the core of Eckhart's mysticism in the transformative power of the godhead through which human subjects can come to metanoesis. Under Otto's influence, I am persuaded that there is a coincidence between Eckhart's mysticism and metanoetics with respect to the for-itself structure of self-consciousness. This is not to say that there is anything like a complete identity or absolute parallel between them. As I stated earlier, insofar as the former is mysticism, its immediacy or in-itself character of intuition and contemplation necessarily implies a tendency toward the unity of identity, with the result that the spiritual aristocracy of Eckhart's "noble person" takes on the sense of the self-power freedom of saints and sages. In this, he stands diametrically opposed to Other-power metanoetics. It is within these limits that we may interpret his thought metanoetically, and even then not without reservations.

It is also possible to approach Eckhart's thought from the opposite angle and see it as a "philosophy of freedom" that has nothing at all to do with metanoetics. In this regard we may mention K. Oltmanns's *Meister Eckhart*,[8] which was published after Otto's study and is a no less valuable piece of work in its own right. In contrast with Otto, Oltmanns sets out to interpret Eckhart from the standpoint of Heideggerian existentialism, and ends up finding nothing in Eckhart's thought that inclines it toward metanoetics. Indeed, her book gives the impression of interpreting Eckhart mainly in order to confirm Heidegger's philosophy. Thus it is only natural that Eckhart's thought should be expounded as a theory of human existence based on a self-power freedom whose absolute actualization is God. The self-power existentialism she develops is the very opposite of Other-power metanoetics, and as such orients her in an altogether different direction from Otto. This shows how Eckhart's philosophy is actually susceptible to conflicting interpretations. To repeat, it is only within certain limits that Eckhart's thought coincides with metanoetics, beyond which elements at odds with metanoetics have to be acknowledged. In terms of both similarities and contrasts, however, the comparison gives shape to problems of great moment.

So far I have attempted to explain absolute mediation by Other-power chiefly in terms of similarities between metanoetics and Eckhart's thought. We may now take the equally important step of turning to another aspect of his mysticism which is completely opposed to metanoetics. This should enable us to recognize those features that distinguish metanoetics from the action-intuition of mysticism. On the one hand, we have an intuition of the union of the divine and the human wrought through self-power; it is based on the freedom and self-reliance of the sage and the saint. On the other, we see a circular movement charged with the tension and crisis of *zange*; it is based on conversion and salvation of the ordinary and the ignorant through Other-power. The philosophical character of the former resides in an in-itself action-intuition that experiences absolute truth in everyday life, while the latter insists on the necessity of a for-itself mediative action that realizes truth through revolutionary praxis. It is no exaggeration to say that the problem this presents is so important as to affect the very life and death of philosophy: in the final analysis, metanoetics is a mode of being that is for itself and in crisis, revolutionary and circular.

As noted above, Eckhart's thought agrees with the philosophy of metanoetics to the extent that it recognizes the divine power of meta-noesis as mediating salvation and transformation, but directly opposes metanoetics to the extent that it asserts freedom through self-power and regards self-reliant nobility as deliverance, which it proclaims as a com-munion and union of the divine and the human in the form of the birth of the Son of God in the depths of the soul. In order to distinguish the two, I have outlined the scope of their similarity and opposition by drawing a clear dividing line between them. As far as Eckhart's thought is con-cerned, these two contradictory aspects actually function as comple-mentaries. They are not bound and coordinated to each other as if repre-senting distinct realms, but rather interpenetrate each other so as to form a dialectical unity in dynamic tension. This means that in his thought the factor of metanoesis and transformation and the factor of self-reliant freedom oppose and penetrate each other as transcendent and immanent. For metanoetic conversion to take place, the element of spontaneity and freedom should be present. It is through this spontane-ity that metanoesis can direct its mediation toward transformation and salvation. Without it, there would be no transforming mediation. If metanoesis is actuated entirely from the standpoint of self-power, or self-reliant freedom, it cannot establish communion between the divine and the human, that is, the power of mutual transformation between the self-renunciation of the soul and the self-generation of God.

If we grant that Eckhart's theory of deliverance is not a mere self-consciousness of idealism but represents a mediated synthesis of on-tological realism and self-conscious idealism expressed in terms of the birth of the Son of God, there can be no doubt that the freedom of self-power and the transformation by Other-power must "co-respond" to each other and penetrate each other. This is why, despite the fact that Eckhart is generally regarded as the main source of German idealism, his thought is thoroughly dialectical and cannot simply be identified with idealism. The element of realism is clearly present as a negative mediat-ing factor of idealism. In other words, his thought consists not only of an ethics and a doctrine of salvation but also of an ontology that mediates between the two.

In a comparison of Eckhart's thought with Kant's doctrine of radical evil, these traits stand out more clearly. In his theory of religion, Kant maintains that it is not through human self-power but through the transforming aid of divine grace—through a "revolution of sentiment (*Gesinnung*)"—that radical evil can be transformed into the good, and the sentiment toward the good be recovered in the rebirth into a new life. Thus, in Kant's view, by means of a "higher grace unfathomable to human beings" and working as Other-power, it is possible after a revolution of sentiment for self-power to renew its ability to actualize the "ought" and make gradual improvement toward the good.

Despite the dualistic unity this sets up between salvation by self-power and salvation by Other-power, or between revolution and improvement, it is clear that the Kantian revolution of sentiment remains idealistic, a matter of "sentiment," because it lacks a self-negating dialectic within this unity and lacks ontological reality. At the same time, the Kantian concept of Other-power is not sufficiently mediated by self-reliant freedom and spontaneous self-consciousness. In short, Kant's theory of religion stops short at a synthesis of a critical philosophy that adheres to idealism and a realistic ontology required by transcendent religion—a synthesis that does not yet fully attain the level of dialectical mediation. In my view, the revolution of sentiment should not be only a matter of disposition and feeling, but should be based upon being. Moreover, the basis of this being must, at the same time, be mediated and subjectified by the freedom of spontaneous self-consciousness. It is for this reason that the transformation of the subject, consisting of a reciprocal mediation between being and self-consciousness, may be called "inner action" (*innere Handlung*). I would argue that the Kantian revolution of sentiment should be such an "inner action" wrought by the mediation of being–*qua*–self-consciousness. In Kant's theory of religion, however, this dialectical mediation is prone to drive a wedge between idealism and realism, and it is difficult for the revolution of sentiment to reach self-consciousness as a negative mediation brought about from the standpoint of inner action—a defect which it inherits by virtue of belonging to the line of critical philosophy and which has passed down to modern philosophies of religion of Kantian stamp.

I am firmly convinced that the key to solving this problem rests with the dialectic of twofold mediation. It was Schelling's theory of freedom that perfected this tool. This is why it is regarded as a further development of Kant's philosophy of religion. The only difficulty is that in Schelling's thought a speculative construction reminiscent of Greek ontology is so predominant that the aspect of his philosophy we want to consider as a development of "inner action" in faith-witness recedes into the background. Its speculative character sets it in direct confrontation with the self-conscious characteristic of existential philosophy.

As we have already seen, Eckhart's standpoint places him in the latter camp, whence it is natural to expect a dialectic centered on a mutually mediated transformation of being and self-consciousness. In Eckhart, the work of ontological transformation performed by Other-power and the self-consciousness based on the freedom of self-power interpenetrate while maintaining their opposition. If we may identify the former element with metanoetic transformation and the latter with the self-consciousness of self-reliant freedom, Eckhart's thought arises at the very point at which the two elements mediate each other negatively. If either is missing, the dialectical structure cannot stand. In this sense Otto's interpretation—which puts metanoetic transformation at the center—and Oltmanns's existential reading—which regards self-conscious freedom as the main axis—need to mediate each other dialectically. Neither interpretation is of itself sufficient to grasp Eckhart's spirit, and yet neither seems to have realized this dialectic.

There is no question that Otto was correct in locating the core of Eckhart's mysticism in an act of mediation based on metanoetic conversion. But he has failed to work out the implications of this act of mediation, and thus does not bring Eckhart's thought completely into line with Paul's "twofold faith" discussed above, wherein the dynamic of faith overcomes crisis in a radically dialectical manner. Instead, Otto simplifies the dualistic elements in Eckhart's thought into a "twofold intuition" of mysticism, and reduces the tension in polarity to the level of a subjectivity of irrational introspection, finally ascribing it to a "feeling of numinosity" which he sees as the essence of religion. In following this procedure, Otto inevitably overlooks the ontological features in Eckhart's thought, internalizing the dialectic to the point that the real Other-power mediation of metanoetic conversion gets lost. For all of its superb insight, therefore, Otto's interpretation moves in the wrong direction and dissolves Eckhart's thought into mere idealistic introspection.

Oltmanns's existential interpretation does a remarkable job of preserving the element of dialectics and succeeds in bringing systematic unity to Eckhart's thought in a coherent treatment grounded in existential ontology. Nevertheless, her standpoint of self-power and absolute human freedom leads her to identify God with actual reality and to lose sight of the metanoetic element in Eckhart's thought as it is awakened within the existential self-consciousness by a transcendent transforming power in order to become a mediator of Other-power. This flaw in her interpretation also blinds her to the authentic ontological nature of existential self-consciousness in Eckhart's thought, which she treats from start to finish in terms of idealistic self-consciousness. In this way, the dialectic in her interpretation is diluted into a form of idealism. No doubt it is due to the strong influence of the atheistic existentialism of Nietzsche and Heidegger that Oltmanns swings her interpretation toward an anti-Christian position based on self-power similar to what we find in Zen Buddhism. This gives it an element of what Hegel called "unhappy consciousness," devoid of hope in transformation or salvation.[9] In this regard, Oltmanns's effort to interpret the relationship of God and the soul in terms of the "analogy of being" is far from dialectical. For all the attention this gives to the independence of relative being, does it not in fact pursue the idealistic goal of identifying the transcendent One and relative Existenz analogically?

The negative mediation of dialectics, or the relation of interpenetration in mutual transformation, is in essence the exact opposite of the analogy of being. The absolute transformation of dialectical nothingness does not simply set nothingness over against relative, finite understanding as a transcendent being that surpasses the predicative "thusness" (*Sosein*) of being. It is a nothingness of absolute negation and absolute transformation for which relative being always serves as a negative mediation. Both absolute nothingness and relative being belong to a mutual mediation as opposites that negate each other, as correlatives that diametrically oppose one another. Even in the case of Plotinus's further development of the Aristotelian idea of God as being into the idea of God as the One that completely transcends being, we still come up short of the concreteness of Eckhart's idea of God. For him, God does not surpass being but reveals it as absolute, as a self-consciousness–*qua*–generation that always and everywhere mediates relative being. The eye of self-consciousness with which God sees God is the same eye that holds all things in creation by seeing them. Apart from this generative act of seeing creation, there is no self-generating life in God. This is what Eckhart means by revelation. In revelation, God consummates the divine for-itself. Here *"egressus est regressus"* and motion is stillness. In a word, time and eternity become one.

In contrast with ancient Greek ontology, which considers time to be a shadow of eternity and places emphasis not so much upon what is movable as upon what is immovable, we have here a Christian type of mediatory thinking based on revelation. Eckhart's thought must not be turned into a mere ontology in neglect of this fact. Without strictly preserving the relation of transforming mediation, a mediation of negation in which God and humanity suffer together, there can be no gospel of salvation. This negation is the mutually self-negating transformation of absolute nothingness and relative being, the exact opposite of the analogy of being in the sense that the terms in relationship continually repel each other as well.

Absolute nothingness cannot simply be identified with a transcendent being that rises above the totality of being and becomes accessible to self-transcendence after it has reached its limit on the way of spiritual ascent. Since absolute nothingness is nothingness, it contains within itself the negation of being. Nothingness cannot become manifest as nothingness without a self-consciousness of the determination of being as the self-negation of nothingness itself. The self-revelation and self-consciousness of God is also dependent on a self-negation within the finitude of being, in particular the finitude of human being. But at the same time, the soul within which the revelation of God takes place must consider God as its own ground. The eye of God that sees the human soul must be the eye of the soul that sees God. Each of them, God and the soul, sees its opposite in the other in the act of becoming conscious of itself. Furthermore, through this reciprocal transformation of self-consciousness, the eye of God and the eye of the soul merge into one. This is why we may speak of the eye of God as dual. It is impossible for nothingness as the negation of being to be conceived of in terms of the being of beings. The analogy of being simply does not apply in this case. It was because Oltmanns's dialectic lacked the transformative dynamic of Other-power vis-à-vis Existenz that her interpretation of Eckhart was forced to turn itself into a theory of the analogy of being. As we shall see, this points to a limitation within existentialism as such.

Speaking first more broadly, we may say that the ontology of Western philosophy in general has inhibited the full development of dialectical thought by conceiving of the absolute in terms of being (even when it was a question of the loftiest transcendent being). Only in the Mahāyāna doctrine of emptiness (śūnyatā) is the absolute so thoroughly dialectical that the negative mediation of absolute nothingness can be brought to term. Relative beings, which function as mediators of the emptiness of absolute nothingness, are not allowed to rest in the immediate tranquillity of being but are to negate themselves as "phenomenal beings" (ke). Only when they have been restored through the negation of negation to become mediators of the absolute can they find the self on the middle path of "true emptiness, wonderful being" (shinkū-myōu). Even though this relationship of mediation through emptiness orients absolute nothingness on the one hand, and relative beings and being on the other, in opposite directions, by being transformed into one another they inter-penetrate and establish a relation of dialectical unity in dynamic tension. This relationship is much closer to an "analogy of nothingness" than it is to an analogy of being. It is precisely because of this analogy of nothing-ness that the Buddhist doctrine of emptiness is able to carry the dialectic successfully to term. To the extent that the analogy of being is a direct contradiction of the analogy of nothingness, it can lead only to the sort of negation of dialectics that we find in Oltmanns's interpretation of Eckhart.

If we now turn our attention from ontology in general to the stand-point of existentialism as an ontology of self-consciousness, we are able to see how Oltmanns's interpretation exposes the limitations inherent in existentialism. It will also help us to see the weakness of atheistic doc-trines of deliverance based on self-power. As we saw earlier in touching on Kant's theory of religion, which rends the system of idealism asunder by pointing out its limitations, Kant held that the radical evil of human nature can never be overcome by the self's own power, since the very proof of its radicalness consists in the fact that it has already eradicated one's disposition toward good. Only a higher power unfathomable to us can evoke the revolution of sentiment needed to convert us away from this evil. Without the aid of this Other-power, the human freedom of self-power is closed off to us. But it is precisely this that logic cannot grasp with its principle of identity. Only the dialectic of reciprocal mediation can bring about self-consciousness of the fact that the real grace of Other-power is activated through the spontaneous freedom of self-power, and conversely, that the realization of human freedom in self-power becomes possible only through the assistance of Other-power. By means of this dialectic we are able to understand *jiriki-qua-tariki* and *tariki-qua-jiriki*.

Kant was confronted in his theory of religion with this problem of the dialectic of mediation and came close to acknowledging its validity. In the end, he lacked the means to develop it in a positive form and was compelled to content himself with the negative admission of the limita-tions of human reason in the face of radical evil. To break through this problem dialectically, one must perform for oneself the action of trans-forming mediation and bear witness to "the aid of Other-power"–*qua*–"the realization of self-power." Existentialism would appear to be headed in this direction, and to that extent its standpoint is possessed of a dialectical structure. At the same time, to the extent that it remains at its present level of awareness and obstructs its own path by ignoring the transforming mediation on which its own standpoint is based, existentialism cannot succeed in bringing self-consciousness of this dialectical structure to term. By persisting in its adherence to the principle of self-power, it forsakes, for-itself self-consciousness of the transformative mediation of Other-power for a self-consciousness of the autonomous spontaneity of self-power.

It is unfortunate that, despite the laudable consistency of her method and the meticulousness with which she carried it out, Oltmanns got caught in such a one-sided existential interpretation of Eckhart. The fault lies in the fact that her existentialistic standpoint was too abstract. Still, it is worth nothing that both Oltmanns's and Otto's interpretations not only represent noteworthy contributions to scholarship on Eckhart but have each suggested close parallels in Eckhart's thought to metanoetics and the theory of freedom. This may have led me to venture too deeply into details regarding Eckhart, but my point was only to clarify structural similarities to metanoetics.

As Otto's interpretation has shown, Eckhart's doctrine of salvation argues for a mystic notion of essential simplicity based on a twofold intuition—that is, the oneness of God's eye that sees God, and the oneness of God's eye that sees all the things of the world—in terms of which God and all things unite in the birth of the Son of God in the soul. This leads him to the conclusion that divine salvation is not a matter of grace but of natural necessity based on an identity between God and nature. This prevents the metanoetics contained in Eckhart's thought from unfolding to the full, so that salvation through the Great Compassion of Other-power gets displaced by the freedom and deliverance of self-power. This makes it easy to see how Oltmanns's existential interpretation should have grasped only half the truth of Eckhart.

Delacroix's well-known *Essai sur le mysticisme spéculatif en Allemagne au quatorzième siècle*[10] presents a balanced, clear, and reliable reading of Eckhart. The work's success seems to stem from the fact that, while Delacroix clearly recognized the two opposing tendencies in Eckhart, he was able to see how they came together in Eckhart's mysticism. He depicts the noble human soul as a mountain standing tall and firm under a gentle wind, and details the process of self-consciousness in which the soul shakes off its various attachments to transient things in self-abandonment and self-detachment on its way into the deepest recesses of the soul, until at last it breaks through the essence of eternity at the very foundations of self-awareness and there kindles the spark of the godhead. In reading it, I could not help feeling the closeness of Eckhart to Zen.[11]

Because of my difficulties with Middle High German, I have not read Eckhart in the original. But a reading of Büttner's two-volume translation into modern German has filled me with admiration for the depth of thought to be found in such pieces as "Vom Schauen Gottes und von Seligkeit" and "Vom Gottesreich: Ein Sermon," [12] the latter in particular for its treatment of the role of Other-power in transformation and conversion. There Eckhart argues that for the soul to break through to the eternal essence of God, an experience that he refers to as a "second death," the same inner action of self-power is required as with its "first death" in which the self dies to itself and to the world by renouncing all attachment to temporal things. But for the soul to receive the light of the godhead in the second death, another power is required in addition to self-power: the transcendent Other. [13] As Delacroix has pointed out, [14] we have to do here with a unity of action and intuition: the transforming element of action and the unitive element of contemplative intuition fuse into one. The similarity to the convergence of practical mediation and contemplative union in Zen Buddhism is obvious. The "death in the Lord" that takes place in the soul of the noble person is itself freedom and deliverance. But this second death must always be preceded by the first death of self-abandonment. Once the barriers that the creature erects to separate the soul from God have been removed through the first death, the soul can die the second death in God of breaking through its selfhood and returning naturally to the godhead. Conversely God, who opposes the soul, breaks through God, returns to the godhead, and renders the soul capable of restoring itself to life. The first death is the death of the soul before created things; the second, the death of the soul before God. By overcoming its opposition to the godhead in the second death, the soul is resurrected in the spark of the godhead and spontaneously displays its own divinity. This is its deliverance. It is rather similar to the Zen idea that by putting the Great Death above all else and dying to oneself, one lets go both of oneself and of the Buddha whom one has been seeking, thereby reaching the state of "no-Buddha."

This profound insight of Eckhart's recalls Dōgen's concept of nothingness. Dōgen prefers the doctrine that all sentient beings are *without* the Buddha-nature to the doctrine that all sentients *have* the Buddha-nature, arguing that neither sentient beings nor Buddha-nature ought to exist:

> It is not that sentient beings are from the first endowed with the Buddha-nature. Here the essential point is: even though you seek the Buddha-nature hoping to endue yourself with it, Buddha-nature is not something to appear now for the first time. [15]

Dōgen clarifies the wondrous nature of the mutual transformation through which a sentient being realizes its Buddha-nature and the Buddha-nature realizes itself in the sentient being's performing the action of its own nothingness in and through the realization of the nothingness of the Buddha-nature.

It is through the realization of nothingness, then, that soul and godhead are restored to unity. Eckhart says that God extinguishes God in the soul,[16] that the soul returns to God in empty being, and that God demands that the soul let go of everything, including the soul's own God. Here again the insight is close to Dōgen's thought. Both of them regard the state of mind of forgetting God or the Buddha as deliverance or salvation. For Eckhart, this locates godhead beyond any kind of being in which God preserves the opposition of being between God and humanity, bringing it close to absolute nothingness. At the same time, the freedom of the soul becomes a "doing of nondoing" in which the soul, abandoning God and all concern with God, practices its own truth unreservedly.

Eckhart's mysticism displays exact parallels with Zen Buddhism here on two important points. First, in spite of being a mystic, he maintains a strict and sober doctrine that brings to self-consciousness the freedom of the noble person's soul, which is altogether different from fanciful and sentimental types of mysticism. And second, both are based on an action of self-power that is the exclusive property of brave and noble persons of profound wisdom. The one notable point of contrast is that while Eckhart harks back to the tradition of Western philosophy and elaborates a uniquely consistent form of philosophy, Zen offers a unique method and discipline for bringing *satori* into the everyday realities of life. In terms of fundamental spirit, however, the strong similarity remains. We see this in the fact that although mysticism in the West represents a continuous tradition of wide-ranging intellectual variety that continues right up to the present, Eckhart's mysticism differs from all other forms in virtue of its proximity to Zen as a unity of action and intuition. We may say that both share the same fundamental feature of being doctrines of deliverance and freedom. But for this very reason it should not escape our attention that Eckhart's thought remains bound to the same limitations of self-power as Zen. This has been the main focus of my attention here.

Zen's insistence on self-salvation is guilty of a certain circularity in the sense that while its doctrine of putting the Great Death before all else is a method for the wise and saintly to reach enlightenment, these latter are able to practice the doctrine precisely because they are already wise and saintly. Or in other words, they are able to awaken to the nothingness of the self precisely because in attaining genuine self-consciousness they are already the Buddha. This circularity is ongoing, self-identical, and in-itself, in contrast with the disjunctive and discontinuous for-itself mode of self-consciousness which is brought about through faith in Other-power as a transformation wrought through the merit-transference (*ekō*) of the Great Compassion. This is why I have argued that Zen is always in danger of getting stuck in the merely subjective and immanent.

Let the wise and the courageous be as *subjectively* confident as they may that the freedom they exercise through self-power is at one with the autonomous being of the absolute—there is no way this conviction can be confirmed *objectively*. Let the ordinary and commonplace believe as they may that they are participating in *objective truth* when, having driven their rational capacities to the limit, they cast the self aside and submit to the facts of reality just as they are—there is no way for them to escape the bounds of a *subjective belief* that gainsays objective proof.

The same holds true of practical reason. Try as we may to free ourselves from the bondage of our particularity by dying to ourselves, we cannot dispel the doubt that the death we die falls short of confirming our intention—indeed, that it may only demonstrate how much we still cling to our particularity. Even should we die sacrificing our life for an ideal, the doubt lingers: are we not merely defending a particular self enslaved to an ideal? Is the mere fact of having died a martyr's death any proof that in clinging to its convictions the self does not remain as deeply rooted as ever? Even a death in the name of God or Buddha does not ensure that one has truly died to God and let go of the Buddha. The tenacity of egoity can never be avoided in any act brought about directly by will. This is our radical evil. We may speak of overcoming it through *satori* or self-awakening, but precisely because it is *radical* evil we are powerless to do so. If this evil is to be uprooted through self-power, it can only be because this self-power originates in the liberated freedom of divine reason.

To focus more closely on the problem of death, consider the state of mind of the brave warrior who joins a death squad and goes off to die in battle, serenely composed. This seems not unlike the state of mind of one wise and saintly who has attained the liberation of self-abandonment and is able to say, "For me, there is neither life nor death." This disposition is commonly spoken of as one in which "life and death are one" (shōji-ichinyo). It is not, of course, that life and death have been compared and found to share the undifferentiated identity of a common genus. Quite to the contrary, it means that they penetrate each other at a level where there is neither life nor death, in the absolute detached state of "having no-thing by nature." It is the state of mind of those who have themselves become God or Buddha. For myself, I can only stand before these wise and brave persons in admiration and awe. To my shame, I must confess that theirs is a way closed off to me. This does not mean that it is altogether impossible for me even to prepare myself for death. At times I, too, have risked the sort of actions that can be performed only by one who is ready to die; but it has never occurred to me that in so doing I have experienced a state of mind that I could describe in terms like "For me, there is neither life nor death." This sort of ethical position arrived at through the efforts of self-power has nothing to do with what is called "the continuous state of true mind (shōnen-sōzoku)." It is no more than a special situation arising intermittently at times of crisis.

Neither before nor after—and indeed not even during—such critical situations is radical evil ever eradicated. Only when the darkness has been vanquished by metanoesis and transformed into the light of Great Compassion like a sort of differential point, only when the darkness itself has become a medium for sparking that light, is the Great Compassion of Other-power witnessed to in a standpoint of action-faith corresponding to the self-power of ethics. In Zen the situation of differentiation-qua-nondifferentiation is described as "Light and darkness, side by side." The light of Great Compassion is rather a "shining darkness" and the instant of ethical action a "spark in the darkness." In that sense it is like "Light and darkness, side by side" preceded by a minus sign. The point of speaking in symbolic terms is to show that while the one is related to the freedom of the sage, the latter belongs to the metanoetics of the ordinary and commonplace individual. Those who rely on an ethics of self-power and yet, because they are unable to maintain a "continuous state of true mind," find themselves within the darkness of radical evil at every moment of their action, must, as Kierkegaard has shown, keep in a state of perpetual repentance. This ongoing metanoesis gives rise neither to integral continuity nor to simple discontinuity, but to a differential transformation where light and darkness stand side by side. This is why I have insisted that metanoetics is the basis upon which an ethic devoted to gensō through action-witness of the Great Compassion becomes possible.

Here the impossibility of death through self-power is mediated by Great Compassion through the boundlessness of metanoesis and stimulated to the point of conversion into a spontaneous possibility. What self-power cannot accomplish by itself is made possible when the grace of Great Compassion manifests itself in response to one's self-abandonment through metanoesis, which in turn manifests itself in response to the grace of Other-power. In this way, the reciprocal mediation between the absolute and the relative is brought to fulfillment in a circular movement that involves a "returning" for both. I use the term "fulfillment," but this should not be understood in the sense of a static state of perfection. It rather points to an unending process in which each completion represents a new beginning and each development a return to the source. Metanoesis is simply the axis on which this reciprocally transforming mediation turns. It is not a mere psychological phenomenon only incidentally related to ethics and religion. As Kierkegaard has made clear, repentance is the fundamental and defining quality of ethics for the human person who, as a finite creature, is incapable of breaking away from bondage to original sin and radical evil. It is itself symbolic of the finiteness of ethics.

Through its fundamentally metanoetical character, ethics is led to confess in shame and remorse to its own powerlessness to stand steadfast in autonomy. At the same time, absolute dialectics requires that the finite should serve the infinite in a mediatory role. In mediating the absolute through metanoetic confession of its own finitude and powerlessness, the relative ethical subject cooperates to make manifest the absolute nothingness of religion. Religion mediates itself to ethics through metanoesis in order to actualize an absolute mediation of absolute-*qua*-relative. Metanoesis is both the gate through which ethics passes over into religion and the axis around which religion converts to ethics.

Thus, metanoesis is really a *kōan* mediating a dialectical transformation between ethics and religion. It is only through metanoesis that ordinary sentient beings, the finite and relative subjects of ethics, are received into the grace of God or the Buddha and thereby restored to life as coworkers of God or the Buddha, without ceasing to be the ordinary, ignorant persons they are. In metanoesis relative, finite beings forsake the vanity of aspiring to identity with the infinite and the absolute. Conscious of their own finitude and relativity, they abandon their claim to existence through self-power. This enables them to participate in *nirvāna* without being released from bondage to worldly passions (*bonnō*). They no longer need trouble themselves over the limitations of self-power and bondage to finite subjectivity. Metanoetics turns all of these limitations into mediators for manifesting the infinite. Metanoesis can transmute even its own impurities and imperfections into a medium for the manifestation of the absolute. Through *zange* the ordinary and ignorant are allowed to cooperate with God to the same extent as the wise and heroic. Metanoetics is conscious of shame and preserves a sense of humility, and yet knows peace of heart.

Even though by myself I am unable to come to the point of being able to say, "For me, there is neither life nor death," metanoesis enables me to participate in the absolute even as I am overwhelmed with shame and repentance for my own powerlessness. Through it I come to absolute submission—the submission of living life to the full and dying death to the full. The state of mind in which one realizes this truth is never free of suffering, and yet even suffering itself becomes a state of spiritual peace full of joy and gratitude. The poison of radical evil and the thorns of anguish are withdrawn, while evil and anguish themselves are transformed into incentives for a life of compassion through the operation of the Great Compassion of Other-power which converts them without taking them away. Terms like "the lotus in the fire" (*kachūren*) and "the lotus blooming in the mud" (*odeige*) are fitting descriptions of this process.

But because this transforming mediation is always transforming and always mediative, it is always brought about in action, not in intuition. Metanoesis is not an in-itself mode of being with an inner tendency toward self-identity, but a for-itself mode of being that mediates between the opposites by generating them from within itself and restoring them to unity in the absolute through their mutual transformation. The consciousness that grounds this in-itself mode of action-transformation is faith and witness: a coming together of the way of ascent and the way of descent. Unlike the in-itself immediacy of intuition, faith-witness sets up a dynamic circularity in which a leap ahead is also a step back to the immovable source. This is what is meant by action-faith-witness.

When Zen emphasizes the importance of faith and witness, it is in order to distinguish its standpoint of the identity of action and contemplation from one of merely static contemplation. Faith, of course, bespeaks an attitude of trust in which one entrusts oneself to what is transcendent; and witness, a consciousness of the immanence of what is transcendent. But from its standpoint of immediacy and identity, Zen naturally equates faith with witness as the two faces of practice and discipline. In Zen, action, faith, and witness become one. But what this gives us is not the transforming mediation of a for-itself mode but the unity of an in-itself mode. For this reason, to speak of practice and discipline, of faith and belief, or of witness and *satori* is all the same. Each of them subsumes the others into itself. In the for-itself mode of meta-noetics, however, the three elements are mediated by one another so as to form a sort of trinitarian wholeness. Here we cannot speak of any one of them necessarily subsuming any other into a unity. By being distin-guished from one another, they are able to determine a relationship of mutuality.

These, then, are the differences between the in-itself and the for-itself modes of being, between the unity of identity and transforming mediation. Although the two converge in their concern with action and transformation based on absolute nothingness, Zen cannot escape its tendency to mysticism by reason of its insistence on in-itself unity. And in any event, Zen differs from the transformation by Other-power of metanoetics insofar as it agrees with self-power doctrines based on a theory of freedom. We must not overlook the difference between the standpoint of the wise and heroic and that of the ordinary and ignorant.

Before embarking on an explanation of Shinran's doctrine of the three stages of transformation, which represents a consummate treat-ment of the latter standpoint, I should like first, by way of introduction, to take up the idea of salvation expressed in Pascal's *Pensées*.

Chapter 6

From Pascal to Shinran: Metanoetics as Absolute Gensō

Pascal's Pensées and metanoetics contrasted · The mediating role of thought in salvation · The essentials of Shinran's theory of the three vows · The relationship between ōsō and gensō merit-transference · The absolute gensō of absolute mediation · The relationship of the Tathāgata to the community of Buddhas and sentient beings · "From truth to upāya," "from upāya to truth" · The philosophical significance of the gensō ideal

Like Kierkegaard, Blaise Pascal has had a profound influence on modern philosophy of religion. Few thinkers can rival his penetrating insight into the suprarational nature of faith and the experience of conversion through love and grace that passes beyond the limits of human rationality in order to lead to faith in God. It is a simple matter to find traces of *zangedō* in his *Pensées*. It is clear that the metanoetic impulse played a major role in leading him to conversion and that he was fully conscious of this. Even in his final years as he drew nearer to death, and despite the loftier heights and more profound depths of saintly purity toward which his life ever moved, one theme remained constant in his prayer and repentance: his ties to the world. Even though these ties had been reduced to the slender thread of an attachment to mathematics, Pascal's passionate love of truth brought him time and again into vigorous discussion with others, which in turn was an endless source of pangs of conscience.

From the biography written by his sister, we know that after Pascal's coversion, prayer and repentance were the main elements of his religious life. For instance, we read in his *Pensées*:

Instead of saying: "If God were not merciful, we should have to make every effort towards virtue," we should on the contrary say that it is because God is merciful that we must make every effort.[1]

This is precisely what I have been speaking of in this book. But if one were to ask further whether the core of his thought in the *Pensées* is strictly identical with metanoetics, the answer would have to be in the negative. This is in no way to cast doubt on the authenticity of his faith or to accuse his thought of being shallow. Nothing could be further from the spirit of metanoetics. Quite to the contrary, it seems to me that Pascal was such a pure and noble spirit by nature that he would never have felt the inner impulse to metanoetics. Metanoetics is the way of the ordinary and the foolish, not that of the holy sage of pure and noble spirit. Metanoetics is the way of Other-power; the latter belongs to the path of self-power.

Like Pascal, Spinoza took his start from Cartesian philosophy, passing beyond it to attain purity of heart and nobility of mind. There is, to be sure, a striking contrast between Spinoza's pantheism and Pascal's theism, as also between Spinoza's adaptation of geometrical methods and Pascal's depreciation of *l'esprit de géométrie*. It is clear that when Spinoza, unlike Pascal, rejects repentance as reduplicated powerlessness,[2] he is doing so in sympathy with Descartes's conviction that human emancipation is to be wrought by the perfection of intellect. Here we see an attitude to wisdom and intellect that is fitting for the sage but is the exact opposite of metanoetics. Pascal's famous "wager"[3] retains the quality of decision by self-power, and therefore shares in this standpoint of the sage and the saint, despite its similarity to the core of conversion in faith as a transformation by Other-power. One may also take his original doctrine of probability[4] as further evidence of self-power.

In addition to passages like that cited above, however, there are clear traces of the dominance of Other-power in Pascal's religious thought. We see this for instance in his emphasis on faith as something bestowed by God,[5] and in his remarks that "we are satisfied the moment we give will up,"[6] and that "God makes simple people love him and hate themselves."[7] For all that, the fact that he repeatedly speaks of the significance of learned ignorance as the ultimate knowledge of human existence, and of self-consciousness as that which accounts for the grandeur of being human,[8] betrays an unmistakable tendency to self-power. This is also decisively manifest in the fact that his *Pensées* were drawn from material prepared for a massive unfinished work on apologetics, intended as a verification and vindication of religious truth in the way of positive (self-)affirmation, which runs counter to the obedience and submission through self-negation of metanoetics. It is only natural that in his apologetic writing, as in the *Pensées*, certain metanoetic elements should be included. But on the whole, it is hard to see how apologetics can be carried out properly in a spirit of metanoesis. The reason is this: apologetics consists in the positive attitude of a direct affirmation of one's religion, while the religious attitude of metanoetics inclines toward the passive negativity of humility and obedience.

Besides this formal distinction between metanoetics and the thrust of the *Pensées*, there is a difference in content that stands out no matter how closely the two approach one another. This difference becomes more apparent and concrete the closer we look at the *Pensées*. It is commonly acknowledged that Pascal's chief concern there is to establish an anthropology based entirely on the contrast between "the misery of humanity without God" and "happiness of humanity with God," an anthropology whose apologetic function is to vindicate the truth of the Christian religion. In classifying the stages of human existence from an anthropological viewpoint and characterizing each stage in terms of the ascending rungs of a ladder, Pascal does not view God as Other-power that descends from above to the human stage. This would break the continuity of the hierarchy of the ascent from misery to felicity and reverse the direction of the stages in such a way that the human individual would be made to respond through action in faith-evidence (*shin-shō*) to the mediative activity of the absolute. Even though Pascal's stages of human ascent can be given religious significance by its association with the divine, his anthropology remains contemplative in the sense that God is considered only from the immanent standpoint of human existence and is not confirmed through an action-faith (*gyō-shin*) prompted by a transforming transcendent power. Pascal's standpoint is that of the sage and the saint who aims at unity with God. His anthropology is designed to make intelligible the contrast between the misery of humanity without God and the happiness of humanity with God in order to effect a conversion from the one to the other through an intellectual awakening. As a result, his anthropology lacks the concreteness necessary for a doctrine of salvation. In this it differs altogether from metanoetics, which deals with self-consciousness in concrete subjectivity.

A brief word about the essence of Pascal's anthropology. In his early period of concern with epistemological problems, Pascal distinguished between *l'esprit de géométrie* and *l'esprit de finesse*, the object of the former being universal truth demonstrable by reason, and that of the

latter, individual value apprehended in the form of an immanent understanding of heart and feeling. In his later period, he divided human
existence into three stages: (1) a material, corporeal existence that belongs to the order of the intellect and is the object of *l'esprit de géométrie*;
(2) an order of the heart, a realm of individual value and teleology
apprehended by *l'esprit de finesse* (and which is in turn divided into three
stages); and (3) an order of grace situated above the order of the heart and
corresponding to divine providence.[9] Given his religious viewpoint, it
stands to reason that he should set the order of grace higher than the
teleological realm in such a way as to stress the overall transcendence and
independence of religion. Teleology belongs to the natural order since it
is the object of *l'esprit de finesse*, of *le coeur*, or in Kantian terminology, of
"the reflective judgment" of feeling. In this way, Pascal established
providence as the foundation of all teleology.

The faculty of believing in divine providence is what Pascal calls
pensée de derrière, by which he understands the power of insight to grasp
raison des effets. This latter lies behind the teleological order of nature
and hence cannot be reasoned out from the teleological standpoint as
such. With good reason Chevalier stresses this point, which he refers to
as "Pascalian dialectics." *Raison des effets* cannot supply a given fact with
sufficient reason in a direct and affirmative way; yet to negate the fact
would run counter to teleological order as such. Hence we have no choice
but to describe the rationality of the fact indirectly, from the viewpoint
of its effects. In this sense *pensée de derrière* is "hind-thought." This
corresponds to providence, to an order of grace higher than the order of
teleology with its head-on approach. Its *pensée de derrière* is believed
indirectly, through negation. The dialectic is clear here, particularly in
Pascal's insistence that one's learned ignorance (the self-consciousness
of ignorance and misery) is at the same time one's greatness.[10] This
reversal belongs to divine providence[11] as it is ascribed through *raison des
effets*,[12] and is also evident, we may suppose, in his assertion that the
recognition of one's misery through *pensée de derrière*[13] brings one greatness.[14] This means, however, that one who believes in God and thus
contemplates the world in terms of the order of grace is able to effect the
transformation of the misery of "being without God" into the happiness
of "being with God" within the realms of thought. This is also implied in
Pascal's celebrated image of the "thinking reed" in which the human
being is transformed from weakness into greatness like a reed.[15]

But is it really possible for thought to transform a human being?
Anyone possessed of such power would have to be a holy sage, not an

ordinary, ignorant person. As one who clearly belongs to the latter class of human beings, whose thought is able to reach no further than the self-consciousness of my own miserable state, I stay put and do not experience the transformation into greatness. This is testimony to my ignorance, in the face of which I have been forced to relinquish my qualifications as a philosopher. However much shame this brings me, however painful the confession, it is my destiny from which I cannot escape and for which I have no excuse. For me, the very idea that "thought" should have the power to transform one's being is no more than the ideal of the wise and the holy, an "ought" that cannot become real for me. It is forever an "ought" of self-power, not the manifestation of Other-power. Ignorant and ordinary man that I am, I cannot share with Pascal in the glory of the "thinking reed." For one of such rare genius, such saintly purity of heart, and such a noble mind, it is hardly to be wondered at that thought could reach such heights of luminosity. I regard this as evidence of his wisdom as a holy sage. In contrast, I lack the wisdom of his thought and his freedom from suspicion and doubt. This I regard as evidence of my own folly.

Hence Pascal's understanding of thought as the agent for human existence to transform itself and my advocacy of metanoetics as the mediation of absolute transformation rest on different standpoints. *Zange* is not to be seen as "thought" but as action, and not as the mere action of self-power but as the action of Other-power, one moment in the trinity of action-faith-witness (*gyō-shin-shō*). It is not a matter of self-power, but points to the activity of absolute mediation which can coordinate both self-power and Other-power mutually by converting the former to the latter and thus make transcendent, absolute nothingness manifest. It is for this very reason that we speak of metanoesis in terms of action-faith-witness to a real transformation brought about by the natural spontaneity of Other-power.

In contrast with the self-consciousness wrought in thought of Pascal's learned ignorance, which experiences a continuity of ego before and after conversion, metanoetics is a consciousness of death and resurrection: the ego is given up once and for all, but this initial negation is then transformed into new life as a manifestation of Other-power. As a medium of Other-power, metanoesis is also an activity of self-power needed to solicit the activity of Other-power. In this mutual mediation the absolute shares in the suffering of relative beings who are subjects of metanoesis and brings them the grace of salvation through its unfailing compassion and support. Seen in terms of this salvific mediation, a confessed sin is no longer merely sin, but becomes a medium of grace. This is why we may speak of a *felix culpa* or "the grace of sin." Referring to the tragic event at *Rājāgṛiha*, Shinran notes that

> Devadatta succeeded in persuading King Ajātaśatru to commit a deadly crime. Thereupon, Śākyamuni came out into the world to make the mind of Vaidehī turn towards the Land of Peace and Happiness.[16]

And elsewhere Shinran observes that we are destined to enter into membership in the realm of *nirvāna* without extinguishing our evil passions.[17]

Here we can see how Pascal's notion of transformation or conversion entails a relationship of "in spite of" that contrasts sharply with the metanoetic emphasis on "because of." That is to say, for Pascal it is *in spite of* our misery without God that we achieve happiness and greatness when we are with God. In metanoetics, however, it is *because of* our misery that we are accounted great in God. Even though for Pascal the *raison des effets* can be grasped as providence through *pensée de derrière*, this does not amount to a recognition of the significance of sin as a negative mediatory element. The dialectic of the *pensée de derrière* does not therefore develop beyond the state of the *an sich*, and indeed it is only through reflection that has reached the state of *für sich* that we are able to understand its failure as a dialectic.

Our dialectic of "because of," in contrast, is based on the negative mediation of metanoesis which qualifies it as authentic dialectics: absolute negativity functioning through negative mediation as the mediation of absolute nothingness. This is the difference between Pascal's conversion of thought and what we have been speaking of as conversion through the action of metanoesis. Pascal's determination of the true God as a *Deus absconditus*[18] who is known as unknown and unknown as known, as well as his designations of the dualism of human nature,[19] the bond between misery and misericordia,[20] the parallel between true religion and pseudoreligion,[21] the blessedness of human being as lying within itself and without itself at the same time,[22] and so forth, may at first glance appear to belong to an authentic dialectic. But there is a qualitative difference between his self-consciousness based on thought and the self-consciousness of metanoetics based on the transformation by Other-power. We must be careful not to confuse the two.

Seen in this light, the "Order of Grace," which, according to Pascal, belongs to the highest stage of human being, remains a determination of thought regarding the idea of providence and should not be identified with the manifestation of transcendent Other-power through the mediation of metanoesis. His notion of grace contradicts itself no less than the practice of the *nembutsu* (praise and recitation of the name of Amida Buddha) by self-power does, as we shall see presently. The concept of grace, like that of the *nembutsu*, points to a negation of the self and hence to a negation of self-power. But if the negation of self-power is carried out according to the principle of thought which is based on self-identity, and not, as it should be, according to the principle of no-self or empty self awakened by the transforming activity of Other-power, it can only proceed from the same, as yet unconquered self-power. The contradiction is patent. In general, the unmediated contradiction of objective being is not the contradiction of mediating action performed by the self-consciousness of authentic subjectivity, and accordingly it forfeits its unity as a concept. The concept so entangled in contradiction moves of necessity toward self-negation to become the negative element of the concrete which is dialectical in the authentic sense. That is to say, the idea of self-power can only be seen as the mediating element of the authentic *nembutsu* of transcendent Other-power, of *nembutsu* as a manifestation of metanoetic action corresponding to this Other-power. From the Pure Land Buddhist viewpoint of Other-power with its unity of action, faith, and witness (*gyō-shin-shō*), the "thought" of the holy sage, based on self-power, has to be seen as such a negative element here. That is, the holy sage represents the abstract conceptualization of Other-power and serves as its negative element.

Furthermore, the true standpoint of Other-power itself is always in danger of losing that authenticity by failing in its mediatory action (*gyō*) and removing itself from the suffering of *zange* to the level of mere thought. Self-power is always behind Other-power like a negative lining. The ignorant are always exposed to the risk of regarding themselves as wise and good and to the temptation to self-conceit. The reason is that we are easy prey to the radical sin of selfishness. Here we see the alienation involved in religious "thought" and concepts. When the highly esteemed ideals of truth, goodness, and beauty lose the significance of serving to mediate salvation and become absolutely independent ideals, they tend in the opposite direction of hypocrisy, sin, and ugliness. In truth they are only relatively independent and function as mediators of absolute nothingness. Although Pascal is clearly conscious of this in the *Penseés* and comes very close to the position of metanoetics, he never quite shakes completely free from a contradiction similar to that of the "*nembutsu* of self-power" in the praise he accords "thought." As a result, his dialectic ends up as a unity of thought that does not reach the point of transforming action based on absolute nothingness.[23]

Shinran's idea of the *sangantennyū* (the three stages of transformation corresponding to the three original vows of Amida Buddha) as developed in the *Kyōgyōshinshō* seems to touch the very core of this problem. Looking back from the vantage point of the faith in Other-power that he had gained after wrestling with his own religious experience, Shinran leveled criticisms against the dominant mood of his times, which was one of attachment to self-power. The final book of the *Kyōgyōshinshō* entitled "Hōbenkeshindo" was intended to develop this critique, centered on an explanation of the *sangantennyū*.

"Hōbenkeshindo" refers to Amida Buddha's skill-in-means of using the phenomenal world to promote his aim of saving sentient beings. In the preceding five books of the *Kyōgyōshinshō*, Shinran explains in detail the Pure Land of the absolute where salvation by Other-power is accomplished. In order to become the means for all sorts of people to be led into the Pure Land, Buddha manifests himself in a phenomenal, relative world, establishing there an "adjacent land of *upāya*" [24] in order to take advantage of the opportunities it affords for bringing about salvation. In the "Hōbenkeshindo" book, the stages of religious existence preceding the achievement of true faith are classified and ordered in terms of a process of successive transformations. Woven into this reflection on the respective stages leading to the world of true faith is Shinran's critique of the spirit of his times.

It is worth noting here that Shinran presupposes a scheme of reckoning periods in Buddhist eschatology known as the three periods of *shō-zō-matsu*. The Age of Right Dharma or *shō-bō* is reckoned to cover the first five hundred years after the death of Gotama Buddha. It is the period of saints and sages of pure and noble character. The next thousand years are called the Age of Semblance Dharma or *zō-bō*, and mark the period after the loss of the Right Dharma when only its imitation remains. The following age of ten thousand years is known as the Age of Decadent Dharma or *mappō*, a great stretch of time during which the Right Dharma has become entirely extinct and the world sinks into sin and defilement. In this age there cannot be any saints at all. The practice of self-power, which is the way of the holy sage, is incapable of meeting the demands of the age and can only produce disorder. Only the Other-power way of *nembutsu* has concrete relevance to the condition of this epoch. The abstractions of thought can only serve the mediating role of skillful means or *upāya* for promoting this way.

In the *Sukhāvatīvyūha Sūtra* (or Larger Sutra), mention is made of the forty-eight vows made by Amida Buddha in order to save all sentient beings. Among these, three vows—the nineteenth, twentieth, and eighteenth—are intended, according to Shinran, to show the process of conversion to authentic faith in Other-power. The nineteenth and twentieth vows correspond to the abstract stages whose respective roles are to mediate the highest and most concrete stage of the eighteenth vow, which corresponds to the Way of Other-power in the Pure Land. To the extent that they assume an independent significance apart from their mediatory role, they become a cause of sin and defilement for all sentient beings and produce the disorder of this age. This is especially clear in the case of the nineteenth vow, which is called the "Vow of Recommending Purity of Heart and Establishing *Bodhi-citta*" (stable religious mind or decision), or the "Vow of Performing Virtuous Deeds." In this vow Amida Buddha makes the following oath:

> After I have attained Buddhahood, there will be sentient beings in the ten quarters who raise the Bodhi-Mind, practice various meritorious acts, and desire to be born in my land with sincere aspiration; if, on the eve of their death, I should not appear before them surrounded by a host of (sacred) beings, may I not attain the Perfect Bodhi.[25]

This suggests the ethical stage of religion in which persons try to attain the pure absolute good by their own self-power efforts and by accumulating merit.

If they be saints, free from radical evil by nature, then all the moral merit accompanied by their own religious vow could be the cause of their rebirth in the Pure Land, and their pure mind, in which desire naturally accords with moral precepts (to borrow the terms of Confucius), would give evidence of their religious freedom. That is, their ethical ideal would at the same time mean the realization of that ideal by their self-power, which is identical with the achievement of religious emancipation. To this extent one may say that saints in the age of Right Dharma correspond to this vow without qualification. One may even say, to go a step farther, that in the naturalness of their minds there should be no need for thought and reflection, since they would be able simply to follow their natural desires without any pressure to do so out of moral obligation.

But even in the purity of such saints, there might still be a tendency to bondage insofar as they live in this world in bodily form. It is therefore necessary for them to make their vow and to await moral perfection at the end of their life. Although they can be called saints, as long as they are human it is surely more proper to speak of them in the concrete as "sages." The virtues and merits of the sage cannot of themselves give cause for rebirth in the Pure Land. There is still a need for a self-consciousness before the absolute as the principle of all their virtue and the ground of all their merit. We see this expressed in the content of the twentieth vow:

> If, after I have attained Buddhahood, beings in the ten quarters who, having heard my Name, direct their thoughts towards my land, plant various roots of virtue, and desire to be born in my land by sincerely turning their merits (towards it), should not ultimately attain Birth, may I not attain the Perfect Bodhi.[26]

Shinran refers to the twentieth vow as the "Vow Assuring the Aspirant of the Unfailing Birth," the "Vow of Sincere Mind and Mind to Trans-fer," and the "Vow of Planting the Roots of Virtue." The reference to the "roots of virtue" is to the recitation of the *nembutsu*, which is an expression of one's self-consciousness of the relationship between the absolute and the relative as the ground of all good deeds. But even reciting the name of Amida, if performed by self-power, is no more than conceptual thinking about planting the roots of virtue. It is of course possible for a sage to do this satisfactorily, but in the present age, in this defiled world of sinfulness, there is no such sage. Those who, unaware of this fact, presume to be sages in this age are attached to self-power and incapable of discriminating the true way from the false.

The Love of Amida is concentrated on saving sentient beings in this sinful age, and the eighteenth vow transforms them into persons able to perform the authentic religious action of reciting his name through faith in Other-power. Shinran cites the vow as it is recorded in the Larger Sutra:

> If, after I have attained Buddhahood, the sentient beings in the ten quarters who have Sincere Mind, Serene Faith, and Desire to be Born in my country, should not be Born, even with ten utterances (of the Nembutsu), may I not attain Perfect Enlightenment—excepted are those who have committed the five dead-ly sins and abused the Right Dharma.[27]

Shinran calls this eighteenth vow the "Vow of Sincere Mind and Serene Faith" or the "Vow of Attaining Birth through the Nembutsu." Just as the nineteenth vow is transformed into the twentieth, so does the twen-tieth become the eighteenth. This is the transformation referred to above as *sangantennyū*. Before proceeding to a treatment of these stages of religious existence, let us take a brief look at the overall structure of Shinran's *Kyōgyōshinshō*.

According to Shinran's interpretation, the nineteenth vow is explained in detail by the *Kammuryōju-kyo* or Meditation Sutra, the twentieth by the *Amida-kyō* or Smaller Sutra, and the eighteenth by the Larger Sutra. Together these three texts form the canon of Japanese *Jōdoshin-shū*, the Shin sect of Pure Land Buddhism. In the first five books of the *Kyōgyōshinshō*, Shinran develops the elements that make up the eighteenth vow. Its doctrine (*kyō*) is that of the Greater Sutra; its religious action (*gyō*) is the *nembutsu* or the recitation of the name of Amida Buddha; its faith (*shin*) is sincere mind and authentic faith; its witness (*shō*) is the accomplishment of two movements of the transforming love of Other-power, the *ōsō-ekō* or "going to the Pure Land" and *gensō-ekō* or "returning from the Pure Land to this world"; and in the fifth book entitled "True Buddha and Land" Amida Buddha and his Pure Land are revealed as "Infinite Life and Light." In contrast with these first five books of the *Kyōgyōshinshō*, the concluding book, "Hōbenkeshindo" ("Transformed Buddha and Land of Expediency"), consists of Shinran's explanation of the nineteenth and twentieth vows. In it he clarifies the process by which these vows are transformed successively into the eighteenth vow.

The first stage of religious existence, according to Shinran, corresponds to the nineteenth vow. As one of its alternate names, the "Vow of Being Born into the Pure Land at the End of Life," suggests, those in this first stage, as persons who devote themselves to the accomplishment of ethical ideals, must wait until the end of life for this vow to be fulfilled. Those who wish to be born in the Pure Land merely by transference of their own accumulated merits must hold fast to belief in "resurrection by self-power alone." But this involves a contradiction similar to that of the Kantian antinomy of perfect good (*bonum consummatum*). By doing good and accumulating merit, one cannot conform to the principle of negatively mediated being—that is, of "empty being"—which brings about birth into the Pure Land. For in so doing, one places one's reliance on self-power and affirms the self immediately, thus failing to function as the negative mediating element for absolute nothingness. Only when such persons let go of their self-affirmation at the moment of death and recognize the futility of self-power can they achieve the self-abandonment that qualifies them for the hope of rebirth. It is for this reason that Shinran also speaks of the nineteenth vow as the "Vow of (the Buddha's) Coming to Lead (the Aspirant) to Birth." To speak of sentient beings entering into the ranks of sages through death means that the conversion from the nineteenth vow to the twentieth is brought about through the self-reflective realization that the good accomplished by self-power is never able to effect rebirth into the Pure Land.

The nineteenth vow is thus aimed at those who seek to be born into the Pure Land by transferring their good acts and merits. Theirs is the state referred to in the doctrine of the "Three Minds" as *ekō-hotsugan-shin* or "Mind of Aspiring for Birth by Merit-transference." Of that, more in the following chapter. At any rate, it has to do with the element of the future in religious belief. But if *zange*, or metanoetic consciousness of the futility of self-reliance through the performance of good deeds and the accumulation of merits, is still unable to lead one beyond the conceptualizing level of mere thought that sees the *nembutsu* as the principle of all good and merit, conversion remains at the stage of the twentieth vow of "assuring unfailing birth" or "planting the roots of virtue." Only under the impulse to carry metanoesis through to completion, and thus to become fully aware of the contradiction contained in the notion of "*nembutsu* by self-power," is one enabled to break free of the deep-rooted illusion that has held one captive and to be of Amida Buddha's mind. This signals conversion to the authentic faith of the eighteenth vow, thus completing the cycle of the *sangantennyū*.

The import of the nineteenth vow, "rebirth into the Pure Land at the end of life," thus needs to be mediated by the confession and metanoesis of the self-disciplined person who now realizes that he or she is a sinner in a state of despair. Insofar as the vow is thus mediated by the obedient despair of a religious self-consciousness that despises self-power, one can overcome the mere thought of self-power *nembutsu* and arrive at the truly religious stage of the eighteenth vow. Here self-power is converted into Other-power, and self-negation into the affirmation of a new self. Through this authentic metanoesis one confirms, at each moment of life in the present, the truth that was expected to come only at death. This is what is known as the state of "not falling back" or "irreversibility" (*avaivartika*). Since everything is here done through the mediation of the absolute, this state allows, on the one hand, for a rebirth and resurrection into new life mediated by metanoesis, and on the other, for "action in naturalness" that is an "action of no-action" or "action without an acting self." The former is termed *ōsō-ekō* (merit-transference on the way to the Pure Land), and the latter *gensō-ekō* (merit-transference on the way returning to this world.) The witness (*shō*) in which the two are brought into harmonious coincidence brings to fulfillment this eighteenth "Vow of the Inconceivable Birth" or "Vow of Sincere Mind, Serene Faith, and Desire to Be Born."

Since the stage corresponding to the twentieth vow represents a necessary element of negation that mediates the way to the eighteenth, the two are bound inseparably to each other. If one begins from consciousness of the fact that the good deeds and merits one has accumulated by self-power are all in vain as far as their ability to mediate the way to salvation and effect rebirth in the Pure Land is concerned, and if one then conceptualizes this self-consciousness into a norm for oneself and a discipline for others, the *nembutsu* takes on the nature of an abstract idea about the cause of rebirth in the Pure Land, and this idea ends up becoming the principle for all good deeds and merits. But this *notion* of the *nembutsu* is not what is meant by authentic action through Other-power mediated by the name of Amida Buddha. Other-power is at work in this world as the transformative power of the absolute, that is, as the Original Vow, so that authentic faith should lead rather to action without any activity of self-power, to an "action of no-action" and a "transferring of no-transferring."

When the conceptualized *nembutsu* is regarded as a cause of rebirth into the Pure Land, one is still engaged in the action of an acting self, which makes it proper to speak of self-power *nembutsu*. What is needed is that one deepen self-consciousness to the point of confessing the powerlessness of one's own efforts as internally self-contradictory. Through this kind of radical metanoesis, one's *nembutsu* is transformed into absolute Other-power, and rebirth in the Pure Land is assured. Only under the condition of this transformation does the vow to effect rebirth become the Buddha's twentieth vow of "inconceivable birth" and "accomplishing ultimate salvation." Thus the twentieth vow guarantees the fulfillment of the eighteenth vow of "rebirth through the *nembutsu*" by mediating it. The condition of "sincere mind and mind to transfer" contained in the twentieth vow is accomplished only by a "transferring of no-transferring," or the transferring activity of Other-power working within and flowing forth from the bottomless depth of one's mind. It is the very negation of "transferring by self-power" and the affirmation of the transferring power of Amida Buddha.

As just noted, however, even after the authentic conversion of metanoesis, and after rebirth and transformation into a new life has been confirmed in pure faith, the temptation surfaces again to harden genuine faith into an abstract notion that quickly contents itself with the status quo and forgets the need for ongoing transformation and conversion.

This is the easy-going approach to reliance on providence and *upāya*. One must be ever on guard against the lure of such thoughts. The abstract conceptualization of the *nembutsu* forever trails the concrete *nembutsu* of Other-power like a shadow, and it is only through continual metanoesis that the shadow can be lifted. The assurance of rebirth is confirmed only in such ongoing metanoesis. This is the import of the twentieth vow.

In the preceding, the twentieth vow has been related to sages and the "thought" of their self-power *nembutsu*. Since sages have already reached through thought a point that the sinful and ignorant can reach only through metanoesis, it seems reasonable to suppose that for them the twentieth vow can stand on its own. But in this defiled *mappō* age, no such sages exist. Those who forget their ignorance and presume themselves to be wise are easy prey to the pride and arrogance of self-attachment, which leads them even farther away from true salvation. Only when self-power is converted to Other-power through metanoesis can thought take on the significance of *upāya*. This is why the twentieth vow needs to be converted into the eighteenth.

In terms of the order of logical development, the twentieth vow stands midway between the nineteenth and the eighteenth: even though it has already overcome the contradiction of seeking rebirth into the Pure Land by the good deeds performed by self-power, it still falls short of authentic faith in the transforming love of Other-power, so that its conversion remains at the conceptual level of a mere "idea" of conversion. This accounts for its "in-between" position. This means not only that the twentieth vow functions as a negative mediating element in the conversion to authentic faith, which corresponds to the eighteenth vow, but also that it tends to degrade the eighteenth into the nineteenth. This alienation from authentic conversion takes place when the transformation wrought by the transcendent activity of absolute Other-power shirks the mediatory action of the grief and compassion in *zange* and settles into the idle existence of thinking about the *nembutsu*. In this sense, the twentieth vow harbors a contradiction within itself as a negative moment in the dialectical process. If the dialectic runs its full course, the twentieth vow will be resolved only when it has arrived at the concrete stage of the eighteenth. But the other side of this concreteness is the permanent hue of the abstraction of self-estrangement. Without the continual mediatory activity of *zange* transforming this process, one is forever liable to fall back into the self-contradictory thought of self-power *nembutsu*, and the twentieth vow cannot help being reduced to the stage of the nineteenth. For even the religious action of the *nembutsu*, to the extent that it originates in self-power, cannot be anything more than the self-affirmation of a relative being and cannot really take on the sense of a transformation by absolute Other-power; to the extent that merits are transferred to the Pure Land by one's own power, they lack the "naturalness" (*jinen-hōni*) of the "transference of no-transference."

Philosophy and theology, insofar as they are both forms of immediate thought lacking the mediation of metanoesis, do not get beyond the transference and accumulation of merits by the particular ego. In this they are like the cultured intelligentsia in general who stop short at the improvement of rationality. This is the very thing that we have spoken of as the degradation from the standpoint of the twentieth vow to that of the nineteenth. The way of the sage lures the ignorant into this pitfall. At first, self-power *nembutsu* seems to conform to the "true way to the roots of goodness and virtue" (*zenpon tokuhon no shinmon*) as a religious and ethical ideal. But this ideal is in fact unrealizable, and as one comes to reject it as such, self-power *nembutsu* inevitably sinks to the level of doing good by one's own power in the sense of ordinary secular activities. The only way to avoid such a pitfall is through continual *zange* wherein the activity of Other-power works its transforming mediation.

As will be explained when we come to the doctrine of the "Three Minds" in the following chapter, Zendō's interpretation of the "Sincere Mind" as the religious mind striving for the ideal of the highest good (good conscience) is inverted by Shinran into the painful remorse of *zange* for one's sinfulness (bad conscience). This same relationship needs to be seen functioning between the idea of doing the good stressed in the twentieth vow and the metanoetic conversion stressed in the eighteenth.

Thus the twentieth vow mediates the nineteenth and the eighteenth vows through *zange*, thereby not only elevating the *nembutsu* of the twentieth vow to that of the eighteenth but also mediating a circular movement in which the *nembutsu* of the twentieth vow is degraded to that of the nineteenth and then raised to the level of the eighteenth. In this dynamic of ascent and descent, a spiral dialectic initiated within religious consciousness is realized in which the twentieth vow is set up "in between" the other two vows. This dialectical quality, which is thoroughly self-negating, preserves a duality of affirmation-*qua*-negation that keeps the circular dynamic ever in sight—something that could not happen in a static view of self-identity. Herein lies the difficulty of passing beyond the twentieth vow. The only way to do so successfully is by the continual performance of *zange* which mediates self-power by Other-power and transforms it by letting go of it. This is the action-faith-witness (*gyō-shin-shō*) of the Original Vow of Other-power *nembutsu*.

Through the element of continual *zange* the eighteenth vow is realized in action-faith-witness, so that the notional conversion of the twentieth vow can, by virtue of transcendent Other-power, take concrete form and be made real as the authentic transformative activity of the *nembutsu*. This is absolute Other-power at work in its characteristic naturalness (*jinen-hōni*). The "sincere mind and mind to transfer," which is prerequisite to the satisfaction of the religious content of the twentieth vow, is made real in the present as a purity of heart by purging the mind of its past through *zange*. This is why the twentieth vow is termed the "Vow of Accomplishing the Ultimate Salvation." That the guarantee of this accomplishment—of the twentieth vow being transformed into the eighteenth—is to be found in the purging function of *zange* is already implicit in the notion of the "sincere mind and mind to transfer." It is the negative conversion of Other-power *nembutsu* working to transform the twentieth vow to the point that it can be accepted, in sincere mind and authentic faith, as a "transferring of no-transferring." All of this is similar to what we find in the nineteenth vow.

But what distinguishes the twentieth vow from the nineteenth is the fact that in the former the power of negative transformation does not come from outside in the form of a natural event such as the moment of death, but arises from within the self in a negative dialectic prompted by a self-contradiction in thought. This means that self-power *nembutsu* has been elevated to a higher level by making its contents of action, faith, and witness concrete and the Other-power quality of the *nembutsu* more thoroughgoing, thus effecting the conversion to the eighteenth vow. In a word, here we see the Vow of Great Compassion at work. Speaking of the vow of the assurance of salvation, which he sees as emerging entirely from the "oceanlike vow" of Great Compassion, Shinran has this to say of his own religious development:

> I . . . had forever left the temporary gate of the thousands of practices and various good deeds and departed from the teaching for the Birth under the Twin Sāla Trees [the nineteenth vow, anticipating rebirth into the Pure Land at the end of life], and having converted to the True Gate of the roots of goodness and virtue [the twentieth vow, the *nembutsu* of self-power], I raised the aspiration for the Incomprehensible Birth [the eighteenth vow, rebirth in the Pure Land by

self-power]. However, I have now left the provisional True Gate and turned to the Sea of the Best Selected Vow; having abandoned at once the aspiration for the Incomprehensible Birth, I am now assured of attaining the Inconceivable Birth.[28]

Shinran's reference in this statement of the *sangantennyū* to having "left" the provisional True Gate denotes the independent self-power performance of *zange* by one who had been revived from despair over the contradiction involved in the *nembutsu* of self-power, a problem that had previously tormented him with a sense of his own impotence. The phrase he uses refers to the spontaneity of religious action ushered in by the Other-power of the Original Vow. The conversion from the twentieth vow to the eighteenth is also mediated by the performance of *zange*. The entire process of the three stages of transformation is thus based on metanoetics, without which it could not be understood. There can be no doubt that Shinran's standpoint is one of *zangedō*.

But if the content of the twentieth vow were nothing but the "self-alienation" of the eighteenth, the former being an abstract moment of the latter; and further, if the twentieth vow were merely the middle stage in between the movements of ascent and descent, then the twentieth vow would need to be negated and abolished as an element in the dialectical dynamic. If that were so, this vow could never possess positive significance as an independent stage of human existence with its own *raison d'être*. Seen in terms of the movement toward the Pure Land (*ōsō-ekō*), this is a natural conclusion, and is in fact the standpoint on which the Larger Sutra is based. But in the Meditation Sutra, another point of view is advanced, according to which the Larger Sutra is shown to interpret the vows by proceeding "from absolute truth to *upāya*" (*shinjitsu-hōben*), while this later sutra proceeds in the opposite direction, "from *upāya* to absolute truth" (*hōben-shinjitsu*).

Taking salvation, or absolute transformation, by itself, the Larger Sutra expounds the true order, and the content of the meditation Sutra is actually in accord, albeit in an "implicit" sense. Its "explicit" explanation of the stages of development of truth is of another sort, however, and gives the sutra its distinctive significance. In the Larger Sutra, relative being is considered a negative element for absolute nothingness, since it takes its starting point as absolute truth and from there proceeds to *upāya* (*hōben*). From this *ōsō* standpoint, relative being has significance only as a negative mediating element, and in this role is spoken of as *upāya*. This orientation entails a sense of "empty being" insofar as relative being mediated absolute nothingness. It is only natural that the way to the absolute (ōsō) should represent the chief concern of religion, since faith is always a matter of one's own salvation.

For Pure Land Buddhism, however, Amida Buddha's vow of Great Compassion is mediated by the pre-enlightenment discipline and work of Dharmākara (Hōzō-bosatsu), which as a whole already presupposes the notion of gensō-ekō or the compassionate "return to the world" of Amida Buddha. Thus the circularity within Amida Buddha sets up a twofold dynamic which we can only call a gensō-qua-ōsō: the Buddha's coming to himself (the reflection of the absolute within itself) is at the same time his going out to the relative world. And this corresponds, in turn, to a dynamic within sentient beings: their movement toward salvation is at the same time a return from nirvāna.

This characteristic in the doctrine of the Pure Land school, which developed historically into a crystallization of Mahāyāna's original and characteristic bodhisattva-ideal, bespeaks a vivid and concrete spirituality. In general, transference means converting one's own merits in order to be born into the Pure Land, as we see in the word ekō, which is composed of two characters signifying respectively "to turn or convert to" and "to direct or carry to." For the way of self-power, rebirth in the Pure Land is the result of accumulating one's own merits. This we have seen already in our treatment of the nineteenth and the twentieth vows. For the way of Other-power, however, every action and thought of the self is turned around in a new direction and becomes the activity of Amida Buddha toward all sentient beings. This transference then becomes the object of authentic faith as we saw in the eighteenth vow. The acting and thinking self is converted by faith into a mediating element of transforming Other-power.

Ekō must thus be elevated from its original meaning of transferring one's own merits to a transferring of the grace and merit of the compassionate Buddha to all sentient beings for their salvation. Consequently, those who accept and believe in the transferring of Other-power come to the conviction that they cannot effect their own salvation by themselves alone. This is what we mean by the conversion of thoughts and deeds into a "transferring of no-transferring," where they have meaning only as mediating elements in the establishment of authentic faith. This redirection of action and thought to sentient beings is called ōsō-ekō, "transferring one's going to," insofar as it is aimed at their own rebirth in the Pure Land; and gensō-ekō, "transferring one's return," insofar as it is aimed at returning from the Pure Land to this world in order to teach and save others. Other-power transferring is thus twofold. Moreover, the "going to" and the "returning from" are wrought by the Other-power of Amida Buddha and at the same time are established by authentic faith.

In the Larger Sutra, the absoluteness of Amida Buddha is attributed to his performance of various disciplines and accumulation of manifold merits over a period of five *kalpas* as the bodhisattva Dharmākara. This points to a circularity or transformation within the absolute in the form of *ōsō-qua-gensō*. In this sense Dharmākara is merely a symbol for sentient beings as relative beings, that is, as the negative mediating element of Amida Buddha's absolute transformation. The absolute mediation of Amida Buddha makes possible an *ōsō* transferring through the absoluteness of his return to this world of sentient beings, a return that is also mediated by the authentic action-faith (*gyō-shin*) of sentient beings. This internal transformation within the Buddha with its circularity of *ōsō-qua-ekō* is the symbolic import of the Dharmākara's long history of self-discipline.

As we come to understand the symbolic power of this mythical story, we realize further that the self-discipline of Dharmākara must have been carried on in a spirit of continual *zange*. If we take his self-discipline as a transformation of the past into the future, this would imply a mediation of the element of creative development contained in the future by a negation and transformation of the past. In terms of its structure as authentic action (*gyō*), we may note that the transformation of the past into the future always has the quality of *zange* to it. In truth, there is no genuine self-discipline without *zange*. In this sense, even the self-discipline performed by Dharmākara has to be seen as something accomplished through continual *zange*. It is the absolute symbol of *zange* for us sentient beings.

Since the self-discipline of Dharmākara is at the same time an image of the Great Compassion of the Amida Buddha's absolute *gensō* with its circularity of ascent-*qua*-descent, of *egressus est regressus*, it carries a sense of the salvific transformation of *zange*. This is why the zealous self-discipline of Dharmākara can become the transcendent ground for the metanoetic activity of sentient beings. Dōgen has observed that the bodhisattva-ideal consists in a compassion that seeks to lead others to *nirvāna* rather than attain it oneself. This is, of course, impossible in the ordinary realm of temporal relations. But insofar as saving oneself means performing an act of absolute self-negation which is only brought fully to consciousness when one can sacrifice one's own self compassionately for the sake of others, we can see an essential logic to it. Seen basically as an expression of the bodhisattva spirit, the idea is of extraordinary importance. In all of Mahāyāna Buddhism—and I mean to include here even Zen Buddhism with its emphatic rejection of thinking as a way to enlightenment—no sect has developed the doctrine of this relationship between *gensō* and salvation in such a *für sich* manner as Pure Land Buddhism. Donran (Chin., T'an-luan, 476–542) merits special attention here as the first to introduce the notion of the two ways of transferring. Little wonder that Shinran was an ardent admirer of his.

From the standpoint of *gensō-ekō*, there is great significance in the fact that the Meditation Sutra opts for a progression from *upāya* to truth (*hōben-shinjitsu*), the reverse of the Larger Sutra. This points to the dialectical function of logic as a mediator between ontology and the philosophy of history or the phenomenology of mind. The dialectic of being mediates itself negatively in actual reality. This is concrete logic. It provides a principle for the reverse transformation of being in history. The progression from *upāya* to truth points to the appearance of absolute nothingness as absolute actuality insofar as absolute nothingness is mediated by historical reality.

The standpoints of the Larger Sutra and the Meditation Sutra are identical in the sense that they mediate each other, but this identity is only implicit; explicitly, they move in opposite directions. The mediatory significance of relative being may be understood in the two senses. First, the relative has being and significance only as a mediator of the absolute, as an *ōsō*. But second, this function is fulfilled in a higher stage of self-consciousness: the vertical relation of *ōsō* must also be mediated by the horizontal relation between relative beings, which is the true import of the *gensō*. In other words, the absolute-relative relationship has also to be mediated by a relative-relative relationship wherein each relative being fulfills a mediating role in the salvation of other relative beings. This is the concrete from of "returning to" mediated by the activity of the relative. Hence the absolute itself is able to perform its *gensō* function only if it is mediated by the relative.

The compassionate "returning to the world" of Amida Buddha cannot take place directly but must be mediated by the activity of transferring, such as we see in the *gensō* of the historical Gotama Buddha and others. Still more radically put, even Amida Buddha is but one Buddha among many, and is not himself identical with absolute nothingness. Taking the form of a personal Buddha called Amida Buddha, his manifestation is a particular form of *gensō* with its own historical affinities. His being is merely that of a symbol, no more than an *upāya* for leading sentient beings to the truth. Seen in this light, the metaphorical significance of the long period of self-discipline of Dharmākara becomes intelligible. To refuse this sort of philosophical interpretation and insist on the unmediated absoluteness of his being and on his solitary activity of saving sentient beings without the aid of their mediatory function is inevitably to fall into the error of converting Pure Land Buddhism into a kind of theism akin to Christianity, and thus to get trapped in the mythological scheme. The result would be that one would no longer be able to sustain the notion of absolute truth in religion.

The absolute is absolute Other-power, and this implies absolute mediation, which is also the key to understanding history as the mutual mediation between relative beings making the absolute manifest in the actual world. In short, the structure of history is nothing other than the dynamic correlation of the two ways of ōsō and gensō. The point is important and constitutes the special characteristic of the Buddhist approach to the absolute: as absolute nothingness that is at the same time transforming mediation. The unique significance of the Pure Land Buddhist understanding of the "return to the world" as upāya stems from the important interpretation given this idea by Shinran, who raised it beyond the level of a philosophy of history, or phenomenology of mind in the Hegelian sense. Here Pure Land teaching represents Buddhist thought at its most concrete. But if the doctrine is deprived of its notion of absolute mediation and is turned into a brand of theism, its original contribution is lost. It must be said that this danger is already latent in the Pure Land doctrine of salvation by Other-power.

It is natural in the context of Western thought to conceive of the absolute as being or transcendent being. But this is to reduce the relative to something imperfect whose independent, positive significance can be sustained only vis-à-vis the absolute. It is for this reason that the relationship between the absolute and the relative in the West is merely one of "negative mediation" and falls short of the radical absolute mediation, without which there is no way of assuring the relative of a *für sich* existence. If we are to give the relationship between the absolute and the relative the concrete form of mutual mediation—neither falling into the error of dualism and mere relativity, nor sinking into a *unio mystica* where the difference between monism and dualism disappears—we must have recourse to an absolute dialectic grounded on a radical notion of negative mediation. From this position the absolute is seen as absolute mediation and relative being enjoys a *für sich* independence as the mediator of the absolute. This is to give the relative the initiative within its own relativity. The relative is allowed to work on the relative in the role of a spontaneous mediator, leaving the absolute to carry out its proper activity of absolute compassion in response to this process.

In other words, without the mediative role of the authentic *gensō* action performed by the relative on the relative, there can be no salvific *ōso-ekō* of the absolute embracing the relative in compassionate love. Of course, the mere relationship between relative beings does not circumscribe the way of *gensō* in its entirety. This would never solve the problem of salvation. The relationship of relative to relative needs also to be mediated by the transformative power of the absolute. Only the "natural" (*jinen-hōni*) activity of relative being serving as a mediatory element for the absolute can become an *upāya* for absolute transformation, that is, for the work of salvation which belongs to the absolute alone. Only such an "action of no-action," an action performed without an acting self, can participate in the absolute's work of saving others. Without this participation by the relative, even the absolute would be powerless to save the relative.

The mediating activity that goes on within the absolute itself and is symbolized by the mythical figure of Dharmākara reaches logical self-consciousness in the mind of Shinran as the concrete idea of *gensō-ekō*, the "transferring" of "returning to." This is the concrete development of absolute transformation implied in the Original Vow of Great Compassion. Truth, taking the form of *upāya*, is the mediated phenomenal absolute that allows for the independence of the relative. If the "phenomenal way" (*kemon*) of the nineteenth vow were to remain as it is, and if the accumulation of merit were considered capable of existing apart from the absolute negativity of life coming to its end in death, there would be no salvific mediation. Such a state of existence would not yet carry the sense of *upāya*. For that to happen, certain conditions must first be fulfilled. First, existence must be mediated by absolute nothingness; or put conversely, it must be transformed into "empty being," the mediator of absolute nothingness. Second, at the level of reflection, this process must carry over into a transformation in thought as the abstract counterpart to transformation in action. Third, with the transformation of thought as the original unifying principle, self-power *nembutsu* must be idealized as "the root of all goodness and virtue" and become a refined means to prompt other sentient beings to salvation. And finally, insofar as the *nembutsu* is adopted to lead to the transforming activity of absolute Other-power, it is transformed into the "Vow of Accomplishing the Ultimate Salvation" and thus takes on the significance of *upāya*. Hence *upāya* is not a mere "phenomenal way" but the "true way" (*shinmon*). In the case of the phenomenal way, being is simply negated. But here, being is restored as absolute negativity in the form of "empty being" and recognized as having independent meaning in virtue of being a relative that mediates nothingness. In contrast with the eighteenth vow where the ōsō of rebirth through the *nembutsu* is absolute truth, here we have truth under the cloak of *upāya*. Because it is absolute transformation and absolute mediation, the absolute is incapable of performing its activity of Great Nay–*qua*–Great Compassion without the mediation of *gensō*. To this extent the absolute truth of ōsō is concretized and made real in the progression "from *upāya* to truth" of *gensō*.

As *tathāgata* (the one who has "gone to" and "returned from"), Amida Buddha performs his salvific works for sentient beings only as a result of the mediation of his self-discipline, that is, the merits accumulated over an immeasurable past by the bodhisattva Dharmākara. As mentioned above, this is the absolute *gensō* of the Tathāgata himself. Concretely speaking, his salvific activity is actualized in reality through the praise and recitation of his name in the community of many Buddhas. Amida Buddha himself is, in fact, nothing other than this "communion" constituted by the absolute mediation between one Buddha and another. Hence Shinran remarks, "Buddha-nature is Tathāgata." [29] This does not mean that Tathāgata is merely the universal concept of Buddhahood abstracted from many real historical Buddhas, but rather that Tathāgata and Buddhahood both need to be recognized as concrete universals. Not that there is any Tathāgata apart from the communion of Buddhas; if that were the case, Shinran could not have said that "Buddha-nature is Tathāgata." The Buddhas and the Tathāgata cannot be distinguished from one another. The equality of the mutual relationship that obtains among the Buddhas, their "*tathāgata*," is the development into the stage of self-consciousness (*für sich*) of the Buddha-nature realized in the community of Buddhas. Thus a concrete relationship of absolute mediation, of one-*qua*-many and many-*qua*-one, pervades the entire structure of the notion of Buddha.

Thus there is no Amida Buddha, no Tathāgata, apart from the communion of all Buddhas; and apart from the "oneness and unity" (*tathāta*) in Amida Buddha (Tathāgata), there would be no community of Buddhas in the one Buddha. This is why the name of Amida Buddha developed into the practice of being recited. The *nembutsu* of the Original Vow is one of the mutual praise of all Buddhas, as we see in Shinran's reference to the seventeenth vow as the "Vow That the Name Shall Be Lauded by All Buddhas." If sentient beings become Buddhas in their rebirth through the power of Amida Buddha, they establish a "correspondence" (*sōsoku*) with Amida Buddha and all other Buddhas (sentient beings reborn through their faith), thus bringing to completion the mediation and correspondence of the absolute and the relative. This means that the relation of *ōsō-qua-gensō* and *gensō-qua-ōsō* should be accomplished not along the way of *ōsō* but along that of *gensō*. What from the viewpoint of Amida Buddha is a process unfolding within himself, from the viewpoint of sentient beings is his acceptance and salvation of them. The mediating role of relative sentient beings vis-à-vis the activity of the absolute Buddha is actualized in a communion of equality among them, and this in turn represents the manifestation of Amida Buddha in his *für sich* existence. This twofold mutuality constitutes the absolute mediation of Amida Buddha, whose structure can be described only as *ōsō-qua-gensō* and *gensō-qua-ōsō*.

According to the original doctrine of the Pure Land Buddhism, of course, Amida Buddha is to be worshiped as supreme over all other Buddhas, and the way of "going to the Pure Land" should be kept distinct from the way of "returning from the Pure Land to this world," since the former belongs to action-faith in this world, whereas the latter belongs to the activity of saving others after one has been reborn in the Pure Land. On the one hand, the conclusion flows naturally from a soteriology that does not allow for interpretations made on the basis of mere logical mediation such as I have advanced here. But on the other, does not Pure Land Buddhism need to take a step further in virtue of the fact that it has already reached the concrete state of a personal relationship between Amida Buddha and sentient beings? Does not the communion of mutual praise among the Buddhas through the recitation of Amida Buddha's name need to be "returned to the world" as *upāya*-mediation? Does not the way of "going to the Pure Land," as the *an sich* stage of the salvation of sentient beings, need the mediation of a *für sich* stage that correlation with the way of "return" would provide?

The problem here is not unlike that of developing an understanding of human relationships not only in personal but also in social terms. Just as the idea of personality takes on its full significance only when it is set in the context of the social community, so too "rebirth through the *nembutsu*" is really possible only when one has been brought, through the transforming power of Amida Buddha, into the spiritual community of Buddhas and believers. Transformation cannot come about apart from its own context. As absolute transformation, absolute nothingness cannot exist apart from the transformation among relative beings. For if it could, it would be neither absolute nor nothingness nor the true absolute, but would itself have to become relative being. Relative being, as relative, has to become annihilated through the mediation of absolute nothingness; and by the same token the absolute, as the transforming power of absolute nothingness, has to become mediated by the mutual transformation going on among relative beings. Even as absolute nothingness grants relative beings the independence of forming the temporary axis of their own transformation, it also transforms them into a coequality with one another in the form of an independence-*qua*-dependence, thereby annihilating the axis of transformation; and when relative beings, through the *für sich* level of existence reached in this reciprocal mediation, mediate the absolute, we have *gensō*.

The mediating progression from *upāya* to truth that characterizes the path of *gensō* represents the self-conscious stage of *für sich* existence, whereas the progression from truth to *upāya* that marks the path of *ōsō* remains at the state of immediacy of *an sich* existence. This means that the former represents an independent and more concrete stage of religious consciousness. Although the Meditation Sutra seems at first to be no more than an example of the doctrine of *upāya* spelled out more fully in the Larger Sutra, it is in fact more than that. It is an *upāya* that represents a historical bond of affinity with Gotama Buddha, who entered the world in order to teach the truth, and as such it incorporates the ontology of the latter into a real history, giving it the significance of a "phenomenology of spirit." Yet it is more than a "phenomenology of spirit" in the usual Hegelian sense, where "spirit" is still limited to the consciousness of an individual. Here, spirit belongs to a historical community whose self-consciousness emerges in the authentic action of the true subject awakened to religious existence. Here, *upāya* is not an illustrative example lacking its own independent significance. As an axis of nothingness that serves to mediate the work of absolute nothingness, the independence of relative being means no more than the manifestation of nothingness as an independence-*qua*-dependence. The concrete development of this relationship between the absolute and the relative lies in the equality that obtains among relative beings as *upāya* on the way of *gensō*. In the context of the *sangantennyū*, the *upāya*-mediation of the relative as we see it in the twentieth vow should be distinguished from the merely negative mediation that occurs on the path of *ōsō*. It denotes the unique and positive independence of an axis of transformation.

It is worth noting that we have to do here with the same double meaning of negation that characterizes dialectics in general: the simultaneous presence of annihilation and preservation. These two meanings, or two aspects of one and the same dynamic, interpenetrate with the accent shifting now to one, now to the other as the situation changes. This may help to clarify the opposition between the progression from *upāya* to truth and that from truth to *upāya*. It is further noteworthy that the temporal order of the three aspects of the three minds—past, present, and future—is the reverse of what we have seen in the *sangantennyū* (to which we shall return in the following chapter). The reason is that in *ōsō* the stress falls on the past, on what has been, whereas in *gensō* everything concentrates on the future, on what is yet to unfold. Thus the three minds are arranged in the sequence of past-present-future, whereas the three vows of the *sangantennyū* emphasize the future by reversing the sequence to future-past-present. In the *sangantennyū*, the mind of "Desire to Be Born" (*yokushō*), which represents the aspect of the future, is mediated by metanoesis (repentance for one's past deeds) and converted to faith in the present through the "Sincere Mind" (*shishin*). In this sense, in the *sangantennyū*, faith in the present consists in the mutual transformation and interpenetration of the future and the past. Therefore one cannot attain rebirth in the future without metanoesis for the past. The ongoing continuation of metanoesis is the positive element that brings about assurance of rebirth. In this sense the "Vow of Accomplishing the Ultimate Salvation" suggests the mediatory unfolding of *gensō-upāya*.

It is because of this positive aspect of *upāya* that Shinran interprets the *sangantennyū* on the basis of the Meditation Sutra, and that the concluding book of the *Kyōgyōshinshō*, "Transformed Buddha and Land of Expediency," is developed directly from a treatment of the *sangantennyū*. *Upāya* is the self-conscious (*für sich*) development of absolute nothingness, wherein independent, self-conscious relative beings also become conscious of one another (*für anderes*). Seen from this viewpoint, even the matter of accumulating merits by self-power treated in the nineteenth vow can be understood as the absolute return to the world of the Tathāgata himself, insofar as such accumulation is transformed and included in the pure faith of the eighteenth vow through the mediation of metanoesis, and thus made into an "action of naturalness" (*jinen-hōni no gyō*). This means that the source of all of these good deeds and merits is the *nembutsu* itself, without which they would have no value on their own. Furthermore, although this notional *nembutsu* is still nothing but a "transformation in thought" and still holds within itself the self-contradiction of a self-power *nembutsu*, it can be effective as a means of teaching others and converting them to authentic faith. That is, it can mediate the performance of metanoesis as the abstract element of the authentic transformation in action that is treated in the eighteenth vow: the *nembutsu* of rebirth in the Pure Land. Hence conversion at the level of thought can give shape to the true path of *upāya* treated in the twentieth vow.

At the same time, as the working of self-power, the *nembutsu* remains at the stage of the nineteenth vow. Even if it is termed a "source of merits and good deeds," what is accumulated is accumulated in reliance on self-power. The authentic transformation of the *nembutsu* is the work of Other-power and cannot be achieved directly by the twentieth vow. It requires a metanoesis in the self-reliance on one's own thoughts and deeds whereby one strives for rebirth by self-power. The role of the nineteenth vow is therefore to mediate the way to the twentieth. Metanoesis arises because of the independence of relative beings and as such needs to be carried on without ceasing.

This is how the matter of the twentieth vow, as it is mediated by the nineteenth vow, comes to have a relatively positive significance as *upāya* on the way of *gensō*. And this is why the three vows are arranged in ascending order and connected to one another as a series of successive transformations. Yet this does not bring us any further than the recognition of relative independence to the extent of being mediated by the absolute transformation of *ōsō* and hence changed into the mediatory role of *upāya* in a dynamic that moves from truth to *upāya*.

The way of *ōsō* should therefore be given precedence over the way of *gensō*. Relative beings "are" only as beings in nothingness; theirs is but an "empty" independent existence. In other words, no deed or thought can be transformed into absolute nothingness directly and just as it is, but only through metanoesis. Mediated by the authentic faith of the eighteenth vow, every thought and deed becomes an "action of no-action," an action performed in "naturalness," and thus an action belonging to *gensō*. Relative sentient beings can serve others as *upāya* for salvation by acting as a temporary axis of absolute transformation. In this function, each relative being enjoys the power to make its own *gensō* a skillful means for the salvation of others, and thus the recognition of an independent existence vis-à-vis others. But this also means that its relativity is complete, lacking the privilege of special election or the right to cling absolutely to its independence. Relative beings must become aware of themselves as equal with all others, bound to them in a relationship of complete reciprocity that entails both transforming and being transformed. This is the only way that the axis of nothingness can itself become a true nothingness. This is why we speak of an independence–*qua*–dependence, a self-reliance that is at the same time a reliance on others. This is why *ōsō* can be seen as a prerequisite for *gensō*.

In the terminology of Avatamsaka (Kegon) philosophy, *ōsō* corresponds to the view that sees a harmonious correspondence between facts and reason (*riji-muge*), and *gensō* to the view that sees harmony among facts themselves (*jiji-muge*). Absolute mediation is accomplished perfectly only in the latter: there is no true reason in reality other than the mutual mediation between facts. In the same way, in the altruistic activity of *gensō*, "being as *upāya*" enters into an equality arising from a reciprocally mediated transformation, and through the manifestation of an *an und für sich* nothingness, the *ōsō* performed for one's own sake is made to repeat itself from an *an sich* to a *für sich* state. Prior to such repetition, there can be no unmediated *ōsō* repetition of the former in the latter. In this sense, *gensō* is the mediator of *ōsō*. Perfect reciprocal mediation of this sort is the very essence of absolute mediation.

More concretely, Tathāgata as *tathāta*, or the absolute truth that penetrates the inner core of all beings equally, is present in the community of Buddhas engaged in praising one another and reciting the name of Amida Buddha, and in the derivative mutuality of sentient beings teaching and guiding one another for the sake of salvation. It is, in other words, a matter of *gensō-qua-ōsō* and *ōsō-qua-gensō*. The mediating character of *gensō* is none other than the metanoetic conversion that takes place in *ōsō*. Through the self-transforming activity of metanoesis, the former pride of accumulating merits by one's own power is converted into faith in Other-power. And in the same way and through the same act of metanoesis, the notional quality of self-power *nembutsu* is converted from the desire for rebirth in the Pure Land into a pure faith in Other-power. In other words, despite the provision in the nineteenth vow for rebirth into the Pure Land by a "mind of aspiring for birth by merit-transference" in the future (*ekō-hotsugan-shin*), this mind is actually to be converted at death to an authentic and pure faith, a "deep faith" (*jinshin*) related to the present through metanoesis for the pride of one's past deeds. And it is through the mediation of metanoesis that the twentieth vow, which represents the *nembutsu* of self-power as the negation of the nineteenth vow, albeit a merely abstract and notional negation, should be purified and transformed into the "deep faith" of the present by the "sincere mind" of Amida Buddha which can purge the mind of its past sin and pride. This is a confirmation in the present of the "Vow of Accomplishing the Ultimate Salvation" in the future.

Thus the *sangantennyū* means that the future-oriented desire for rebirth is transformed by metanoesis for the past into the sincere mind of "action of no-action." Faith in the present thus becomes the axis for the transformation of the past and the future, and the vertical orientation is unified into an absolute transformation that is horizontal in nature. As a result, the orientation is reversed, mediating the mutuality between the three vows. Even the nineteenth vow ceases to be a merely provisional way but takes on the quality of a true way of *upāya* insofar as it is able to mediate the twentieth vow. This is so, as we have seen earlier, because the future and the past interpenetrate each other and are transformed into each other. In other words, provisional actuality is turned into truth through the mediation of *upāya*.

By now it should be clear that the principle pervading the whole of mutual transformation as we have been discussing it is in fact metanoetic practice. In Kant's critique of practical reason, all relative good deeds and actions are based on absolute goodwill, which in turn is given a foot-hold in the notion of duty in the categorical imperative. Furthermore, his process of arriving at salvation by Other-power in the philosophy of religion by turning absolute goodwill around to the antinomies of funda-mental evil displays a mutual transformation of deed, idea (thought), and faith that may well be compared with Shinran's *sangantennyu*. But if we search the Kantian philosophy of religion for the sort of social solidarity for the sake of salvation that we have seen in the approach of *gensō*, at best we find only hints in his advocacy of the establishment of the Kingdom of God on earth as necessary for the permanent conquest of evil in the world. Compared with Shinran's idea of the "return to the world from the Pure Land," Kant's approach falls short in the concreteness of its logic of mediation.[30] We cannot help sensing the importance of the idea of *gensō* with its thoroughgoing reliance on metanoetics, since it is here that the difference between Kant's standpoint and ours is made clear.

Metanoetics does not always and of necessity adhere to the doctrine and tradition of Pure Land Buddhism. It is rational in terms of its demand that ethical theory provide *zange* with its distinctive foundation. In this sense, it is closer to Christianity. At the same time, it is obvious that the *Kyōgyōshinshō* of the Pure Land is fundamentally metanoetic in motivation. This is why it has been my guide. Still, I would insist that my metanoetics developed its distinguishing traits under the inspiration of both sources and cannot strictly be identified with either. As a product of my own reflective experience, it cannot but be colored by personal history, and this I regret. I cannot exercise my own *zange* otherwise than in this metanoetic philosophy of mine. Despite all my meanderings and detours, I feel that much still remains to be said. And while I regret, too, that I may have been able only to circumscribe the periphery without touching the heart of the matter, this only prompts me, ordinary and ignorant individual that I am, to undertake further efforts to progress beyond my present stage. In essence, metanoetics is a synthesis of the standpoints of *nembutsu* and Zen Buddhism, a sort of "Nembutsu-Zen" if you will. Through its notion of "transformation in action," it attempts to open a new way to faith, one that combines the aims of a dialectical theology of crisis that sees Christianity as an ethical religion with the opposing aims of mysticism. Insofar as metanoetics may be seen as a new synthesis of faith and witness, I am convinced that what may at first seem to be based only on my own particular experience of "action-faith-witness" can in fact bring about a concrete and universal synthesis. My only hope is that the notion of "absolute mediation" in metanoetics may be carried out more thoroughly than any other similar way of thought has been.

Chapter 7

Metanoetics and the Theory of the Three Minds

The guiding inspiration of Shinran for metanoetics · The suggestiveness of the Kyōgyōshinshō for resolving dialectical problems in the contemporary philosophy of religion · The gist of the Three Minds as a theory of the mediatory structure of metanoetic consciousness · Shinran's Three Mind theory as a dialectic radicalization of Zendō's theory · Metanoetics in Shinran's understanding of the Three Minds · The discipline of Dharmākara Bodhisattva as a symbol of metanoetics · The mediatory nature of "recitation of the name" · Absolute mediation in the soteriology of twofold merit-transference · The transformation and interpenetration of "is" and "ought" through the mediation of metanoesis · The mediation of past and future through metanoesis · The dialectical unity of the Three Minds · The unity of action, faith, witness · The meaning of the nembutsu · "All is zange" · The Gate of the Sages and the Gate of the Pure Land · The gensō guidance of Shinran for philosophy as metanoetics

In the foregoing chapters I have discussed the origins in my personal history of what I call "philosophy as metanoetics" and have singled out those confrontations with Western philosophy that were influential in shaping my thought and help to shed light on its particular traits. My aim in so doing was not, of course, to reread the entire history of Western philosophy from the viewpoint of metanoetics, but simply to acknowledge the inspiration of certain thinkers and my continued sympathy with their work in order all the more clearly to distinguish metanoetics from what they were about. No doubt there are many other thinkers who have developed systems of thought with similarities to my own, but this is not the time to pursue further comparison.

As mentioned earlier, it was at a time when I found my thought caught in a deadlock—generated and sustained by the Western philosophical tradition in which I had been trained—that a wondrous experience opened me up to the way of metanoetics. For the first time, Shinran's path of Other-power *nembutsu* took on meaning for me, even though I had had a passing familiarity with his thought through the *Tanni-shō* (*Notes Lamenting Differences*) and other works. The more I came to understand his writings and then to discipline myself to their guidance, the more I found them a powerful motivating force in developing the philosophy of metanoetics. In addition to this direct influence, I also received a great deal of enlightenment and stimulus from Shinran's commentators, but it was really through an unexpected act of grace that metanoetics was drawn into the heart of the *Kyōgyōshinshō*, and for this I cannot express sufficient gratitude. By directing me along the way of *gensō*, Shinran has disciplined my understanding of metanoetics and helped me to see it as a philosophy of *tariki* comparable to the way of *nembutsu* in Pure Land Buddhism.

My relation to the *Kyōgyōshinshō* is not unlike Shinran's relation to the Larger Sutra, which he believed to represent the preaching of Gotama Buddha, his *gensō-ekō* as it were to Shinran himself. The doctrine of Other-power *nembutsu* offered consolation to the common people of his day in a way that traditional Buddhism could not. At the time the Tendai sect and many of the old Nara sects had degenerated into ritualistic forms of religion suited only to serve the court aristocrats by praying for their prosperity and providing them with a diversion from the gathering storms of political unrest that were soon to prove their undoing. Zen Buddhism, meanwhile, was serving chiefly as a way to spiritual peace through religious training for the *samurai* class.

A somewhat similar development can be seen in the fate that befell German idealism. After reaching the heights of Hegel's philosophy, it turned into a mere object of academic discussion, a pastime for philosophical specialists that was completely worthless as a critical guide for scientists and practical-minded individuals. As a result, a shallow positivism and naturalism became fashionable in the intellectual world, against which Nietzsche was to rise with his call for the "transvaluation of all values." Somewhat the same reaction is visible at present in Heidegger's development of an existentialism of profound self-awareness in response to the superficial idealism of neo-Kantian and phenomenological schools. On this point, both figures share Zen's self-power approach to spiritual discipline. No doubt both their philosophies deserve high esteem as philosophies of intellectuals and sages, but their spiritual aristocracy puts them beyond the reach of the common populace. In contrast, I found my way to metanoetics as a philosophy for the ignorant and ordinary, such as I consider myself. As a way of action-faith through absolute criticism, it has a great deal in common with Kierkegaard, and thus also coincides on not a few counts with Barth's theology of crisis, which has carried Kierkegaard's tendencies over into the present. But here we leave religion for the world of theology.

Is there any living religion today capable of bringing peace of soul to a people driven to war and self-sacrifice for the interests of the privileged classes, almost to the point of forfeiting their livelihood? The *tariki* teaching of Shinran came to birth as a religion centered entirely on the common people. But nowadays, as a look around makes plain to see, it has degenerated into a sect that covets prestige and prosperity above all else, a lifeless corpse from which the spirit has departed. I once incurred the wrath of the Zen sect by suggesting that Zen Buddhism should be emancipated from its bondage to particular sects and schools. It seems to me that a similar emancipation from narrow sectarianism is called for in present-day Pure Land Buddhism, where charges of heresy have erected barriers impeding free research into its doctrine. Shinran's valuable thought goes largely unexplored and undeveloped, when it should be investigated thoroughly in a spirit free of the bonds of sectarianism. It needs to be reinterpreted in the light of our current spiritual situation and brought to bear on the religious needs of today. Its philosophical foundations as a way of faith for the common people have to be reclarified. Shinran's religious thought deserves special attention in our times precisely because it is relevant to the needs of present-day intellectuals. Its profound and wide-reaching truth can appeal to the hearts of our people—nay, to all people everywhere. I have no doubt that of all the sects of Buddhism, the doctrine of Pure Land Buddhism is the most accessible to the Christian world. It is comparatively easy to read its mythological elements in symbolic terms, and its doctrine makes no appeal to miracles or anything that contradicts the scientific mind. If, as we shall see shortly, the core of Shinran's thought lies in metanoetics, it has internal affinities with science through the principle of absolute criticism described earlier. In this sense, we might even say that it is more accessible to the modern scientific spirit than Christian theism is.

For my part, I am convinced that Shinran's religious thought is first and foremost a metanoesis. Metanoetics is not just one element among others, but the very ground of his faith. For this reason, he does not treat it as a particular problematic but infuses the whole of the *Kyōgyōshinshō* with its spirit. To illustrate this, and at the same time to deepen our understanding of metanoetics, we shall consider the notion of the Three Minds, which scholars of Pure Land Buddhism generally see as the core idea of the work, and how it unfolds into a dialectic of faith-consciousness that ushers in a Pure Land philosophy of religion. If my reading is not too wide of the mark, as I trust it will not be, this idea should also shed light on the question of methodology in the philosophy of religion, which is currently attracting a great deal of attention, and may also make a contribution to philosophical methodology in general.

Unlike religion, philosophy cannot be based on the beliefs of a particular historical tradition; it must begin from the academic demands of reason. But because its very nature is to seek absolute knowledge, philosophy must ultimately enter into higher realms it shares in common with religion. Religion, meantime, in order that it can interpret and systematically organize its faith in the interests of teaching others along the way of *gensō*, needs to adopt the forms of thought, and thus inevitably to develop a "theology." Here we see how the philosophy of religion crystallizes the most difficult problems of philosophy, in particular those of philosophical method. In the philosophy of religion, the demand for unity between contradictories—immanence and transcendence, relative and absolute, and so forth—appears in so compelling and acute a form that it is impossible to avoid dialectical mediation. On the one hand, it is necessary for philosophy to be based on analytic logic and to display a systematic structure coherent with the law of identity, since it is a discipline like the other sciences. On the other hand, its irresistible tendency to achieve systematic unity leaves philosophy no choice but to seek the absolute and unconditional. Yet insofar as it does this, it cannot elude the pitfall of the antinomies of reason spelled out by Kant in his *Critique of Pure Reason*. This is why the critique of reason has to be pursued radically to the point of an absolute critique of reason.

It is no longer possible for us, in our day and age, to assume the abstract, ahistorical viewpoint of the Kantian critique and to assume the facts of science as unshakable and beyond criticism. Quite to the contrary, science, the critique of science, and the historical viewpoint need to mediate one another and interpenetrate in a circular process of development. Dialectics cannot therefore be rejected out of hand as mere illusion the way Kant did in his *Critique of Pure Reason*, but needs to be developed into a positive method. On a dialectical standpoint, the absolute and the relative achieve a harmony and coincidence in spite of their contradiction, transcendence and immanence interpenetrate and mediate each another, and religion unfolds within philosophy itself. Philosophy inserts itself into the realm of science and then in turn finds religious faith inserted into its own inner life. Hence philosophy takes the position of mediator between science and religion. As we saw earlier, Kant's aim in his philosophy of religion to develop religion within the limits of reason alone overlooked the inherent self-contradiction in what he was doing and failed to see how it was rupturing the very framework of his critical philosophy. Given the nature of religion, the philosophy of religion cannot avoid contact with the transcendent and the absolute. That is, it requires the dialectical mediation of both philosophy and religion. If the philosophy of religion stops at the immanent stage, it cuts itself off from the essence of religion. (The so-called phenomenology of religion involves the same self-contradiction as Kant's quest for religion within the limits of reason alone; not even Hegel's *Phenomenology of Mind* could avoid it. How much the worse for contemporary transcendental phenomenology, which lacks sufficient method to be established as a philosophy of religion.)

One way or another, we must assume a standpoint of mediation that allows for a transcendence-*qua*-immanence witnessed to in action-faith. And this is precisely what metanoetics offers. The concrete form that absolute mediation takes in the religious consciousness of one performing metanoesis includes the following: that the aspect of ascent (*ōsō*) and the aspect of descent (*gensō*) should be mediated in action (*gyō*); that the way of *ōsō* becomes possible through the mediation of an absolute *gensō*; and that the absolute *gensō* should pass over into the *für sich* stage of a relative *gensō* and from there develop into a merit-transference (*gensō-ekō*). The doctrine of the Three Minds represents the most careful and lucid analysis of this to be found in Buddhism. In it we see the very core of the Pure Land faith with its distinctive profession of participation in *nirvāna* without extinguishing our evil passions. Here, too, light is shed on the three phases of temporality—past, present, and future—in the transcendental structure of faith-consciousness. In short, the doctrine of the Three Minds holds a central place in the teachings of the Pure Land sect, comparable to that of the Trinity in Christian theology.

In metanoesis the Original Vow of the transcendent Amida Buddha becomes active in a direct manner, entering immanently into the consciousness of sentient beings, converting it to the way of absolute *gensō*, and thus completing its work of salvation. The Three Minds represent the structure of metanoetic consciousness as a mediating activity. That is, it is a Buddhist development of metanoetics that opens the way to a philosophy of religion on a standpoint of action-faith-witness that supersedes phenomenology. In this way, philosophy as metanoetics not only receives substantial insight from this doctrine but confirms itself on the path of philosophical understanding by exposing the element of metanoesis at the foundations of the doctrine. It is on this basis that I shall undertake a metanoetic reading of the notion of the Three Minds in what follows. I cannot do so, though, without first expressing a certain uneasiness that my insufficient appreciation of the doctrines of Pure Land Buddhism and lack of training in its disciplines may render my views shallow and premature. But the fear I sense more keenly than any other is that my faith in Other-power is still too weak. Still I carry on, in the belief that even my misunderstandings can be redeemed by metanoesis.

In this regard I would note that the idea that the Three Minds refer to a temporal structure was first proposed by Soga Ryōjin,[1] to whose outstanding interpretation I owe a great deal. I am deeply appreciative of the penetrating insight he brings not only to this notion but to the teaching of Pure Land Buddhism in general. The fact that his interpretation is, as far as I can see, metanoetic at heart, lends support of the highest authority to my own metanoetic reading and strengthens me in my resolve.

It is not just my own private view that the most important part in all the six books that make up the *Kyōgyōshinshō* is Shinran's interpretation of the Three Minds. Scholars of Pure Land Buddhism generally acknowledge that the interpretation of Zendō (Chin., Shan-tao, 613–681)[2] was epoch-making in the history of Pure Land doctrine. Shinran's original contribution lies in the fact that he took Zendō's interpretation, which was based on the Meditation Sutra, and reread it in terms of the Original Vow of attaining rebirth through the *nembutsu* (the eighteenth vow), thus developing a new interpretation of his own. The daring twist he gave to Zendō's text by deliberately misreading the original meaning of the Chinese stems entirely from Shinran's demand for metanoesis, a fact which no one can gloss over. The objective evidence of his turn to a most profound faith in Other-power could not be clearer.

What is more, the question of the Three Minds is a matter of philosophical significance in that it corresponds to the phenomenological analysis of the structure of existential time-consciousness in Western philosophy, whose origins go back to St. Augustine and which has, we might say, reached the peak of its development in recent existential philosophy. More than this, the notion of the Three Minds goes deeper than these attempts of Western philosophy because it is in touch with a deeper dialectic. Not only the theory of time but Western dialectics in general was given more concrete form by Augustine's doctrine of the Trinity, which converted it from the standpoint of classical ontology into one of phenomenology and gave it a subjective orientation. The doctrine of the Three Minds is concerned with the same problem as the doctrine of the Trinity is in the Western world, and arrives at a deeper structure of dialectics.

In the West, this "deeper" dialectic mode was pursued to no avail, either because it clung to a position of self-power in an ontology of self-consciousness or because it took the path of mysticism. In the doctrine of the Three Minds, however, such a dialectic shows up unmistakably in the transforming function of Other-power which provides the foundation for the interpretation of the Three Minds. Naturally, as noted earlier, Shinran's standpoint is essentially one of faith-interpretation and thus merely presupposes the mediation of metanoesis as part of its background without developing to the full its latent implications. Only when we pass beyond the surface of the text and sound its hidden and latent significance are we forced to recognize the dialectical mode of metanoesis. On the surface, the subject of *zange* is not taken up, except for a description of the "three sorts of *zange*" in the final book of the *Kyōgyōshinshō*, and the word is even omitted from the index of some editions of the work.[3] But seen in terms of content, there can be no doubt that beneath all the books of the *Kyōgyōshinshō* flows a deep wellspring of *zange* that feeds and sustains them. In this sense, the doctrine of the Three Minds has to be seen as merely one point at which the metanoetic element breaks through the surface and gushes over into the text. It is only natural that we should see this passage as the core of the *Kyōgyōshinshō*.

The Three Minds are explained in Meditation Sutra as follows:

> If there are sentient beings, who wish to be born thither into the Pure Land, they can satisfy their wishes by establishing Three Minds. What are these three? The first is the Sincere Mind; the second, Deep Mind; and the third, the Mind of Aspiring for Birth by Merit-transference. With these Three Minds they can surely be born into the Pure Land.[4]

It was Zendō's interpretation of this passage that gave Shinran his starting point. According to Soga, the gist of the distinction between the "minds" comes to this: The salvation of ignorant sentient beings can be attained only through the Compassionate Vow of Amida Buddha. Faith consists in a wholehearted reliance on the power of the Vow of Amida Buddha. But faith is composed of three elements. The first is the Sincere Mind (*shijōshin*), which believes in the sincerity and purity of one's past thoughts, words, and deeds. The second is the Deep Faith (*shinjin*) of the self in the power of salvation achieved by Amida Buddha. The third is the unshakable faith and firm resolve of the Mind of Aspiring for Birth by Merit-transference (*ekō-hatsugan-shin*) in the future. Since these three form one faith, we may speak of "Three Minds–*qua*–One Mind." These Three Minds are the proper cause of rebirth in the Pure Land. Thus the Sincere Mind is mind as a subject of action, responsible for what has been done in the past; Deep Faith is mind of present trust in Amida Buddha; while the Mind of Aspiring for Birth is the desire for rebirth in the Pure Land in the future. The object of the first mind is the deeds we have performed, and the mind that practices it is called Sincere Mind because of its purity and authenticity. The object of the second mind is Amida Buddha, who is trusted by sentient beings, and the mind that embraces this trust is called Deep Mind (*jinshin*) in virtue of its deep faith. The object of the third mind is the goal that is sought for, and the mind that so desires is called the Mind of Aspiring for Birth by Merit-transference.[5]

According to Zendō's commentary, the Sincere Mind is the true mind that has never involved itself in fraud or untruth. Everything one does, be it thought or word or deed, should be performed with this Sincere Mind. To make an outward display of wisdom, virtue, and effort while inwardly one's heart is filled with untruth is the very antithesis of the Sincere Mind. If one is full of avarice, anger, vileness, and deceit; if one makes use of cunning and deceit to carry out one's wicked inner designs; if one's heart is like a nest of snakes and scorpions, then even the good that one practices in thought, word, and deed is to be called a poisonous good, an act of untruth, but never an act of sincerity. One who wishes to perform a good deed must do so with the Sincere Mind. The deed should be genuine and true, both inwardly and outwardly, whether it is performed in the shadows of darkness or in the bright light of day.

The Deep Mind is the mind that believes deeply. Here we distinguish two sorts of faith: the deep realization of sinfulness (*ki no jinshin*) and the deep acknowledgment of Amida's Merciful Salvation (*hō no jinshin*). The former implies a deep and resolute conviction in our entrapment in the unending samsaric cycle of birth and death in the three worlds with no prospect of liberation. The latter embraces two phases: the resolve to a deep trust in Gotama the Buddha and other Buddhas, and the resolve to a deep trust in the five sorts of authentic actions for the sake of rebirth in the Pure Land.

The Mind of Aspiring for Birth by Merit-transference refers to a firm and unmovable resolve to be born in the Pure Land by transferring all one's good deeds and merits to others. Rebirth in the Pure Land is possible only when all of the Three Minds are present. If one of them is lacking, it becomes impossible.

According to Zendō, the Pure Land sect represents a doctrine of salvation designed especially for ignorant and sinful persons like ourselves who live in the decadent age of *mappō*. In his compassion, Amida Buddha could not look on with indifference as we sentient beings with our evil passions piled up sin and evil day after day, drowning ourselves in the sea of *samsāra*. It was for this reason that he pronounced his great vows, set up the Pure Land on the yonder shore, and drew us up into the bark of his saving vows. Zendō was further convinced that without relying on this doctrine, there would be no escape from the great sea of *samsāra*. The same deep faith that he himself professes in Pure Land doctrine he therefore taught to others as well. It is said that while he took an extremely rigorous approach to his own moral discipline, his attitude to others was one of great compassion and love. In addition to swaying the minds of his contemporary Buddhists in China with the eschatological doctrine of *mappō*, his experience of his own ignorance and sinfulness and his sense of himself as a lost soul brought him to faith in the Original Vow of Great Compassion of Amida Buddha.

As the originator of an epoch-making doctrine promulgated in defiance of the theories of other Pure Land scholars, Zendō's importance to the Pure Land sect is considerable. It was his conviction that ignorant, sinful persons who confess their sin to Amida Buddha and trust in his Original Vow are the sole guests invited to His Pure Land. Hōnen (1133–1212), the founder of the Pure Land sect in Japan, found this sentence in Zendō's *Compendium on the Meditation Sutra*:

> Those who continually recite Amida's Name single-mindedly and exclusively in daily life without regard to time or place or circumstances, and never let go of it, are called believers of Right Established Practice because they comply with the purport of the Buddha's Vow.[6]

This opened his eyes to the Purport of the Vow of Amida Buddha and brought him to the convicton that

> even ordinary, ignorant persons are sure to attain to rebirth at the end of time if they recite the name of Amida, since this accords with the purport of the Buddha's Vow.[7]

Even these few brief words leave no doubt about the important position Zendō holds in the development of Pure Land doctrine.

But if we go a step further and ask whether his interpretation of the Three Minds is so clear as to cause no further problems, we have to admit that this is not the case. A closer look discloses deep contradiction not only in the nature of the relationship between the Three Minds but within the description of each Mind itself. (In a sense, this comes as no surprise, since a dialectical situation naturally implies that any contradiction in the outward relation between elements will correspond to a simultaneous contradiction within the elements themselves.) Moreover, the contradiction at issue here does not seem to be of the shallow sort that can easily be corrected and dissolved through the manipulations of conceptual analysis. On the contrary, it obliges us first to investigate the matter and try to get to the very bottom of the antinomy, and then break through to a point where the contradictories can be brought into dialectical unity by the transforming mediation of absolute nothingness. This is in fact the path that Shinran followed in attempting to come to grips with the spirit of Zendō's interpretation of the Three Minds and resolve its difficulties by means of action-faith. The key to his solution is none other than *zange*.

It is clear from his *Compendium* that the inner inspiration of Zendō's interpretation of the Three Minds lay in metanoesis, even though externally he appears to go no further than the self-reflection of a rigorous conscience unable to escape the idealism of moral obligation. In the case of Shinran's way of *zange*, we see someone unable to stand the demands of moral obligation and pushed to the limits of his own self-existence, to the very core of evil and sin. Breaking through this core, he willingly accepted the self-negation of destroying and abandoning that very self-existence itself. While Zendo's treatment of the Three Minds of *sentient beings* speaks of the moral ideal of an "ought" and implies the contradiction presupposed by the self-effort that accompanies that obligation, Shinran's interpretation speaks rather of the Three Minds of *the Original Vow*, that is, as Other-power that allows sentient beings to enter the Pure Land by converting them to obedience. Thus Shinran develops the Three Minds in terms of the bodhisattva Dharmākara, seeing them as the *ōsō* aspect which, when seen as the *gensō* taking place within the Tathāgata himself, can also be called an absolute *gensō*. This effects an absolute transformation of the Three Minds of sentient beings in terms of which they become mediators of absolute nothingness. The result is that the antinomies generated in the Three Minds by Zendō's approach are elevated to a higher unity in nothingness, the unity of a *neither/nor*.

The action of metanoesis is necessary in order for this mediation by absolute nothingness to take place. Hence Shinran's interpretation, which develops the notion of the Other-power transformation of the Original Vow, presupposes as a necessary condition his own practice of *zange*. Though difficult to understand as metanoesis at first sight, the idea of accumulating merits and good deeds in order to fulfill the vow made by Dharmākara is simply a religious symbol of metanoetics. The discipline of Dharmākara (*inni*), which represents the *ōsō*-aspect of the Tathāgata, is interpreted by Shinran solely on the basis of his own experience of *zange* as the transcendent ground of metanoetics through merit-transference. Of course we cannot forget that it was Donran (Chin., T'an-luan, 476–542) who first inspired him to seek the deeper implication of the Three Minds by tracing a path from the Meditation Sutra back to the Larger Sutra. This is why his *Gāthā of True Faith in the Nembutsu*[8] expresses the quintessence of his faith. The merits of Shinran as a disciple of Hōnen who surpassed his teacher in securing a solid basis for Pure Land doctrine lie in the fact that he grasped the mediatory significance of the discipline of Dharmākara as a transcendent foundation for metanoetics in terms of an *ōsō* that corresponds to the absolute *gensō* of the *nembutsu*, and that he saw in it a *für sich* development of the Original Vow of the Larger Sutra. It is only natural then for Shinran that the doctrine of the Three Minds in the "True Faith" book of the *Kyōgyōshinshō*, which is mediated by the "True Practice" book through the "Gāthā of True Faith in the Nembutsu," not only awakened him to metanoetics by means of the contradiction contained in the mind of all sentient beings but prompted him to develop it into a dialectic. The content developed in this way falls naturally into line with the development of Shinran's *zange*.

Zendō's interpretation of the Three Minds was drawn from the Meditation Sutra. As noted in the previous chapter, this sutra develops the structure of mediatory being in terms of *upāya*, a standpoint quite different from what we find in the Larger Sutra, which develops the structure of absolute transformation into the Three Minds of Sincere Mind, Sincere Faith, and Desire to Be Born of the Original Vow. It follows as a matter of course that the Three Minds in the Meditation Sutra should imply a dialectic and set up a dynamic within the self whereby the Three Minds arrive at an absolutely mediated synthesis. The fundamental cause or primary impulse to this dynamic is to be found in the Three Minds of the Larger Sutra, which together represent the mediatory unity of absolute transformation.

To look at this contrast a bit more closely in terms of the doctrine of the various "bodies" of the Buddha, the Three Minds of the Meditation Sutra represent a structure of minds which, when realized in the mind of sentient beings, becomes a "body of expediency" (*hōben-keshin*), a *für sich* stage of existence. In the Larger Sutra, however, the Three Minds point to a substantial *an und für sich* stage of existence symbolized by the Three Minds of Dharmākara. Insofar as the former is mediatory in the sense of becoming manifest in the mutuality between one relative being and another as absolute nothingness, and since, as a transforming axis of "nothingness," it becomes the subject of *für sich* activity vis-à-vis other relative "beings," it shows a dialectical structure of an *upāya*-body in the sense of "being" that can exist autonomously. The latter, in contrast, shows the speculative structure of absolute mediation in the sense of a "true reward-body" (*shinjitsu-hōjin*) which is the absolute negation of the former. In short, the latter is both the efficient cause and the final cause of the former.

The self-discipline of Dharmākara as it is described in the Larger Sutra, therefore, points to the process whereby the Original Vow of the Tathāgata arrives at a *für sich* state. This is the source and ground of Other-power, as explained in the Meditation Sutra, in the sense that it enables sentient beings to attain rebirth. Here Other-power neither works out of natural necessity, as is the case with the forces of nature, nor corresponds to the workings of personality. Between Tathāgata and sentient beings there exists a gap that no "interpersonal relationship" can bridge. It is impossible to understand the relationship between the absolute and the relative in terms of the "I-Thou" relationship of theism. Between being and nothingness there can be no such relative relationship. The relative existence of sentient beings can be transformed into new being by absolute nothingness so that it can mediate Other-power. But the work of Other-power, because it is nothingness and absolute transformation, cannot appear in the pure passivity of the relative that is transformed by it, nor can it simply be set alongside the relative as a "one" to an "other." If the absolute were to be placed in such an opposition to the relative, it would of necessity become another relative. Absolute Other-power means obedience to an absolute seen as a "naturalness" that supersedes the opposition between self and other. Hence, when we say that the self becomes a mediator of Other-power, we cannot mean that it cooperates with the Other-power that confronts it. Properly speaking, we mean that the self is transformed under the influence of an absolute nothingness which is neither the self nor an other, and is drawn into a "naturalness" in which the self loses itself: Other-power is action (*gyō*) seen as the transformation of the self. This "mediation-through-action" is the most fundamental of all mediated relationships; all other relationships among relative beings are abstractions of it. Absolute mediation itself is the most concrete and unique relationship that can be experienced.

The story of Dharmākara's discipline is symbolic of this power of transformation. While the metanoetic mediation of sentient beings is moved by this power, it also makes that power real in the world. The bodhisattva's discipline served essentially as a continual renewal of that power and mediated its way into the future, thus transferring the eternal now into the dynamic development of the future. As a religious symbol, the discipline of Dharmākara represents the transcendent ground of the metanoesis of sentient beings. The Three Minds of the sentient being simply refer to the recognition and mediation of this source. This transcendent ground is the source and substance of the Three Minds, at the same time as the latter symbolizes the *für sich* mediation of the former in the world. Because the determination of the Tathāgata in the form of Dharmākara, his "departing descent," is at the same the "returning ascent" of the Tathāgata to himself, an internal circular dynamic of departure-*qua*-return or descent-*qua*-ascent is the Original Vow of Amida Buddha, identical with the name of *Namu-Amida-Butsu*. Because Dharmākara is simply a self-determination of the Tathāgata seen from the standpoint of the Tathāgata, and because the Tathāgata represents absolute mediation, we may speak of a "self-determination"– *qua*–"other-determination." Accordingly, as the negative mediatory element within the Tathāgata, Dharmākara symbolizes nothing other than the power of absolute negativity by means of which sentient beings, who are "other" to the absolute, are mediated to the dynamic unity of the Tathāgata. All sentient beings are encompassed within the compassion of Amida Buddha (Tathāgata) and can be determined to realize their wish to be born because they are mediated by the absolute *gensō* whose symbol is the bodhisattva Dharmākara.

The aspect of *ōsō* that corresponds to this absolute *gensō* is the aspect

of Dharmākara's discipline before his enlightenment. Through Dharmākara, Tathāgata makes himself *für sich*; only by mediating a mutual
gensō among relative sentient beings does he make real the absolute
transformation of his Great Compassion. Thus determined, the Tathāgata cannot be an unmediated transcendent being that simply embraces
relative beings within itself. Tathāgata allows the relative a full mediatory role; he works with and suffers with the relative, and as such represents absolute mediation performing the Great Compassion–*qua*–Great
Nay.

This quality of absolute transformation that characterizes nothingness does not exist apart from the relative being of sentient beings who
are given the independence of *upāya* to serve as the axis of absolute
nothingness. In other words, it expresses itself in the equality that
pervades all sentient beings in their reciprocity. For all relative beings
are independent-*qua*-dependent and as such are converted to nothingness. In his negative mediatory aspect, therefore, Tathāgata works in
accord with the metanoesis of sentient beings and grants them a mediating role. In their mutual equality of independence-*qua*-dependence,
each is raised to a *für sich* state and made an axis of transformation for the
salvation of every other, and is thus granted provisional independence as
an *upāya* of the absolute nothingness. This is what is called the "transformed body of expediency" (*hōben-keshin*). Precedence among relatively independent beings, or the sequence of relative *gensō*, indicates
merely a temporal and historical relationship. The aseity that absolutely
negates and at the same time eternally affirms the totality of this order is
the "true reward-body" (*shinjitsu-hōjin*). In terms of the salvation of
sentient beings, the "true reward-body" belongs to the way of *ōsō* while
the "transformed body of expediency" belongs to the way of *gensō*. But
seen from the viewpoint of the Tathāgata himself, the *ōsō* of establishing
himself in a *für sich* state by undertaking the discipline of Dharmākara
and returning to a process of development within himself is already
absolute *gensō* because it is the transforming work of Other-power aimed
at salvific merit-transference in the phase of *ōsō*. In this sense we speak of
ōsō as *gensō*. But the salvific merit-transference in the phrase of *gensō*
makes absolute *gensō* manifest through the mediation of the relative and
brings it to an *an sich* state. Thus we may also speak of *gensō* as *ōsō*. On
the one hand, the relative is relative in virtue of its opposition to other
relatives, and can confront the absolute only by way of this relative-to-
relative relationship. On the other, the absolute is able to function vis-à-
vis the relative only through the mediatory action of other relatives.

The logic of this absolute mediation is clearly expressed in Shinran's notion of the "two kinds of merit-transference" which gives more concrete form to the structure of salvation. Dharmākara and the mind of sentient beings are differentiated and set in opposition to each other in such a way that the former grasps identity in terms of the aspect of the absolute in itself, while the latter grasps it in terms of the aspect of negative mediation.[9] In the sense that both regulate the opposition between one and the same identity, however, they are the same. This is why it is said that the Three Minds of the Meditation Sutra are the same as those of the Larger Sutra in spite of their differences,[10] and different in spite of their identity;[11] and that the two doctrines differ in their outward significance but unite in their inner core.[12] The pure mediation of absolute transformation, a circular dynamic within the self in which the inner and the outer correspond harmoniously to one another, is the work of mediation implied by the notion of merit-transference (ekō).

Shinran believes that the rebirth of sentient beings in the Pure Land can be accomplished only through the nembutsu of the Original Vow, that only insofar as the self is converted to the power of the Great Compassion of the Original Vow as a mediator of absolute nothingness can it reach the "Rank of Nonregression" (futai no kurai) as "empty being." From the standpoint of this faith, Shinran draws the doctrine of the Kyōgyōshinshō from the Larger Sutra and argues that only the attainment of birth through the nembutsu can constitute the "true reward-body." Since the "transformed body of expediency" mediates this process but cannot accomplish it, the Meditation Sutra, which is based on that standpoint, can only offer a way of upāya. This explains why Shinran takes the sense of Zendō's understanding of the Three Minds as he found them in the Sanzengi[13] and turns it around to fit the Original Vow of the Larger Sutra, reading the one in terms of the other. In this way the idea of the Three Minds in Zendō's Compendium, which presents an ideal structure of the moral conscience that sentient beings must have to attain salvation, becomes a notion of the Three Minds that shows the für sich structure of the Original Vow in Dharmākara. The absolute transformation that Zendō's idea undergoes in being made to mediate transcendent Other-power is like the change from immediate life to death-and-resurrection, from expression to symbol, from immediate thought to action-faith, from being to nothingness. This is how Shinran's interpretation took Zendō's Three Minds out of their context in the Meditation Sutra and reread them into the Original Vow of the Larger Sutra.

What sort of contradiction does Zendō's notion of the Three Minds contain to prompt this dialectic transformation? And what is the form of the dialectic contained in the Three Minds of the Meditation Sutra? First of all, we may consider the relationship between the Sincere Mind and the Deep Mind. As we have already observed, the Sincere Mind is concerned with our past actions and deeds; it calls for a purity of heart in which the good we do outwardly is in harmony with our inward state. In the Deep Mind, however, a deep trust in salvation through faith in Amida Buddha is accompanied by a self-consciousness of our deep ignorance and sinfulness, as persons permanently adrift in the sea of *samsāra* with no prospect of deliverance. Obviously these two sides of self-consciousness contradict each other. We cannot but admit the existential fact of our deep sinfulness to which the doctrine of the Deep Mind speaks, and thus recognize that the Sincere Mind can never be more than a moral ideal, a demand that lies irremediably beyond the reach of our own ignorance and sinfulness. But this discrepancy between the ineluctable "is" of our radical sin on the one hand, and the "ought" on the other, between our existential actuality and our essential nature, cannot simply be left in a state of dualistic antagonism. If that were the case, we would have no right to speak of Three Minds—*qua*—One Mind.

How is it possible to reconcile these contradictories? Only through the metanoetic confession of our inability to achieve the ideals of moral obligation and humble acceptance of the fact of our own existential finitude. Through the workings of the wondrous power of absolute transformation which mediates this self-abandonment of metanoesis, our mere self-negation is turned into a negation of negation—that is, a self-affirmation—and death is turned to resurrection. The essence of moral obligation is transferred to the "action of no-action" of absolute Other-power, and through this experience metanoesis mediates the Deep Mind which confesses deep ignorance and sinfulness to the truthfulness of the Sincere Mind. Thus the Sincere Mind, which is unrealizable by self-power alone, does not stop at the mere notion of an "ought" but is mediated by the transforming activity of Other-power and realized in the action of transferring gratitude, which is an "action of no-action." All of this is due to the wondrous power of the Original Vow and its absolute transformation wrought through the mediation of metanoesis. The metanoetic recognition of the inability to achieve the Sincere Mind through self-power because of ignorance and sin at the same time mediates a process whereby what was once impossible because of ignorance and sin now becomes possible through submissive gratitude for the transference of Other-power. In this wondrous power, Sincere Mind and the Deep Mind are brought into a dialectical unity grounded in metanoesis. Mediated by metanoesis, the Sincere Mind that was an impossibility for self-power is realizable by Other-power as "the truthful mind" (*shishin*) of obedience and gratitude. Insofar as it is performed in a spirit of metanoesis, the action of obedience, gratitude, and indebtedness for the absolute transforming power of the Original Vow enables sentient beings to keep their minds true and pure, however deeply sinful and ignorant their minds may be, by the continual cleansing of metanoesis. A Sincere Mind toward one's past deeds cannot remain pure by itself; it requires continual metanoesis.

Zendō's interpretation of the Sincere Mind, we recall, contained the following comment: "Do not show wisdom, virtue, and effort in one's outward acts, while your inward heart is fraught with vice and fraud." Here we are presented with a moral "ought." But Shinran retranslates the passage into a confession of *zange*: "No wisdom, virtue, or effort can there be outside, for falsehood sits within." [14] In this bold rereading of the original meaning, it is impossible not to see the pervasive significance that he gives to *zange*. The discipline of Dharmākara works in us sentient beings as the power of the Vow, prompting us to metanoesis. Shinran, who believes in the power of the Original Vow, is impelled by it to the actual practice of metanoesis, and thereby to the reinterpretation of Zendō's standpoint of moral obligation, which seeks to clarify the ideal structure of the Three Minds by negating the standpoint of sentient beings, by redirecting it toward the transcendence of the Original Vow. Shinran's metanoesis is not a work of self-power but is the manifestation within himself of absolute Other-power, and as such represents an "action of no-action," or an *an sich* action of absolute negation. This is why it needs to be based on a pure and sincere heart.

Second, let us turn to the contradiction between the Deep Mind and what was referred to earlier as the "Mind of Aspiring for Birth by Merit-transference" (*ekō-hotsugan-shin*). This latter refers to the firm resolve to be reborn both by transferring all of one's own good deeds and by sharing in the good deeds of others. But really to possess this mind is a direct contradiction of the "Deep Mind of Dharma" (*hō no jinshin*) which binds faith to the power of Amida Buddha's Vow and implies that one would no longer feel the need for performing any supplementary good. In this case, the aspiration for rebirth by merit-transference would become completely unnecessary, and one would end up betraying Deep Faith in the power of the Vow.

To overcome this contradiction, it is necessary to preserve Deep Faith fully and to believe deeply that rebirth depends entirely on the power of the Original Vow. It means applying all good deeds, one's own and those of others, to the aspiration for rebirth as a transference of gratitude for having been converted to faith in Other-power by the power of the Original Vow. That is to say, the aspiration for rebirth is not the unmediated working of self-power, whose impotence has already been recognized as unstable and liable to collapse. Moreover, the notion of unmediated aspiration for rebirth harbors the inevitable contradiction of not being able to shake free of the dilemma of seeking after the Buddha who was himself a person who sought for nothing. Only a hope for rebirth that is mediated by Deep Faith and supported by Deep Faith can enjoy the stability and resoluteness of a "hopeless hope" or a "seeking of no-seeking" whose absolute negation rests on the Original Vow. Shinran is clear on the point:

> Next, the Desire for Birth is the Tathāgata's command which summons all sentient beings. The substance of the Desire for Birth is the True Serene Faith. Indeed, this is not (the mind of) merit-transference with self-power as conceived by Mahāyānist or Hīnayānist, common men or sages, or meditative or non-mediatory persons; hence, it is called "(the mind of) non-merit-transference." [15]

Just as we have seen that the Sincere Mind cannot be achieved merely by self-power, but requires that one be converted by Other-power to an "action of no-action" performed out of gratitude to Other-power, so Deep Faith in the Dharma comes about only when one has Deep Faith in the existential fact of one's profound ignorance and sinfulness, drowning in a sea of *samsāra* without any prospect of rescue, and when this latter faith mediates the former. This means that Deep Faith must be mediated by metanoesis and grounded in a recognition of one's own existential plight. Like the Sincere Mind, the Mind of Aspiring for Birth by Merit-transference is made possible only through the mediation of metanoesis, since the Deep Faith opened up by means of metanoesis is the ground of both of them. While both stand in contradiction to Deep Faith, they are also unified dialectically in virtue of metanoesis, which serves as a pivot of this transformation and mediation. In this way, we have already seen how the Sincere Mind and the Mind of Aspiring for Birth are both mediated jointly by the Deep Mind. From there we may see how this third and final contradiction is resolved in dialectical unity.

The contradiction between the Sincere Mind and the Mind of

Aspiring for Birth is not hard to understand, given that they represent past and future respectively and share in the same contradictory relationship that characterizes the past and the future. Those who possess the Sincere Mind of believing in the purity of their past deeds find no reason to turn toward the future, aspiring for rebirth and transferring their merits, since rebirth would appear to follow as a natural consequence of continuing and extending the deeds of the past. If some need is felt to aspire for rebirth in the Pure Land and to transfer merits for that purpose, this can only point to a failure of the Sincere Mind in the past. The self-identical, unbroken continuity of the past and the creative transformation of the future are directly incompatible and contradictory. It is only through the mutually transforming mediation of the two in the present that this antagonism can be reconciled. That is, in this mutual mediation, the past ceases to cling to its identity despite its continuity, and undergoes a conversion in metanoesis so that it can accept the continual renewal of its meaning as a mediator that propels the present into the future. The future, meanwhile, needs also to realize that it cannot produce any creative content without the tradition of the past. It must accept the determinations of the past as a negative mediation, obedience to which can renew the past from its own deeper sources and bring about creativity through the transforming activity of absolute nothingness. In this way a new creative synthesis can be effected which is neither past nor future but revitalizes both through their negation, establishing a transcendent unity in the present as the absolute transformation through which both the past and the future are mutually reconciled into a harmonious whole.

While the Sincere Mind and Mind of Aspiring for Birth are antagonistic in their immediacy, Deep Faith brings them to unity in mutual negation and transformation. This is the negative dialectical unity of the Three Minds. In metanoesis the past is completely negated, but within the pure passivity of this negation the continuity of the past is renewed and transformed into the "naturalness" of an "action of no-action." The past, therefore, is resurrected to a life that is "brought to life in its dying." This is salvation. It is a conversion in which the Mind of Aspiring for Birth through Merit-transference is achieved and rebirth determined as a "non-transferring." Through the mediation of metanoesis, rebirth in the future is already contained in the past as a destination; and apart from the absolute transformation of resurrection in the future, there can be no negation and transformation of the past by means of absolute nothingness. Mediated by the future, the past can be transformed absolutely. Metanoesis, the transformation of the past through negation, also mediates salvation in the sense of determining rebirth in the future. In short, the mediative unity in the eternal now, in which the past and the future mutually transform and penetrate each other, is brought about by metanoetic action.

A consciousness that has reached a *für sich* state in this action of faith and has become aware of itself as the absolute transformation between the transcendent absolute and the self *is* this Deep Faith, and hence represents the unifying center of the Three Minds. This unifying function, as we observed earlier, consists in the mutual mediation of a "twofold Deep Faith," the self-negation of Deep Faith in our own being and the absolute affirmation of Deep Faith in the Dharma, whence it goes on to display the internal structure of a negative dialectic. As such, it merits closer attention.

We have seen three sorts of contradictions among the Three Minds, and have seen how it is due to the unifying work of Deep Faith that they are mediated dialectically with one another and brought to a unity. The Deep Faith that forms the center of this unity is of two sorts, neither of which can be understood if treated directly and in isolation from the other. Deep Faith in the ignorance and sinfulness of our human condition, caught in a never-ending and inescapable cycle of life and death, is based on Deep Faith in the Great Compassion of the Dharma in the Original Vow in the sense that the former reaches consciousness and is sustained there by it. At the same time, Deep Faith in Dharma cannot exist without being accompanied by Deep Faith in the human condition. It is metanoesis that effects a transforming mediation between the two and provides a background for their dynamic and dialectical unity.

Sincere Faith (*shingyō*) in the Vow of Amida, which is the driving force and prime mover of each of these aspects of Deep Faith, is possible only in metanoesis, even as metanoesis is possible only through the transcendent Other-power of Sincere Faith. As Shinran writes:

> Next, the Serene Faith is the ocean of Faith consummated with the Tathāgata's Great Mercy and the complete, all-merging, and unhindered Wisdom. For this reason, it is not mixed with doubt; hence, it is called the Serene Faith. The essence of the Serene Faith is the Serene Mind endowed by the Other-Power. All the ocean-like multitudinous beings, since the beginningless past, have been transmigrating in the sea of ignorance, drowning in the cycle of existences, bound to the cycle of sufferings, and having no pure, serene faith. They have, as a natural consequence, no true serene faith. Therefore, it is difficult to meet the highest virtue and difficult to receive the supreme, pure Faith. All the common and petty persons at all times constantly defile their good minds with greed and lust, and their anger and hatred constantly burn the

treasure of Dharma. Even though they work and practice as busily as though they were sweeping fire off their heads, their practices are called poisoned and mixed good deeds and also called deluded and deceitful practices; hence, they are not called true acts. If one desires to be born in the Land of Infinite Light with these deluded and poisoned good acts, he cannot possibly attain it. Why is it so? Because when the Tathāgata performed the Bodhisattva practices, His three kinds of actions were not mingled with doubt even for a thought or a moment.

Since this mind (Serene Faith) is the Tathāgata's Great Compassionate Mind, it necessarily becomes the rightly determinant cause for (Birth in) the Recompensed Land. The Tathāgata, pitying the sea of suffering multitudes, endowed the unhindered, great Pure Faith to the ocean of all beings. This is called the True Faith of the Other-Power.[16]

The two types of Deep Faith that Zendō lines up parallel to each other in his interpretation are here united clearly in a mutually transforming mediation; the transforming transcendent power of the absolute (Tathāgata), as the source and cause of this unity, is located on the way of *gensō* in the discipline of Dharmākara; and the transformation that takes place in the metanoesis of sentient beings is attributed to Other-power. All of this is expressed in terms of Shinran's own driving *zange*. The sense of urgency and personal torment in his style leaves no doubt as to how truthful and painful was his metanoesis.

Faith that consists of trust in Other-power may seem at first sight an easy-going affair without suffering, and indeed is commonly referred to as the "easy way" in the doctrine of the Pure Land school. But anyone who can detect the tincture of sorrow that pervades the whole of Shinran's works and can sense how close it is to despair will readily understand that True Faith (*shinjin*) comes about only through the painful truthfulness of metanoesis. This does not mean, of course, that it is a notional ideal such as we find in self-power *nembutsu*, a mere self-affirmation that conceives of all good deeds and merits as one's own activity without recognizing the transforming power of Tathāgata. Such an idealistic conception with its notion of a moral "ought," however pure, remains the property of the self and is bound to the context of the self's own life. It does not rise to the higher level of an existence mediated by a self-surrender that negates life, by a death in which one lets go of the existence of the self in an act of despair toward the self. (Obviously, what we mean by "death" here is not the same as suicide. Suicide is not a negation of self-will, but its affirmation, and therefore belongs to life, not to death. The death we have in mind is the death of a self-negation that is concerned neither with death nor with life, a surrender of the self in a self-surrender of pure passivity and complete submission.)

The self-affirmation of the principle of all good deeds and merits is a continuation of self-centeredness, not its conversion. No conversion in a positive sense has yet taken place. Hence, however much one may hypothesize that the spirit of this standpoint approaches the moral ideal, or even unites with it at some ultimate stage, one cannot speak here of authentic True Faith. As before, it remains within the realms of confused practice. There is no final peace of soul in such "idealism." Only those arrive at the authenticity of True Faith who are converted through metanoesis to share in practice of Dharmākara on the way of *gensō*, whose self is completely reoriented in conversion and for whom death becomes the principle of life; only those who are taken up into the Compassionate Vow of the Tathāgata through the action-faith-witness of nothingness as the ground of being can come to the joy of True Faith. This is Deep Faith truly come to concrete unity.

Without the practice of metanoesis, there is nothing that can mediate this process. As explained earlier, only the ongoing development of metanoesis supplies the infinite element for transforming relative beings into mediators of nothingness as the absolute negation of life in death, so that merit-transference in *ōsō* can come about. Shinran's True Faith in Other-power rests on the unfathomable depths of a serious practice of *zange*. The fact that he is brought to his proper share in Amida Buddha's salvation of merit-transference in *ōsō* by being converted to the absolute merit-transference in *gensō* of Dharmākara is due to the mediation of metanoesis which allows his action of merit-transference in *ōsō* to conform to the thought of *gensō* through an inner relationship of the two in the form of *ōsō-qua-gensō*.

Metanoesis represents a breakthrough of self that is an action-*qua*-thought. As such, it mediates the absolute transformation of Amida Buddha's *ōsō-qua-gensō*. To the absolute *gensō* of the compassionate Amida there corresponds an *ōsō* manifested at the moment of Dharmākara's invocation and fulfillment of the Original Vow. In the True Faith that is transferred here, the conversion of the mind of sentient beings is not directed by the mere thought of Deep Faith. It must rather be a transforming affirmation of self-surrender in metanoesis, a turnabout of the self through death and resurrection, a transformation through reversal.

Shinran's sentiments of sorrow in his experience of metanoesis, which not only pervade the background of his description but overflow into his manner of expression when he is treating True Faith, leave no doubt about the fact that he means to turn it into the confession of metanoesis and to consider the Three Minds from the viewpoint of action (*gyō*). In so doing, he surpasses the standpoint of idealistic thought that marks Zendō's interpretation to speak of the Three Minds of Dharmākara as representing the aspect of absolute *gensō*. Shinran's devotion to Donran underwrites what I have been saying here.

We have seen the conflict between the two kinds of Deep Mind, the Sincere Mind and the Mind of Aspiring to Birth by Merit-transference, and have seen further how each of them is involved in contradiction with Deep Faith, but we have also seen how they are rendered mutually complementary. This makes it amply clear that the whole of the Three Minds is based on the transformation and mediation of metanoesis and thereby enjoys the unity expressed in the saying, "Three Minds–*qua*–One Mind." Shinran sheds light on the inner dialectic of the relationship between the Three Minds (or Three Faiths) and the transforming mediation of immanence-*qua*-transcendence that stems from this relation when he redirects Zendō's demand for a moral ideal into the transforming action of *zange*. While Pure Land doctrine had previously taken as its principal authority Zendō's commentary on the Meditation Sutra, Shinran developed his doctrine under the influence of Donran, deepening the notion of the Original Vow into faith in Other-power. This being the case, it is clear that metanoetics represents the pillar on which he set up the sect known as the True Pure Land sect or Shin Buddhism.

To carry our treatment a step further, we may note that the three elements that combine to form action-faith-witness, a notion that contains Shin doctrine in its entirety, correspond respectively to the Three Minds. This allows us to conclude that it is metanoesis that provides a principle of unity to the whole. Thus, by action is meant the action of metanoesis with regard to the past, through which we come to understand the true significance of the Sincere Mind. Faith, of course, means the Deep Faith in the present, and witness corresponds to the aspiration for rebirth in the future.

Properly speaking, action in the sense of the Pure Land school refers to the *nembutsu*, the recitation of the name of Amida Buddha expressed in the six Chinese characters *Na-mu-a-mi-da-butsu*. The *nembutsu* is a symbol of a personal relationship of absolute mediation between Amida Buddha and a sentient being in the form of a call and a response. But through this personal relationship, the *nembutsu* also symbolizes the Original Vow of the Buddha's Great Compassion as it is expressed most fully in the community of all Buddhas reciting Amida's name. The *nembutsu* is believed to have the power of absolute transformation and to establish a mutual transformation and exchange between Amida Buddha and the sentient being in an act of transference; and praise of the name of Amida is seen as the action of the *nembutsu*.

In terms of content, the *nembutsu* signals a participation in the transformation wrought by absolute Other-power of the Original Vow, whose symbol is the name of Amida Buddha. Furthermore, inasmuch as absolute Other-power is pure passivity without an agent, the *nembutsu*, as the action of this Other-power, needs first of all to be mediated by metanoesis, the act of negation and transformation performed by sentient beings. If this were not the case, numerous difficulties would be unavoidable, even if it were granted that Other-power is manifest in the action of reciting the name. In the collection of texts known as the *Anjinketsujō-shō* (*On Assurance and Determination*) we read:

> The *nembutsu* is not necessarily limited to the oral recitation of "*namuamida-butsu.*" It is an awakening of faith in the sense that one is made aware of the established merits of Amida Buddha which, from the moment of his enlightenment ten kaplas ago, he has been ready to bestow on the believer who does him reverence (*namu*). The comprehension of this Buddha's Grace is expressed by *namuamidabutsu.* . . . To grasp the core of *namuamidabutsu* as an expression of genuine faith is to attain the Three Minds.[17]

In the *Songō-shinzō-meimon* (*Notes on the Inscriptions on Sacred Scrolls*), Shinran comments on an inscription on the portrait of Zendō (here given in italics):

> *To say the Buddha's six-character Name*: to say namu-amida-butsu. *Is to praise the Buddha*: To say namu-amida-butsu is to praise the Buddha. Further, *it is to repent*: To say namu-amida-butsu is to repent all the karmic evil one has committed since the beginningless past. *It is to awaken to the aspiration for birth.* . . . To say namu-amida-butsu is to desire to be born in the Pure Land of peace.[18]

In this brief but rich passage, Shinran suggests that the recitation of the name, or the development of the name on the way of *gensō*, is substantiated by the practice of *zange*. To this extent, it is completely identical with metanoetics, which is why I believe that Shinran's doctrine of faith is centered on a metanoetics. There is, of course, no denying the historical fact of his intention to clarify the authentic doctrine of the Pure Land sect and to set it up against what was being taught by the influential disciples of Hōnen at the time. In the development of the Pure Land sect, there was much discussion about the significance of the recitation of the *nembutsu*, leaving no doubt that Shinran was influenced by the ideas of his predecessors and elders, in terms both of positive appreciation and of negative criticism. But here I must submit my judgment to competent religious scholars.

It is a special mark of the doctrine of Pure Land Buddhism, according to the scholars, that action and faith are related in an order opposite to that of other schools. Specifically, action precedes faith in the Original Vow, yielding a unity of action-faith (*gyō-shin*) instead of the usual faith-action. Furthermore, for Shin Buddhism the *nembutsu* is not a form of prayer but an expression of gratitude to Amida Buddha. But all of this seems to conform better to a metaphysical-ontological consideration of the transference of Other-power in the Original Vow than it does to our immediate experience. For us, it is impossible to perform the act of praising the name of Amida and expressing gratitude without the enlightened awareness or witness (*shō*) of salvation, just as it is not possible to have faith in the Original Vow without any hint or foreboding of such witness. In the temporal order of our experience, one cannot think of action as prior to faith. On the contrary, in our religious consciousness *nembutsu* begins with the Mind of Aspiring for Birth in the future, and then passes over into the Sincere Mind of metanoesis for the past, converting our desire into a "desire of no-desire," that is, a desire for rebirth in spite of our lack of any qualification for harboring such a desire. From there, consciousness ripens into a Deep Faith of submission in the present to Other-power. The conviction that one has been destined for rebirth gives rise to a sense of indebtedness that develops in turn into the act of gratitude. In this action of gratitude, salvation is the proclamation of a completeness: one's own salvation is witnessed completely in the transference of the Tathāgata's transforming act of absolute nothingness to the salvation of others, so that one takes on the role of a mediator to cooperate in their salvation on the way of *gensō*. Thus action, faith, and witness make up a triune one through the mutual transformation of each with the others.

When we have faith in the saving power of the Original Vow through the doctrine or teaching (*kyō*), we are merely recognizing the fact that it is the structure of salvation itself that maintains the order of teaching-action-faith-witness as it has been explained above. We see this in Shinran's *Tanni-shō*, for instance, when he expresses his absolute trust in the teachings of Hōnen. It is also patent from both the content and the structure of the *Kyōgyōshinshō* that the whole of Pure Land Buddhism has developed on the basis of a tradition of doctrine extending from a "beginningless past" up to the present.

But this is looking at the matter from the viewpoint of spreading the faith, whereas philosophy must put weight on the evidence of one's own experience. If one wishes to develop one's thought through the mediation of experience, one must pursue another course. It is the same with religion: insofar as it is concerned with developing thought, authoritative tradition has to be mediated by self-witness (*jishō*) in the sense of the self's own witness to what is evident to the self itself. In the case of religious faith *per se*, however, we always have to acknowledge the priority of doctrine. Hence, religious thought is by nature the opposite of philosophy, which begins from a critique of doctrine and makes self-witness the main thing. In philosophy, we begin from what is "prior to us" and trace a path back to what is "prior in itself." But this commitment to self-power that insists on affirming the standpoint of philosophy without any outside mediation is no guarantee that the absolute self-power of philosophy will actually be able to achieve its goal. Our path of ascent to unity with the absolute is cut short by the fact that we are relative beings. On the contrary, it is distinctive of a metanoetics based on action-faith-witness that this way opens up for us through a posture of *zange* and through the obedient despair of absolute critique vis-à-vis the immediacy of a self-power philosophy. This is why philosophy must be said to contain a dialectic at its very foundations. Looking at the question from this standpoint, we are forced to conclude that philosophical self-consciousness, in order to set itself up as the working of autonomous reason, requires the mediation of a metanoesis of despair toward the philosophy of self-power which begins from a critique of the teachings of tradition.

The only action we can perform with regard to the past is metanoesis, but this metanoesis is mediated by the wondrous power of absolute transformation through which an initial self-negation is turned into a self-affirmation, through which death is resurrected to new life. In this resurrected life, philosophical thought and other cultural activities of a moral nature that were once abandoned in despair are reinstated—though not now as moral obligations of self-power but as something transferred to self-consciousness by Other-power, as a selfless "action of no-action" performed in "naturalness." This is self-witness in the sense of the gratitude befitting the mind we have called the Mind of Aspiring for Birth by Merit-transference. Here, witness is mediated by the action of metanoesis as the past opening up to the future, so that an orientation to future rebirth becomes implicit in the metanoetic transformation of the past and faith comes to birth in a present consciousness of the change that has taken place in witness, a self-consciousness based on absolute

Other-power. Faith is usually said to consist in believing that which is not clearly evident, but there would be no impulse for us to believe without any presentiment at all. An orientation to the future provides the present with a hint as to the direction in which the transformation of the past should be pushed. The present reaches the *für sich* state of self-consciousness only by serving as a transforming mediator between the past and the future.

Logically speaking, the past is a "particular" whose conversion into the "individual" of future witness through the action of metanoesis constitutes a transformation through negation comparable to the *Ur-teil* (original, fundamental division) of judgment in the Hegelian scheme. As a result, the "universal" of synthesis in the present is set up as a dynamic self-consciousness of eternity. This is faith in its function of transforming mediation between immanence and transcendence. And behind it, as its *an sich* backing, is the action of metanoesis. In contrast with Hegel's "all is judgment," I would prefer to say "all is metanoesis." Odd as this might seem at first, if we think of everything as a symbol manifesting absolute nothingness realized through metanoesis, there is nothing surprising about it at all. Judgment, as we observed earlier in the case of Hegel, is unable to break through the unity of reason by means of inference and thus cannot escape from the standpoint of idealism: trapped within the limits of rationalism, it cannot come to a concrete freedom with radical evil as its element of negation. If the judgment of *Ur-teil* is the sole principle in terms of which all individuals are constituted, these individuals must at the same time be converted to a "submissive freedom" as mediators of nothingness. And this means metanoesis. Only in the case of judgment based on metanoesis is it proper to say that "all is judgment," which is why we insist that "all is metanoesis." In metanoesis, the judgment of *Ur-teil* is naturally included as the element of negation.

Existence bespeaks metanoetic transformation. Its knowledge is grounded on faith. According to traditional teaching, the power of the Original Vow, which is the object of faith, is mediated in the *für sich* action of the community of Buddhas engaged in mutual praise and takes shape on the way of *ōsō* as action-faith. This means that it precedes the way of *gensō* in terms of the sequential order of salvation. But this order is the very reverse of the order of our self-consciousness and needs to be transformed through its mediation. This is what the relationship between existence and consciousness requires, and what we mean by the relationship between doctrine and witness. Looked at from the order of our self-witness, the sequence action-faith-witness reflects the synthetic character of faith in the Original Vow in the sense of a transforming interpenetration between the action of metanoesis and the witness of a resurrection to an "action of no-action" in gratitude.

As mentioned in the preceding chapter, the notion of the *sangan-tennyū* found in the final book of the *Kyōgyōshinshō* describes the developmental mediation and interpenetration of the three aspects of the mind of sentient beings in terms of the independence of the "expediency body." In this process, the three aspects are arranged in a sequence running from future to past to present, while the interpretation of the Three Minds in terms of the "true reward-body" sets up a sequence from past to present to future. In both, the modes of time are based on the self-transformation of the past, making it clear that metanoesis mediates action-faith-witness. It is only through the mediating action of metanoesis—that is, not along the path of *ōsō*, which is concerned only with the structure of the Vow itself, but along the way of *gensō*, which is concerned with the *für sich* state of consciousness—that transcendent, absolute nothingness becomes manifest in the course of transforming the minds of sentient beings.

This leaves no room for doubt that the *Kyōgyōshinshō* is constructed in such a way that its entire system is grounded on the *an sich* action of metanoesis. It is difficult to deny the fact that salvation is not something that comes about simply as a result of a temporary act of faith, but is mediated by continual metanoesis. It may be that only the foolish and ordinary need to assent to this fact, while the wise and sagacious have no such need. As for us ignorant and ordinary people, we have no right to deny the existence of such people. But because a tendency to the arrogance and presumption of classing ourselves among them lurks in our hearts, we are in need of continual metanoesis. For myself, I need both to carry on metanoesis without fail because of my abysmal ignorance and shamefulness, and honestly to acknowledge others for their wisdom and goodness. I have been brought to the belief that just as the wise and intelligent can find peace in enlightenment by virtue of having no sin or evil passions for which to perform metanoesis, so I, in my ignorance and sin, can participate in *nirvāna* just as I am and without extinguishing my evil passions.

This wondrous transformation wrought in metanoesis is none other than the power of Amida's Vow of Great Compassion. As Shinran explains:

From the beginningless past to this day and this moment, the ocean of multitudinous beings has been defiled, evil, and filthy, and they do not possess the pure mind; again, they have been deluded, flattering, and deceitful, and do not possess the true mind. Hereupon, the Tathāgata, pitying the sea of all the suffering sentient beings, disciplined Himself in the Bodhisattva practices for inconceivable and innumerable kalpas. During that time, his three kinds of actions [of body, mouth, and mind] were not impure nor untrue even for a thought or a moment. The Tathāgata with a pure and true mind perfected the complete, all-merging, unhindered, inconceivable, indescribable, and ineffable supreme virtue. The Tathāgata bestows His Sincere Mind on the sea of all the multitudinous beings filled with evil passions, evil acts, and perverted knowledge. The Sincere Mind is the true mind endowed by Him to benefit the beings; hence, it is not mixed with doubt. The substance of this Sincere Mind is the Blessed Name of the supreme virtue.[19]

By means of this altruistic transference of truthfulness from the Compassionate Mind, our being, fraught with sin and lust and sunk in a state of misery in the present, is suddenly lifted up and promised *nirvāna* and rebirth. In Shinran's *Jōdo Monrui Jushō (Passages on the Pure Land Way)* we read:

When, through Amida's directing of virtue to them by the power of the Vow, the foolish beings ever floundering in birth-and-death hear the true and real virtues and realize supreme *shinjin*, they immediately attain great joy and reach the state of non-retrogression, so that without being made to sunder their blind passions, they are brought quickly to the realization of great *nirvāna*.[20]

The miracle of salvation is thus bound inseparably to *zange*. But this does not mean that metanoesis is simply the work of self-power. It is rather a work of self-negation and self-abandonment. Only those who are prompted by the transforming power of the absolute and who can submit obediently to it are capable of metanoesis. In other words, when metanoesis is performed, it is believed already to have been mediated by the transference of Other-power. Therefore the Sincere Mind (*shishin*) of the Original Vow, which is the aspect of absolute Other-power of the Sincere Mind (*shijōshin*) made manifest by means of metanoesis, is described as "embodied" in the "Blessed Name."

At the same time, it is impossible to open the mind to faith in Other-power without metanoesis. In contrast to the views of the self-power sect known as the "Gate of the Sages" (*shōdōmon*), for which faith is prior to action, the path of faith is characterized by seeing action as prior to faith. As indicated already, the idea of giving *für sich* action priority over faith is not without its problems. Still, it is necessary that the *an sich* action of metanoesis be prior to faith in order for self-power to be emptied out, brought to self-negation, and made into a mediator of Other-power. Without the mediation of metanoesis, there can be no foundation on which to establish faith in Other-power. In itself, faith in the Original Vow may be prior, but for us it is metanoesis that is prior. That is to say, metanoesis that has been prompted and given rise to by the Original Vow, develops in us into a faith in Other-power. It is not simply a matter of *ōsō* coming before *gensō*; it must at the same time be mediated by the absolute *gensō* that corresponds to the discipline of Dharmākara. The two ways are mediated and made manifest in the action of metanoesis in a relationship of action-*qua*-faith or faith-*qua*-action. Hence it is no exaggeration to say that Pure Land Buddhism is the "Dharma Gate of Metanoesis."

Even before Shinran, Hōnen himself had been impressed by the way of *nembutsu* found in Zendō's commentary on the Meditation Sutra, as exemplified in the following expression of the metanoetic standpoint: "The darkness of my own ignorance lights up for me the Great Compassion of the Buddha's mind; my own inability testifies to the rebirth in the *nembutsu*." The "Gate of the Pure Land" leads to *zange* only for those who become aware of their own powerlessness, recognize the complete inability of self-power, and let go of the self. Given the fact that after the time of Nāgarjūna most teachers of Mahāyāna Buddhism accepted the Pure Land's "easy way" at least as one element in their own doctrine, we may conclude that the self-power "Gate of the Sages" and the Other-power "Gate of the Pure Land" are not really separate and antagonistic schools within Buddhism. The former takes up immediately a general standpoint of reason, from which the relation between the absolute and the relative is seen as a unity of opposites, thus developing only as far as an ontological-phenomenological method. The latter, in contrast, begins from a standpoint that views individual realities through the mediation of the self in an existentialist-soteriological way, leading to the action-faith-witness of the mutual interpenetration and transformation of the absolute and the relative. Inasmuch as only saints and sages can awaken to and understand the reason of the former way, its doctrine is limited to the contents of their self-consciousness. It is not a way for the ordinary and ignorant. Those who awaken to their own ignorance and sinfulness and come to believe in the transforming power of the Original Vow can only have recourse to the "easy way" of Other-power, for theirs is a "Faith bestowed by the Tathāgata" and a salvation brought about through the mediation of metanoesis.

In Pure Land doctrine, the "easy way" is accomplished by the mutual transformation of salvation and metanoesis. Like two aspects of one and the same process, it consists in a mutual mediation wherein each collaborates with the other and urges it on to further progress. As religion, this way is naturally more concrete than the way of self-power, which is no more than a philosophical development of the symbolic side of the way of Other-power. That is to say, in the way of Other-power, those who are brought to the grace of salvation through the mediation of metanoesis become self-conscious of the fact that only the self that submits to Other-power and mediates its absolute transformation is resurrected into new life; they affirm the life of the self in its negative mediating role for Other-power as occurring only in the gratitude of action performed on the way of *gensō*; they let go of the self in an act of self-detachment and offer it to Other-power, embracing a life of gratitude and "naturalness" in the "action of no-action." To this extent they are able to accomplish in negative mediation what those who walk the path of self-power seek to accomplish in unmediated fashion.

The enlightenment that develops through the Gate of the Sages is simply an abstract determination, wrought on the general standpoint of reason, of what the Gate of the Pure Land confirms through faith-witness to be the transforming structure of salvation; its description from an idealistic, nonexistential standpoint lacks the mediation of the death-and-resurrection of metanoesis. When this way speaks of nothingness, it is no more than as an *idea* of nothingness. Indeed, existentially considered, it is actually a form of being. By setting up the absolute in opposition to the relative, it is itself made a relative; by excluding the relative completely from the absolute, transcendence turns into immanence. In being degraded into a relative, the absolute becomes no more than an *idea* of the absolute, and as such is but one more relative among other relatives. Action seen as the mutual transformation of the transcendent and the immanent is impossible here: everything is reduced to the realm of the notion. Because the standpoint of reason, on which the absolute-relative relationship is reduced to an opposition, does not require the absoluteness of the absolute to be mediated concretely, it inevitably passes through absolute negation to end up as a standpoint that sees things as individual existences.

Here we see why the Pure Land sect represents the apex of Buddhism's development, and why it is no exaggeration to claim that metanoetics represents a concrete principle for the whole of Buddhist teaching. If indeed there is no other way but metanoetics for such an ignorant person as I, it is only natural that Pure Land Buddhism as the "Gate of Metanoesis" should play a particularly leading role in philosophy. Of course, this is not to say that only Buddhism can have this significance. Quite to the contrary, we have already seen the leading role that metanoetics can have in Western philosophies of religion as well. But as I think I have demonstrated, it is difficult for metanoetics to be carried through as thoroughly in such a context as it can in Pure Land Buddhism. And this is what forms the distinctiveness as well as the limits of Western thought. It is no less a matter of historical fact that I, as an individual trained in Western philosophy, have found meaning in Pure Land Buddhism for breaking my way through those limits. This is where metanoetics has acquired its existential foundations.

Through the legacy of his *Kyōgyōshinshō*, Shinran walks the path of *gensō* and cooperates in the work of Amida's Great Compassion to spur me on in metanoetics, to provide me with disciplined guidance, and to inspire in me a sense of the unbounded breadth and depth of that Great Compassion. He urges me on along the path of "philosophy as metanoetics" in the self-consciousness of metanoetic action-faith. He inspires me to transfer it in turn to others and to communicate my faith-witness to others by walking the way of *gensō* myself. As a philosophy of Other-power, metanoetics begins from the initial mediation of Shinran's return to the world to teach others and opens up into my own conversion and awakening to metanoetics. Conversely, the logic of absolute mediation, which is brought to consummation in philosophy as metanoetics, demonstrates its usefulness for mediating and systematizing the central notion of the *Kyōgyōshinshō* as "thought." Hence one might say that my philosophy is "returned to the world" in an act of gratitude, to serve as a medium for spreading faith in Other-power. In this way, metanoetics becomes a philosophical witness of action-faith in Other-power.

Chapter 8

Metanoetics as a Religious View of Society

Great Nay–qua–Great Compassion as the core of metanoetics · The absolute mediatory nature of absolute Other-power · The mutuality of good and evil · Metanoetics, the manifestation of absolute mediation · Metanoetics and philosophy · Metanoetics as the conclusion of the critique of reason · Metanoetics and Western philosophy compared · The unique place of Kant · Metanoetics and the Kyōgyōshinshō · The historical problematic of contemporary philosophy · The abstractness of culturalism · The place of the mediatory theory of metanoetics vis-à-vis idealism and materialism · Absolute realism and materialism · Material existence and symbolic existence · The meaning of human life: the enjoyment of social reconciliation and cooperation, the satisfaction of love · The unique value of social existence · The ethical and religious views of society of Aristotle and Kant · The notion of the Kingdom of God in Christianity · Hegel's theory of religion · "God is society" contrasted with "God is nature" · The contemporary view of religious society · The religiosity of "closed societies" · Bergson's social theory of religion · The limits of Hegel and his thinking on the relationships between God and the state · The social nature of Buddhism · The notion of solidarity in metanoetics · The social nature of metanoetics · Shin Buddhism's religious view of society · The mediatory nature of theory · The absolute mediating quality of absolute knowledge · Self-consciousness of "empty being" as the mediation of absolute nothingness · The transformation-through-action of the faith-witness of absolute mediation · Nothingness-qua-love in the self-consciousness of nothingness · The absolute gensō of the absolute · The mediatory nature of absolute Other-power · The opposition between relatives and their mutual mediation in the

In the preceding chapters I have attempted to show the vital significance that metanoetics has for ordinary and ignorant people such as I. Unlike the philosophies of sages and saints, which presuppose a standpoint of the infinite and the absolute, metanoetics is thoroughly conscious of its finite and relative limits. Since the critique of reason cannot avoid entangling itself in antinomies, and is finally brought by "absolute critique" to its complete undoing, reason has no choice but to let go of itself and acknowledge its own ineffectiveness. But once reason itself, shattered by antinomies, decides to die in the midst of contradiction, the gate to a "middle way" that is neither thesis nor antithesis opens up unexpectedly, and one is taken up into transcendent nothingness. Transformed into a mediator of an absolute transformation that supersedes the opposition between life and death, one is brought to faith-witness of the Great Compassionate Action (*taihigyō*), which we saw to be the core of metanoetics.

This is why we may speak of self-consciousness of the Great Nay–*qua*–Great Compassion, or of Nothingness–*qua*–Love, as the core of metanoetics. Here the self is resurrected from the death it once died of its own decision and is raised up to a new life beyond life and death, or a "life-in-death." The self is restored to a state of "empty being" as a mediator of absolute nothingness. In our gratitude the self is led to cooperate in a mediating function in the absolute's work of saving other relative beings. It is here that the Great Compassion of the absolute, which revives the relative self by its transcendent power, realizes its quality of absolute mediation: it makes independent relative beings a skillful means (*upāya*) to serve the workings of its own Great Nay, and yet allows them their relative existence as an "other" to serve as mediators of absolute Other-power. Hence we may speak of its quality of "absoluteness–*qua*–absolute *gensō*," in contrast with the return of the relative to other relatives that mediates this return of the absolute (*gensō-ekō*). In this way, the salvation of the self is witnessed in the action of gratitude, which this return to other relative beings represents. It is the action-faith of metanoetics that mediates this witness and through it salvation becomes grounded in the absolute transforming power of *ōsō-ekō*, the way of ascent to the Pure Land on which salvation is acheived. Hence the action of the self enters into a relationship of mutual mediation with the Great Action of the Great Compassion of Other-power.

Logically speaking, absolute Other-power means absolute mediation, which is simply an absolute reciprocity in which all things form a dynamic, transforming unity of opposites in terms of a mutually mediating relationship of *neither/nor*: neither one nor two, neither identity nor difference. This is realized in the innermost self through action-faith, where, under the influence of this absolute transformation, one casts oneself into absolute mediation. This is what metanoetics is. Without this action, we could not be taken up into nothingness to participate in the transforming mediation of the absolute.

If philosophy is thought to attain absolute knowledge only by means of absolute mediation, then metanoetics is just such a philosophy. Only metanoetics considers the absolute as the transcendent ground of a self conscious of the fact that it can never be identified with the absolute, that it is no more than a finite relative mediating the absolute, and that as such it is bound inseparably to the absolute in the form of a "unity-in-opposition." Only metanoetics can bring about a mutual transformation of the absolute and the relative in which the relative transcends itself in an ascent to the absolute and the absolute makes itself immanent in a descent to the relative.

The absolute is essentially nothingness. It cannot be being, because being is relative to nothingness and therefore cannot itself be absolute. Only nothingness can rightly be called absolute, because only nothingness transcends the relativity of being and nothingness as absolute transformation. Being simply fulfills the function of a negative mediating element. But a word of caution: "negative" here does not mean simply that being is to be wiped away without a trace. As a mediating element it is to be preserved, only preserved in a state different from before. The "egoity" (*gashō*) that represents the root of all evil cannot be extinguished so long as the self remains. Its extinction would get rid of good along with evil. Even if the good as absolute good transcends relative good and evil, this does not remove it away to the abstract realms of a holiness free of all inclination to evil. It means rather that under its sway the orientation toward evil is reversed so that evil can be purified and changed into a mediator of good. In this way the good also becomes an absolute good beyond all opposition and discrimination between good and evil. For this reason we must distinguish the relative good that belongs to the realm of ethics from the absolute good that is proper to the realm of religion.

Even though religion does not set up an opposition between evil and absolute good, the egoity that constitutes the root of evil lives on in its very foundations. Hence the words of Shinran referred to in the previous chapter: "without being made to sunder their blind passions, they are brought quickly to the realization of great *nirvāna*." Clearly, even one destined for rebirth in the Pure Land and promised the attainment of *nirvāna* is not able to witness rebirth as such or to enter into *nirvāna* in this life. As long as we are alive, we cannot escape the egoity that limits us. When the *jiriki* Gate of the Sages adopts expressions such as "becoming Buddha immediately in this bodily life" (*sokushin-jōbutsu*), it presupposes the position of the sage or saint who is by nature one with the Buddha, a belief that the *tariki* Gate of the Pure Land does not permit. Ordinary sentient beings lack the self-power to walk this path. The self-conscious despair arising from this deficiency is precisely what we mean by metanoesis. In this sense, metanoesis corresponds to the Other-power faith of the Pure Land.

Given the overwhelming predominance of the self-power path in philosophy, talk of a "philosophy of Other-power" sounds ridiculous at first, if not outright contradictory. Yet, as I have argued in this book, the critique of reason carried through to a radical critique of science drives us ultimately to set up such a starting point for philosophy. Moreover, in the realm of practical reason, the antinomy of radical evil brings the critique of reason face-to-face with the limits of reason and turns evil itself into an absolute good transcending reason. This, too, leads to a philosophy of *tariki* as the only foundation for establishing the Kingdom of God on earth, the only firm basis for history. Critical philosophy ushers in metanoetics because absolute critique is the logical outcome of the critique of reason.

The fact that Kant's philosophy, with its insistent demand for allowing full rein to the autonomy of reason, should lead us to the metanoetics of *tariki* seems strange, but this is the inevitable result of absolute critique. Surely this is a remarkable demonstration of the fruitfulness of Kant's philosophy. Indeed, this is the most significant aspect of his philosophy of religion. The philosophies of Schelling, Hegel, and, in our own time, Heidegger all developed historically out of Kant's philosophy. While each of them may be seen as having developed and carried through one aspect of Kant's thought, it is clear that they have all neglected the religious factor of *tariki* as we find it in Kant. From our viewpoint, they have either forfeited the spirit of critical philosophy or taken the standpoint of sages and intellectuals. This same standpoint of union with the absolute is equally present in Eckhart, Pascal, and Nietzsche. Even though their notions of conversion or transformation have some points in common with the *tariki* philosophy of metanoetics, their deepest inclinations lead in the opposite direction.

When we look further into Western thought to consider such figures as Augustine in ancient times, and Kierkegaard and Barth in modern times, we find that they elevate religious faith above philosophy, putting special stress on the suprarational character of faith. This brings them closer to metanoetics, but their theistic notion of revelation prevents them from arriving at the point of the transformation and mediation of absolute nothingness, such as the conversion and transformation of absolute critique in metanoetics. In this regard we may note the tendency in Barthian theology to effect a complete split between faith and reason and to prefer the *credo quia absurdum* to the *credo ut intelligam*. On the one hand, we have a rejection of philosophy's position of the self-power of reason, and on the other, an absolute acceptance of the truth of Other-power as the object of faith, without any connecting link between the two. This sets their thought off completely from the self-consciousness of action-faith as is realized in the philosophy of *tariki* based on the logic of absolute mediation.

It is for these reasons that I did not find help anywhere in Western thought, aside from Kant, for developing my metanoetics as a philosophy of *tariki*. This is not to say that I have a low esteem of Western philosophy or wish to level criticisms against it. There is no need for philosophy as metanoetics to engage in this sort of thing. On the contrary, as *jiriki* philosophies for sages and intellectuals, those Western systems serve the important function of clarifying the limits of reason to which metanoetics must devote its attention. In a direct and unmediated manner they circumscribe a field into which metanoetics can enter only by way of self-negating transformation, and as such they assume the role of indirectly guiding metanoetics to its fulfillment. I now find that I have every bit as much respect for and attachment to those Western philosophies in which my philosophical thinking was cultivated and nurtured as before. The only difference is this: whereas I had previously taken up the standpoint of wisdom without sufficiently taking into account my own limitations, and consequently landed in a self-contradictory predicament from which I could not escape, the subsequent metanoesis to which this gave rise brought me to a point where, quite against my will, I was converted to the philosophy of *tariki*. It is precisely this standpoint that enables me now to take a new approach to understanding affinities between my present thought and Western philosophy. Since being converted to metanoetics, the aspects of self-power in my own philosophy have been transformed into mediating elements in the philosophy of *tariki*, shedding light in turn on the deeper significance of the philosophy of *jiriki*. The fact that metanoetics allows for such mediation-through-transformation constitutes for me proof of its truth, since the truth of metanoetics can only be witnessed in the action-faith of metanoesis.

In the dialogue with Western philosophy, this metanoetic philosophy of *tariki* leans in a special way on the guidance and instruction provided by Shinran's faith in Other-power. I do not mean by this that Shinran's doctrine merely presents me with problems to be solved in the philosophical tradition of Shin Buddhism. It rather provides an impulse to reorient philosophy itself in the direction of *tariki* and to set up a new goal toward which philosophy can move on its own, carrying on from the illustrious example set by Shinran. In this sense, Shinran is truly the master and the teacher of my philosophy.

Of course, this requires a certain understanding and interpretation of the *Kyōgyōshinshō*. I selected the sections dealing with the explanation of the Three Minds and the *sangantennyū* as the focus of a philosophical interpretation in terms of metanoetics because I consider these two ideas to be pivotal to that work. In doing so, I have discovered for myself that Shinran's faith and thought are metanoetical to the core—indeed, far more profoundly metanoetical than can be understood at a first reading of the *Kyōgyōshinshō*—and lay the foundations for the entire work. The sincere and profound *zange* expressed throughout his principal works, his "confessions and remorseful reminiscences," are like an inner fire bursting into flame, an inner fire that lies always just beneath the text. I am convinced that metanoetics alone provides the key to understanding the *Kyōgyōshinshō*, and that the two permeate each other and derive strength from each other.

Although my interpretation of the *Kyōgyōshinshō* frequently relies heavily on the commentaries of scholars of Shin Buddhism, I fear that my own failures of insight and ignorance of Buddhism in general, and of Shin doctrine in particular, may have led me into error at times. Nevertheless, my conviction that I have found in metanoetics the key to the interpretation of the entire *Kyōgyōshinshō* leads me to believe that I am on the true path that leads to the very marrow of Shinran's doctrine. Furthermore, the logic of absolute mediation, which pervades my interpretation of the *Kyōgyōshinshō*, has rarely been applied to its study before. Provided there are no grave errors in my interpretation, I trust that this may contribute to a deeper understanding of the work. If so, I believe I shall have paid back in some way the debt of gratitude which I feel toward the Great Compassion of Other-power and which was mediated to me under Shinran's guidance and instruction. The help that Shinran's *Kyōgyōshinshō* afforded me at a critical moment when my philosophy had to be converted metanoetically into a *tariki* philosophy is almost too great to be measured. I am also thankful for the grace of Tathāgata's Great Compassion through which Eastern and Western thought, in mutual dependence, seem to be developing in the direction of metanoetics. My own efforts in this line are nothing other than an act of gratitude for that grace.

Philosophy as metanoetics, for reasons of its structure of historicism explained in chapter 3, has necessarily to deal with absolute critique and metanoetic conversion in the field of contemporary science and ethics. I hope also thereby to have given some new direction for the future to the foundations of mathematics and the methodology of physics. But in addition to all of this, we are faced today with the general task of finding a guiding principle of both international and national dimensions. By this I mean some concrete principle that will enable us to overcome the dichotomy of conflicting principles represented by the United States and the Soviet Union. Such a principle should be rooted in the awareness of the historical mission that fate has accorded our own country of Japan. We should not look for it in such abstract principles as "establishment of the state on morality" or "cultural reconstruction." I have to investigate whether, in the philosophical solution of this truly vital and pressing issue, metanoetics actually functions differently from the philosophical methods employed up to now. I wonder whether the same sort of epoch-making significance that Shinran's faith in Other-power came to have in the history of Buddhism as the faith of ignorant and voiceless people of his time might not also exist in philosophy as metanoetics.

The opposition between liberal idealism and socialist materialism has already entered the phase of political struggle. This antinomy of principles confronts us as an urgent problem of the philosophy of history that demands an immediate solution. Is not this the very touchstone of present-day philosophy? In this regard, I must say that I have my doubts about the "culturalism" that characterizes the current philosophical mainstream in our country. More than once I have already pointed out the abstractness and ineffectiveness of this school of thought. And when I see how, at this crucial moment of our national existence, we are looking to such outmoded culturalism as a principle to guide the reconstruction of our nation, I cannot but bewail the lack of seriousness of our philosophers.

As philosophies, culturalism and metanoetics stand diametrically opposed. Basically culturalism is nothing but an artistic hedonism that flatters its proud proponents with an awareness of their own privileged status. This is why it has been able to reach a high-water point in modern capitalistic regimes. For the misled and impoverished proletarian class to follow in their wake and intoxicate themselves with culturalism amounts to suicide. In contrast, existentialism from Nietzsche to Heidegger raises a critical voice against the degeneration of bourgeois society and advocates the heroism of the morally free individual. As such, it takes on the marks of a philosophy of the intelligentsia in much the same way as Zen Buddhism became the religion of the *samurai* class in the medieval period. Here we see grounds for a really serious critique of culturalism based on moral principles. Moral principles have nothing at all to do with culturalism, which may even be said to lack moral principles in the true meaning of the term in the sense that culture does not include the self-negating transcendence that is the special mark of morality; it is a mere affirmation of life, a merely immanent development of the immediate formative power in life of life itself. The only thing the two have in common is the stress they put on individualism.

When we ask further whether, instead of either of these two approaches, socialist materialism with its so-called dictatorship of the proletariat might truly be the philosophy of the people, the many contradictions such materialism contains, as well as the various correctives and compromises that aim at their removal, are sufficient to prove that the answer can hardly be in the affirmative. In particular, when it comes to the obvious opposition between internationalism and nationalism, it is completely impossible to settle such disputes diplomatically through the arbitration of an overriding realism. In order to find a real solution to this problem, a much more concrete logic of social existence is needed. The establishment of an ontology of social existence is the greatest and most urgent task of our times.

To the extent that metanoetics, as an absolute realism, is opposed to idealism, it cannot be said to be opposed to materialism to the same degree that it is opposed to culturalism. Unlike its relation to culturalism, metanoetics has an affinity with materialism insofar as both are basically realistic. Moreover, both have in common a high respect for science as the guiding principle of practice. Science accords the factual content of actual reality priority over the idealistic "ought" of mere reason, continually renewing the latter through the mediation of the former in the attempt to make reason conform to reality. The two are especially close in the sense that both seek not to become slaves of the prevailing "ought" of the status quo but to put the revolutionary idea of freedom into practice in accord with the absolute necessity of historical reality.

At the same time, insofar as the realism of metanoetics is an absolute realism, it differs essentially from the relative realism of materialist socialism. That materialism still contains idealistic tendencies and that socialism is still confused with individualism may be inevitable, given their respective historical development; nevertheless, this shows that the position of materialistic socialism is not altogether pure and consistent in its realism. An absolute realism cannot be satisfied with the sort of relative realism that brings materialism into opposition with idealism. The reality that mediates the historical subject through its action is not matter but "empty being" in the sense of a mediatory existence that absolutely negates it. As a mediator of nothingness, reality can never simply be the immediate or restored existence of matter. On the contrary, it is always mediated by our action and, as a symbol of the subject's reciprocal mediation on the way of *gensō*, becomes absolute reality. It must be something comparable to the symbolic existence that makes up the content of contemporary physics. The human "mind" of idealism and the "thing" of materialism have to be mediated by the "action" of the theory of metanoetic mediation. The relativity of mind and thing gain independence as elements of action mediated by absolute nothingness. The material existence and spiritual meaning of the symbol do not coincide immediately and inseparably here as they do in expression, but are independent by being mutually autonomous. They constitute a symbol by being united relatively through action in the present of individual subjects. Mathematical symbols are simply formulas of experimental practice. Only when we come to theoretical physics with its abstract objectivity can the statistical universality of mathematical probability be established.

But perhaps in speaking this way we shall be attacked for espousing idealism ourselves or trafficking in daydreams and delusions that face us directly away from the fact of nuclear energy as a material entity of alarmingly gigantic power. But nuclear energy is not simply material; it is a subjectified entity mediated experimentally, which means that we can manipulate it and control it by means of the symbolic formulas of theoretical physics. The awesome force of the atomic bomb does not lie in matter but in an absolute reality mediated by human subjects. It is not an immediate natural entity but a technologically fabricated entity, guided by a mere mathematical formula symbolizing experimental activity in the realm of physics.

Materialism is based on presuppositions about nature drawn from classical physics, and its methodology cannot rise above the relativism of pragmatism any more than the idealism of liberalism can. Because it does not assume the standpoint of absolute mediative action such as we find in the new physics of our times, materialism is inadequate as a philosophy for the masses of this new age. What is more, the presence of abstract contradictions and blindness to its own limits in the economics that grounds it as a social science betray how inadequately materialism is mediated by concrete science. The most pressing need that a new philosophy has to meet is to assure its own mediation by new science. And the fact that this new philosophical standpoint is based on the method of dialectical mediation can only lead us to the conclusion that it will conform to the absolute and mediatory realism of metanoetics. As paradoxical as it may sound—or rather, precisely because it is paradoxical— the insistence that the new science opens up into a new religious faith should be accepted as true. Far from excluding or opposing each other, science and religion mediate each other, transforming and permeating each other. If this were not the case, they would not be capable of fulfilling the historical needs of this new era, they could not be the science and religion of a new class suited to carrying out the leading role as subjects of the new era, and they could not issue in a philosophy that mediates the two self-consciously.

In this context it must be remarked that it is not the individualistic hedonism of culturalism or the individualistic austerity of moralism that can give meaning to human existence, but only the joy of a trans-individual unity of mutual reconciliation and instruction at work within the human community of individuals mediating individuals. Pleasure, even the refined enjoyment of artistic beauty, can only end up in tedium; on this point, there are no grounds for preferring artistic pleasures over material ones. Moreover, insofar as pleasure tends to preclude the enjoyment of others and to become the exclusive license of a privileged class, it proves itself completely unworthy of serving as the ultimate goal of humanity. This is why moralism rejects pleasure. But is moralism with all its radical austerity any better suited to provide fullness of meaning to human life? Kant's antinomy of the highest good shows that it is not. The well-known dissatisfaction that Schiller, one of the leading poets of the age, felt toward Kantian ethics offers further indirect proof of how moralism goes against human nature.

All of this leads us to see that a positive and adequate principle of human existence is not to be found in the individualistic standpoint but only in the joy and fulfillment of love in human social existence. Love is a concrete relationship of transforming mediation in which self-negation turns into self-affirmation. Truly, as we remarked earlier, love is nothingness, and at the same time nothingness is love. In the negativity of the Great Nay, love has something in common with moralistic austerity; and in the gratitude and joy of the Great Compassion, it can also partake of the aesthetic enjoyment of culture. Love synthesizes both as aspects of itself and transforms negation into a mediator of affirmation. Hence this synthesis is not a mere compromise but is truly the product of concrete mediation through action. This is where the goal of human being as social being is to be found. Even the "equality" that materialistic socialism sets as its goal becomes concretely meaningful only through the mediation of this love.

The philosophy of metanoetics, which takes its lead from Shinran's *Kyōgyōshinshō*, finds a positive principle here that is not readily seen in any of the systems of Western philosophy. It is a source of great joy to me that this falls in line with the "logic of species" which I have long been advocating and provides it with a religious foundation. Since it seems to me that this is the most comprehensive perspective that the philosophy of metanoetics can offer, I should like to discuss the point in some detail by way of conclusion to this work.

Western philosophy has devoted not a little effort to the quest for those unique and positive values in human social life that are absent in individualized human existence. In ancient times, Plato's ethics sought to concretize justice, one of the virtues of individual existence, through the principle of social duty according to which each individual would make a contribution to the state according to his or her particular position within the state. For Aristotle, friendship, as a principle of human relations that exists apart from the virtues of individuals, performs an integrating function in the state that justice cannot. His idea merits attention in that friendship is not advanced as something connected immediately (*an sich*) with the social quality of human being, but as an independent (*für sich*) principle distinct from the principle of individual existence and transcendent to it.

In modern times, Kant suggested in the third part of his work on religion that since most of our human passions have their source in human coexistence, the permanent subjugation of evil must also presuppose social cooperation. He then went on to advocate the founding of a "Kingdom of God on earth" as a society in which people would be united under the laws of virtue (morality). God was to be looked up to as the legislator of these laws—though not in the sense of state legislators who establish regulations merely from a standpoint of legality—while the church is the society based on the religious recognition of God's command as our moral duty. Here religion is clearly thought to be the principle on which society is constructed.

The idea of the Kingdom of God of course goes back to Judaism, and with Christ was spiritualized to form the core of a new religion. As is well known, Augustine contrasted the City of God with the earthly city and considered the meaning of history to lie in establishing the City of God in this world, a city in which love would be the pivotal mediator of unity and whose aim would be the peaceful coexistence of those who are justified by God's grace. The fundamental principle of Christianity, that God is love, is a social principle. If God's love is not mediated by love of neighbor, and if it is not actualized in interhuman relationships, the existence of God has no witness on earth. To this extent, Christianity may be said to be social by nature. Compared with primitive Buddhism, for example, whose aim was to provide the individual with escape from *saṃsāra*, it is easy to see how early Christianity's gospel of love speaks a social message of an altogether different sort.

Hegel has an important remark in this regard in his *Phenomenology of Mind*. The self-righteous attitude of the "beautiful soul," so absolutely confident and sure of itself as to exclude all others, emerges as a one-dimensional phase in the development of the moral worldview. For Hegel, this attitude needs to be converted into one of reconciliation and mutual forgiveness in order for the mind to ascend to the level of religion. Even though his conclusion clearly betrays the fundamental inspiration of Christianity, it is exceedingly important as an expression of the social nature of religion. Still, it seems to me that the mutual tolerance and respect which he considers to be the driving force of reconciliation are superficial and negative, and furthermore, that his standpoint did not succeed in providing a solid basis for a society that promotes the salvation of its members in a positive sense, a society where the more developed guide the less developed. In other words, the weakness of Hegel's approach lies in this, that he did not present *salvation* as the positive principle of social construction, that he did not bring mediation to the concrete level of sociality.

From the standpoint of the logic of absolute mediation, Hegel's failure to bring mediation to the point of what Shin Buddhist doctrine calls the way of *gensō* points to a lack of thoroughness. If metanoetics had developed only under the tutelage of Western philosophy, its social ideal should hardly have moved beyond Hegel's mutual respect and reconciliation. At the same time, it is to his credit that, in his effort to pursue the reality of mind in a thoroughly logical and *für sich* manner, Hegel was moved by the fundamental spirit of Christianity to elevate the psychological and *an sich* sociality of Aristotle and Kant from the level of politics and ethics to that of religion, and to describe absolute mind, the subject of religion, in terms of mutual respect.

The idea that God is society, eccentric though it may seem at first, has its basis here. This idea opens up a new field of religious inquiry that contrasts with the religious view that God is nature. Indeed, Hegel's idea of reconciliation through the love of God renders the goal of Augustine's City of God more concrete by giving it an emotional tone. Hegel's idea of a religious society in which Christianity's gospel of love is systematized through a logic of mediation makes his view of religion an extremely important one. In Kant's teleology, as well as in Schleiermacher's theory of religion, the prevalent theme is surely the nonevangelical and unorthodox idea that God is nature. Such a tendency, it should be noted, brings religion perilously close to art and runs the risk of refracting our gaze from the essence of religion. This is no doubt why certain representatives of the "theology of crisis" concentrate their attacks on Schleiermacher. Kant's theory of religion transcended the theology of teleological nature and penetrated deeply into the problem of evil, forsaking the view of God as nature in order to arrive at a standpoint of negation and mediation. In spite of that, he did not develop this thought fully enough to bring the *für sich* dimension into his social conception of religion. He goes no further than the standpoint of the individual personality, leaving him stranded halfway between the view that God is nature and the view that God is society—in a position that seems to say that God is personality. As a result, his view of the church is psychological-anthropological. That Hegel's conception of religion went further to achieve a new social standpoint is a matter of epoch-making significance.

Of late, sociologists of religion belonging to the Durkheimian school have been investigating the religious life of primitive peoples, demonstrating the intimate connections between primitive religion and the structure of primitive society itself. These scholars have further shown how the supernatural forces that are seen as the fundamental elements of human life and believed to be the source of life are manifest in the forces that control a society and function as principles of its social structure, and therefore how it is these latter that constitute the object of religious worship. This gives positive corroboration and clear expression to the idea that God is society.

As is well known, Bergson makes use of the work of the Durkheimian school to set up a contrast between the primitive religion of "closed societies" and the mysticism of love of an "open society" which he presents as the purest form of religion, thus arguing for two sources of morality and religion. While Bergson's views need to be seen as a further development of the social view of religion, it is hard to see how the unmediated intuition of mysticism and the mutual love and service of all people that is supposed to result simply by dispensing with the borders of a closed society—a society of "species"—would actually bring society to a *für sich* state that would provide it with a principle of spiritual deliverance. It fails to give sufficient attention to the reality of radical evil that is always latent in the individuation of personality and works contrary to the spirit of love. On such a view, it is unavoidable that the "egoity" that is the principle of evil and the "egolessness" that is the principle of love are opposed to each other without mediation, the one conceived as the direct negation of the other so that individuality seeped in selfishness is dissolved in the universality of a selfless love. This is where Bergson's version of monism leads us with its nondialectical mysticism and unmediated intuitionism that sees religion only in terms of the way of *ōsō*, only as a fusing of the finite with the infinite.

Even though this is called a "social" view of religion, because it lacks the mediation of negation resulting from the consciousness of evil in personalistic religion, it cannot avoid the tendency to flow over into a "natural" view of religion. At the *an sich* level, it may be social; at the *für sich* level, it is not. This brings us back again to Hegel's unique contribution: by struggling to preserve the mediation of personalistic religion, he made sociality the principle of religion in *für sich* terms. In that sense, we may rightly credit him with inaugurating a new age in the philosophy of religion. Still, his treatment of absolute spirit as mutual respect amounts to nothing more than a direct extension of the Christian ideal of love of neighbor, unmediated by the national determinations of objective spirit. Unavoidably, momentous issues in the philosophy of history, such as the rivalry between the earthly kingdom and the eternal peace of the Kingdom of God that we find in Augustine's *City of God* came to be dissolved by his rationalism into a facile optimism. In the process, the radicality of evil passed by unnoticed. For despite the fact that evil appears in the formation of the individual, Hegel forgets that the absoluteness and totality that egoity tries to usurp as its own are no more than unmediated relative claims entangled in the oppositions and struggles peculiar to the "species." Thus instead of the national determination of objective spirit being considered as the negative mediator of the Kingdom of God, nations are subsumed under the Kingdom of God, much the same as species is subsumed under genus in formal logic.

The reality of the nation does not begin and end simply with objective spirit. As objective spirit, a people are mediated by the absolute spirit and endowed with the status of "God on earth," which leads to a contradiction with religion, the self-consciousness of absolute spirit. The same can be said of the estrangement between world history, which has national peoples as its subject, and the religious ideal of the Kingdom of God. In more formal terms, what we have here is a contradiction between the relative historical determinations of the species and the absolute unity of the universal. It falls to each individual's action-faith to solve this contradiction, in the eternal now, by initiating a circular mediation among individual, species, and universal. And it is not just a conceptual solution worked out in reason that is called for, but a coordination of the universal and the particular through the mediation of absolute nothingness in action, a conversion of nothingness to manifest being and a conversion of being to the emptiness of nothingness.

If Hegel's logic had consummated its commitment to absolute mediation, it would have come to this point. Instead, Hegel clung to an ontological mediation of absolute spirit. This was probably unavoidable, given the Christian theism under whose inspiration he developed his thought. But this ensnarled his philosophy in difficulties when it came to elucidating the relationship between state and religion, landing it in a serious contradiction. Because of the extraordinary significance of Hegel's social view of religion as precursor of a new standpoint, it is all the more regrettable that he limited it to the abstract *ōsō* understanding of reconciliation through mutual respect and did not develop it into the more concrete *gensō* understanding of positive mutual instruction. Hegel's view diluted the gravity of the Kantian conception of evil based on personalism and returned it to the rationalistic standpoint of identity. In so doing, he neglected the transformation in action of absolute mediation and left no room for metanoetics to develop. Against the attacks of Schelling and Kierkegaard in this regard he stands defenseless.

Buddhism, which began simply as an intellectual doctrine about the human condition aimed at delivering the individual from the cycle of birth and death, moved beyond primitive Buddhism's standpoint of solitary enlightenment to a communitarian approach according to which the Dharma is transmitted from master to disciple. A parallel evolution took place on the doctrinal level. With the development of the bodhisattva-ideal in the Mahāyāna tradition, Buddhism developed the ideal of "benefiting oneself–*qua*–benefiting others." This evolution culminates in the Shin doctrine of *gensō*. Strange as it may seem, this process is but the natural unfolding of the essential Buddhist teaching of *muga*—that there is no self or ego in all of reality—which is the principle of absolute nothingness. This paradox is the very hallmark of Buddhist truth. Under the guidance of Shinran's attitude of total *zange*, metanoetics is thus able to develop a social doctrine inaccessible by way of Western philosophy alone. I have tried to touch on this as one of the promising aspects of metanoetics.

Logic begins in syllogism; in other words, mediation is the essence of logic. As absolute knowledge, philosophy takes absolute mediation as its logic. Basically, absolute knowledge means a wisdom that knows the absolute. If this were understood in the sense of making the absolute an object of one's knowing, all knowledge of the absolute would have to remain relative, and there could be no attaining to absolute knowledge. Absolute knowledge can only mean that knowledge as such belongs to the absolute, that it is the self-consciousness of the absolute. That on the one hand. On the other, philosophy is something that takes place in us relative beings, so that if absolute knowledge is limited to the self-consciousness of an absolute apart from us, it has to be relative as something opposed to our consciousness. Hence absolute knowledge must be the self-consciousness of the absolute and at the same time our knowledge. And if it is not to be knowledge of an absolute that stands opposed to us, the self-consciousness of the absolute must at the same time signify our self-consciousness.

How is this possible? The absolute, because it is self-consciousness, makes use of the self-consciousness of us relative beings, who are other than the absolute, as its mediation. Thus our relative knowledge is forced to a limit at which relative being confronts antinomies that it cannot, because of its relativity, escape and there negates itself, obediently merging with the absolute as its other. Conversely, this is the very conversion that takes place when the relative is taken into the absolute as its mediation and is affirmed in being negated. The Great Nay of absolute critique turns into an affirmation at the outermost limit of its negation, and resurrects the relative that had died behind the negation to serve as a mediator of the absolute without ceasing to be relative, affirming it as "empty being" that has passed beyond life and death or that has life in its very death. This Great Nay witnesses to the Great Compassion of affirmation and resurrection, and out of this witness emerges metanoetics as the absolute transformation of the Great Nay–*qua*–Great Compassion. This is what accounts for the possibility of absolute knowledge in philosophy.

This is why I have chosen metanoetics as my philosophical method. But since this transformation is action, its faith-witness can be attained only by practicing it oneself. The self-consciousness of action witnesses to the fact that the negation of self and reliance on the absolute as other is also a process of mediation in which the self is affirmed as "empty being." Since this transformation in action is a manifestation of nothingness, it cannot be intuited as self-identical being. Indeed, as the contradictory unity of an antinomy, it is something that can be realized only through a transformation in action. This self-consciousness is not the awareness of a self-identical reality, then, but an awareness of a transcendent conversion occurring in the nothingness of self-consciousness. It is not that self-consciousness arises because there is a self; rather, the self is conscious of itself as a unity because the absolute nothingness that lies at the ground of the process of change represents a transcendent unity mediating the transformation of the self in nothingness. Through this self-consciousness there comes about the "empty being" of the self which has nothing to do with either being or nothingness. The unity of this transformation brings about the "empty being" of the self as its resurrected existence: though nothingness, it is yet being, and though being, it moves back and forth through nothingness; like a flickering star, its extinction is its appearance and its appearance extinction. The self-consciousness of action signifies the faith-witness of this absolute transformation. Metanoetics comes about in this action-faith-

272 METANOETICS AS A RELIGIOUS VIEW OF SOCIETY

witness. It is simply the direct expression of absolute mediation in the self.

As I have noted many times already, the absolute must be absolute nothingness. Being, even though it be called absolute being, is self-identical and therefore must dissolve and absorb the relative within itself without being able to grant it independent status; instead of exhibiting its own absoluteness through the mediation of relative being, it relegates the relative to the darkness of nothingness. Or again, were absolute being to permit the independence of the relative, it would lose its character of absoluteness because of this opposition to the relative. Being cannot but fall into one or the other of these contradictions. Aside from nothingness, there is nothing that can truly be called absolute.

Nothingness cannot, however, exist directly, for anything that exists directly belongs to being. Nothingness must manifest itself in the mediation of negative transformation. Of course, since nothingness is the principle of negation, nothingness in itself must precede negation. A nothingness that exists previously without being realized mediatively in negation would already be being and not nothingness. Nothingness does not allow itself to be treated ontologically. It is simply brought to faith-witness in action. Only a faith-witness in which negative transformation acts and is acted upon can bring about self-consciousness of nothingness. Insofar as nothingness is the transcendent ground of that action-faith, it is made self-conscious in accord with the self-witness in which the immanent self is negated and transformed. Hence we are obliged to conclude that as far as we are concerned, this self-witness is prior to the self-consciousness of nothingness.

Aristotle's paratactic distinction between what is prior by nature (πρότερον τῇ φύσει) and what is prior for us (πρότεπον πρὸς ἡμᾶς) is typical of ontology and at the same time displays the limits of that standpoint. In setting the two up as opposites, ontology betrays its own imperfection as a system of identity since it still contains contradiction and opposition. Only the self-consciousness of action can transform this opposition and bring it to a unity where the two types of priority are transformed into each other without either being determined as absolutely prior. For the two are united mediatively, and it is action that makes this mediation actual. In mediation, priority is accorded neither side; rather, each is transformed into the other and penetrates the other in a reciprocal and circular manner. Mediation is not a relationship in which one party is subordinated to the other, but one in which both enjoy and maintain an independence made possible by the other. There is no question here of a causal connection that would make one party subordinate to the other as its effect. Mediation is always and only a matter of a reciprocal relationship of independent participants, albeit one in which the independence of the one relies on the independence of the other. Unlike a cause-effect relationship, it cannot be understood in terms of the logic of identity in that it is simply a unity of contradictories in which the affirmation of independence is made possible only through the negation of dependence, and in which the self-negation of dependence is made possible only through the affirmation of independence. This is why mediation is the core of dialectics and why absolute mediation constitutes the logic of absolute knowledge. It obliges us to the conclusion that absolute nothingness becomes self-consciousness only in the mediatory unity of action.

If we grant, then, that the absolute is nothingness and that this nothingness is something that can be believed in and witnessed to only in a process of mediation consisting of transformation through action, the absolute must be something that of necessity makes the relative its mediator. Far from functioning in an unrestricted manner, therefore, the absolute makes room for the independence of relative being, and to that extent imposes a restriction on its own determinative functioning, and through this self-negation functions affirmatively.

Of course, this restriction is not imposed from outside. The absolute as absolute retains its original absolute spontaneity throughout. Restriction can refer only to a self-negation that the absolute freely imposes upon itself. At the same time, the absolute is truly absolute only when, through self-negation, it makes room for the independence of relative beings, permitting them to function as its mediators. This is why the absolute is nothingness. As the reality that realizes its own character of absolute nothingness in mediation with relative beings, it is a principle that, of its own accord, provides a basis for the independent existence of relative beings. And this is nothing other than love.

Love must be selfless. In other words, love is nothingness. And at the same time, nothingness is love. Or again, it is the Great Nay–*qua*–Great Compassion. It is absolute mediation in its self-consciousness and concreteness. And this is why it is the center of metanoetics, the philosophy of *tariki* that gives logical structure to the core of *tariki* faith.

To express the same thing in symbolic terms: Tathāgata, who is the absolute, does not rest peacefully on some distant summit of absolute perfection, but is forever on a journey of descent to relative beings below. Tathāgata is not poised sedately within the inner sanctum of his home, but is ever ready to set off, at the first sign of alarm, to save relative beings. Tathāgata cannot exercise his absoluteness apart from this descent to save relative sentient beings. It is for this reason that the essence of Tathāgata is taken to be absolute *gensō*. Meanwhile, as the subject of absolute mediation, Tathāgata makes room for the independence of relative beings, thereby restricting his own work in an act of self-negation in order to collaborate with the spontaneity of relative sentient beings as his mediators. Thus he instructs all sentient beings by providing an example of action which sentient beings can learn from him and imitate. This is his salvific work, aimed at elevating all sentient beings and directing them into the realm of the Buddha.

In fact, as I shall explain later, the absolute *gensō* performed by the bodhisattva Dharmākara is embodied in the relative *gensō* of the relationship between relative beings in which the more advanced on the way of *ōsō* guide the less advanced, quite apart from the order of seniority that would characterize them as members of a society of "species." The work of the absolute Tathāgata begins as a work of mediation between one relative being and another. To simplify this twofold relative mediation for a moment and treat it as one, the meaning of the doctrine comes down to this: Amida Buddha, as Dharmākara, performs absolute *gensō* as the more advanced who provides a model of the action that less advanced sentient beings must perform to be saved, and he does so at the stage of Dharmākara—that is, prior to his enlightenment or while he is at the stage of disciplined preparation for enlightenment (*inni*). All sentient beings who enter upon the path of salvation are promised Buddhahood and participation in *nirvāna* if they take the discipline of Dharmākara as their guide and model, and of their own accord make their action conform to his through absolute negation. This is *ōsō-ekō*, merit-transference on the way toward the Pure Land. It is understood to mean that, mediated by the absolute *gensō* of Tathāgata, stimulated and supported by his transforming power, one offers up one's self-power to mediate the Great Action of Tathāgata.

By placing too much emphasis here on Other-power, we end up in the usual position of claiming that whatever action sentient beings perform is done *qua* the Great Action of Tathāgata. But this "*qua*" refers to mediation, not to a mere causal relationship. If this latter were the case, we would be forced to conclude that the Great Action is itself the action of Tathāgata, or at least its effect, so that the meaning of action by sentient beings would be completely lost. By the same token, persistence in this position lands us in a sort of mysticism that places the action of the Tathāgata and the action of sentient beings in a relationship of contradictory self-identity. Obviously neither of these solutions is suited to the spirit of metanoetical transformation. In my view, Shinran's *zange* has nothing at all to do with such ideas, but is rather concerned with absolute mediation. The rather detailed explanation of the theory of the Three Minds presented in the foregoing chapter bears this out.

At the same time, it is clear that in making *jiriki* a mediator of *tariki*, salvation is not achievable by *jiriki* alone without *tariki*. If this were so, it would be self-power deliverance and not Other-power salvation. In speaking of *tariki* salvation, we have necessarily to presuppose the power of an absolute "other" as the basis of salvation. This absolute does not act directly, however, but in every case requires its "other," namely relative beings, for mediation. This is the meaning of absolute Other-power, and it is only in this sense that we can claim that the absolute is not being but nothingness. To opt for the idea of an unmediated absolute urging and upholding *jiriki* directly is truly to forfeit the meaning of "absolute." The absolute cannot be understood as such a self-identical substance, but must always be interpreted in terms of negative mediation in nothingness. It is able to be absolute because in making *jiriki* its mediator and leaving room for its spontaneity, it works in a self-negating manner.

The relative, which is saved through the mediation of absolute *tariki* in the sense that its *jiriki* mediates *tariki*, makes the absolute something mediated. Simply put in these terms, the relative looks to be on a level with the absolute and to lose its proper significance as a relative. If the relative has only the absolute as its "other" and does not also confront other relative beings in the same way, there is no way to distinguish it as relative being from the absolute, or absolute unity, that transcends all oppositions.

Thus *jiriki*, the mediator of absolute *tariki*, enters into salvation through the mediation of *tariki* and is transformed into "empty being" as the mediator of absolute nothingness (the way of *ōsō*); and at the same time, it serves an additional mediatory function for the absolute's salvation of other relative beings, who stand opposed as relative beings, and must therefore collaborate with the absolute (the way of *gensō*). As that which mediates this *gensō* relationship among relative beings, the absolute *gensō* of the absolute makes its meaning apparent: in order to save relative beings on the way of *ōsō*, the absolute gives relative beings a model for action in the form of the discipline and action of Dharmākara, the symbol of absolute *gensō*. And at the same time, the action of the relative itself, undertaken in imitation of the absolute and under its guidance, becomes a mediator of the action performed by the absolute for the salvation of other relative beings.

Only in this way can the work of the absolute always imply the use of the relative as a mediator; only in this way can the absolute avoid falling into the contradiction of working directly, which would make it being and not nothingness. In other words, the salvific work of the absolute toward relative beings is performed in two ways and uses relative beings as its mediators in two ways: first, as the relative being that is the object of the salvific work of the absolute; and second, as the relative being more advanced than other relative beings.

So far I have spoken about the absolute's opposition to and collaboration with the relative as a single relationship in order to deal with it abstractly and in analytical terms. In actuality, the absolute makes the relative its mediator in the two senses just mentioned—in the relationship it sets up between itself and the relative, and in the relationship it sets up between one relative being and another. This twofold relationship accounts for the *gensō* of the absolute serving as the basis for the *gensō* of the relative. The relative that provides a model of action for less advanced relatives who are the objects of salvation is not itself the absolute, but simply a more advanced relative being engaged in *gensō* in a relative sense, as a mediator of the absolute. Both relative beings in this case are mediated in terms of a mutual opposition located within the "species" they share in common. Hence the absolute is nothing but the absolute mediation at work in the mutual relationships between relatives. Essentially, what is relative is relative because it confronts another relative. Without this mutuality, its distinction from and opposition to the absolute would vanish. Nevertheless, the mutual relationship between relative beings is possible only because they are mediated by the absolute.

The relationship between the relative beings who are the object of salvation and the relative beings who are collaborating in the work of salvation is mediated by the *gensō* of the more advanced, who provides guidance and instruction to the less advanced, so that after the former have been saved on the way of *ōsō*, they may in turn follow the way of *gensō* to guide and instruct those less advanced than they. The order of more or less here is maintained in a manner similar to that between elder and younger siblings. Unlike Aristotle's idea of friendship and the Christian ideal of love, which are based exclusively on equality, this relationship is based on the twofold dynamic of *ōsō* and *gensō*—an extremely odd but concrete idea. At the same time, just as the brothers and sisters who maintain an order of seniority among themselves maintain their equality as children of the same parents, relative beings are of a kind and equal to one another vis-à-vis the absolute.

The eternity of the present is disclosed in the mutual mediation of the past and the future wherein each reverses direction to conform to the other and to form a reciprocity. In the same sense, ōsō and gensō display not only a rigid order of priority but also a reciprocal relation in which the truth of the former is made manifest in the latter, and the comparative stage of "advancement" between relative beings shows a circularity in which their relationship can be inverted. This is the concrete aspect of absolute mediation. From this point of view, the relationships of equality and reciprocity between relative beings are the same as they are between siblings, displaying the essential structure of mediation by the absolute. If the prescribed order were final and immovable, absolute mediation would be utterly impossible. Hence the circularity of absolute gensō comes into existence in virtue of the fact that both ōsō and gensō, while establishing an order of priority on the one hand, are equal and reciprocal on the other.

Because of this reciprocal equality, absolute gensō takes on the quality of transcendence in mediating the transformation of relative beings and is thus absolute vis-à-vis relative beings. At first glance it would seem as if this reciprocal activity were something uniting the opposing directions of the cause-and-effect relationship. In fact it creates a kind of unity that not only cannot be reduced to talk of causality, but transcends it to form an equality at a transcendent location that enables the transformation to occur freely in both directions. This transcendent "location" (bamen) cannot be intuited apart from actual transformation in the way that "locus" (basho)[1] can. It becomes self-conscious only in the action of actual conversion and transformation. Just as there is no reciprocal transformation in intuition that does not belong to a causal relationship, the equal reciprocity of relatives does not become self-conscious except through the action of transformation according to the order of priority. Without it, nothing at all, even apart from this equality, could become self-conscious.

The equality of siblings is always realized in the order of priority, but this order is not fixed and can be inverted so that the position of the more advanced who instructs and guides one less advanced necessarily comes to imply that the former has also to learn from the latter. Hence the saying, "To teach is to learn." This does not mean that the more advanced becomes inferior to the less or that an elder brother turns into a younger brother. From the standpoint of absolute mediation, all are equal because all are reciprocally transforming yet maintain their order of priority throughout.

It is much the same in the case of time treated earlier, where past and future preserve their sequential order rigidly, and yet are converted into each other and become equals in the present. In the present these two phases of time are mediated by eternity, which transcends time and thereby makes manifest a spatial simultaneity that accords with the dynamic evolution of time, thus bringing about the temporal-spatial evolutionary unity of the world. Relations between siblings, which are not simply a matter either of elder and younger or of simple equality, seem to be a concrete expression of the historical structure of the world.

In this regard I would argue that the three ideas that form the slogan of the French revolution, *liberté*, *égalité*, and *fraternité*, are not independent but mutually mediating notions. Left on its own, freedom ends up in inequality. There can be no doubt that democracy and liberalism are producing the inequality of today's capitalistic societies. Socialism, meanwhile, sets up equality as its goal, but there is no disputing the fact that the socialist system invariably limits freedom and in that sense negates it. Freedom and equality are not concepts that can easily be linked together into a formal identity, but are contradictory concepts that oppose each other. The only thing that can unify them is the transforming action of those who make up the membership of a society, but this is no easy task. The standard for such unification would seem to be a kind of fraternity that retains the literal meaning of "brotherhood." It is conceivable that the social order that freedom provides can be preserved in this way and at the same time the demand for equality be realized, thus disclosing a concrete unity that would actually synthesize the two.

Ordinarily when we speak of fraternity, the emphasis is put on equality, as is the case with brotherly love, and this makes it hard to distinguish it clearly from friendship. But if we insist on the true meaning of brotherhood, priority joins equality as an essential element, or rather as *the* main aspect of fraternity. In the case of brothers, the guidance that the elder brother gives the younger affects the latter's entire personality; it is literally a learning and an imitation. The instruction that goes on between them can be compared to that of the master-disciple relationship. As Kierkegaard has remarked, a true master exists only in religion. In other words, there is no absolute master who does not allow for equality except for the absolute as such, as is the case when God—or Christ—is said to be the master. As relative beings, teachers, however eminent they be, retain an aspect of equality with their disciples as fellow travelers. The fact that the absolute *gensō* of Amida Buddha takes as its mediator the discipline and practice of Dharmākara means that the absolute humbles and restrains itself to take on relativity for the sake of mediating the way for relative beings. This is the Great Compassion of Other-power.

It has been pointed out as a defect of modern education that the element of "personal imitation" has been replaced by an external system of imparting and receiving knowledge and a formalistic moral guidance, with the result that the sort of master-disciple relationship that molds the entire personality has fallen by the wayside. Might not this be amended by a revival of "fraternal" guidance? The element of equality is relatively weak in the master-disciple relation and requires a specialized system of education to come to the fore. In this regard, we might look on brotherhood as the relationship that combines concretely a fully personal relationship of trust and imitation similar to that between master and disciple with a relationship of equality. As such, it is able to spread to all members of society and embrace a variety of social differences.

When one stops to consider how religious communities (for example, Roman Catholic communities) still use the title of Brother or Sister, one cannot but see the special importance that the idea of brotherhood has in religion. We may wonder whether nowadays these amount to anything more than formal titles that have lost their spiritual significance, but it seems to me that the notion of *gensō* can offer a principle of fraternal instruction through which meaning can be infused into brotherhood to forge a new social ideal. In other words, people should be bound together by a brotherhood (fraternity) that synthesizes the freedom of capitalistic society and the equality of the socialistic state. The ethics of the masses might then be said to consist in a "way of brotherhood" and their faith to consist in a "Dharma Gate of Brotherhood."

The theme of justice that Plato focused on in his *Republic* is developed by combining the way of brotherhood with the division of labor in society. In Zen temples, the custom has arisen of greeting one another as a brother or sister, and there is ample testimony in Zen literature of masters who addressed their disciples in like manner. In Zen, where special importance is attached to personal direction and trust, the master-disciple relationship is developed into a concrete relation of brotherhood, and equality is brought to the fore. Shinran, for his part, consistently rejected the master-disciple relationship, treating the faithful as fellow pilgrims. Contrasted with the hierarchical system that prevails in the other Buddhist sects or in the Roman Catholic church, it must be admitted that these two traditions contain a profound inner significance.

Be that as it may, along with revolutions in the social system it is necessary to develop and restore brotherly relations. Again I would stress that the idea of *gensō* is of the utmost importance as the basic principle in brotherly relations. It is particularly worth noting how the bodhisattva-ideal of Mahāyāna Buddhism harmonized deliverance and instruction into the idea of "benefit to oneself"–*qua*–"benefit to others." Furthermore, starting from the social sense implied in the "mutual correspondence among Buddhas" (*Butsubutsu-koō-sōshō*), Mahāyāna Buddhism advanced to the idea that the content of the most basic truths is fulfilled in sociality, expressed in the Lotus Sutra's statement that "only a Buddha and a Buddha can exhaust their reality."[2] Finally, by means of the concept of *gensō* this social sense is now elevated to the status of an important aspect of Buddhist doctrine itself.

Truly remarkable is the way that Mahāyāna Buddhism took up this idea of the relation of discipleship and went beyond the idea of equality common to many religions to provide a principle of order. Before the absolute, differences among relative beings in ability, natural talent, and social status, are all reduced to naught and replaced with a horizontal equality. That the notion of equality should be universal in religion is natural and easily explained. But that the order of priority in attaining deliverance imposes an order on the social life of a religious sect, and that the transmission of truth from master to disciple is regarded as important, are especially characteristic of Buddhism. The bodhisattva path is no doubt a distinctive feature of Mahāyāna Buddhism, but it merits note that in Shin Buddhism it is given a grounding in doctrine.

This idea of an order based on brotherhood is one of the primary inspirations of metanoetics, which takes its universal significance from the notion of joint social responsibility. Apart from this idea of solidarity, metanoesis would be a phenomenon proper only to guilt-ridden and sentimental minds, and not something able to direct human life in a broad and consistent manner. It would be no more than a particular form of behavior and state of mind appearing only under special circumstances, and would not possess the universal significance required of a philosophical starting point. Philosophy as metanoetics would become so much bombast. If, however, one reflects from a standpoint of social solidarity on how difficult it is to accept responsibility for the totality of social evils, how easily we flee from the very thought of it, and how difficult it is to sustain a sensitivity to the need for social reform and to exert one's best efforts in that direction, then, as Kierkegaard points out, metanoesis and repentance become universal notions that distinguish ethics in general.

My conviction that metanoetics can pave the way for a new philosophy is based on such a notion of solidarity and is essentially social in motivation. But without the influence of the Shin doctrine of Other-power, metanoetics would not have been led to the idea of a social order of guidance and instruction on the way of *genso*. Thus it bears special mention that what metanoetics, as a philosophy of Other-power, has learned from the teachings of Shin Buddhism belongs to its very essence. The fact that I am devoted to the Shin idea of *genso* is not due merely to my appreciation of the kind of social brotherhood through ordered discipline explained above. The idea of a communality in "species" mediating this *genso* also filled the need for a theory of social existence based on the "logic of species" (*shu no ronri*) that I had developed and announced previously. In my view it provides such a theory with a religious footing and enables us to correlate the findings of recent investigations on the religiosity of primitive societies with the faith of Shin Buddhism as a world religion.

My logic of species did not limit itself to the problem of social structure in general, but developed into a logic of the state. I believe that it constitutes an improvement on Hegel's philosophy of the state by carrying the logic of absolute mediation through to completion. I am therefore convinced that it enables us to avoid the difficulties that arise in Hegel's system with regard to the relationship between the state and religion. Moreover, it is my hope that it may shed new light on the problem of the essence of the state—a problem that today stands in urgent need of solution—and that, in the current face-off between democracy and Marxist socialism touched on earlier, it may offer a middle way from a standpoint that transcends them both. I cannot but think that this problem, too, needs to be resolved metanoetically through the logic of absolute critique.

I say this not in order to delude myself into thinking that my imperfectly developed logic of national existence will make it possible to solve all current difficulties related to the state. I mean only that because logic implies mediation, I am convinced that it should not be impossible, with the aid of the thoroughgoing approach to mediation presented in the logic of absolute mediation, at least to point ourselves in the direction of a solution. Naturally more work will have to be done to develop such a logic of the state and carry it further along its way, but I am happy and grateful for the thought that I may have provided the right initial bearings. And here it gives me a special sense of satisfaction to know that the idea of *gensō* offers confirmation from a religious standpoint. This is why, under the guidance of Shin Buddhist doctrine, I would like to draw attention to social existence as an important orientation for the Other-power philosophy of metanoetics to pursue, and why I wish to make it the concluding topic of this work.

It is only natural that the "logic of species" that I came to as a result of what I myself have suffered in connection with the current position that we the people occupy in the state will not readily be understood by those who have not known the same suffering. Since introducing the question, the term "species" (*shu*) has been adopted for a wide variety of uses. For example, proponents of culturalism have maintained that the reason that human culture displays the peculiarity of differing from one people to another is simply that each possesses a "specific" pattern for giving expression to human living. But this use of the term gives it an altogether different conceptual content from what I intended. By limiting itself to a classification of genus-species-individual according to the logic of identity, the term "species" is reduced to the realm of the "particular" that occupies a place midway between the universality of the genus and the singularity of the individual. Even if such a viewpoint can point to the social environment that determines our existence as individuals, it cannot relate to the power of the state that can threaten that existence and deprive us of our lives. If our life controls its surrounding environment, freely altering it and shaping it into its own expression, then the environment is something that can be assimilated into our life. This seems to be the sense of the motto "from the made to the making."[3] But it is precisely this transformation "from ... to ..." that is the crux on which the life of political praxis hangs, and in whose simplistic expression we see the characteristic feature of a culturalism as a life-affirming and aesthetic standpoint. Accordingly, awareness of those realities that call forth the political and ethical responsibility of the individual to resist the controlling power of the state as expressed in laws and customs, even at the cost of position and life, is missing here. Missing, too, is the consciousness that one arrives finally at metanoetic transformation only after concerted reflection on the forms that moral evil can take: for example, in complying opportunistically with what the state requires, one may fail in awareness of joint responsibility, while in rejecting the demands of the state, one may be guilty of ambition and egoity.

It is no surprise, then, that the proponents of culturalism are completely oblivious to the crucial negative significance of "species" as an attribution pregnant with this crisis of social existence. When on occasion they use the words "species" or "activity," they do not treat them as social elements with a political meaning, nor do they refer to action in crisis. Instead, they simply limit the terms to what culturalism can develop by way of artistic production, remaining at the level of a culturalism that begins and ends with "life" and its "expression." It is not unlike the category of spirit that constitutes the subjective existence of the spirit in Plotinus referred to earlier. Completely distinct from Aristotle's category of substance, which is a category of being based on the principle of identity, Plotinus's category of spirit was intended to arise out of the subjective self-consciousness of an active unity of nothingness, and to be understood as an extension and expansion of the position of Aristotle. Instead of actually producing such a standpoint of the active unity of nothingness, Plotinus deviated from Plato's later philosophy and misunderstood his dialectic, combining it with an Aristotelian logic of identity, thereby lapsing into mysticism and diluting his spiritual standpoint. For spirit or mind is not something to be contemplated, but something to be brought to faith-witness in action. If it could be contemplated, the transcendence of the One would become immanent in the intellect and, thus reduced to the level of an abstract infinite, would lose its quality as a concrete unity resulting from the practical transformation of nothingness. As a result, the standpoint of authentic action, which transcends being and nonbeing and is related to neither, would become the mere enjoyment of serenely basking in the abundance of being.

Eckhart, who is thought to have been deeply influenced by Plotinus and to have grasped his spirit well, nevertheless valued the praxis of Martha more highly than the contemplation of Mary. I find this in harmony with the spirit, if not the letter, of the Gospel and of great religious importance. Regrettably, the culturalism of artistic production and the standpoint of "life and its expression" usurp the role of religion and do away with it. For it results in a situation where ethical praxis— including, of course, political praxis—vanishes into contemplation. Religion then becomes indeed an opiate of the people. The sage and the intellectual may be able to abide serenely in contemplation, but the ordinary and ignorant must take the path of praxis.

A religion of the people must offer peace of soul and inspire trust in action. Culturalism is the worldview of the inwardly or outwardly privileged classes; the masses can have no part in it. The peace of soul of the masses of ordinary and ignorant people, who are poor in possessions and are obliged to struggle for their livelihood, requires a different worldview. It is my private hope that metanoetics and Other-power philosophy and the way of brotherhood may somehow be able to rise to that demand.

Culture mediates an ulterior social harmony. The purpose of human life is not the enjoyment of culture but the joy of social harmony. The concept of "species" as I understand it refers primarily to the political existence of society which confronts us as individuals and controls us from without. It points to the existence of a force that crushes and eliminates the individual who opposes society. The state displays this trait because it is an objective entity that cannot avoid self-alienation in one degree or another. Naturally, those who do not feel the reality of this oppressive power will not be able to recognize it. For the privileged, the concept of species does not even exist.

I do not of course mean to imply that species and individual *necessarily* oppose each other. On the contrary, in the universal where the two arise through negative mediation, the totality and the individual can coexist in simultaneous and harmonious mediation. Such coexistence is a world of religious expediency (*upāya*), and to the extent that the state actualizes this structure, it, too, can truly become a concrete unity in which freedom, brotherhood, and equality can be realized in simultaneous mediation. In this sense the state can represent a particular determination of the Kingdom of God on earth: in mediating the absolute, it can enjoy the absoluteness of mediating the absolute and take on the quality of the "sacred." But as a mediator of the independence and spontaneity of the individuals that make it up, this sacredness is a thoroughly mediatory mode of being that arises in action, and not something whose existence is a natural given. The harmonious aspect of this mediatory unity in its actual expression we refer to as culture, while politics is said to represent the transforming aspect of conflict and opposition. The action of the individual that mediates between culture and politics is regulated by ethics, and religion is the action-faith in Other-power whereby the crisis of antinomy between the two is resolved in a transforming unity.

Culture is therefore merely one phase of a broader ethical and religious totality. Put in terms of temporality, "specific" culture corresponds to the past, and "individual" activity corresponds to the future. The eternal present in which religious salvation takes place consists in the fact that these two elements, representing tradition and freedom respectively, are mediated in the nothingness of the present and transformed into a "universal" Great Action. Culture provides the underlying basis of continuity here. Specific determination—in particular, the mediating work of *gensō* that has been our concern here—is *one* facet of this cultural unity. When the absolute receives and saves relative beings through absolute *gensō*, it mediates self-power in terms of the structure of absolute Other-power. The spontaneity of sentient beings, who are to be saved (*ki*) and yet need to remain clearly distinguished from Other-power itself, serves in a mediating capacity. At the same time, the absolute, which does not act by direct intervention in the relative world but always makes the relative its mediating function, is at work in the mutual mediation of one relative being to another. Only thus does the absolute cause the relative to be relative and to witness through its own mediating activity to the fact that it is the absolute. It is too clear to leave room for doubt: an absolute that works mediatively as a transforming nothingness is not an object for contemplation but a focus for action.

Even when the absolute mediates the interrelationships, however, if it does not make the *being* that serves as a substratum to its mediation a mediator of *nothingness*, there is no way for absolute nothingness to reach the transforming action and witness of the subject. For action, both the individual, which is the manifestation of nothingness, and the substratum of being of a community of life, which provides the basis for the determination of the individual and at the same time mediates the realization of the individual's subjectivity, are required. This community of life is the "species" that is present as the substratum of being mediating the relationship between relative beings and that lays the foundations for the absolute unity of absolute nothingness.

To put this more concretely in the terminology of Shin Buddhism, when the more advanced sentient beings who have been drawn up into salvation and fixed in their "rightly established state" (*shōjōju*) take the way of *gensō* to share in the salvation of the less advanced and perform that mediatory action as representatives of the absolute, they have to make use of the traditional doctrine common to both, giving and receiving instruction through the terms and concepts of that doctrine. That common substratum is culture, and what passes it on as tradition is the "specific" society. This is how a society seen as "species," by means of its unique and particular tradition, qualifies the existence of the individuals who make it up and provides them with a common basis of mediation. This is precisely what Hegel has in mind in speaking of objective spirit as an ethical substratum. Or again, and in more popular parlance, if we take "brotherhood" to represent the social structure resulting from relationships based on the imparting and reception of instruction among sentient beings, we may say that the Tathāgata is the absolute master, or father, who never extends a hand directly to save less advanced sentient beings but always makes use of the more advanced, the elder brothers, in his place. With one and the same family tradition as a common substratum, the elder and the younger children communicate with one another. The father places his complete trust in the elder son and urges the younger sons to exert themselves to collaborate with their older brother, bringing about a salvific conversion to the absolute through the mutual dependence and mutual support of all the brothers. Each family then, to carry on with our image, takes on the particularization of a species and accordingly must oppose every other family, leading immediately to rivalry and a struggle for survival. The same could be said of the relationship between one country and another.

Individuals, however, transcend the limits of the specific society, even though they belong to it directly. They can communicate and commune with one another as subjects of nothingness who, while being determined by their respective societies, can also transform and determine them in return. To the extent that specific societies can thus be transformed into subjects of nothingness and become mediators of salvation, they can communicate with one another and find communality in their mediation of nothingness, even as they remain delimited by the particularity of their being. The unity of the absolute resulting from this practical transformation of the species may be termed the universal. The notion of the human race (or genus) has its origins here. From such a standpoint, the unity that results from the nothingness of transformation through action must entail the action of an absolute metanoetics that presupposed the absolute crisis of this opposition. Insofar as individuals are the subjects of this unity, they can attain a mutual love and sympathy that reaches out to the full breadth of their humanity, quite apart from whether their particular countries are at war or peace with one another. Insofar as cultures generate and intensify the peculiarity of their "species," they open themselves up to the understanding and influence of a more pervasive communality, thus enabling them to possess a universal validity. Mediated by the freedom and spontaneity of the individual, cultures can communicate with one another at the profound level of nothingness.

The fact that such an advanced state of culture always goes along with a flowering of national strength can also be explained in terms of the mediation we have been discussing here. A devastated nation has no culture. One cannot expect the autonomous and free development of a culture without the freedom and autonomy of the state. Every once in a while, of course, some individual of rare genius manages to break through the general pattern, escaping the mediation of the species and moving far beyond it to communicate directly with the universal ground of the human. But even in such cases, if we look closely enough, we find the mediation of species at work.

In Buddhism the Tathāgata performs his salvific work by "preaching" the Dharma in a variety of different manifest forms according to the species of sentient beings he wishes to save: to save a bodhisattva, he appears as a bodhisattva; to save Devas and devils, he appears as a Deva or a devil; to save a woman, he takes the form of a woman.[4] The idea may sound somewhat eerie at first, but if we stop to consider that salvation must have a specific society as its substratum and some specific culture as its medium, and if we are convinced that the salvation of the individual must be mediated by specific particularization, we must surely concede that any clarification of the question of species is bound to take extremely concrete form.

To understand—or to prevent the recurrence of—the strange fact that the representative democratic and socialist states proclaiming freedom or individual equality in our day betray the causes they profess when they turn from a "specific" nationalism to the other extreme of imperialism, a strict and detailed investigation of the significance of "species" is necessary. It is because we do not take the situation seriously but simply leave events to follow their natural course that we get trapped and manipulated by them. The evils of nationalism are hardly preferable to the evils of a perverted democracy or socialism. Surely our own misguided nationalism stands in need of metanoesis, but at the same time so do the nationalistic perversions that infect democratic and socialist states alike. The first step in reflecting on this matter must be to direct our attention to the problem of "species." Only from the standpoint of "species" are we able to find a clue to the solution of the difficult problem of nationalism, and this holds true even if conceived in terms of the "class" problem that socialism takes as uniquely definitive. Classes originate, after all, because the power of the controlling society, which originally belongs to the totality of the species, falls into the hands of one social stratum as a result of an economic division of labor, which would seem to suggest that the problem of class is incomprehensible without the notion of species. I would go further and suggest that the solution does not lie in a nationalism conceived in terms of states as relative beings, but in a nationalism conceived in terms of action mediated by absolute nothingness.

The Shin Buddhist idea of the way of *gensō* offers a religious solution to this problem by interpreting "species" as a mediator of salvation. The idea of absolute *gensō* symbolized in the religious discipline of the bodhisattva Dharmākara is extremely helpful in clarifying the significance of the community of species as an *upāya* that mediates the guidance of exemplary action in *gensō*. The fact that the notion of *gensō* not only introduced the notion of a society of salvation into doctrine but even took into consideration the specific structure of such a society gives it a special importance and claim on our attention.

In his *Critique of Teleological Judgment*, Kant defined the specification of nature from the standpoint of the conceptual knowledge of nature, and the specification of history and society, which do not belong to nature, from the standpoint of religious symbolism. The approach is profoundly significant for our understanding of the "specification" of the Buddha's appearance in different forms suited to the salvation of different types of sentient beings. Moreover, the fact that this happens to correspond to the notion of "specific" substratum in the logic of absolute mediation makes it all the more important. All of this can aid us to see how metanoetics can open up a perspective for religion on the most urgent problems of the state that face us today.

To begin, let us draw attention to a problem latent in the relationship between metanoetics and religious action-faith. Even granting the significance we have been claiming for metanoetics, there is no doubt that its basic motivation lies in the accompanying notion of evil and sin. This should be amply clear from the foregoing chapters. But religion—and Buddhism in general is clear on this point—is not based on the notions of evil and sin but on the claim to offer deliverance from *samsāra*, the endless cycle of birth-and-death. Metanoetics, or so it would seem, is not equipped to deal with this issue, and this gives us pause to wonder whether it might not be limited to Other-power religions like Christianity and Shin Buddhism which have been developed under the impulse of the ethical antinomy, and whether it is really suited to any but overtly ethical religions. In other words, it may be that metanoetics applies only to doctrines of salvation and not to doctrines of deliverance from the samsaric cycle of birth and death.

As suggested before, however, this disjunction is not a final one. On the one hand, the desire for deliverance from *samsāra* does not directly mediate an ethic. As a demand of nature, it cannot be spoken of as an "ought." From its earliest period, Buddhism has based itself on the problem of *samsāra*, which is an immediate fact of life that has no connection to ethics. The contrast this sets up between Buddhism and religious traditions of a strong ethical stamp like Judaism and Christianity could not be clearer, and may well stem from strong differences in social life between the Jews and the people of India. On the other hand, going a step further we find the belief in primitive Buddhism that our samsaric existence is in fact an illusion, and that deliverance consists in insight into the truth of this illusion. In other words, even if its original motive is not ethical but based directly on life, from the moment Buddhism becomes a religion and a value-differentiation is set up between truth and falsehood, enlightenment and illusion, it is clear that an obligation is imposed to actualize what is valuable and reject what is without value. In this sense, Buddhism entailed a morality in the broad sense of the term from its first beginnings.

Reason is not something opposed to life or merely appended to it from without. It is the faculty of reflective activity proper to human life as such, and thus something that develops from within life itself. The idea of human life without rationality and ethical concern is a pure abstraction that has nothing to do with actual reality. Because the ideas of illusion and enlightenment derive from a distinction of intellectual values, they immediately flow over into an ethical "ought." To wallow in illusion, unable to attain clear insight into the truth, is nothing other than the very sin and evil that characterizes human finitude itself. Its roots lie in the self-entanglement of egoity, our bondage to radical evil. Even in Shinran's Buddhist hymn entitled "The Hymn of Remorseful Reminiscences," one finds frequent reference to compunction and regret for intellectual illusion. To be caught in the cycle of *samsāra* and be unable to escape is itself evil and sin. True knowledge ultimately lies on the way of right action, an action that includes *satori*, or enlightenment. The way of enlightenment is deliverance, and *samsāra* is sin and evil: though conceptually distinct, the two necessarily belong together in human self-conscious existence. Indeed, the genesis of self-conscious existence in action may be said to consist in a dynamic that correlates the two.

Metanoetics begins from the consciousness of evil and its concomitant remorse and despair over sin, but there is absolutely no reason to conclude that it therefore lacks a doctrine of deliverance based on a consciousness of the illusion of *samsāra* and the demand for escape and liberation. In line with the structure of self-conscious existence itself, metanoetics acknowledges this dimension of the human. We have therefore every reason to dispel the fear that viewing metanoetics as philosophy narrows the reach of philosophy. On the contrary, it is making self-deliverance the sole issue that is evil. There is no way actually to escape the entanglements of egoity merely by yearning for escape. Relative beings can return to the absolute only through a relationship that makes other relative beings its mediators; only through the action of offering oneself up for other relative beings can one be delivered from the egoity of self. If the desire for merely *an sich* deliverance therefore necessarily converts into a demand for *für sich* salvation that entails reconciliation and cooperation between self and others, we may rightly view metanoetics as a necessary consequence of the spirit of Mahāyāna Buddhism, and therefore as possessing universal significance.

Through metanoetics, we are truly promised an existence without bonds or attachments. In the peace of soul of a conversion that carries us beyond all distinction between being and nonbeing, we shall be able to enjoy a sense of harmonious cooperation in an "ordered equality" where all work together for mutual instruction and guidance. Culture is the medium of such a community, and the control of nature aims to ensure that the restraints nature imposes on us do not obstruct our cooperation with one another. Experience has taught us that when science is viewed merely as a way to satisfy natural human desires, it not only brings happiness but becomes a source of unhappiness as well. The unhappiness of being used by science rather than using it, of applying technology for our own purposes and ending up being ruled by that technology, is something of which we are all too painfully aware in our times. An approach to life that makes human happiness its ultimate goal can only frustrate our expectations and issue in unhappiness instead.

Moreover, human existence is not simply a human project. As it is written, "He who finds his life will lose it, and he who loses his life for my sake will find it." [5] Everything in this world exists correlatively to everything else. To seek existence for oneself alone by destroying all others is to forfeit one's own existence as well. Only by giving life to those who exist as others, by seeking coexistence despite the tension of opposition, and by collaborating for the sake of mutual enhancement can the self find life in its fullness. The absolute does not allow the self-indulgence of relative beings who seek to adhere to the existence of the isolated self and to attach themselves to material things in such a way as to exclude others and lord it over them, monopolizing their possessions to advance their own worldly success. Such persons will eventually end up in their own destruction. The absolute is absolute mediation, mediating relative beings to one another and thereby mediating itself as well. And this process means continual transformation for relative beings: grounded in a nothingness that ensures mutual self-transcendence, each relative being finds itself in every other.

The relative is thus being whose principle is nothingness: a re-surrected existence brought to life through death. This "existence in nothingness" through absolute transformation—or "empty being"—represents the truth of existence: an existence without attachments, clinging to nothing. But the nothingness of absolute transformation can be achieved only through reciprocal mediation in society. The nothing-ness of absolute transformation is realized only in mediating the dynamics of "empty being" in society. The world of absolute transformation whose principle is nothingness is not the world of nature but the world of history.

Unlike nature, history has no structure that provides it with an unchanging substratum on which changes of attribution and relation-ship take place. It has no structure within which a self-identical universal can regulate all phenomena according to its own laws, or within which all things can be directed toward the realization of their essential nature; it lacks a *telos* for things to progress from the possible to the real, from the potential to the actual. All these things belong to the substratum or substance of being, and the logic that regulates them is the logic of identity. It is otherwise with history, which has no permanent and unmediated substratum. History is set up in terms of "specific" spheres of fixed duration, and is held in existence as a cycle of activity in the sense that the individuals who are determined by a specific sphere are able to actualize nothingness by negotiating their own freedom and subjectify-ing it through action. The periods of history correspond to particular "specific" societies. Both the individual and the society are limited relative beings involved in a continuous process of renewal and trans-formation. Strictly speaking, any given period of time, far from main-taining an absolute constancy, is ultimately undergoing transfigurations at every moment. So long as time does not stop—that is, so long as time remains the principal determinant of reality—reality is incessantly changing, an elliptical field with two focal points generating spheres of activity that move in cycles.

As is well known, the Greeks took constancy to be the essential determinant of being, and saw the heavenly bodies rotating eternally within their fixed orbits as representing that constancy in the natural world. The periodicity of history, in contrast, is changeable and prone to deviations. Within its "specifically" different and noncoincidental cycles, history forms a circularity continually shifting from one cycle to another. Its periodic nature should not be conceived in terms of orbits running on strictly coincidental cycles but in terms of a circular movement of continually deviating cycles. This means that the specific societies that correspond to these cycles are also in constant flux and transformation in the actuality of history through the death-and-resurrection of the individuals who mediate these societies. As the subjects of action mediating the historical transformations of "specific" societies, individuals may be considered axes of nothingness as it moves in and out of the realm of species. That it to say, as "turning points" for nothingness through whose action-faith-witness the "eternal now" is realized, the individual self is the subject of Existenz; and conversely, Existenz is grounded on nothingness and becomes a manifestation of nothingness. Moreover, by practicing—and being made to practice—a nonattachment based on nothingness, individuals actualize a society of "ordered equality" based on coexistence, cooperation, and mutual instruction. Such a society, as it passes through the course of history, is continually renewed through their action-witness. It is a world of brotherhood founded on human cooperation and reconciliation, providing meaning to human existence for those who rejoice in building it up and inhabiting it.

The absoluteness of nothingness that brings us into this society of brotherhood is love; it is Great Compassion. Nothingness is love; and the Great Nay of absolute transformation is the Great Compassion. The action-witness of this fact is itself the building of the Kingdom of God and the fulfillment of faith in rebirth into the Pure Land. It is here that we find the meaning of history: that the Kingdom of God is made actual in the course of history through the action-witness of nothingness. This is not to be confused with the "goal" of history or the "end" of history in an eschatological sense. Such thinking locks us into the conceptual constructs of a teleological view of nature. My view is rather that the Kingdom of God already exists in each "present" insofar as the realization of eternal nothingness in one's individual existence is brought to action-witness, enabling us to say in the words of the New Testament, "The Kingdom of God is within you." [6] At the same time, it is also proclaimed that "The Kingdom of God is at hand." [7] This "already"–*qua*–"not yet" is not something that exists naturally, but something being brought to faith-witness through transforming action.

This action-faith-witness of nothingness, a unity that can never become the object of contemplation, displays what is distinctive about history. Nonbeing is ever present in the depths of being, continuously transforming it and converting it. The self-consciousness of action freely performed in a spirit of detachment and impartiality, moving in and out of being and nonbeing, represents the consummation of the Kingdom of God in history. Even in Augustine's *The City of God*, the Roman Empire, as historical state in the secular world, is not simply set up as the earthly kingdom to contrast with the Christian church which is then identified directly as the Kingdom of God. Augustine recognizes that even within the Roman Empire there are persons of faith practicing a religious life, just as there is impurity and worldliness within the church, and therefore that the two kingdoms intermingle, their members forever moving between the one and the other. It is the same with the historical world where being and nonbeing are ceaselessly being transformed into each other, interpenetrating and intermingling with each other, so that it cannot be circumscribed systematically by a logic of identity or comprehended in unified form by intuition. Light and darkness continually give way to each other like the flickering of a lantern; things are ever turning inside out and outside in; being and nonbeing are engaged in incessant interchange each with the other. In action the inner workings of this transformation reach self-consciousness as the core of nothingness. Such is the historical world.

The transformation through action in which the center of each self mediates other selves and where past and future are converted into each other stops at self-consciousness of this unity. Without centers of action there is no historical world. A world of contemplation without them is in fact not the historical world. This does not mean merely that a world of mere conceptual construction cannot be considered as the historical world, but also that even a world of "life and expression" or of artistic "formation" does not belong to the world of history. The idea that historical realities can be thought of as objects whose unity we can contemplate as modalities of a basic archetype comes about because the essence of history has been lost sight of. Ultimately, such a view comes down to replacing the three-dimensional self-consciousness of absolute nothingness, with its characteristic interpenetration of being and nonbeing through "action-transformation," with a two-dimensional "action-intuition."

Allow me to take the image of the pompon dahlia to symbolize what I have in mind. It is customary in Buddhism to use the "lotus in the flames" as a symbol of the state of deliverance and salvation. The image is well suited to suggest the immaculateness of the lotus flower. Emerging from the mud and mire and yet preserving its purity, the lotus blossom ringed with fire easily comes to represent the constancy of a faith that is not extinguished by the raging fire of the passions. The symbol is profoundly touching, yet I wonder whether the pompon dahlia would not be better suited to symbolize the action of "empty being" in nothingness that corresponds to historical reality.

Pascal, it will be recalled, likened nature to an infinite circle whose center is everywhere and whose circumference nowhere. The development of the historical world, however, may better be compared to an ellipsoid whose rotation can generate an infinite number of ellipses with foci of finite distance at the plane sections (image surfaces) of the cross sections (ways of seeing). If we take the pompon dahlia as the symbol of that ellipsoid, the petals or florets that make up the flower correspond to the individual selves of a "specific" society, and the central floret situated on the floral axis corresponds to the manifestation of God. If next we rotate this flower at different angles and project it on the surface of a flat mirror, the ellipse formed by two foci at an equal distance on either side of the absolute center would appear in the mirror in various aspects and different shapes, and the successive transformation of their figures would symbolize the historical world. Then the elliptic cycles that are produced at different angles by successively changing the flower's image surface may be seen as the periods of history. The divine center, the floral axis, is reflected in the sphere of action as the faith-witness of absolute transformation according to each individual's position and inclination. Each such reflection of the mirror image is a floret of the total flower which in turn represents a cyclical unity of all the reflections. Thus the rotation of the pompon dahlia becomes a symbol of the historical world and at the same time a symbol of the contents of philosophical consciousness. In Buddhism, the true wisdom of the Buddha, the state of deliverance, is represented by the picture of sacred figures drawn in concentric circles known as a mandala. I trust it will not be considered improper if I take this image of the pompon dahlia as the mandala of a metanoetics based on historicism.[8]

In nature, myths have no significance. It is the business of natural science to replace myths with laws. The object of its knowing is eternal and universal order, not contingent occurrences. But history cannot avoid absolute contingency. Why is there being? How does existence exist? These are questions about primary contingency that necessarily arise in connection with history. And yet there is no way rationally to explain the why or wherefore of this contingency; if we could, it would not be absolute. What is more, the mystery extends not only to *Dasein* but also to *Sosein*, for existence is incomprehensible to us not only because it is contingent but because it has the particular form of contingency that it does. Thus an ineluctable antinomy arises with regard to history: on the one hand, we must ask the question about the origin of the world and the reason for existence, and on the other hand, we can never answer our question. All we can do in our predicament is base ourselves metanoetically on a self-consciousness of the contents of our action-faith and turn our imaginations to mythical symbols and their interpretation.

Plato reckoned true knowledge to lie in the contemplation of the realm of ideas, and saw this as the self-conscious activity of true eternal being. Yet when it came to the realm of opinion of the phenomenal world, he made use of myths to interpret the origins of the world. The point has great significance even for present-day epistemology in clarifying the difference between nature and history. It is not, however, Plato's "two-world" theory that we need, but a theory of absolute mediation through action whereby the two worlds transform and interpenetrate each other. In this regard, the doctrine of the absolute *gensō* of the bodhisattva Dharmākara's religious discipline, when viewed from the standpoint of religious salvation, gives meaning to the historical world and contains a profound significance almost without parallel. To return to our image of the dahlia, the central floral axis may be said to correspond to the content of self-consciousness of Dharmākara as an absolute *gensō* representing the absolute. As the firstborn son of the Tathāgata entrusted with the supervision of his father's house, Dharmākara always represents his father and stands before all other sentient beings as their absolutely more advanced, as the teacher and elder brother that guides and instructs them as they advance toward the absolute. In my view, the emphasis on historical society in religious communion symbolized in these myths is the most important lesson metanoetics has to learn from the Shin Buddhist doctrine. Moreover, when we pause to reflect on the quality of *gensō* characteristic of Amida Buddha, as we have in the previous chapters, the "seniority" of Dharmākara is also relativized into a symbol of an ideal that can be realized only through the "ordered equality" of mutual instruction in the human community.

At present our nation faces the task, imposed on it externally, of performing *zange* for its past nationalism. That we, as a vanquished nation, should now be forced by others to do what we should surely have done before and of our own accord, occasions the very height of shame and remorse. Yet even at this late hour we can at least perform our *zange* out of deep inner conviction and so ensure our inner freedom. A liberalism imposed from the outside is both nonsensical and contradictory. The opportunistic advantage we take of this relative "other-power" to announce our own liberalism and culturalism is hardly less shameless and unconscionable a posture. The turning point for a new beginning lies in *zange*. Without it, we have no way to rebuild our nation.

And it is not only our own nationalism that stands in need of *zange*. That liberalism finds itself in the same situation is clear to see both from the inner contradictions that infect its representative countries and from its opposition to the socialism represented by other strong nations of the allied powers. Does it not look as if the socialist states who have been brought to an impasse by insistence on their political theory are revising their standpoints in large measure and falling with liberalist nations into the trap of a nationalism that is as much the antithesis of socialism as it is of liberalism—the very path that our nation has been forced to abandon—and thus landing themselves in the tragic contradiction of boldly leading one another into the morass of imperialism? Obviously we are not the only country that needs *zange*. Other nations, too, should undertake its practice in a spirit of sincerity and humility, each acknowledging its own contradictions and faults, its own evil and sin. *Zange* is a task that world history imposes on all peoples in our times.

I repeat: metanoetics possesses profound significance as a philosophy for the present turning point in history. History is calling on people of all nations to practice *zange* in order to build up societies of fellowship. This is how I understand the meaning of philosophy as metanoetics.

Notes

1: THE PHILOSOPHICAL MEANING OF METANOETICS

1. [Literally these terms refer to two "aspects" or "phases" of a single process that will be treated at greater length in chaps. 6 and 7.]

2. [The "*qua*" here refers to the Sino-Japanese copulative "*soku*," which functions as a sort of pivot around which two terms revolve and interchange with each other as mutually defining elements in a single dynamic.]

3. [Wherever possible, references to the *Kyōgyōshinshō* will be taken from the abridged English version, *The Teaching, Practice, Faith, and Enlightenment*, vol. 5 of the Ryukoku Translation Series, published in 1966 in Kyoto (RTS). Suzuki Daisetsu's translation, *The Kyōgyōshinshō* (SD), was published in 1973 by the Eastern Buddhist Society in Kyoto. Passages unavailable in either of these translations will be taken from the more complete but dated translation of Yamamoto Kosho, published in 1958 by Karinbunko in Tokyo (YK).]

In the passage cited here, Shinran is quoting Zendō; see YK, p. 133.

4. *Enneads* 3.8.6.

5. English translation by Lee M. Capel (New York: Harper & Row, 1965). [Tanabe read Kierkegaard in the German.]

6. *Kyōgyōshinshō* 6:10; see YK, p. 251.

7. The passage is cited in Shinran's *Yuishinshō Mon I* (*Exposition of the Words of Seikaku*). See 『親鸞著作全集』 (*Collected Writings of Shinran*), ed. Kaneko Daiei (Kyoto: Hōzōkan, 1979), pp. 563–564. Hereafter references to this collection will be abbreviated as SZ.

8. 4:11; see YK, p. 138.

9. SZ, p. 457.

10. [*Ekō* refers to the transference of merits by Amida Buddha to sentient beings. In its *gensō* phase, it enables those who have been saved to return to the world to save others; in its *ōsō* it is composed of action, faith, and witness.]

11. See especially the *Philosophical Fragments* and *Concluding Unscientific Postscript*.

2: ABSOLUTE CRITIQUE: THE LOGIC OF METANOETICS

1. *Critique of Pure Reason*, trans. Norman Kemp Smith (New York: St. Martin's Press, 1929), p. 9.

2. [Tanabe understands the term here in the sense of a task thrown existentially before us for the performing.]

3. [Tanabe often cites this passage from Shinran's *Shōshin-ge* (*The Gāthā of True Faith in the Nembutsu*), line 26 (Ryukoku Translation Series edition, Kyoto, 1961, p. 23), without indicating its precise source. At times, as here, his wording is closer to the final sentence of the *Jōdo Monrui Jushō* (SZ, p. 362). Its English translation, *Passages on the Pure Land Way* (Kyoto: Shin Buddhism Translation Series, 1978), renders the passage as follows: "... so that without being made to sunder their blind passions, they (foolish beings floundering in *samsāra*) are brought quickly to the realization of great *nirvāna*" (p. 57).]

4. *Enneads* 3.8.6.

5. See E. Gilson, *Introduction à l'étude de s. Augustin*, 3d ed. (Paris, 1949).

3: ABSOLUTE CRITIQUE AND HISTORICITY

1. See Heidegger, *Sein und Zeit: Erste Hälfte* (Halle: Max Niemeyer, 1935), p. 192.

2. Ibid., pp. 192, 223.

3. Ibid., p. 192.

4. Ibid., pp. 284–285.

5. [The edition Tanabe was using of *Was ist Metaphysik?* (Bonn, 1929) predates Heidegger's later additions of an introduction and postscript.]

6. [Tanabe translates this term of Heidegger's idiosyncratically as *dassai jizai*. The first two characters are a classical Chinese term that implies "leaving the world of everydayness," and the last two the ordinary expression for "at will."]

7. A paraphrase from *Thus Spoke Zarathustra*, "On Redemption" (II, 20). Compare fragment 1041 of *The Will to Power*, and the following passage from *Ecce Homo*: "that one wants nothing to be different, not forward, not backward, not in all eternity" (trans. Walter Kaufmann [New York: Vintage, 1967], p. 258).

8. *Was ist Metaphysik?* p. 26.

9. Ibid., p. 285.

10. "Vom Wesen des Grundes," in *Festschrift Edmund Husserl zum 70. Geburtstag gewidmet*, Jahrbuch für Philosophie und phänomenologische Forschung, Ergänzungsband (Halle: Max Niemeyer, 1929).

11. *Enneads* 3.6.

12. For my assessment of the work on Eckhart done by Oltmanns, one of Heidegger's followers, see chap. 5 below.

13. *Sein und Zeit*, pp. 375 ff.

14. Ibid., pp. 366–368.

15. Ibid., p. 385.

16. See S. Kierkegaard, *Repetition: An Essay in Experimental Psychology*, trans. W. Lowrie (Princeton, N.J., 1941).

17. *Sein und Zeit*, pp. 428–435.

18. See *Twilight of the Idols*, trans. R. J. Hollingdale (Baltimore: Penguin, 1968), pp. 35 ff.

19. Ibid., pp. 37–38.

20. On this point, compare Jaspers.

21. *Thus Spoke Zarathustra*, trans. Walter Kaufmann (New York: Viking, 1966). See "On Redemption" (II, 20) and "The Convalescent" (III, 13).

22. Ibid., "On Old and New Tablets" (III, 12).

23. Ibid., "On the Great Longing" (III, 14).

24. Ibid., "The Other Dancing Song" (III, 15).

25. E. Förster-Nietzsche, *The Lonely Nietzsche*, trans. P. V. Cohn (London: Heinemann, 1915).

26. *Thus Spoke Zarathustra*, "Retired" (IV, 6).

27. See Ernst Bertram, *Nietzsche: Versuch einer Mythologie* (Berlin: Bondi, 1918).

28. *Thus Spoke Zarathustra*, "The Magician" (IV, 5).

29. See Nietzsche, *Vom Nutzen und Nachteil der Historie für das Leben*, in *Gesammelte Werke* (Munich: Musarion, 1920–1929), 6:227–326; Heidegger, *Sein und Zeit*, pp. 396–397.

30. [Tanabe seems to be referring here to Nietzsche's idea that the various perspectives on history are like differing interpretations of a text whose original has been lost.]

4: METANOETICS AND THE PHILOSOPHY OF FREEDOM

1. These are the words that Daitō Kokushi, a Zen priest of the Rinzai sect (1282–1337) and founder of Daitoku-ji in Kyoto, is supposed to have uttered on attaining enlightenment.

2. [Literally, *jinen-hōni* means "being what one is of oneself in virtue of the Dharma that makes things to be what they are." In the fifth Letter of his *Mattōshō*, Shinran notes that the term refers to the fact that what one is "of oneself" one is "made to become through the working of the vow of Tathāgata." While this is consistent with Tanabe's approach, he does not elaborate on the term. Hence the simple translation: "naturalness."]

3. See his *Six Theosophic Points*, I, 12, 15.

4. *Sein und Zeit*, pp. 286–287.

5: ABSOLUTE MEDIATION IN METANOETICS

1. The 信心銘 (*Hsin-hsin-ming*) is a short text of 584 characters composed by Sêng-ts'an (d. 606), the third patriarch in the lineage of Chinese Zen.

2. SZ, p. 74.

3. The poem is by Bunan, 1602–1676.

4. *Mysticism East and West*, trans. B. Bracey and R. Payne (New York: Macmillan, 1960), pp. 141–148.

5. Ibid., pp. 146–147.

6. Ibid., p. 217.

7. Ibid., p. 218.

8. Käte Oltmanns, *Meister Eckhart* (Frankfurt: Klostermann, 1935).

9. Ibid., p. 213.

10. Henri Joachim Delacroix, *Essai sue le mysticisme spéculatif en Allemagne au quatorzième siècle* (Paris: Alcan, 1900).

11. Ibid., pp. 210–218.

12. [Tanabe read Eckhart in the older Büttner edition, *Meister Eckharts Schriften und Predigten*, which we shall cite here.]

13. Ibid., 2:166.

14. *Essai sur le mysticisme spéculatif*, p. 216.

15. "Shōbōgenzō Buddha Nature," Part III, trans. Norman Waddell and Abe Masao, *The Eastern Buddhist* 9, no. 2 (1976): 75.

16. Büttner, *Meister Eckharts Schriften und Predigten* 1:202.

6: FROM PASCAL TO SHINRAN

1. *Pensées*, trans. A. K. Krailsheimer (New York: Penguin, 1966), no. 774.

2. See his *Ethics*, IV, Prop. liv.

3. *Pensées*, no. 418.

4. Ibid., no. 599.

5. Ibid., no. 7.

6. Ibid., no. 960.

7. Ibid., no. 380.

8. Ibid., nos. 656, 111, 759.

9. Ibid., no. 933.

10. Ibid., no. 83.

11. Ibid., no. 14.

12. Ibid., no. 93.

13. Ibid., no. 91.

14. Ibid., no. 106.

15. Ibid., no. 200.

16. SD, p. 3. See RTS, p. 18.

17. See above, chap. 2, n. 3.

18. *Pensées*, nos. 741, 445.

19. Ibid., no. 629.

20. Ibid., nos. 774, 192.

21. Ibid., nos. 734, 735.

22. Ibid., nos. 407, 564.

23. Ibid., no. 257.

24. [The *Hōbenkeshindo* is envisaged as a purgatory surrounding the Pure Land.]

25. RTS, p. 165; see SD, p. 176.

26. RTS, p. 194; see SD, p. 184.

27. RTS, p. 90; see SD, p. 88. [This is also referred to as the Original Vow of Amida Buddha.]

28. RTS, p. 197.

29. SZ, p. 110.

30. This will be taken up again in chap. 8.

7: METANOETICS AND THE THEORY OF THE THREE MINDS

1. [The relevant works of Soga Ryōjin (1875–1971) are not yet available in English, but a helpful reconstructed synopsis of his interpretation can be found in "Dharmākara Bodhisattva," in *The Buddha Eye*, ed. Frederick Franck (New York: Crossroad, 1982), pp. 221–231.]

2. See his *Compendium on the Meditation Sutra (Kangyōgi)*.

3. For example, there is no reference to *zange* in the index to the three volumes of Yamanobe Shūgaku and Akanuma Chizen, *Kyōgyōshinshō Kōgi* (*Lectures on the "Kyōgyōshinshō"*) (Tokyo: Hōzōkan, 1913–1917).

4. [The Chinese rendering condensed the fuller Sanskrit, which can be found in *Buddhist Mahāyāna Texts*, vol. 49 of *Sacred Books of the East*, ed. F. Max Müller (Oxford: Oxford University Press, 1894), 2:167.

To bring as much consistency as possible to the overlapping of terms, the translations of RTS (p. 167, n. 2) have been adopted throughout this translation. Thus the Three Minds of the Larger Sutra, which refer to the three aspects of faith contained in the eighteenth vow *of the Buddha*, are Sincere Mind (*shishin*), Serene Faith (*shingyō*), and Desire for Birth (*yokushō*); and the Three Minds of the Mediation Sutra, which refer to the three aspects of faith required *of the aspirant to faith*, are Sincere Mind (*shijōshin*), Deep Mind (*jinshin*), and Mind of Aspiring for Birth by Merit-transference. Though explicitly distinct, these two classifications are implicitly the same.]

5. See his "Tradition and Evidence," in vol. 3 of 『曽我量深論集』 (*Collected Essays of Soga Ryōjin*) (Kyoto: Teishiya, 1948).

6. See YK, pp. 96–97.

7. [See *Shinran*, vol. 11 of the 『日本思想体経』 (*Library of Japanese Thought*) (Tokyo: Iwanami, 1978), p. 78.]

8. See above, chap. 2, n. 3.

9. [The translation was adjusted to suit the context, though Tanabe reverses the order in his text.]

10. See, for example, *Passages on the Pure Land Way*, pp. 47–57.

11. This is the view expounded in his *Exposition of the Words of Seikaku*. See SZ, pp. 556–557.

12. See RTS, p. 173.

13. The *Sanzengi* is the fourth part of Zendō's *Compendium*.

14. YK, p. 93; see SZ, p. 92.

15. RTS, p. 109; see SD, p. 114.

16. RTS, pp. 106–108; see SD, pp. 108–109.

17. One of the sacred texts of Shin Buddhism, of undetermined authorship and composed somewhere between 1270 and 1351.

18. *Notes on the Inscriptions on Sacred Scrolls*, ed. Ueda Yoshifumi (Kyoto: Shin Buddhism Translation Series, 1981), p. 50.

19. RTS, pp. 104–105; see SD, p. 105.

20. See above, chap. 2, n. 3.

8: METANOETICS AS A RELIGIOUS VIEW OF SOCIETY

1. [Tanabe is clearly referring here to Nishida's final essay, "The Logic of Locus and a Religious Worldview." While Nishida's "place" (*basho*) is commonly rendered by the Greek word "topos," "locus" seems preferable here, both because it preserves the everyday quality of the Japanese word and because it conveys the play on words that Tanabe intends by "location" (*bamen*).]

2. *Scripture of the Lotus Blossom of the Fine Dharma*, trans. Leon Hurvitz (New York: Columbia University Press, 1976), p. 22.

3. [The allusion is to Nishida's final essay. See above, n. 1.]

4. *Scripture of the Lotus Blossom*, pp. 314–315.

5. Matt. 10:39.

6. Luke 17:21.

7. Mark 1:15.

8. [This final image of Tanabe's is difficult to understand, both mathematically and visually. It is hard to see how the "rotation" of an ellipsoid makes any difference to cross-sectioning. The main point in his choice of the ellipsoid seems to be to set up a contrast with Pascal's circumferenceless circle whose center is everywhere (actually a much older idea that goes back to a Gnostic text, the *Liber Trismegisti*, Cod. Par. 6319 and Cod. Vat. 3060), by insisting that each "center" is only one of two determining foci of "finite distance" from each other. (Foci of infinite distance would generate a straight line, and foci that coincide would generate a circle.) The pompon dahlia is made up of elliptical shaped petals folded around a central floret rising up to about the middle of the whole blossom (and thus midway between the foci of the ellipses), giving a globular, and hence perhaps "cyclical," effect to the whole.]

Index

Designer:	U.C. Press Staff
Compositor:	Asco Trade Typesetting Ltd.
Text:	$10\frac{1}{2}/13$ Plantin Light
Display:	Plantin
Printer:	Edwards Brothers, Inc.
Binder:	Edwards Brothers, Inc.